# CIVIL PROCEDURE

## Examples and Explanations

# CIVIL PROCEDURE

## Examples and Explanations

## Joseph W. Glannon

*Professor of Law*
*Suffolk University Law School*

**LITTLE, BROWN AND COMPANY**
Boston    Toronto

Library of Congress Catalog Card No. 86-82424

ISBN 0-316-31595-8

*Fourth Printing*

*Published simultaneously in Canada by Little, Brown & Company (Canada) Limited*

Printed in the United States of America

**FG**

*I wish to dedicate this book to my parents,*
*Edward and Helen Glannon.*

# Contents

# Preface to Students

Everyone comes to law school with some idea of what a contract is or of the meaning of assault and battery, but who ever heard of ancillary jurisdiction, impleader, or res judicata? Abstract concepts such as these make civil procedure the most unfamiliar and intimidating of the basic law school courses.

However, civil procedure can also be fascinating if you can get by the initial strangeness. Many of the topics covered in the course appear baffling upon first acquaintance but begin to make sense when you see how they apply in particular cases and how they relate to other topics in the course. The goal of this book is to demystify civil procedure by providing concrete examples of procedural doctrines and rules in operation, together with full explanations of how these abstract concepts apply to each example.

Most case books contain major or representative cases but provide little discussion of what the cases mean or "what the law is" on a particular topic. I hope that you will find, as my students have, that the discussion in this book helps to tie the cases together into a coherent picture of the law. In addition, the opportunity to try your hand at the examples and then to compare your answers with mine will provide an incentive to analyze the examples and make that process more rewarding—perhaps even enjoyable.

Each chapter (except for the pleading chapters in Part Five) includes an introduction that gives a basic explanation of the relevant procedural concept followed by a series of questions. The "Analysis" section of each chapter presents my analyses of the examples in that chapter. The most effective way to use the book is to read each chapter when that topic is covered in your civil procedure course and to try to answer the questions yourself, based on my introductions and your reading for class. To keep yourself honest, write out your own analysis of each question, if only in a few sentences, before comparing it to mine. You may also want to review the chapter again after class coverage or discuss with your civil procedure professor any issues that you don't fully understand.

One of my principal frustrations as a first year law student was that the questions posed in the casebooks were too hard. (Many are still beyond me, even after teaching procedure for a number of years.) I think you will find that the questions in this book are geared to covering the basics as well as more sophisticated variations; you really will be able to answer many of them, and the explanations will help to deepen your understanding of the issues.

You certainly will want to use Civil Procedure: Examples and Explanations for reviewing your civil procedure course at the end of the year. My students have found that these chapters provide an excellent way to test their understanding of each topic and to fill in any gaps in class discussion or case reading. The examples provide an efficient means of learning the material because they help you to actively apply the concepts. You will learn a lot more by doing that (even if you get some questions wrong) than by passively rereading cases. In addition, the process will give you a sense of mastery of the material. As the year progresses, you will find that your ability to analyze the examples improves markedly, and that this positive feedback will help you feel more confident of your analytical skills. Surely every first year law student will be thankful for that.

# Acknowledgments

I would like to express my appreciation to Dean David J. Sargent of Suffolk University Law School for his support for this project and to Professors Karen Blum, Charles Burnim, Gerard Clark, Victoria Dodd, Nancy Dowd, Marc Greenbaum, Russell Murphy, Marc Perlin, Robert Wasson, and Timothy Wilton for reviewing parts of the manuscript. I especially wish to thank Steven P. Perlmutter, of the Massachusetts bar, for his considerable assistance on the pleading chapters.

I also appreciate the efforts of my able research assistants at Suffolk Law School, Richard Howe ('86), Patti Reitz ('86), and Lou Storrow ('88), as well as Linda Foulsham ('87), Heather Kaval ('89), Phyllis Parham, and Lynette Vetrano, who helped prepare the manuscript. Thanks too, to Dana Wilson of Little, Brown for her capable and good-humored assistance in editing the manuscript.

Richard Heuser of Little, Brown, who provided helpful advice and support for this project throughout, deserves special thanks. So does my wife, Annie, both for patiently enduring my preoccupation with this project and for her able reference help—such as finding out who built the Suez Canal and that there really is an Alton, New Hampshire.

Last, I want to thank my civil procedure students of the last four years, whose enthusiasm for these materials has encouraged me to persist in developing them.

# Special Notice

For several frequently cited treatises I have used shortened forms after the initial citation to the work. These are as follows: Casad, Jurisdiction in Civil Actions (1983), cited as Casad; Friedenthal, Kane, and Miller, Civil Procedure (1985), cited as Friedenthal, Kane, and Miller; James and Hazard, Civil Procedure (3d ed. 1985), cited as James and Hazard; Moore's Federal Practice, cited as Moore's; Wright, Federal Courts (4th ed. 1983), cited as Wright; and Wright and Miller, Federal Practice and Procedure, cited as Wright and Miller. (My apologies to supplementary co-authors of the Moore's and Wright and Miller treatises.) For multivolume treatises (Moore's and Wright and Miller) the volume number has been retained before the authors' names.

# CIVIL
# PROCEDURE

## Examples and Explanations

# PART ONE

*Choosing a Proper Court*

# 1

## Personal Jurisdiction: The Enigma of Minimum Contacts

## Introduction

There is no place to start like the beginning, and the usual beginning for the defendant is the receipt of a summons from the court with an order to appear and defend a lawsuit. It is never a prospect that evokes much enthusiasm, but the reception is likely to be even chillier if the suit has been filed in a distant state. The defendant will want to know why on earth the plaintiff has chosen to sue in a court a thousand miles away and, perhaps more to the point, whether she *can* sue there. The answer to the second question lies shrouded in one of the foggiest realms of civil procedure, the doctrine of personal jurisdiction.

Ever since the landmark case of *Pennoyer v. Neff,* 95 U.S. 714 (1877), the Supreme Court has consistently held that plaintiffs are not free to bring suit wherever they choose. The fourteenth amendment to the United States Constitution forbids the states from "depriv[ing] any person of life, liberty or property, without due process of law." A state would violate this guarantee if its courts entered judgments against defendants without following a fair judicial procedure, and fair procedure includes not only such traditional elements as the right to counsel or to cross-examine witnesses, but also appropriate limits on the places where a defendant can be required to defend a lawsuit.

The Supreme Court has repeatedly attempted to define the appropriate limits on the power of state courts to "exercise personal jurisdiction over" defendants, that is, to require them to come into the state to defend lawsuits there. A number of bases for personal jurisdiction have evolved, including domicile, consent, physical presence, and the enigmatic "minimum contacts" standard. In many cases in which the defendant is not from the forum state (the state where suit is brought), the only basis for exercising personal jurisdiction over her will be the minimum contacts test developed in *International Shoe v. Washington*, 326 U.S. 310 (1945). This chapter focuses on the meaning of that test.

In *International Shoe*, the Supreme Court held that the courts of a state may exercise personal jurisdiction over a defendant if she has such minimum contacts with the state that it would be fair to require her to return and defend a lawsuit in that state. The Court did not elucidate this somewhat circular proposition by providing a list of what minimum contacts are sufficient, nor did it say how many contacts are needed. Instead, the Court suggested that whether jurisdiction is permissible depends on the "quality and nature" of the contacts with the state. 326 U.S. at 319. In some cases, the Court indicated, even a single contact will do, but not "casual" or "isolated" contacts.

This language is too vague to provide much guidance in applying the minimum contacts test, but the rationale of *International Shoe* is more helpful. The *Shoe* Court suggested that a corporation that chooses to conduct activities within a state accepts (implicitly, of course) a reciprocal duty to answer for its in-state activities in the local courts. A defendant should understand that her activities within the state will have an impact there, that they may lead to controversies and lawsuits there, and that the state has a right to enforce the orderly conduct of affairs within its borders by adjudicating disputes that arise from such in-state activities. The defendant who deliberately chooses to take advantage of the "benefits and protections of the laws" (326 U.S. at 319) of a state will not be heard to cry "foul" when that state holds her to account in its courts for her in-state acts.

This rationale suggests an important limitation on minimum contacts jurisdiction. Since the court's power to exercise jurisdiction derives from the defendant's voluntary relation to the state, the power should be limited to cases arising out of that relation. *International Shoe* implies such a limitation, and subsequent cases have confirmed that minimum contacts jurisdiction is limited to claims arising from (or, perhaps, related to) the defendant's contacts with the forum state. In *Shoe*, for example, the corporation was held subject to personal jurisdiction in Washington for claims arising out of its shoe sales in that state, but the corporation could not have been required to defend a claim in Washington arising from shoe sales in Texas under a minimum contacts analysis. (We will leave aside for the moment the possibility that International Shoe would be subject to general in personam jurisdiction in Washington.) Sales in Texas are unrelated to Washington; the corporation would certainly not expect to be sued in Washington by a Texas shoe buyer; nor does the corporation take advantage of the benefits and protections of the laws of Washington by its activities in Texas. In analyzing minimum contacts cases, you must always consider the relationship between the contacts that gave rise to the suit and the state where the suit is brought. Miscellaneous contacts are not minimum contacts. It is the contacts that spawned the lawsuit that are crucial to the *International Shoe* analysis.

Several important aspects of the minimum contacts test have been settled by cases since *International Shoe. First,* the minimum contacts test applies to individual as well as corporate defendants. See, e.g., *Kulko v. Superior Court,* 436 U.S. 84 (1978). This makes good sense, because individuals benefit from their voluntary in-state contacts just as corporations do and should likewise understand that those benefits may carry with them the burden of related litigation. *Second,* the limitations on personal jurisdiction found in long-arm statutes are distinct from the constitutional limit imposed by the minimum contacts test. (See Chapter 2, which compares these two related concepts.) *Third,* it is clear that a defendant may have minimum contacts *with* a state without having acted *within* the state. *Calder v. Jones,* 465 U.S. 783 (1984). If a defendant commits acts outside the state that she knows may cause harmful effects within it, or that enable her to indirectly conduct business with or derive profits from the state, she will be amenable to minimum contacts jurisdiction in the state for claims arising out of those contacts.

For example, if a Florida lawyer calls a Missouri client on a regular basis to give her legal advice and bills the client for that advice, the lawyer derives benefit from conducting business in Missouri and will have to answer there for a claim of legal malpractice arising from this deliberate business relationship with a Missouri citizen. Similarly, if a manufacturer makes lawnmowers in Illinois that are routinely distributed through wholesalers to stores in Michigan and resold there to consumers, the manufacturer directly benefits from Michigan commerce. Although it is the wholesaler who actually brings the mowers into the state, the manufacturer knowingly obtains economic benefit from indirectly doing business in the state. It is that deliberate benefit for which the state may fairly demand that the manufacturer submit to personal jurisdiction for claims arising out of the in-state business.

There is also much talk in the cases about factors other than the defendant's in-state contacts, such as the interest of the forum state in providing redress to its citizens, the interest of the plaintiff in obtaining relief in a convenient forum, and the extent of the inconvenience to the defendant if she is forced to defend away from home. The cases have consistently cited these factors as relevant to the determination of whether it would be unfair to exercise personal jurisdiction over the defendant. Indeed, the recent cases appear to give them increased weight. See *Keeton v. Hustler Magazine,* 465 U.S. 770, 775-780 (1984); *Burger King v. Rudzewicz,* 105 S. Ct. 2174, 2182-

2183 (1985). However, the cases also reiterate that these factors are not sufficient in themselves to support jurisdiction. *World-Wide Volkswagen v. Woodson*, 444 U.S. 286, 294 (1980); *Burger King*, 105 S. Ct. at 2183. Due process requires first that the defendant have "purposely avail[ed] itself of the privilege of conducting activities within the forum state, thus invoking the benefits and protections of its laws." *Hanson v. Denckla*, 357 U.S. 235, 253 (1958). It is only where deliberate contacts exist between the defendant and the forum state that other factors may then be weighed in determining whether the exercise of jurisdiction would comport with fair play and substantial justice.

Another legitimate source of confusion in personal jurisdiction analysis is the related doctrine of "general in personam jurisdiction." As indicated above, minimum contacts analysis focuses on claims that are related to the defendant's contacts with the forum state. Because that analysis focuses on the specific contacts that gave rise to the claim, it is frequently referred to as "specific in personam jurisdiction." In several cases, however, the Supreme Court has suggested that a defendant may sometimes be subject to jurisdiction even for claims that are completely unrelated to in-state activities. See *Helicopteros Nacionales de Colombia, S.A. v. Hall*, 466 U.S. 408 (1984); *Perkins v. Benguet Consolidated Mining Co.*, 342 U.S. 437 (1952). See generally Friedenthal, Kane, and Miller, Civil Procedure §3.10 (1985) (hereinafter cited as Friedenthal, Kane, and Miller). Although the Court has never definitively set forth the factors that will support such broad jurisdiction, the cases suggest that general in personam jurisdiction is appropriate if the defendant's activities in the state are so substantial and continuous that it would expect to be subject to suit there on any claim and would suffer no inconvenience from defending suits where it conducts such substantial activities. This is roughly analogous to general jurisdiction over individual defendants based on domicile, approved by the Supreme Court in *Milliken v. Meyer*, 311 U.S. 457 (1940).

Under general in personam jurisdiction analysis, for example, a major American oil company would be subject to personal jurisdiction in many, if not all, states regardless of whether the claim arose in the state where suit was brought. These companies generally have such extensive activities and facilities in the states where they operate that they may fairly be considered "at home" in each of these states and therefore subject to the burden of submitting generally to jurisdiction there.[1]

---

1. Be careful not to confuse general in personam jurisdiction over a corporation with the corporation's domicile for diversity purposes, under 28 U.S.C. §1332(c). A corporation will almost certainly be subject to general in personam jurisdiction in the states where it is incorporated and has its principal place of business, but it may also be subject to general in personam jurisdiction in many additional states, as in the oil company example described above. General in personam jurisdiction is explored more fully in Chapter 9.

Thus, although some principles are established in the minimum contacts area, the test still remains difficult to state and even more difficult to apply. Over the course of your lawyering life it will take on clearer meaning as you handle personal jurisdiction issues and begin to see how courts give flesh to the bare bones test. The following questions will provide a start in that direction. In answering them, focus on the constitutional issue of minimum contacts only; do not worry about statutory problems under long-arm statutes. Also, assume that the contacts mentioned are the only contacts the defendant has with the forum state.

# QUESTIONS
## Opening Rounds

1.   Austin is a travelling salesman who lives in North Dakota and sells Fuller brushes in parts of North Dakota, South Dakota, and Minnesota. While en route to deliver brushes to a Minnesota customer, he is involved in an auto accident in Minnesota with Healy, a Minnesota citizen. He brings suit against Healy in North Dakota for his injuries in the accident. Does the court have personal jurisdiction over Healy?

2.   As a result of the same accident, Healy brings suit against Austin in South Dakota. Does the court have jurisdiction over Austin based on minimum contacts?

3.   To be on the safe side, Healy also files suit against Austin in Minnesota. Does that court have personal jurisdiction over Austin based on minimum contacts?

## A Parade of Perplexities

4.   *The Volkswagen.* Many of the most difficult personal jurisdiction cases involve commercial contacts, that is, contacts that arise out of business done in the state, either directly or indirectly, by a corporation acting outside the state. *World-Wide Volkswagen v. Woodson,* 444 U.S. 286 (1980), sets out the basic framework for analyzing these cases. The motorcade of hypotheticals that follows may help you to assess the importance of various contacts with the forum state.

Hudson, an Ohio citizen, buys a Volkswagen from Smoky Mountain VW, located on the east side of the Smoky Mountains in North Carolina, while she is on vacation in North Carolina. Shortly after she returns home all four wheels fall off while she is driving, and Hudson is injured. Understandably upset, Hudson sues Smoky Mountain in an Ohio court for negligence, breach of contract, and breach of warranty. Does the court have personal jurisdiction over the dealer?

5.   *The Chevy.* After Hudson leaves, Ford pulls into Smoky Mountain's lot with his engine belching smoke. His car is clearly a total loss, and he tells De

Soto, the salesman, that he must have a car to get back home to Florida. De Soto sells him a (very) used Chevy. After crossing into Florida, Ford pushes the windshield wiper button and the engine automatically ejects into the Everglades. Ford sues De Soto and Smoky Mountain in Florida. Is personal jurisdiction proper there?

6.  *The Maserati.* De Soto has an eye for fast cars. At the moment, he has a nice Maserati on the lot, with all the extras (engine, wheels, brakes). A customer tells him that a trucker buddy of his, Packard, from Pennsylvania, might be interested in buying the Maserati. De Soto calls Packard in Pennsylvania, extolls the Maserati's virtues and encourages her to come in and test drive the car on her next delivery in North Carolina. Packard does stop to see the car, likes it, and buys it. She makes the mistake of towing it home, only to discover upon arrival that the engine, lights, carburetor, and exhaust system are missing. She sues De Soto in Pennsylvania. De Soto has no other contacts with Pennsylvania and has never before sold a car to a Pennsylvanian. Will the Pennsylvania court have personal jurisdiction over De Soto?

7.  *The Audi.* After lunch, Rambler comes in. Rambler lives across the border in Tennessee, where he read Smoky Mountain's ad in a Tennessee paper for a one-year-old Audi for $1,100. Because the Smoky Mountain dealership is located ten miles from the Tennessee border, it advertises frequently in Tennessee, as well as in North Carolina. Rambler visits the dealership, talks De Soto down to $1,025 and buys the car. He barely gets across the Tennessee line when the steering wheel comes off in his hand and the body comes entirely loose from the frame of the car. He sues Smoky Mountain in Tennessee. Does the court have personal jurisdiction over Smoky Mountain?

8.  Assume, on the facts of question 7, that Smoky Mountain only advertises occasionally in Tennessee, and derives only 5 percent of its business ($20,000 of its annual gross sales of $400,000) from sales to Tennessee customers. The rest of its sales are in North Carolina. Rambler sees the ad and buys the Audi at Smoky Mountain's dealership; it breaks down in Tennessee on the way home. Can Rambler sue Smoky Mountain in Tennessee?

## A Hard Case

9.  Assume the same facts as question 7, except that Rambler never read the Tennessee ad. Instead, he happened to notice the dealership while passing through the Smokies on his way home from the outer banks of North Carolina. He buys the car from De Soto and it expires on the drive home. Can Rambler sue Smoky Mountain in Tennessee?

## Another Hard Case

10.  *The Rabbit.* Assume that Smoky Mountain does 10 percent of its business with Tennessee buyers. Valiant, a Texan who vacations in the Smokies,

buys a used Rabbit from Smoky Mountain and obliviously heads for her Texas home. Twenty miles into Tennessee, the car auto-destructs. Can she sue Smoky Mountain in Tennessee?

11. *The Ferrari.* You can't work all the time. When De Soto relaxes, he likes to go to the Georgia coast for some deep sea fishing. While drinking at a bar in the fishing lodge there, he gets to talking with Lenoir, another sportsman. Lenoir asks De Soto about his work. The two get into a car lovers' debate over the relative merits of various sportscars. Before leaving the bar, Lenoir asks De Soto for his card.

Two months later, Lenoir visits Smoky Mountain and buys a jazzy looking Ferrari from De Soto. Imagine for yourself what happens to the Ferrari when Lenoir gets it back to Georgia. Lenoir sues De Soto in Georgia. Will the court have personal jurisdiction over De Soto?

12. *The Toyota.* Nippon Auto Unlimited is a Japanese corporation that purchases used cars in Japan for resale in the United States. It imports the cars to the States and resells them to wholesalers on the West Coast who resell them to dealers who ultimately sell them to customers. Nippon buys a used Toyota and sells it to a California wholesaler who sells it to Al's Used Car Emporium of Reno, which sells it to Lincoln in Reno, Nevada. When Lincoln discovers that the engine has been replaced by an elaborate system of tightly wound rubber bands, she sues Nippon in Nevada. Can she do so?

13. *The Edsel.* Andretti is an Indiana race car driver whose hobby is collecting antique cars. He notices an ad in *Antique Auto,* a national magazine, for a mint condition Edsel for sale by a Michigan collector, Studebaker. He calls Studebaker, gets further information on the car, and decides to go up to look at it. While he is in Michigan, he and Studebaker discuss price but do not settle the deal. After Andretti returns to Indiana, he calls Studebaker back, agrees to his price, and arranges to pick up the car the following month. After buying the car and returning with it to Indiana, he discovers that it is a cleverly disguised Dodge Dart. He sues Studebaker in Indiana. Will the court dismiss for lack of personal jurisdiction?

## Fundamental (Un)truths

14. Every year, the following statements sprout like dandelions in civil procedure bluebooks. What is wrong with them?
   (a) "Even if the defendant lacks minimum contacts with the state, the plaintiff may be able to get jurisdiction over him if he has taken advantage of the benefits and protections of the laws of the state."
   (b) "If the defendant does not have minimum contacts with the state, the court may have jurisdiction based on the state's long-arm statute."

# ANALYSIS

## Opening Rounds

1.    In this case Austin has brought suit in a state with which he has contacts, but Healy has none. As far as the question tells us, Healy has never been there, has not formed any deliberate relationship to, or performed acts within, the state, and has done nothing to derive benefits from North Dakota. Consequently, she has no reason to expect to be sued there and has not impliedly swallowed that bitter pill in exchange for the benefits of in-state activity. She lacks minimum contacts with North Dakota and may not be sued there on this claim.

As this conclusion suggests, the personal jurisdiction rules are defendant-oriented. The plaintiff's contacts with the forum state will not do; the court must find some basis for forcing the defendant, the unwilling litigant, to appear before it.[2] One might well ask why Austin should have to go to Healy instead of Healy coming to Austin. If someone will have to be inconvenienced by the suit, shouldn't it be the defendant rather than the injured plaintiff? On the other hand, the defendant may be completely blameless: Plaintiffs lose law suits as well as win them. If so, it seems unfair to add the insult of distant litigation to the injury of being sued in the first place. Perhaps more importantly, the defendant (unlike the plaintiff, who has started the suit) has not chosen the forum and ought to have some veto power over unreasonable choices by the plaintiff.

2.    The South Dakota court will not have personal jurisdiction over Austin under the minimum contacts test. It is true that Austin has some contacts with South Dakota because he travels there to sell brushes. However, *International Shoe* does not hold that a defendant may be sued in a state simply because she has some contacts with that state. *Shoe* holds that a defendant may, by committing limited acts within a state, submit herself to jurisdiction for claims arising out of the in-state acts themselves. Here, Healy's claim is unrelated to Austin's brush sales in South Dakota. Austin had no reason to believe that he was submitting himself to the jurisdiction of the South Dakota courts for auto accidents in Minnesota or other states by selling brushes in South Dakota. The situation would be different if the claim were for faulty brushes sold to a South Dakota customer. In that case, the claim would arise directly from Austin's voluntary contacts with the state and jurisdiction would be proper.

However, Healy may still be able to sue Austin in South Dakota for the auto claim. Ever since *Pennoyer v. Neff,* 95 U.S. 714 (1877), it has been

---

2. Conversely, if the defendant has minimum contacts with the forum state, it is irrelevant (at least, for personal jurisdiction purposes) that the plaintiff has none. The plaintiff's contacts may be relevant to the issue of venue, however. See Chapter 8, p. 104.

permissible to obtain personal jurisdiction over a defendant by serving her with the summons in the action within the state where suit was brought. Although this basis for asserting personal jurisdiction has recently been questioned,[3] it has never been explicitly repudiated by the Supreme Court and has been upheld in several recent lower court decisions. See, e.g., *O'Brien v. Eubanks*, 701 P.2d 614 (Colo. Ct. App. 1984). Thus, if Healy is determined for one reason or another to sue in South Dakota, it appears that she may bring suit there and have the process server await Austin's next sales trip into the state.

3.  Healy has gotten it right by suing Austin in Minnesota. For purposes of this claim for injuries suffered in the accident, Austin's act of driving in Minnesota provides a minimum contacts basis for suing him there. Motorists who use the roads of a state should realize that they subject other drivers to a risk by this voluntary activity, that people may be injured, and may sue. It would be unfair to allow drivers to take advantage of Minnesota's highways but not to call them to account there for accidents they are involved in on those highways.

Even if causing the accident in Minnesota were Austin's only contact with the state, it would be sufficient to give rise to personal jurisdiction. The "quality and nature" of the act, and the consequences that may predictably ensue from it, are so serious as to make it reasonable to force the driver to return to defend in the state of the accident. This is true whether Austin causes an accident while in Minnesota on business or in Florida on vacation. Even before *International Shoe* the same result was reached on a rather shaky implied consent theory. See *Hess v. Pawlowski*, 274 U.S. 352 (1927).

## A Parade of Perplexities

4.  As the heading suggests, this case bears a close resemblance to *World-Wide Volkswagen v. Woodson*. Here, as in *World-Wide*, the plaintiff purchased the car in one state and took it to another where she suffered injury from alleged defects in the car. As in *World-Wide*, the plaintiff sues where the injury is suffered, although the defendant acted in a distant state and is still in that state. And, as in *World-Wide*, the court will dismiss this case for lack of personal jurisdiction. Smoky Mountain (like Seaway in the *World-Wide* case) has committed no deliberate act that affiliates it with Ohio. It does not sell cars there, has not availed itself of the protection of Ohio's laws, and has no reason to expect that it will be sued there. Although it is foreseeable that the

---

3. A number of scholars have suggested that such jurisdiction based on "transient presence" of the defendant in the forum state is inconsistent with *Shaffer v. Heitner*, 433 U.S. 186 (1977), which holds that all exercises of personal jurisdiction must be measured against the minimum contacts standard. See, e.g., Friedenthal, Kane, and Miller at §3.17; see also the third-party defendant's memo in *Schulansky v. Ronan*, infra pp. 385-386.

car will be driven through or end up in Ohio, it is equally foreseeable that it will go to most other states. A rule that such foreseeability establishes jurisdiction would essentially subject the seller of any portable product to nationwide jurisdiction, making "the chattel [product] his agent for service of process" (*World-Wide Volkswagen* at 296) wherever the buyer takes it.

5.    This case is somewhat stronger than Hudson's, since De Soto at least knew that he was dealing with a Florida citizen who would use the Chevy in Florida. However, it is very doubtful that this knowledge is enough to support jurisdiction over De Soto or Smoky Mountain in Florida. Personal jurisdiction is the price defendants pay for deliberate efforts to derive benefits from or conduct activities in a state. These defendants did not solicit any business in Florida. They did not even solicit business from a Floridian; Ford rolled into the dealership under his own steam (and smoke). He initiated the transaction in North Carolina. It was only by chance that he told them why he needed the car; it is reasonable to infer that it was irrelevant to De Soto that Ford planned to drive it to Florida. (A sale is a sale, right?) In this case, De Soto and his employer derived benefits from dealing with a Floridian, not from doing business in Florida. Ford's Florida domicile is essentially a unilateral contact of the *plaintiff* — not the defendant — with the forum state. See *Hanson v. Denckla*, 357 U.S. 235, 253 (1958).

It is true that the Supreme Court cases, especially the recent ones, emphasize that the plaintiff's interest in a remedy and the forum state's interest in providing one are part of the personal jurisdiction calculus. See, e.g., *Keeton v. Hustler Magazine*, 465 U.S. at 775-776. However, before those factors can be weighed in favor of jurisdiction, the defendant must be shown to have minimum contacts with the state asserting jurisdiction. *Burger King Corp. v. Rudzewicz*, 105 S. Ct. at 2183. I would characterize De Soto's relation to Florida on these facts as too attenuated to support such a finding.

Nor is it sufficient that the defendants could anticipate that the car would be used in Florida. If that were sufficient to support jurisdiction, then the local store that sells a defective mountain climbing rope could be sued in any mountainous state, or a farmer who sells rancid tomatoes to railroad dining cars could be sued in any state the railroad serves. The Court has chosen a narrower view of personal jurisdiction, focusing on the scope of the activity of the seller, rather than the predictable area of use of the product by the buyer.

6.    Here, as in question 5, De Soto has consciously dealt with an out-of-stater, but here, unlike the earlier situation, he has voluntarily affiliated himself with the plaintiff's state. He can not only anticipate that his acts will have consequences in the other state, but he has also deliberately set those events in motion by his own in-state act. De Soto voluntarily reached into Pennsylvania to conduct business with a Pennsylvanian. He encouraged Packard to come to North Carolina to buy the car. He can reasonably anticipate that Packard will use it extensively in Pennsylvania and likely suffer harm there

from any defects in the car. De Soto should realize that his deliberate relationship with a Pennsylvanian, which he initiated by calling into that state, may lead to a lawsuit and that if a claim arises out of the sale, Packard will likely bring the suit in Pennsylvania. Thus, De Soto will be subject to personal jurisdiction in this action. His single contact with Pennsylvania is sufficient to support specific in personam jurisdiction (that is, jurisdiction for claims arising out of the contact itself), although it would not support jurisdiction for any claim that did not arise out of the sale.

7.    In this case the dealership has reached into Tennessee to solicit business. It has attempted to draw customers from there into North Carolina, and in Rambler's case it succeeded. Although the actual sale took place in North Carolina, the claim arises directly out of deliberate efforts to serve the Tennessee market, to derive profits from doing business with Tennessee citizens. Smoky Mountain can hardly plead unfairness or surprise when suits that arise from that business are brought in Tennessee. Cf. *Keeton v. Hustler Magazine*, 465 U.S. at 780-781.

It is important that the dealership is the defendant in this case, instead of De Soto, because it is the dealership that solicited the business in Tennessee, not the salesman. Although an argument could be made that De Soto derives benefits from working for a dealership that serves the Tennessee market, it is unlikely that the dealer's contacts would be imputed to all of its employees. Thus, if Rambler wanted to sue De Soto and Smoky Mountain together, he would probably have to go to North Carolina.

8.    This hypo makes an important point. Personal jurisdiction is not based on the most contacts or the best contacts but on minimum contacts. Here, Smoky Mountain has a great deal more contact with North Carolina than it has with Tennessee, but the dealership has solicited business in Tennessee, and the claim arises out of its efforts to obtain that business. That is enough to support jurisdiction in Tennessee. Smoky Mountain will not be able to defeat jurisdiction there by arguing that it has more contacts with North Carolina.

A corollary of this point is that a defendant may be subject to jurisdiction in more than one state for a claim if a claim arises from a transaction that involves contacts with a number of states. Indeed, if general in personam jurisdiction is considered, jurisdiction may sometimes be proper in many additional states, as in the oil company hypothetical.

## A Hard Case

9.    This case is more difficult than the last one, because the sale here did not arise directly out of the advertising in Tennessee; Rambler happened upon the dealership on his own.

However, jurisdiction is still appropriate in this case. The minimum contacts analysis focuses on the deliberate acts of the defendant, not on the state of mind of the plaintiff. Smoky Mountain has chosen to locate its business on the Tennessee border. It certainly anticipates and relies upon customers from Tennessee as well as North Carolina, and it has attempted to serve that market by advertising in Tennessee. While the sale to Rambler does not result directly from advertising, it does arise in a more general sense from Smoky Mountain's deliberate choice to serve the eastern Tennessee market area. Any dealership hopes to sell cars not only to solicited customers but also to area residents who come in off the street. It is certainly predictable that Tennesseans such as Rambler, who live close to the dealership and circulate in the area, will happen upon the lot or hear about it from friends and end up buying cars there. When that very predictable scenario unfolds, the dealership will not be heard to say that it didn't specifically solicit Rambler's business or hope to profit from it.

The situation in question 5 is distinguishable. In that case there was no deliberate effort to serve the Florida market. Although De Soto did consciously sell a car to a Floridian, the sale did not result from any deliberate activity directed at the state of Florida.


## Another Hard Case

10. This case also resembles the situation in *World-Wide Volkswagen*. As in *World-Wide*, the plaintiff bought the car in one state and took it to another where the injury occurred and suit is brought. As in *World-Wide*, the defendant committed an act outside the forum state — selling a defective car — that has a harmful effect within it. The Court in *World-Wide* concluded that that contact in itself is not a sufficient basis for personal jurisdiction over the out-of-state seller. See question 4.

However, in this case the defendant not only caused tortious injury in the state by a negligent act done elsewhere, he also does business in the forum state by selling cars to Tennessee residents. The Court in *World-Wide* concluded that an out-of-state defendant who serves the market for his product in a state may be subject to personal jurisdiction in that state when one of these products causes injury there, even though the negligent act that led to the injury took place outside the forum state. 444 U.S. at 297-298. Thus, in *World-Wide* the Court suggested that Audi, the manufacturer of the automobile, would be subject to personal jurisdiction in Oklahoma, since it indirectly sold Audis in that state, even though the Robinsons' Audi was sold in New York. In this case Smoky Mountain is analogous to Audi in the *World-Wide* case; in question 4, it was analogous to Seaway, the local dealer in that case.

This is one of the most confusing situations to conceptualize, because the court relies both on contacts that directly give rise to the claim (causing the tortious injury in the state) and on broader contacts (the defendant's sales of the same product — but not the specific car at issue — in the forum state).

Although causing the tortious effect in the state is not sufficient to subject Smoky Mountain to jurisdiction (compare Seaway in the *World-Wide* case), Smoky Mountain's deliberate business activity in the state makes it foreseeable that it will be sued there and lessens the argument that it is unfair or inconvenient to litigate claims in the state that relate (albeit indirectly) to its business there.

Smoky Mountain might also be subject to general in personam jurisdiction in Tennessee based on its substantial and continuous business dealings with Tennessee buyers. Most cases that have upheld general in personam jurisdiction have involved corporations with permanent facilities or employees in the state, but these are probably not necessary if the volume of in-state business is high enough. On the other hand, 10 percent of the sales of a local auto dealership — without in-state facilities or employees — is probably not enough.

11. In my estimation, this is the kind of "casual" or "isolated" contact (*International Shoe*, 326 U.S. at 317) that is insufficient to subject the defendant to personal jurisdiction. Although De Soto did act in the state, he was not soliciting business and did not initiate the conversation for business purposes. He gave Lenoir his card at Lenoir's request. He did not encourage him to go to North Carolina to buy a car. In the "but-for" sense this contact did give rise to the claim Lenoir asserts, but it was not a purposeful act intended to take advantage of the benefits and protections of conducting activity in Georgia. De Soto would be justly upset if this off-hand interaction led to suit in Georgia. He would hardly expect that to be the consequence of responding to a request for a business card, and jurisdictional doctrine is largely based on a common sense appraisal of what people should expect.

There is room for debate on this case, but it is hard to argue that this represents deliberate in-state activity intended to exploit the local market or have effects on local citizens. In this regard, it is clearly distinguishable from the Maserati case, in which De Soto deliberately initiated a business contact with the in-state plaintiff.

12. This is the classic situation of indirect contact with the forum state. Nippon does not do anything in Nevada, yet it derives profit from the resale of its cars there by others. *World-Wide Volkswagen* clearly supports jurisdiction over such out-of-state (or out-of-country) suppliers who deliver "products into the stream of commerce with the expectation that they will be purchased by consumers in the forum State." 444 U.S. at 298.

Here, Nippon has purposely taken advantage of the benefits and protections of the laws of Nevada by importing cars to that state and deriving a profit from those sales. It cannot insulate itself from the jurisdictional consequences of that activity by using wholesalers to channel the goods into the state. For an extreme example of this "market area" doctrine, see *Nelson v. Park Industries Inc.*, 717 F.2d 1120 (7th Cir. 1983) (Hong Kong shirt manufacturer that sold shirt to Hong Kong distributor that resold to American retail chain subject to personal jurisdiction in Wisconsin in action for personal injuries suffered when shirt ignited).

13. This is a close case indeed, perhaps too close to call. Studebaker does have a contact with Indiana: He advertised in a magazine circulated there with the express purpose of selling his Edsel. On the other hand, the magazine is a specialty publication circulated nationally. Studebaker was not specifically soliciting an Indiana buyer but was willing to sell to anyone, in or out of the state. Once Andretti learned of the car's availability, he took the initiative. He went to Michigan to see the car. He called back to make an offer. He picked the car up. Studebaker remained in Michigan and passively responded. It was irrelevant to him that Andretti was from Indiana. He may not even have known where Andretti was from. Compare *Droukas v. Divers Training Academy, Inc.*, 376 N.E.2d 548 (Mass. 1978) (holding jurisdiction lacking on somewhat analogous facts).

I think this is a case in which the defendant does have a deliberate minimum contact with the forum state, but the totality of the circumstances weighs against jurisdiction in Indiana. Once a jurisdictionally significant contact with the forum state is found, the court must consider whether it would be fair and reasonable under all the circumstances to take jurisdiction. *World-Wide* at 292. Given the lack of deliberate acts by Studebaker in Indiana, that all the negotiations took place at Andretti's initiative, and that Studebaker never left Michigan, it appears unreasonable to expect Studebaker to defend this claim in Indiana. But again, reasonable minds might disagree.

## Fundamental (Un)truths

14. (a) This statement implies that taking advantage of the benefits and protections of the laws of the state is an alternative basis for personal jurisdiction, independent of the minimum contacts test. On the contrary, the purpose for asking whether the defendant has taken advantage of the benefits and protections of the state's laws is to *evaluate* the defendant's contacts with the state in order to ascertain whether they are of the "quality and nature" to support jurisdiction. If the defendant's in-state acts demonstrate a deliberate effort to take advantage of the benefits and protections of the forum state's laws, it is a fair inference that these acts satisfy the minimum contacts test, since minimum contacts jurisdiction is based on the defendant's deliberate decision to act in the forum state for her own purposes.

(b) Never, never, never. As Chapter 2 should make clear, a state court's exercise of specific in personam jurisdiction must be authorized by a "long-arm" statute. However, while this is necessary to support jurisdiction, it is not sufficient; the exercise of jurisdiction must also be consistent with due process analysis. A long-arm statute cannot grant personal jurisdiction in situations in which there is no constitutional basis (such as minimum contacts) for exercising it, since a court may never act outside of constitutional limits. If a long-arm statute purported to confer jurisdiction beyond the reach of due process, that exercise of jurisdiction would be unconstitutional. For example, a long-arm statute that conferred jurisdiction over any defendant who interacted with a resident of the forum state would be held unconstitutional as applied to the facts of question 1 above because Healy has no minimum contacts with North Dakota in that case.

# 2

## Statutory Limits on Personal Jurisdiction: The Reach and Grasp of the Long-Arm

## Introduction

As we discussed in Chapter 1, the due process clause of the fourteenth amendment to the Constitution imposes fundamental limitations on the power of state courts to exercise personal jurisdiction over defendants in civil suits. Under that clause states may only assert jurisdiction over defendants who have established a significant relationship to the forum state, such as domicile, in-state presence, continuous and substantial business within the state, consent to suit in that state, or minimum contacts with the state that gave rise to the claim in suit. If the defendant is not subject to personal jurisdiction within the forum state on one of these limited bases, the court will be unable to adjudicate the plaintiff's claim.

However, even if it is constitutionally permissible for a court to exercise personal jurisdiction in a case, that court may still lack the power to call the defendant before it. The due process clause does not actually confer any jurisdiction on state courts: It only defines the outer bounds of permissible jurisdictional power. It is up to the legislature of each state to actually grant the power to its courts to exercise personal jurisdiction through jurisdictional

19

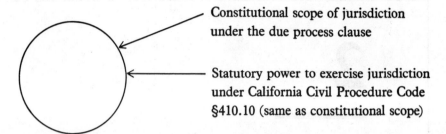

**Fig. 2–1**

statutes. Thus, every personal jurisdiction issue involves a two-step analysis. *First,* the court must ask whether there is a state statute that authorizes it to exercise personal jurisdiction under the circumstances of the case. *Second,* if there is, the court must ask whether it would be constitutional under the due process clause to do so.

State legislatures are free to grant their courts the power to exercise personal jurisdiction to the limits of the due process clause or to confer only part of the constitutionally permissible jurisdiction. In some states the legislature has granted the courts the full scope of personal jurisdiction permissible under the due process clause. California's statute, for example, authorizes its courts to exercise jurisdiction "on any basis not inconsistent with the Constitution of this state or of the United States." Cal. Civ. Proc. Code, §410.10 (West 1973 & Supp. 1986). In states with statutes like California's, the two inquiries are collapsed into one: If the court has the constitutional power to assert jurisdiction, it automatically has the statutory power to do so as well. Visually the relationship may be (somewhat simplistically) portrayed in Figure 2-1.

Other states, however, have not given their courts blanket authority to exercise personal jurisdiction to the limits of due process. Instead, these states have passed "long-arm" statutes, which authorize their courts to exercise jurisdiction over defendants based on specific types of contact with the forum state. Historically, these statutes were passed in reaction to *International Shoe* and its progeny. See generally R. Casad, Jurisdiction in Civil Actions ¶4.01 (1983) (hereinafter cited as Casad). Once *International Shoe* and succeeding cases established that certain types of contacts were constitutionally sufficient bases for exercising personal jurisdiction over nonresidents, the states adopted long-arm statutes to authorize their courts to hear cases arising out of such contacts. Thus, long-arm statutes generally authorize state courts to exercise jurisdiction over cases arising out of contacts such as committing a tortious act within the state, transacting business in the state, or owning property in the state.[1]

---

1. A fairly typical provision is the Uniform Interstate and International Procedure Act, 13 Uniform Laws Annotated 461 (West 1980), which has served as the model for the long-arm statutes of some 20 states. It is reproduced on page 23 for use in the questions in this chapter.

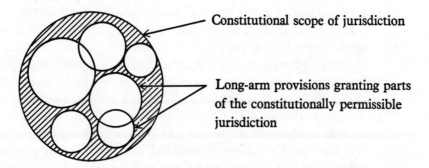

Constitutional scope of jurisdiction

Long-arm provisions granting parts
of the constitutionally permissible
jurisdiction

Fig. 2–2

Visually the relation of such statutes to the due process clause can be
represented as in Figure 2-2. Such provisions convey a good deal of the
jurisdiction authorized by the due process clause, but not necessarily all of it.
Some areas remain (represented by the shaded area in the diagram) in which
jurisdiction could be exercised but the statute does not authorize it.

Long-arm statutes take their colorful name from their primary purpose,
which is to reach out of the state to call nonresident defendants back into the
state to defend lawsuits.[2] Even though a defendant has left the forum state
before he is sued (or in some cases has never been in the state at all) he may be
required to defend a suit there under the *International Shoe* analysis if it arises
out of his prior contacts with the forum. (Compare *Pennoyer v. Neff,* 95 U.S.
714 (1877), which based jurisdiction on the defendant's presence in the state
at the time of service in the action, rather than on prior contacts with the
forum state.) Legislatures tend to grant such long-arm jurisdiction liberally
since it is usually invoked by plaintiffs who live in the state and prefer to sue
at home.

Be careful, however, not to conclude that every assertion of jurisdiction
under a long-arm statute is automatically constitutional simply because the
statute apparently covers it. In the area of personal jurisdiction, it is not
always easy to tell what is and is not constitutional. Consequently, the reach
of the state's long-arm statute may sometimes exceed its constitutional grasp.
Suppose, for example, that an Iowa long-arm statute authorized its courts to
take jurisdiction in all cases brought by resident plaintiffs. It would certainly
be unconstitutional to apply such a statute to a case arising out of the plain-

---

2. Such statutes are usually unnecessary to obtain jurisdiction over in-state defendants. Individuals who are domiciled in the state are subject to personal jurisdiction
on that basis. *Milliken v. Meyer,* 311 U.S. 457 (1940). Individuals present within the
state may be personally served and are subject to jurisdiction under the ancient (but
arguably still viable) theory of *Pennoyer v. Neff.* In-state corporations are subject to
jurisdiction on the basis of substantial and continuous activities in the forum state. See
*International Shoe* at 318. In each of these cases, however, there must also be a
statutory basis for the exercise of jurisdiction. See, e.g., Uniform Interstate and International Procedure Act §1.02 (jurisdiction based on domicile or incorporation in the
forum state).

tiff's purchase of goods from a Colorado defendant in Colorado because the defendant would have no minimum contacts with Iowa. The case is represented by Figure 2-3. But the statute could be applied in other cases without violating due process. For example, if the case arose from a sale by the defendant to the plaintiff that took place in Iowa, the exercise of jurisdiction would be permissible, since the defendant's voluntary contacts with Iowa gave rise to the claim. This case would fall in the shaded area on the diagram. In such cases, where the statute may be constitutional as applied to some cases but not all, the courts do not invalidate the statute entirely; they simply refuse to apply it to cases that fall outside the bounds of due process. Consequently, the statute remains in force and may be applied in other cases that are within due process limits.

All long-arm statutes that base personal jurisdiction on specific minimum contacts require that the claim sued upon arise out of the contact itself. See, e.g., Uniform Interstate and International Procedure Act §1.03(b) infra p. 23. This limitation is rooted in the *International Shoe* analysis, which holds that where jurisdiction is based on limited in-state contacts, jurisdiction only extends to claims that arise from those contacts. See Chapter 1, pp. 4-5. By echoing that limitation in the long-arm statute itself, the legislature insures that the statute will not be used to reach cases beyond the constitutional bounds of due process.

You will frequently read in the cases that a state's long-arm statute is "intended to reach to the limits of due process." This is one of the most frequently misunderstood phrases in the civil procedure lexicon. Although innumerable cases broadly hold that the long-arm statute in question is intended to extend jurisdiction to the constitutional limits, this is *not* generally intended to mean that a statute like the Uniform Act occupies the entire constitutional field, as the California statute does. It would make little sense for the legislature to pass a statute enumerating specific contacts that support jurisdiction if it actually intended all minimum contacts to do so. Instead, this

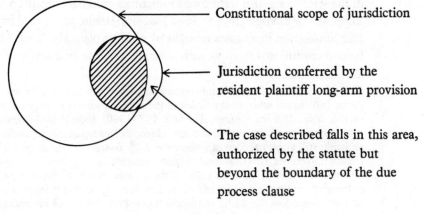

Constitutional scope of jurisdiction

Jurisdiction conferred by the resident plaintiff long-arm provision

The case described falls in this area, authorized by the statute but beyond the boundary of the due process clause

Fig. 2–3

phrase is better interpreted to mean that the specific categories of jurisdiction conveyed by the long-arm statute are to be interpreted as liberally as the due process clause will allow. See generally R. Casad and P. Simon, Civil Procedure 70 (1984).

For example, the phrase "transacting business" in a long-arm statute might be interpreted quite narrowly, to apply only in cases where the defendant has on-going commercial activities and permanent employees within the state. Alternatively it might be interpreted to apply whenever the defendant enters into a single business transaction with an in-state party. If the statute is intended to go to the limits of due process, the court must interpret this language to reach all cases that are arguably within the statutory language and can be reached under the due process clause. See Casad at ¶4.01[1][b]. Since a single business transaction (depending on the facts) may be sufficient under due process analysis to give rise to personal jurisdiction over claims arising out of it, the statute should be broadly interpreted to reach such a case. In other words, the going-to-the-limits-of-due-process language commands liberal interpretation of the specific provisions of the long-arm statute; it does not fill in any interstices that those provisions fail to cover.

In answering the following questions, consider first whether the applicable long-arm statute authorizes the court to exercise jurisdiction. Then consider whether it would be constitutional under the minimum contacts test for the court to exercise jurisdiction on the facts given.

# UNIFORM INTERSTATE AND INTERNATIONAL PROCEDURE ACT

### §1.03. [Personal Jurisdiction Based upon Conduct]

(a)   A court may exercise personal jurisdiction over a person, who acts directly or by an agent, as to a [cause of action] [claim for relief] arising from the person's

   (1)   transacting any business in this state;
   (2)   contracting to supply services or things in this state;
   (3)   causing tortious injury by an act or omission in this state;
   (4)   causing tortious injury in this state by an act or omission outside this state if he regularly does or solicits business, or engages in any other persistent course of conduct, or derives substantial revenue from goods used or consumed or services rendered, in this state; [or]
   (5)   having an interest in, using, or possessing real property in this state [; or
   (6)   contracting to insure any person, property, or risk located within this state at the time of contracting].

(b)   When jurisdiction over a person is based solely upon this section, only a [cause of action] [claim for relief] arising from acts enumerated in this section may be asserted against him.

# QUESTIONS

## Torts and the Long-Arm: Basic Cases

1.  Hardy throws a pie at Fields while the two are making a movie in New York. Fields fails to see the joke and sues Hardy for assault in Pennsylvania, where Fields lives. Hardy has no other contacts with Pennsylvania.
    a.  Could the Pennsylvania court assert jurisdiction over Hardy if the Uniform Act (supra p. 23) applied in Pennsylvania?
    b.  Would it be constitutional for the court to do so?

2.  Assume that Hardy, a comedian, performs occasionally at clubs in Pennsylvania. Fields sues him in Pennsylvania for the New York assault.
    a.  Is jurisdiction proper under the Uniform Act?
    b.  Would it be constitutional for the court to take jurisdiction?

3.  While traveling to Pittsburgh for a performance, Hardy hits Fields while driving on Interstate 81 near Harrisburg. After the performance, Hardy returns to New York. Fields, fast losing his sense of humour, sues Hardy in Pennsylvania.
    a.  May Fields do so under the Uniform Act?
    b.  Would it be constitutional for the Pennsylvania court to take personal jurisdiction over Hardy?

4.  West, in California, learns that Paramount Pictures plans to offer Fields a lucrative contract. She calls the producer in New York and tries to talk him out of it. During the conversation, she offers several vivid and distinctly uncomplimentary opinions concerning Fields's sense of humour. Fields is not amused; he sues West in New York for defamation.
    a.  Does the Uniform Act authorize jurisdiction on these facts?
    b.  Would it be constitutional for the New York court to exercise jurisdiction over West on this claim?

## Torts and the Long-Arm: *Gray* Areas of Products Liability

5.  Chaplin manufactures stunt cars in Michigan for use in movie and television chase scenes. Paramount Pictures of Hollywood, California, a regular customer of Chaplin's, orders ten cars from Chaplin, which are shipped to California. One of the cars is used to film a cliff-hanging scene in Rocky Mountain Park, Colorado. Brice, the star of the show, is injured when the brakes fail at 14,000 feet. Brice sues Chaplin in Colorado.
    a.  Would jurisdiction be authorized by a long-arm statute that allowed jurisdiction for claims "arising out of a tortious act committed in this state"?
    b.  Would long-arm jurisdiction be proper under the Uniform Act if it applied in Colorado?
    c.  Would it be constitutional for the Colorado court to exercise jurisdiction over Chaplin in this action?

6. Assume the same facts as question 5, except that the accident took place on location in Hollywood.

    a. Would jurisdiction be proper under the Uniform Act if it applied in California (instead of California's anything-constitutional-goes version, quoted at p. 20)?

    b. Would it be constitutional for the California court to exercise personal jurisdiction on these facts?

7. In this same case against Chaplin in California, Brice also sues Gleason Brake Corporation, the Michigan manufacturer of the brakes in the stunt car.

    a. Would the Uniform Act authorize jurisdiction if it were applicable in California?

    b. Would it be constitutional to require Gleason to defend this action in California?

8. One more variation: assume that Chaplin ordinarily sells his cars to New York film studios and that the car that injured Brice (in Hollywood) is the only one Chaplin has ever sold in California.

    a. Would the Uniform Act authorize jurisdiction over Chaplin in California in Brice's action?

    b. Would it be constitutional for the California court to exercise jurisdiction?

## Transacting and Contracting

9. Chaplin sells ten stunt cars to Paramount in California. Paramount sues Chaplin for breach of contract and breach of warranty after one of the cars repeatedly breaks down during filming in Hollywood. Assume that suit is brought in California and that the Uniform Act applies. (Assume for purposes of questions 9, 10, and 11 that breach of warranty is not a tort action.)

    a. Does the Uniform Act authorize jurisdiction over the suit?

    b. Does the court have power to hear the suit under the due process clause?

10. Chaplin manufactures stunt cars and sells them to Indestructible Auto, Inc. of Denver. Indestructible in turn sells the cars to movie studios. Indestructible sells ten of Chaplin's specials to Paramount in California. Paramount sues Chaplin in California for breach of warranty after three of the cars break down repeatedly during filming.

    a. Is jurisdiction proper under the Uniform Act?

    b. Is jurisdiction permissible under due process analysis?

11. Tucker, understandably anxious about the chase scene in her new movie, shops around for the best stunt car she can find. She visits Chaplin's plant in Detroit, is impressed with Chaplin's work, and agrees to buy a Chaplin stunt car. When the car is ready, Chaplin calls to find out where to deliver it, and Tucker tells him to deliver it to the movie location in Colorado. The car

breaks down repeatedly, and Tucker sues Chaplin in Colorado for breach of warranty.

    a.   Would the suit be proper under the Uniform Act?

    b.   Would it be constitutional to sue Chaplin in Colorado on this claim?

12.  Lloyd, a Californian, calls Rae, a New York lawyer he has not previously dealt with, to ask her about the advisability of signing a contract to make a movie about an opera. The call is placed from California. Rae advises him not to sign the contract because several key provisions are unenforceable. The contract goes to Marx. Lloyd sues Rae in California for legal malpractice.

    a.   Could the California court exercise jurisdiction over Rae under the Uniform Act?

    b.   Would it be constitutional for the court to do so?

13.  Assume on the facts of question 12, that Rae is Lloyd's primary counsel and that they often conduct their consultations coast-to-coast over the phone. Does the long-arm statute cover the case?

# ANALYSIS

## Torts and the Long-Arm: Basic Cases

1.  Long-arm jurisdiction: No    Constitutional power: No

    a. The Uniform Act does not provide statutory authority for Fields to sue Hardy in Pennsylvania. Although §§1.03(a)(3) and 1.03(a)(4) of the Uniform Act authorize jurisdiction in tort cases, neither applies in the circumstances of this case. Subsection 1.03(a)(3) authorizes jurisdiction over claims arising out of tortious injuries caused by an act or omission in the state (meaning the state where suit is brought). This subsection does not apply because Hardy's act took place in New York. Subsection 1.03(a)(4) allows the plaintiff to sue in Pennsylvania if he suffered tortious injury in Pennsylvania from an out-of-state act and if the defendant does business in the state or derives revenues from goods used or consumed in the state. This doesn't help Fields either. *First,* any injury he suffered took place in New York, where the assault occurred. *Second,* the question states that Hardy does not do business in Pennsylvania or have any other contacts with the state. No matter how liberally interpreted, the long-arm is too short to reach this case.

    b. Had the statute purported to confer jurisdiction over this case, its reach would have exceeded its constitutional grasp. Although Fields has minimum contacts with Pennsylvania, Hardy does not. Nor do the facts suggest any other basis for personal jurisdiction, such as consent or domicile. Fields's domicile in Pennsylvania is irrelevant; it is the defendant who is being forced into the state to defend. Unilateral contacts of the plaintiff with the forum do not create a constitutional basis for requiring the defendant to defend there. *Hanson v. Denckla,* 357 U.S. 235 (1958).

2. Long-arm jurisdiction: No    Constitutional power: No

a. Hardy's occasional forays into Pennsylvania do not lead to a different result from question 1. Subsection (a)(3) of the Uniform Act still doesn't apply because the tortious act took place in New York. Nor does subsection (a)(4) reach this case because the injury was in New York. Even if the injury could be construed to take place in Pennsylvania, it is doubtful that the proviso in (a)(4) could be met. Occasional performances in Pennsylvania probably do not amount to "regularly do[ing] business" in the state or "deriving substantial revenue from . . . services rendered" in the state.

Fields might argue that Hardy has "transacted business" (Uniform Act §1.03(a)(1)) in Pennsylvania by his performances there. Indeed he has, but this is insufficient to subject him to personal jurisdiction for Fields's New York tort claim. The Uniform Act and all long-arm provisions limit jurisdiction based on specific contacts to claims *arising out of* the contacts. Indeed, this point is so fundamental that the Act says it twice, in the first sentence of §1.03(a) and in §1.03(b) as well. Hardy could be sued in Pennsylvania for a breach of contract claim resulting from his performances there, but not for an unrelated claim arising in New York.

b. In this case, Hardy has contacts with Pennsylvania, but the claim doesn't arise from them. Ordinarily, under *International Shoe,* jurisdiction based on minimum contacts requires a relationship among the defendant, the forum, and the specific suit. *Keeton v. Hustler Magazine,* 465 U.S. 770, 775 (1984); compare *Helicopteros Nacionales de Colombia, S.A. v. Hall,* 466 U.S. 408, 413-415 (1984) (discussing circumstances in which a defendant's extensive contacts with the forum may support jurisdiction over it for any cause of action). It is because of this constitutional limitation that long-arm statutes also restrict jurisdiction to claims arising from the listed contacts. Otherwise, their reach would frequently exceed their constitutional grasp in cases like this one.

3. Long-arm jurisdiction: Yes    Constitutional power: Yes

a. In this case, Fields gets the last laugh. The case is clearly covered by subsection (a)(3) of the Uniform Act, since Hardy's tortious act (the negligent driving) took place in Pennsylvania. An argument might also be made, since Hardy was driving to a performance, that the claim arose out of Hardy's doing business in Pennsylvania (subsection (a)(1)). The argument is dubious, and in any event unnecessary because subsection (a)(3) squarely applies.

b. Courts have consistently held that committing a tortious act within the state is a minimum contact of the "quality and nature" that gives rise to personal jurisdiction. Since the claim arises out of this in-state act, jurisdiction is proper under the minimum contacts test. The fact that Hardy left the state before suit was brought does not preclude jurisdiction, because *International Shoe* premises jurisdiction on the contacts out of which the claim arose, not presence at the time of suit.

4.   Long-arm jurisdiction: Maybe     Constitutional power: Yes

a. Assuming that West has no other contacts with New York, the only likely basis for jurisdiction is subsection (a)(3) of the Uniform Act. The problem, of course, is that that section requires that the tortious injury result from an "act or omission in this state," yet West has not entered New York. The legislature has also precluded the extravagant interpretation used in *Gray v. American Radiator and Standard Sanitary Corp.*, 176 N.E.2d 761 (Ill. 1961), by specifying that the act or omission that causes the injury must take place in the state, not the injury itself. §1.03(a)(3). Indeed, statutes such as the Uniform Act, with separate provisions for in-state tortious acts and in-state injuries from out-of-state tortious acts, were a direct response to the statutory ambiguity addressed in the *Gray* decision. Compare §1.03(a)(3) with §1.03(a)(4).

However, a strong argument can be made that West did commit the tortious act in New York. Here, the defamatory statement, the act that caused the harm, rather than the injury, arguably took place in New York, where the producer heard it. Compare *Gray*, in which the tortious act was done entirely in Ohio but the harm was suffered in Illinois. Some courts have concluded in cases like this that the act takes place where the statements are heard, rather than where they are uttered. Other courts have concluded that the act takes place where the actor acts, not where the statement is heard. These courts therefore characterize cases like this as of-out-state act/in-state injury cases and refuse to take jurisdiction unless the defendant has engaged in business or other persistent activity in the state under subsection (a)(4). See generally Casad at 7-62.

This case is a good example of the importance of interpreting long-arm statutes to the full "reach of due process." If this is the governing rule of interpretation, the court should choose the broader interpretation favoring jurisdiction, rather than the narrower interpretation that West's tortious act took place in California.

b. West's act is deliberately aimed at causing harm to Fields in New York. Such an act, undertaken with the intent to injure the plaintiff in New York and involving direct contact with the producer there, constitutes a voluntary affiliation with the forum of the "quality and nature" to support jurisdiction under the due process clause. West can hardly claim surprise when the harm she intended eventuates where she intended it, and Fields sues her there. See *Calder v. Jones*, 465 U.S. 783, 788 (1984).

## Torts and the Long-Arm: *Gray* Areas of Products Liability

5.   Long-arm jurisdiction: (a) Possibly  (b) No
     Constitutional power: No

a. The long-arm statute quoted here is similar to the Illinois statute interpreted in *Gray v. American Radiator and Standard Sanitary Corp.*, 176

N.E.2d 761 (Ill. 1961). In *Gray* the court interpreted this language to apply if the injury occurred in the state, even though the defendant's negligence occurred elsewhere. 176 N.E.2d at 763. However, other courts have refused to accept this strained interpretation. See *Feathers v. McLucas*, 209 N.E.2d 68, 79 (N.Y. 1965), in which the court concluded that the *Gray* interpretation "disregards [the statute's] plain language and exceeds the bounds of sound statutory interpretation," and that the phrase only applies to cases in which the defendant's tortious conduct took place in the state. Thus, whether Chaplin is subject to jurisdiction under this long-arm provision depends on the court's willingness to stretch the language.

b. The Uniform Act does not reach this case. Subsection (3) does not apply; it focuses specifically on the place where the negligent act (negligent manufacture) took place, which was Michigan in this case. Subsection (4) does not apply either. Although Chaplin may have caused tortious injury within the state by his out-of-state act, there is no indication that the additional requirement of regular in-state conduct or profits is met.

c. The only contact Chaplin has with Colorado in this case is that the motion picture company took one of his stunt cars from California to Colorado to make a movie and the brakes failed there. Like the Volkswagen in *World-Wide Volkswagen v. Woodson*, the car reached Colorado by the unilateral act of a third party, not as the result of any deliberate contact by Chaplin with Colorado. Although it may be foreseeable that Paramount will use the car to make chase scenes in the Rockies, this foreseeability is not a sufficient basis for exercising jurisdiction over Chaplin wherever Paramount chooses to do so. *World-Wide Volkswagen v. Woodson*, 444 U.S. 286, 295-296 (1980). On these facts, it would exceed the limits of due process for the Colorado court to exercise jurisdiction over Chaplin.

6. Long-arm jurisdiction: Yes     Constitutional power: Yes

a. If Brice's accident takes place in California, subsection (4) will authorize jurisdiction. Chaplin has caused Brice's injuries in California by an out-of-state act. In addition, he apparently does business with Paramount in California on a regular basis. Note that subsection (4) includes two requirements: an in-state injury from an out-of-state act and an on-going relationship to the state. The second requirement may be satisfied by one of several alternative showings: regular solicitation of business, regularly doing business, any other persistent course of conduct in the state, or deriving substantial revenue from goods or services used or consumed in the state.

It may also be possible to argue that Brice's claim in this case arises from Chaplin's "transacting business" in California, under §1.03(a)(1) of the Uniform Act. Although Brice's claim does not arise directly out of the transaction itself (as a claim by Paramount for defects in the cars would, for example), it does "arise out of" the sale of the cars in California in a more general sense. Some courts would uphold jurisdiction in these circumstances under §1.03(a)(1). See Casad at 4-40 – 4-41. However, others have held that "transacting business" provisions like §1.03(a)(1) are intended to apply to business-related claims such as contract claims, so that a plaintiff such as Brice must satisfy (a)(3) or (a)(4) in order to sue Chaplin on this tort claim in California. See, e.g., *Whitaker v. Krestmark of Alabama, Inc.*, 278 S.E.2d 116, 118 (Ga. App. 1981).

b. There is a constitutionally significant difference between this case and the last. Here, the brake failure and resulting injury is not the sole contact Chaplin has with the forum state. The presence of the car in California arose through deliberate efforts by Chaplin to serve the market for his product in California. This is a voluntary affiliation with the state that changes the "quality and nature" of Chaplin's in-state act of causing injury in California. The Supreme Court's stream-of-commerce analysis in *World-Wide Volkswagen* supports jurisdiction over out-of-state defendants in these circumstances on the theory that a defendant who persistently takes advantage of the benefits and protections of a state's laws may fairly be called to account in the state if his product causes tortious injury there. Chaplin here is analogous to Audi in the *World-Wide* case, rather than Seaway, which did not serve the Oklahoma market. See Chapter 1, question 10. Section 1.03(a)(4) is specifically designed to provide a statutory basis for exercising this hybrid jurisdiction.

7. Long-arm jurisdiction: Yes     Constitutional power: Yes

a. The issue here is whether the component part manufacturer, who has dealt with the final manufacturer but not directly done business or sold goods in California, can be required to defend there in a products liability case arising out of injury in California allegedly resulting from a defect in its product. Gleason is analogous to Titan Valve Company in *Gray*. Gleason caused tortious injury in California by an out-of-state act and derives substantial revenue from goods used or consumed in California (i.e., the cars Chaplin sells there that incorporate Gleason's brakes). Jurisdiction has generally been upheld over component part manufacturers in these circumstances, under §1.03(a)(4) of the Uniform Act.

It will not always follow that the component part manufacturer will fit subsection (4) just because the final manufacturer does. For example, if Chaplin sold only 50 cars in California, this may be enough to constitute doing or soliciting business there or deriving substantial revenue from goods sold there. The company that makes the windshield wipers, however, at $2.00 a pair does not derive substantial revenue from goods used or consumed in California if the only wipers that go there are on Chaplin's 50 stunt cars. If the wipers failed and caused the accident, Chaplin would be subject to jurisdiction under this language but the wiper manufacturer probably would not.

b. Most courts have held that it is within the bounds of due process to assert jurisdiction over the out-of-state component part manufacturer in these circumstances. The manufacturer has derived revenue from the sale of its goods in the state, albeit indirectly. The manufacturer should not be able to accept those benefits from California and then wash its hands of the matter when the product it sends into the state (albeit indirectly) causes injury there. See *Burger King Corp. v. Rudzewicz*, 105 S. Ct. 2174, 2184 (1985). Even if the component part manufacturer is unaware that Chaplin sells his finished cars to Californians, it is subject to jurisdiction if it should realize that Chaplin is engaged in sales in other states, and it is actively seeking to serve the national market for its products by selling to Chaplin. See, e.g., *Bean Dredging Corp. v. Dredge Technology Corp.*, 744 F.2d 1081 (5th Cir. 1984).

8.   Long-arm jurisdiction: Maybe      Constitutional power: Yes

a.  In this case neither subsection (3) nor subsection (4) applies because the tortious act did not take place in the state (though the plaintiff's injury did), and Chaplin does not do substantial business or conduct other activities in the state. An argument can be made, however, that subsection (1) or (2) applies. Most courts would hold that a defendant "transacts business" in a state when it enters into any transaction with an in-state party. See, e.g., *Mouzavires v. Baxter*, 434 A.2d 988, 992-993 (D.C. App. 1981). Other courts, however, interpret this language to require an ongoing effort to exploit the in-state market. See *Droukas v. Divers Training Academy, Inc.*, 376 N.E.2d 548, 551-553 (Mass. 1978). In any case, this was a sizeable sale, presumably resulting from negotiations with the studio in California and would almost certainly constitute "transacting business" under subsection (a)(1). Here again, however, as in question 6a Brice's claim is a tort claim, not a contract or similar commercial claim arising directly out of the business transacted between Paramount and Chaplin or out of Chaplin's contracting to supply the car in California. It arises out of subsequent injury to a third person from use of the goods after the transaction was complete. Thus, it requires an expansive interpretation of the Uniform Act to conclude that it authorizes jurisdiction in this case, but some states would give the Act such a broad reading.

b.  This is a case in which I think it would be constitutional for the court to take jurisdiction. Chaplin has deliberately sent the automobile, which he should realize may cause serious injury if defective, into California. This is a meaningful minimum contact with the state. The injury arises out of that state-oriented act. It is fair and reasonable to make Chaplin defend this action in California.

If the Uniform Act applied in California, and the court concluded that it did not provide a statutory basis for jurisdiction over this case, this would be an example of a case in which the reach of the long-arm statute would be less broad than the due process clause would allow. Of course, under the actual California long-arm statute (supra p. 20), as opposed to the Uniform Act, California courts may exercise all constitutionally permissible jurisdiction. Thus, if my due process analysis is correct, this case would be proper under California's long-arm as well.

## Transacting and Contracting

9. Long-arm jurisdiction: Yes     Constitutional power: Yes

a. This claim squarely fits subsection (2) of the Uniform Act because it arises directly out of Chaplin's agreement to sell the allegedly defective car to Paramount in California. It would likely satisfy subsection (1) as well. Even if Chaplin does not have a business office in California, most courts would hold that he transacts business there by selling his product to a California buyer, at least where the sale is as substantial as this one.

b. The decision to sell goods to buyers in another state is a deliberate, profit-oriented contact with that state. When the sale is substantial (as here) or part of a series of such sales, the seller enjoys the benefits and protections of doing business in the state and may have a significant effect on the commerce of the state. In such cases, the seller should expect to defend suits there arising out of those business transactions with forum-state customers. See *Burger King,* 105 S. Ct. at 2184.

10. Long-arm jurisdiction: Yes     Constitutional power: Yes

a. The subsections of the Uniform Act that might apply on these facts are (a)(1) and (a)(2). Subsection (a)(2), however, was probably meant to reach cases in which the defendant deliberately agreed to supply goods to an in-state party. Here, Chaplin has merely sold them to a distributor who may — indeed, probably will — resell some of them in California, a likely market for movie stunt cars.

However, §1.03(a)(1) probably will support jurisdiction in this case. Although Chaplin has not directly shipped cars into California, he has profited from a predictable resale of his goods in California by the Colorado dealer. It appears likely that the statute was intended to support jurisdiction in such cases, especially if the wholesaler consistently ships Chaplin's cars into the state. Chaplin should not be able to avoid jurisdiction for acts that consistently provide him with profits from the state by using a distributor rather than directly shipping the goods into the state himself.

b. The analysis here is similar to that in question 7b. As *International Shoe* indicates, parties who enjoy the benefits and protections of the laws of a state by conducting business there, directly or indirectly, subject themselves to jurisdiction for claims that arise from those forum-related activities. So long as Chaplin can reasonably anticipate that his cars may be resold to California buyers and derives profits from such sales, it is not unreasonable to require him to defend suits such as this one, which arises from use of the cars in the state where they are ultimately sold to the consumer.

11. Long-arm jurisdiction: Unlikely     Constitutional power: Doubtful

a. It is unlikely that Chaplin's shipment of a single car into Colorado at Tucker's order is sufficient to support jurisdiction under the Uniform Act.

First, it is doubtful that a court would conclude that Chaplin has transacted business (subsection (1)) in Colorado by shipping a single car there at Tucker's request. Although many courts (but not all) have concluded that a single shipment of goods into the state is sufficient to establish "transaction of business" (see Casad at ¶¶4.02[1][a][iv], 8.01[2][a][i]), such cases have usually involved a deliberate effort by the defendant to serve the in-state market or to direct a flow of goods into the state. In this case Chaplin did not deliberately seek a business affiliation with Colorado, or even agree in advance to ship the goods to Colorado. He simply followed the shipping directions of his buyer in delivering previously ordered goods.

It also seems unlikely that jurisdiction could be found under §1.03(a)(2), which authorizes jurisdiction based on contracting to supply goods in the state. This transaction was initiated by Tucker in Michigan. The facts suggest that Chaplin did not know where the car was to be shipped or used at the time that the sale was made. He contracted to supply a car to Tucker, but not to supply it in any particular place; Tucker could have ordered him to send it anywhere. Although the car was ultimately shipped to Colorado, there is a substantial difference between passively agreeing to ship a car to the destination chosen by a buyer and deliberately agreeing from the beginning to supply goods in a particular state. It is clear that the drafters of this section intended to reach the latter conduct, but they probably did not mean to include the former.

b. It is doubtful that this isolated shipment of a single car to Colorado, at the buyer's request, is a sufficient contact with Colorado to support jurisdiction under the minimum contacts test. Chaplin has not deliberately taken advantage of the benefits and protections of Colorado law. The sale was made to a Californian in Michigan, apparently without specific knowledge that the car would be used in Colorado. Tucker's order to ship the car to Colorado is more a unilateral contact of Tucker with Colorado than of Chaplin. See *Hanson v. Denckla*, 357 U.S. 235, 253 (1958). Merely following the buyer's shipping orders is not the type of deliberate affiliation with a state that *International Shoe* contemplates as a basis for personal jurisdiction.

12.  Long-arm jurisdiction: Unlikely     Constitutional power: Also
                                                              unlikely

a. This case could be analyzed as a "transacting any business" case under subsection (1) of the Uniform Act. While there is an argument to be made that Rae has transacted business in California by offering legal advice to Lloyd there, most courts would conclude otherwise. Rae did not initiate the contact, never entered the state, perhaps did not even know what state Lloyd was calling from. This one-shot, passive forum-related activity is probably too fortuitous to rise to the level of "transacting business," which implies a calculated intent to benefit from business activities in the state.

Alternatively, Lloyd might argue, since his claim is for legal malpractice, that Rae committed a tortious act in the state, analogous to West's call in question 4. This is a close issue, but there is a significant difference between the two situations. West deliberately called the New York producer with the intent to affect his actions there. Rae simply picked up the phone and responded to inquiries from Lloyd. It is a fine distinction, but the interpretation of long-arm statutes frequently turns on such delicate judgments about what the legislature must have intended in enacting a statute that uses rather general language.

b.  It is unlikely that it would be constitutional to sue Rae in California on the basis of this single, passive contact with the state. She has not deliberately formed an affiliation to the state but simply responded to a call initiated by Lloyd, which could have come from anywhere. While Rae may receive some protection from the laws of California (for example, the right to sue Lloyd there to collect her fee), this relation to the state seems too casual to make it fair to sue her there. Even if the court concludes that she committed a tortious act in California within the meaning of the long-arm statute, it does not seem fair on these facts to subject Rae to jurisdiction there. See *McBreen v. Beech Aircraft Corp.*, 543 F.2d 26 (7th Cir. 1976) (no jurisdiction over defendant who made allegedly defamatory statements outside the state to a reporter calling from the forum state).

13.  Long-arm jurisdiction: Yes     Constitutional power: Yes

On these facts, Rae would be subject to jurisdiction in California under the "transacting business" provision of the long-arm statute and under the minimum contacts test. Here, the phone call is not just a chance occurrence, but part of an on-going, deliberate course of business between Rae and Lloyd, who (as Rae must know) lives in California. While Rae does not enter the state, she advises Lloyd in much the same way as if her office were in Hollywood and derives benefit from participating in the general business activity created by Hollywood's movie industry. It is not unreasonable to require her to accept the reciprocal obligation to defend suits arising from her advice to a California client in California.

# 3

## Seeking the Home Field Advantage: Challenges to Personal Jurisdiction

## Introduction

Surely one of the most fundamental principles of civil procedure is that the courts of a state may not exercise judicial power over a defendant unless that defendant has, in one way or another, submitted to the jurisdiction of the courts of that state. A century of case law has given some specificity to this requirement. As Chapter 1 indicates, defendants may be subject to jurisdiction under due process analysis on the basis of domicile in a state, in-state service of process, consenting to jurisdiction, continuous or substantial in-state contacts, or as a result of "minimum contacts" with the forum state that give rise to a particular cause of action.

It is not always clear when a plaintiff sues a defendant in a particular state whether one of these bases for personal jurisdiction is met. Suppose, for example, that Wolfe, a North Carolina novelist, gives a newspaper interview in North Carolina in which he disparages Hemingway's writing abilities. Hemingway sues Wolfe in Oregon for libel. When Wolfe is served with the complaint, he may be unsure whether the Oregon court has the right to exercise jurisdiction over him. For example, he may not know whether the newspaper that interviewed him is circulated in Oregon or whether Hemingway has suffered any injury in Oregon as a result of the alleged libel. If Wolfe has no other connections with Oregon, he may well conclude that the courts of Oregon have no right to order him to appear and defend the suit.

This chapter explores the options available to a defendant like Wolfe to present his objection to the exercise of personal jurisdiction over him by the courts of another state. Generally, these options involve a challenge either in the court in which the original action is brought (the rendering state) or in another state where enforcement of the original judgment is sought (the enforcing state).

The defendant's first option is to appear in the original action at the beginning of the suit and object to the court's exercise of jurisdiction over her. For example, Wolfe may decide to appear in the Oregon court and ask the court to dismiss the action for lack of personal jurisdiction. The effect of such an appearance depends on the jurisdictional doctrine of the particular state in which it is made. Some states allow a defendant to make a "special appearance" in their courts to challenge the court's exercise of personal jurisdiction over her. In those states the defendant may appear for the sole purpose of objecting to jurisdiction, without submitting to jurisdiction by the very act of appearing.

In states that follow the special appearance rule, the defendant must exercise extreme care not to raise any other issue: If she raises any objection or argument that the court can construe as a defense on the merits, the court may conclude that she has waived her jurisdictional objection. For example, in *Koplin v. Saul Lerner Co.*, 201 N.E.2d 763 (Ill. App. 1964), the defendant entered a special appearance to object to the court's jurisdiction and also moved to strike the complaint for vagueness. The court held that this hapless defendant, by raising the vagueness issue, had submitted to the court's jurisdiction. The pitfalls of making a successful special appearance are discussed in Casad at 3-18 – 3-25.

A growing number of states have liberalized their approach to jurisdictional challenges in the rendering state, by adopting the flexible approach of the Federal Rules of Civil Procedure. Under Fed. R. Civ. P. 12(b)(2), a defendant may appear before answering to the merits of the complaint and raise an objection to personal jurisdiction. The difference from the special appearance, however, is that under the Federal Rules approach the defendant may also raise other objections at the same time, without waiving the jurisdictional objection. For example, under Fed. R. Civ. P. 12(b), a defendant may move to dismiss for lack of personal jurisdiction and for failure to state a claim upon which relief can be granted (see Rule 12(b)(6)) in the same pre-answer motion. This second objection clearly goes to the merits of the suit; if it were raised by a defendant using the common law special appearance, it would be construed by the court as a waiver of her objection to personal jurisdiction.

Fed. R. Civ. P. 12(b) also allows the defendant to present her objection to personal jurisdiction along with her defenses on the merits by answering the complaint and including the jurisdictional objection in the answer. (See the defendant's answer in *Schulansky v. Ronan,* infra p. 362.) In either case, whether the defendant moves to dismiss before answering or includes the jurisdictional objection in the answer to the complaint along with her defenses on the merits, the objection must still be raised immediately in order to preserve it. Under the Federal Rules approach, as in states that still allow the special appearance, a defendant who answers on the merits and later concludes that personal jurisdiction is lacking will have waived the objection by not raising it at the outset. See generally Chapter 14.

If Wolfe properly enters a special appearance, or raises his jurisdictional objection under Fed. R. Civ. P. 12(b)(2) or an applicable state rule, the court will hold a hearing on the issue. If the court concludes that there is no basis to exercise jurisdiction over Wolfe, it will dismiss the suit. However, if the court concludes that it does have the power to exercise jurisdiction over him (at least for the cause of action asserted by Hemingway), it will proceed with the case.

In most states a defendant who challenges jurisdiction at the beginning of the suit and loses may proceed to defend the merits of the suit without waiving her objection to the court's jurisdictional ruling. If she loses the suit on the merits, she may appeal, claiming that the trial court's conclusion that it had personal jurisdiction was wrong. This scenario is hardly palatable to Wolfe, of course, since it requires him to do exactly what he believes he should not have to do, defend the action in a state that (allegedly) lacks personal jurisdiction over him. However, it at least leaves him an avenue to correct the trial judge's mistake and to avoid being bound by a decision rendered by an improper court.

## Challenging Jurisdiction in the Enforcing Court

The second option for the defendant who objects to personal jurisdiction is to ignore the original suit entirely. If Wolfe is truly convinced that Oregon lacks personal jurisdiction over him, he may view the suit as mere harassment, an ineffective proceeding that can give rise to no binding judgment and that can therefore be ignored with impunity. If the Oregon court lacks personal jurisdiction over Wolfe, any judgment it enters in Hemingway's suit will be unenforceable anyway. If that's true, why bother to respond at all?

Procedurally, it is true that Wolfe has a right *not* to appear in Oregon if the Oregon court lacks jurisdiction over him for the claim asserted in the suit. However, this course poses a serious risk: If Wolfe fails to appear at all in Oregon, either to object to personal jurisdiction or to defend on the merits of the libel claim, the court will enter a default judgment for Hemingway — that is, a judgment ordering Wolfe to pay Hemingway the damages sought in the complaint. If that judgment is enforceable, Wolfe will have lost his suit without ever having had a chance to defend it.

The usual method of enforcing money judgments against out-of-state defendants is for the plaintiff to take her judgment against the defendant to a state where the defendant has property and seek a court order from the courts of that state authorizing the sheriff or other public official to sell the defendant's assets to satisfy the judgment. Hemingway, for example, may take his Oregon judgment to North Carolina, where Wolfe lives, and ask the court to authorize a judicial sale of Wolfe's house to pay off the judgment. However, the North Carolina court will not automatically execute the judgment of another state. Instead, the usual procedure is to initiate a new court proceeding in the enforcing state, in this case North Carolina, seeking a "judgment on the judgment." If Hemingway obtains such a judgment, the North Carolina court can order execution on its own judgment through attachment and sale of the defendant's assets.[1]

The Full Faith and Credit Clause of the United States Constitution (Article IV, §1) requires the courts of each state to honor the judgments of other states by entering judgment on foreign judgments and allowing out-of-state judgment creditors to use court process to collect such judgments. However, one exception to this obligation has long been recognized: The enforcing court may inquire as to whether the rendering state had jurisdiction in the original action and refuse enforcement if it did not. See *Pennoyer v. Neff,* 95 U.S. 714, 732 (1877). For example, if the North Carolina court concludes after a hearing on the jurisdiction issue that the Oregon court had jurisdiction over Wolfe, the North Carolina court must enforce the Oregon default judgment by entering a North Carolina judgment on the judgment and making its procedures for execution of judgments available to Hemingway. However, if the North Carolina court concludes that the Oregon court did not have jurisdiction over Wolfe, it will refuse to honor the Oregon judgment, and Hemingway will not be able to levy on Wolfe's property in North Carolina.

Thus, if Wolfe ignores the Oregon proceeding, he will still have an opportunity to protect his property from being sold on execution in North Carolina. Even though a default judgment will be rendered in the original Oregon law suit, Wolfe may oppose enforcement of that judgment by asserting in the North Carolina enforcement action that the Oregon court lacked personal jurisdiction over him. This scenario is clearly the most convenient for Wolfe because he does not have to go to Oregon, something that from his

---

1. A number of states have adopted the Uniform Enforcement of Foreign Judgments Act promulgated by the National Conference of Commissioners on Uniform State Laws. 13 U.L.A. 173 (1964). The Act provides a registration procedure for state court judgments that eliminates the need to file a second suit in the courts of the enforcing state. There is also a federal statute authorizing registration of federal judgments in other federal districts. 28 U.S.C. §1963. However, under such statutes the defendant will still have an opportunity — as discussed in the text — to challenge the jurisdiction of the court that rendered the original judgment.

point of view he shouldn't have to do. It also allows him to litigate the jurisdictional issue in his home state. While the issue of whether the Oregon court had jurisdiction over Wolfe will theoretically be the same in either state, it is at least possible that a North Carolina court will be more sympathetic to Wolfe's objection than the Oregon court would be.

However, this strategy poses a great risk for Wolfe. The Full Faith and Credit Clause allows Wolfe to question the rendering court's jurisdiction but not to reopen the merits of the underlying libel action. If the North Carolina court concludes after hearing Wolfe's jurisdictional defense to Hemingway's action to enforce the judgment that the Oregon court had jurisdiction over him, the North Carolina court will automatically enforce the Oregon default judgment. If Wolfe's original conclusion that the Oregon court lacks jurisdiction is wrong (and most conclusions in this area are only educated guesses), the default judgment will be valid and enforceable, in Oregon or any other state. The idea is that a defendant has the right to stay away if a court lacks jurisdiction but not if it has jurisdiction. In the latter situation, the defendant is deemed to have waived her defense on the merits by failing to appear. That is a very considerable price to pay to avoid contesting the jurisdictional issue in the plaintiff's chosen forum.

All this is complex enough, but one further wrinkle is also important. It is true that the Full Faith and Credit Clause allows defendants such as Wolfe to challenge the validity of another state's judgment on the ground that the rendering state never obtained personal jurisdiction over them. But there is an exception to this rule as well: A defendant may not challenge personal jurisdiction in the enforcement action if she has already done so in the original action. Suppose, for example, that Wolfe had appeared in the Oregon action and moved to dismiss for lack of personal jurisdiction. If he lost and then defaulted on the merits, he could not renew his challenge to jurisdiction in an enforcement action in North Carolina because he had already litigated and lost on that issue. Once is enough; the rules of collateral estoppel provide that a party who has fully litigated an issue in one action may not relitigate it in another. See Chapter 20, p. 280. Thus, Wolfe gets his choice to raise the objection in one court or the other but not to resurrect it after it has been fully litigated and decided.

While the explanation of these principles is lengthy, their application is fairly straightforward. The following examples should help. Please assume that all cases are brought in state court unless the question states otherwise. Also assume that the special appearance rule applies in Mississippi.[2]

---

2. Until 1982 Mississippi practice allowed defendants to raise objections to personal jurisdiction by special appearance. Mississippi now follows the Federal Rules model, which allows defendants to raise the objection by a pre-answer motion to dismiss. Miss. R. Civ. P. 12(b)(2). Assume for purposes of the questions that the special appearance rule still applies.

# QUESTIONS

## Novel Developments

1.   Assume that Lewis publishes books in Ohio. He agrees to sell a thousand copies of *Brandywine, Ohio,* a popular novel, to Faulkner, a book wholesaler with offices in Mississippi. At Faulkner's request Lewis ships the books to Faulkner's Louisiana warehouse. Faulkner subsequently discovers that the books are damaged and sues Lewis in Mississippi, to recover the price of the books. Lewis claims that the books were damaged later, while stored in Faulkner's warehouse. He also doubts that the Mississippi court has jurisdiction over him because all the negotiations took place in Ohio and the parties contemplated from the beginning that the books would be shipped to Louisiana.

Lewis makes a special appearance in Mississippi to contest the Mississippi court's jurisdiction over him. The court concludes after holding a hearing that it lacks jurisdiction. What will the court do?

2.   When first served with the complaint in *Faulkner v. Lewis,* Lewis is confident that he can win on the merits, and therefore answers the complaint and defends the case on the merits. Just before trial, however, he gets nervous about the outcome and decides to move to dismiss for lack of personal jurisdiction. How will the court respond to the motion?

3.   Assume that Lewis decides to appear in the Mississippi action, despite his doubts that the court has jurisdiction over him. He defends the action on the merits and loses. Judgment is entered for Faulkner. Faulkner brings a suit on the judgment in Ohio, and Lewis opposes enforcement of the judgment on the ground that the Mississippi court lacked personal jurisdiction over him. What will the court do?

4.   Lewis is convinced from the outset that the Mississippi court lacks jurisdiction over him. Consequently, he does not respond to the complaint, and a default judgment is entered for Faulkner, who then brings an action on the judgment in Ohio.

   a.   Lewis defends the Ohio enforcement action on the ground that he is not liable for the damage because the books were damaged after delivery. Assuming that Lewis can prove this, what will the court do?

   b.   Lewis defends the enforcement action on the ground that the Mississippi court never obtained personal jurisdiction over him. Assuming this is true, what will the court do?

   c.   Lewis defends the enforcement action on the ground that the Mississippi court lacked jurisdiction over him. The Ohio court, however, concludes that the Mississippi court did have jurisdiction. What will the court do?

5.   Lewis appears specially in the original suit in Mississippi to challenge personal jurisdiction. The court holds that it has personal jurisdiction. Lewis, convinced that the court is wrong, defaults. Faulkner gets a default judgment and seeks enforcement in Ohio. Lewis defends on the ground that the Mississippi court lacked jurisdiction over him. What result?

6.   Assume that Faulkner's suit is brought in a state that follows the Federal Rules model. Lewis appears and moves to dismiss for failure to join an indispensable party. The motion is denied. He then moves to dismiss for lack of personal jurisdiction. Is the motion proper?

## The Plot Thickens

7.   Assume that Faulkner brings suit in Louisiana, the state where Lewis has agreed to deliver the books, and the Louisiana long-arm statute authorizes personal jurisdiction over a nonresident defendant as to all claims arising out of "contracting to supply goods in the state." The Ohio long-arm statute, however, has no such provision, nor any other that would apply on the facts of the case. Lewis defaults in the Louisiana action. When Faulkner seeks to enforce his default judgment in Ohio, Lewis defends on the ground that the court lacked personal jurisdiction under the Ohio long-arm statute. Will his defense be upheld?

8.   Assume that Lewis is sued in Mississippi, and makes a special appearance to object to the court's exercise of personal jurisdiction over him. The court concludes that it has jurisdiction and therefore refuses to dismiss the case. Lewis, fearful lest he lose his right to defend on the merits, decides to defend the case on the merits in Mississippi and loses. May he appeal the court's initial decision that it had personal jurisdiction over him?

9.   Lewis makes a special appearance in Mississippi to challenge personal jurisdiction and loses. He is frustrated. He knows that decision is wrong. He foresees the following scenario: litigating the merits, losing, appealing on jurisdiction, winning the appeal, case dismissed for lack of jurisdiction, Faulkner starts over in Ohio (where he ought to have started anyway). Is there any way that Lewis can short-circuit this procedural nightmare?

## Double Trouble

10.  Lewis defaults in Mississippi and challenges enforcement of the resulting default judgment in Ohio. The Ohio court refuses to enforce the Mississippi judgment, on the ground that the Mississippi court lacked personal jurisdiction over Lewis. Faulkner, convinced that the Ohio decision is wrong, brings another action on the judgment in Illinois, where Lewis owns property subject to execution. What do you think the Illinois court will do?

# ANALYSIS

## Novel Developments

1.   In most cases, the court will dismiss the case because it lacks the power to render a binding decision if it lacks personal jurisdiction over the defendant. Thus, by entering a special appearance (or an analogous motion to dismiss under Fed. R. Civ. P. 12(b)(2) if the case were brought in federal court), Lewis will avoid litigating the merits in Mississippi, without risking a default judgment that might be enforced in Ohio or some other state where Lewis has property.

In a few cases the court may agree with Lewis that it has not acquired jurisdiction over Lewis yet still refuse to dismiss. For example, if the defendant is subject to jurisdiction in the forum state but has not been properly served with process, the court may simply order process to be served in an appropriate manner and then proceed. See Chapter 4 on the proper methods for service of process. In most cases, however, the defendant's objection will not be to the method of service but to the power of the court to exercise jurisdiction. This objection, if valid, will usually require dismissal.

2.   In this case Lewis has waived his objection to personal jurisdiction by appearing and defending on the merits without raising his jurisdictional challenge. In states that follow the special appearance rule, the defendant waives her jurisdictional objection unless she raises it immediately, before pleading to the merits. The states that follow the federal approach similarly provide that objections to personal jurisdiction are waived unless raised by motion before answering or in the initial answer to the complaint. See Fed. R. Civ. P. 12(g), (h). Thus, under either approach, objections to personal jurisdiction must be raised immediately, or they are waived. Lewis may not hold back on this defense and spring it on the plaintiff later if things go badly on the merits.

3.   The answer to this question follows from the last. Lewis has waived his jurisdictional objection and is barred from raising it either by direct attack in the Mississippi court or by collateral attack in the Ohio enforcement action. It is true that it is ordinarily open to the defendant to defend the enforcement suit on the ground that the original, rendering court lacked personal jurisdiction over her. Here, however, Lewis has waived the objection by his appearance on the merits in the initial action. He may not sandbag the plaintiff by trying to win on the merits in one court and saving the jurisdictional objection to raise in the other.

4a.   Lewis defaulted on the merits in Mississippi. That precludes him from litigating any of the underlying substantive issues that Faulkner had to prove to recover, such as whether the books were damaged and whether the damage resulted from Lewis's negligence. Even if Lewis can conclusively prove that the damage was not his fault, the Ohio court will not listen. The Full

Faith and Credit Clause prevents it from reexamining issues that have been settled (even by default) in another state's courts.

If this seems like a victory of form (or procedure) over substance, consider what would happen if the opposite were true. If defendants could litigate the merits in the enforcement action, they could simply ignore the plaintiff's original suit and have the substantive issues heard in the forum of the defendant's choice instead. The plaintiff's traditional right to choose the forum (subject, of course, to venue and jurisdictional restrictions) would be replaced by the defendant's right always to litigate at home.

b. In this hypo, Lewis has exercised his prerogative to ignore the Mississippi action because he is convinced that the rendering court has no power to order him to appear there. He may raise the defense of lack of personal jurisdiction in the Ohio enforcement action since jurisdiction is the one issue that the enforcing court may consider before giving full faith and credit to the Mississippi judgment. If it is true that the Mississippi court lacked jurisdiction, the Ohio court will refuse to enter a judgment on the Mississippi judgment, Faulkner will be unable to collect on his default judgment, and Lewis will suffer no harm from it — except, of course, the anxiety over whether the Ohio court will agree with him on the jurisdictional question. If I were Lewis, I would prefer to litigate the jurisdictional issue in the Mississippi court, by filing a special appearance there, rather than risk losing the chance to litigate the merits entirely by staking all on the chance that the Ohio court will agree that the Mississippi court lacked jurisdiction over him.

c. As in question b, it is open to Lewis to challenge the personal jurisdiction of the original court in this enforcement action. However, if Faulkner proves that the Mississippi court had jurisdiction, the Ohio court is bound under the Full Faith and Credit Clause to enter judgment on the original judgment and order execution of it on Lewis's assets. Thus, by postponing his jurisdictional challenge, Lewis has abdicated his chance to defend the substance of the claim in either Mississippi or Ohio. This is an extreme price to pay for the convenience of litigating the jurisdictional issue in your home state. This price was paid, for example, in *McGee v. International Life Ins. Co.*, 355 U.S. 220 (1957), in which the insurer ignored the original California suit and the California judgment was subsequently held enforceable in Texas.

5. Once again, Lewis has run afoul of the rules. He has already raised his challenge to jurisdiction in the initial action. One bite at the apple is all that he gets; he may not challenge jurisdiction in Mississippi, lose, and try again in the enforcing court in hopes of getting a more favorable reading from an Ohio judge. See *Baldwin v. Iowa State Traveling Men's Association*, 283 U.S. 522 (1931) (defendant who appeared specially to challenge personal jurisdiction in federal action barred from reasserting that objection in subsequent enforcement action). The plaintiff should not have to prove twice that the

first court had jurisdiction, nor should the defendant be allowed to keep raising the issue until she finds some court that agrees with her. If Lewis insists on challenging jurisdiction in Ohio, he will have to default in Mississippi to preserve his right to do so.

6.    Alas, poor Lewis. All these arbitrary rules and traps for the unwary. Here, he has fallen into another by misconstruing Rule 12. That rule, and state rules modeled on it, allow the defendant to raise the jurisdictional objection along with other objections but not to raise other objections first and then challenge the court's personal jurisdiction in a subsequent motion. Responding with other objections and defenses (such as failure to join an indispensable party, or failure to state a claim, or denials on the merits) without asserting lack of personal jurisdiction operates as a waiver of that objection. See Fed. R. Civ. P. 12(g), (h). The jurisdictional objection must always be raised in the defendant's first response to the complaint. The motion will be denied.

## The Plot Thickens

7.    This question raises two important points. First, the rendering court must have jurisdiction not only under the minimum contacts standard of *International Shoe* but also under the applicable long-arm statute. Thus, even if Lewis's contacts with Louisiana are sufficient to support jurisdiction under the constitutional standard, Lewis could still argue (in the original suit or the enforcement action) that the rendering court lacked jurisdiction under the applicable long-arm statute.[3]

The second point is, what *is* the applicable long-arm statute? Ohio's, where enforcement is sought? or Louisiana's, where the initial suit was brought? The relevant issue is whether the Louisiana court had the right to exercise jurisdiction over Lewis. Therefore, the Ohio court must ask whether the Louisiana long-arm statute authorized jurisdiction in Louisiana, not whether the Ohio statute would have allowed it if Faulkner had sued there. Lewis's defense fails again.

8.    As the introductory discussion indicates, most states[4] allow the defendant, after raising the jurisdictional objection and losing, to take the safer course of defending on the merits and appealing the decision on jurisdiction. This way, Lewis may still obtain appellate review of the decision on personal jurisdiction without abandoning his opportunity to defend the case on its

---

3. Even though Lewis never did anything in Louisiana, he might be subject to jurisdiction there as a constitutional matter under minimum contacts analysis. See, e.g., *Mid-America, Inc. v. Shamaiengar*, 714 F.2d 61, 61-62 (8th Cir. 1983) (defendant subject to personal jurisdiction in Iowa for failing to fulfill agreement to assist in construction of factory in that state).

4. Mississippi follows the majority rule. See *E. B. Kaiser Co. v. Ludlow*, 243 So. 2d 62, 66 (Miss. 1971).

merits. If he wins on the merits, he will be content and will obviously not appeal the decision on jurisdiction. If he loses on the merits, he may appeal the trial court's decision that he was subject to personal jurisdiction in Mississippi. If the appellate court concludes that he was subject to jurisdiction, it will affirm the judgment. If, however, it concludes that he was not subject to jurisdiction in Mississippi, it will order the case dismissed, even though there has been a full trial on the merits.

A handful of states still follow the older, more formalistic rule that the defendant waives the jurisdictional objection by defending the case on the merits. The theory behind this more draconian rule is that it is inconsistent for the defendant to appear and litigate in that court and at the same time claim that the court lacks jurisdiction over her. If you object to jurisdiction, these courts hold, you should stick to your guns by refusing to litigate the merits and appeal solely on the jurisdictional issue. See, e.g., *Jewett v. Jewett,* 296 A.2d 11 (N.H. 1972). The cases holding both ways are reviewed in Annot., 62 A.L.R.2d 937 (1958).

9.   Clearly the most efficient course for Lewis would be to file an immediate appeal of the trial court's decision upholding jurisdiction. That way he can avoid going through a trial on the merits in Mississippi, assuming that the trial judge was wrong.

This strategy would not be open to Lewis in the federal courts. Ordinarily, parties in federal cases can only take appeals from final judgments in the district courts. 28 U.S.C. §1291. The Supreme Court has held that decisions upholding personal jurisdiction are "interlocutory" orders because they do not finally resolve the suit and are therefore not appealable until the end of the suit. See *Catlin v. United States,* 324 U.S. 229, 236 (1945).

However, state practice varies considerably on this issue. Some states allow interlocutory appeals of orders upholding personal jurisdiction or appellate relief through some extraordinary method of review. A good example is *World-Wide Volkswagen v. Woodson,* 444 U.S. 286 (1980), in which the defendants obtained review of such an order by seeking a writ of prohibition in the Oklahoma Supreme Court. Some states even *require* the defendant to seek interlocutory review of these decisions. See Casad at ¶601[5][c]. The lesson is to check carefully the applicable state practice to see whether you may or must take an immediate appeal.

## Double Trouble

10.   This is an interesting strategy on Faulkner's part. Since Court Number Two has held that Court Number One lacked jurisdiction, Faulkner tries Court Number Three, in hopes that it will disagree with Two and enforce One's judgment. It is reminiscent of Lewis's attempt in question 5 to have the enforcing court reexamine the jurisdictional issue already litigated and decided in the rendering court.

For the same reasons, it won't work. The issue of whether the original court had personal jurisdiction over Lewis was litigated and decided in Ohio. Under the principle of collateral estoppel Faulkner will be barred from relitigating the jurisdiction issue in Illinois or any other state. Note that the Illinois court, by refusing to reopen the jurisdiction issue, is not choosing between the two courts and deciding to honor the judgment of one over the other. Only the Ohio court decided the issue of jurisdiction over Lewis in the original action. The Mississippi court never did because Lewis defaulted. Thus, the Illinois court is honoring the holding of the one court that reached the jurisdictional issue.

**Tab. 3–1:** Challenges to Personal Jurisdiction: Some Common Scenarios

| Defendant's Response to the Original Suit | Action in the Rendering Court | Action in the Enforcing Court |
|---|---|---|
| *D* appears, defends on merits, and loses | Enters judgment for *P* | Must enforce the rendering court's judgment, even if *D* challenges its jurisdiction; *D* has waived her objection |
| *D* makes special appearance or 12(b)(2) motion; court agrees that it lacks jurisdiction | In most cases, dismisses action for lack of jurisdiction; in some, may order proper service to cure jurisdictional defect | If original suit dismissed, there will be no judgment to enforce |
| *D* makes special appearance or 12(b)(2) motion; court upholds jurisdiction; *D* defaults | Enters judgment for *P* | Must enforce judgment because *D* already litigated the rendering court's jurisdiction and lost |
| *D* loses on objection to jurisdiction; defends action on the merits; loses; appeals | In most states, appellate court may review decision that jurisdiction was proper; a few treat defense on merits as a waiver of the jurisdictional objection | If jurisdiction upheld on appeal, or objection waived by defense on merits, must enforce |
| *D* defaults, contests jurisdiction in enforcing court | Enters default judgment for *P*, unless lack of jurisdiction is clear from the complaint | Enforcing court may decide whether rendering court had jurisdiction; if it holds it did not, it refuses enforcement. If it holds that it did, it must enforce the judgment |
| *D* defaults, denies liability on the merits in the enforcing court | Enters default judgment for *P*, unless lack of jurisdiction is clear from the complaint | Enforces the judgment; full faith and credit clause precludes reexamination of merits, which are settled by default |

# 4

---

# *The Bearer of Bad Tidings: Service of Process in the Federal Courts*

## Introduction

Some of the most profound protections of our constitutional system are astoundingly simple. "Due process of law" under the fourteenth amendment, for example, guarantees parties the basic right to notice of a court's intention to adjudicate their rights and an opportunity for those parties to be heard before the court proceeds to do so. "An elementary and fundamental requirement of due process in any proceeding which is to be accorded finality is notice reasonably calculated, under all the circumstances, to apprise interested parties of the pendency of the action and afford them an opportunity to present their objections." *Mullane v. Central Hanover Bank,* 339 U.S. 306, 311 (1950). In civil suits, this requirement is fulfilled through service of process.

The term *service of process* is sometimes loosely used to refer to the delivery to a party or witness of various court orders, required by the relevant rules of law to be served upon him, including subpoenas, writs, and other orders that are entered in the course of litigation. However, in a stricter sense the term is used — as we will use it here — to refer specifically to service of the initial notice to the defendant of the filing of a lawsuit against him. Service of this initial summons both notifies the defendant that he has been sued and informs him that the court intends to proceed to adjudicate his rights. The summons in the Schulansky case, for example, (infra p. 334) specifically warns the defendants that they must respond to the plaintiff's complaint, or judgment by default will be entered against them.

All courts, state and federal, have elaborate provisions governing service of this initial notice to defendants. State service provisions may be found in statutes (see, e.g., N.Y. Civ. Prac. Law §§305-318) or in court rules (see, e.g., Mass. R. Civ. P. 4, set forth on pp. 52-53 for use in the chapter). Service of process in the federal courts is governed by Rule 4 of the Federal Rules of Civil Procedure. This chapter explores the intricacies of Federal Rule 4, which has served as a model for service provisions in many states, including the Massachusetts rule used in this chapter.

Rule 4 specifies in detail what documents must be served on the defendant (Rule 4(a)), how they must be served (Rule 4(c), (d), (e), and (f)), when they must be served (Rule 4(j)) and who must do it (Rule 4(c)). For example, look at Form 1 of the Federal Rules Forms that accompany the Federal Rules of Civil Procedure. The summons there complies with each of the formal requirements in Rule 4(b). Compare the summons in the Schulansky case (infra p. 334), drawn to comply with Mass. R. Civ. P. 4(b), which is virtually identical to its federal counterpart.

The most complex provisions of Rule 4 are those governing the permissible methods of service, in Fed. R. Civ. P. 4(c), (d), and (e). Under these provisions, the proper method of service depends on the type of defendant being served: For example, the methods provided for service on individual defendants may not be used to serve process on a municipal corporation or upon the United States. In addition, the Rule provides different methods of service for in-state defendants (Rule 4(c), (d)) and out-of-state defendants (Rule 4(e)).

These provisions governing the methods of service are particularly confusing, in part because they are scattered throughout subsections (c) through (e) of Rule 4. These subsections have been amended a number of times over the years, as Congress and the Supreme Court have expanded the reach and methods of service. It would be a boon to law students (and to practicing lawyers, who also have trouble with these provisions) if the rule-makers would rewrite the rule in a more understandable fashion. Hopefully the descriptions of the service provisions that follow and the questions in this chapter will help you to sort these service provisions out, despite admitted obscurities in the text.

## Service on In-State Defendants

Essentially, Fed. R. Civ. P. 4(c) and (d) provide three different methods for serving process on *individual* defendants (that is, natural persons) within the state where the court sits. The most traditional method of service is that found in Rule 4(d)(1), which authorizes service by personal delivery to the defendant, or by leaving a copy of the summons and a copy of the complaint at his dwelling house or usual place of abode with a person of suitable age and discretion residing there, or by delivering the papers to an agent appointed by the defendant to receive service of process on his behalf.

Until 1983 service by personal delivery under Rule 4(d)(1) had to be made by a United States marshal or a person specially designated by the court to serve process. This provision frequently led to delays in service or motions to the court for appointment of special process servers because the marshals were too busy with other duties to serve process promptly. Consequently, the 1983 amendments to Rule 4 inserted subsection 4(c)(2)(A), which provides that personal service may be made by any person who is over 18 years of age and not a party to the action, except in unusual circumstances set forth in 4(c)(2)(B).

The plaintiff's second option is to serve individual defendants under the provisions for service of process that apply in the courts of the state where the federal court sits. Fed. R. Civ. P. 4(c)(2)(C)(i). The plaintiff in an action in the federal district court in Massachusetts, for example, may use any methods for service of process on individuals that apply in the Massachusetts Superior Courts; that is, any of the methods provided in Mass. R. Civ. P. 4(d) (see infra pp. 52-53). If the suit were brought in Maine, however, the plaintiff would look to the service rules of the Maine courts. Note that the state rules are an alternative to service under the other methods provided in Rule 4(c) and (d); the plaintiff may choose whichever he prefers.

A 1983 amendment to Rule 4 provides the plaintiff yet a third method for serving individual in-state defendants. Under Rule 4(c)(2)(C)(ii), the summons and a copy of the complaint may be mailed to the defendant with two notice-and-acknowledgment forms and a stamped return envelope. Fed. R. Civ. P. 4(c)(2)(C)(ii); see Federal Rules Form 18-A for a sample of the form. The defendant is required to sign one of the forms and return it to the plaintiff or his lawyer. This provides a simple method for insuring notice to the defendant without the expense and delay of personal service. However, if the defendant fails to return the acknowledgment, the rule requires the plaintiff to re-serve the defendant by one of the methods specified in Rule 4(d)(1) or (3), to insure that the defendant receives proper notice of the action.

# Service on Out-of-State Defendants

One of the reasons that Rule 4 is so confusing is that it does not state explicitly that the three procedures described above apply only to service on defendants who are served within the state. If you look at Rule 4(e), however, you will see that it provides methods for service on "a party not an inhabitant or found within the state." This implies that the separate provisions of Rule 4(c) and (d) apply to in-state service, and that is the established reading of the rule. 2 Moore's Federal Practice (2d ed. 1985) ¶4.32[1] (hereinafter cited as Moore's). Service on out-of-state defendants, by contrast, must be made in the manner prescribed in Rule 4(e).

Under Rule 4(e), if there is a federal statute that authorizes service of process outside the forum state in a particular type of case, service may be made on out-of-state defendants in the manner provided in the statute. Fed. R. Civ. P. 4(e), first sentence. Alternatively, if a federal statute authorizes such out-of-state service for the type of case but does not specify a method of service, the defendant may be served by any appropriate method in Rule 4(c) or (d). Id. Last, the second sentence of Rule 4(e) authorizes service on out-of-state defendants by any method for service on out-of-state defendants that is authorized in the courts of the state where the federal court sits.[1]

It is important to understand that the second sentence of Rule 4(e) is an alternative to service under the first sentence. Even though a federal statute authorizes extraterritorial service, the plaintiff does not have to make service under its provisions; he is always free to serve under state law provisions. Advisory Committee Note to 1963 Amendment to Rule 4(e). Even if there is a federal statute that authorizes extraterritorial service *and* specifies a method for service, the plaintiff still has the option to serve by the method provided in an applicable state rule or statute. On the other hand, if there is no relevant federal statute governing out-of-state service, the *only* proper methods for such service will be those in the state statutes or rules, because the first sentence of Rule 4(e) does not apply.

Two other mechanical aspects of service should be briefly mentioned. *First,* the person making service must make proof of service (often called "return of service") by promptly filing with the court an affidavit setting forth the manner in which service was made. Fed. R. Civ. P. 4(g). If service is made by a marshal or sheriff, proof of service is usually inserted on the summons itself. See the *Schulansky* summons (infra p. 334), which contains a printed form for proof of service. *Second,* the 1983 amendments to Rule 4 have added, for the first time, a time limit within which service must be made. Fed. R. Civ. P. 4(j).[2] Prior to the addition of Rule 4(j), service might have been made well after the complaint was filed, so long as there was no unreasonable delay on the plaintiff's part in attempting it. See 2 Moore's at ¶4.06-1. Under the new rule, the plaintiff will have to demonstrate "good

---

1. The "100-mile bulge" provision in Rule 4(f) provides additional authority for serving certain out-of-state parties who are added to the lawsuit under various joinder provisions of the federal rules.

2. This time limit for service of the summons and complaint is separate from and in addition to the requirements of any applicable statute of limitations. The fact that an action is *filed* within the limitations period (which, in many cases, will satisfy the statute of limitations) does not affect this additional requirement to serve the complaint within the 120-day period prescribed in Rule 4(j).

cause" for failure to make service within the 120-day period or face dismissal of the suit.

It is important to distinguish service of process from the related concept of personal jurisdiction. In many cases, particularly older cases, challenges to personal jurisdiction have been framed in terms of "insufficient service of process," although the actual basis of the defendant's objection was that he lacked any contact with the state sufficient to support personal jurisdiction over him. In modern phraseology, a challenge to service of process (a motion to dismiss for insufficiency of service of process under Fed. R. Civ. P. 12(b)(5)) attacks the adequacy of the method used by the plaintiff to give the defendant notice of the action, not the power of the court to exercise personal jurisdiction over him (a motion to dismiss for lack of personal jurisdiction under Fed. R. Civ. P. 12(b)(2)). It is not surprising that the *Pennoyer*-era cases blended the two concepts, however, since at that time service of process on the defendant within the forum state was the predominant means of obtaining jurisdiction as well as giving notice to the defendant of the suit. Thus, under *Pennoyer*, if service was not proper (because it was not made within the state), personal jurisdiction was not obtained, and the two objections were more or less interchangeable.[3]

As noted earlier, many other papers get "served" on parties and witnesses in law suits in addition to the original complaint. All motions, pleadings (other than the complaint), discovery requests, and other papers filed with the court must be served on each party to the action; all parties have a right to notice of these as well as notice of the commencement of suit. Virtually all such papers may be served under the more flexible provisions of Fed. R. Civ. P. 5, which authorizes service of papers subsequent to the complaint by mailing them to the party's attorney, without requiring an acknowledgment. See the certificate of service for the answer in *Schulansky*, infra p. 365 and the accompanying note (pp. 365, 370). The complaint is singled out for special treatment because it is the first notice the defendant receives of the filing of the suit. If he does not receive this notice, he may never learn of the action at all. Once he has been properly informed of the suit, however, the law presumes that he will keep an eye on the docket, and eventually learn of any paper that was served by mail under Rule 5 but, for one reason or another, never reached him.

---

3. Rule 4(e) governs not only the methods for service of process on out-of-state defendants, but also the amenability of such defendants to jurisdiction in the federal court. See Fed. R. Civ. P. 4(e), second sentence, which authorizes service on out-of-state defendants "under the circumstances and in the manner prescribed in the [state] statute or rule." This "under the circumstances" language authorizes each federal district court to assert personal jurisdiction over defendants to the same extent as the courts of the state in which the federal court sits. See Chapter 6, pp. 80-81. For the purposes of this chapter, however, we focus on the other aspect of Rule 4(e), authorizing service of process "in the manner" authorized by any relevant federal statute or state statute or rule.

In answering the following questions, assume that all actions are brought in the federal district court for the District of Massachusetts. Because the state provisions for service of process may apply in some circumstances, you will have to consider the methods of service provided in Mass. R. Civ. P. 4 as well as those in Rule 4 of the Federal Rules. The relevant portions of Massachusetts Rule of Civil Procedure 4 are as follows:

(c) **By Whom Served.** Except as otherwise permitted by paragraph (h) of this rule, service of all process shall be made by a sheriff, by his deputy, or by a special sheriff; by any other person duly authorized by law; by some person specially appointed by the court for that purpose; or in the case of service of process outside the Commonwealth, by an individual permitted to make service of process under the law of this Commonwealth or under the law of the place in which the service is to be made, or who is designated by a court of this Commonwealth. A subpoena may be served as provided in Rule 45. Notwithstanding the provisions of this paragraph (c), wherever in these rules service is permitted to be made by certified or registered mail, the mailing may be accomplished by the party or his attorney.

(d) **Summons: Personal Service within the Commonwealth.** The summons and a copy of the complaint shall be served together. The plaintiff shall furnish the person making service with such copies as are necessary. Service shall be made as follows:

(1)   Upon an individual by delivering a copy of the summons and of the complaint to him personally; or by leaving copies thereof at his last and usual place of abode; or by delivering a copy of the summons and of the complaint to an agent authorized by appointment or by statute to receive service of process, provided that any further notice required by such statute be given. . . .

(2)   Upon a domestic corporation (public or private), a foreign corporation subject to suit within the Commonwealth, or an unincorporated association subject to suit within the Commonwealth under a common name: by delivering a copy of the summons and of the complaint to an officer, to a managing or general agent, or to the person in charge of the business at the principal place of business thereof within the Commonwealth, if any; or by delivering such copies to any other agent authorized by appointment or by law to receive service of process, provided that any further notice required by law be given. . . .

(e) **Same: Personal Service outside the Commonwealth.** When any statute or law of the Commonwealth authorizes service of process outside the Commonwealth, the service shall be made by delivering a copy of the summons and of the complaint: (1) in any appropriate manner prescribed in subdivision (d) of this Rule; or (2) in the manner prescribed by the law of the place in which the service is made for service in that place in an action in any of its courts of general jurisdiction; or (3) by any form of mail addressed to the person to be served and requiring a signed receipt; or (4) as directed by the appropriate foreign authority in response to a letter rogatory; or (5) as directed by order of the court.

# QUESTIONS

## A Comedy of Errors

1. Marvell brings a pro se[4] diversity action against Donne for breach of contract. He serves Donne by having a copy of the complaint delivered to Donne personally at his summer home on Cape Cod, in Hyannis, Massachusetts. Is service proper?

2. The court upholds Donne's objection to the original service and orders Marvell to re-serve Donne properly. Marvell takes a new copy of the complaint and summons, drives to Hyannis, and serves them personally on Donne. Donne moves again to dismiss for improper service of process. Why will the motion be granted?

3. Disgusted with the whole process (no pun intended), Marvell retains Herbert to represent him. Herbert promptly serves process on Donne by having Marple, an investigator from his office, deliver copies of the summons and complaint to Donne in Hyannis. Donne is not home when the investigator arrives, so she pushes the papers under the front door. Donne renews his objection to the method of service. Is the objection valid?

4. Herbert changes tactics and orders Marple to serve the summons on Donne at his year-round residence in Boston. Since the elusive Donne is not at home, Marple serves copies of the summons and complaint by leaving them with Donne's sister, who lives in Texas but is visiting Donne to run in the Boston Marathon. Though not to be found at home, Donne reappears faithfully in court to object once again to the manner of service. Has Herbert cured the defect?

5. If Donne is elusive, Herbert is tenacious. He sends the sheriff to Donne's house in Boston to serve the papers. As the sheriff knocks on the front door, Donne leaves by the back for a pressing appointment. The sheriff slips the papers under the front door and leaves. Is service finally proper?

6. Assume that Herbert is up on the latest changes in the rules and decides to serve Donne under the new mail/acknowledgment procedure instead of any of the methods in the prior questions. He sends copies of the summons and complaint to Donne, along with the required acknowledgment forms and a stamped return envelope. See Fed. R. Civ. P. Sample Forms, Form 18A. Nothing happens. Consequently, he re-serves Donne by having the sheriff take the papers to Donne's Boston home and (Donne being predictably unavailable) leaving them there under the door. Is service proper?

---

4. A pro se action is one brought by a party who is not represented by a lawyer.

## Variations

7.    Herrick sues Marlowe for personal injuries arising out of an accident while visiting Marlowe's truck repair garage in Revere, Massachusetts. Marlowe is from Massachusetts, and the action is again brought in the federal district court for the District of Massachusetts. Herrick serves copies of the summons and complaint by having them delivered in hand to Daniel, Marlowe's service manager, at the garage. Is service proper?

8.    Herrick sues both Marlowe and Daniel (also a Massachusetts citizen) for his injuries arising out of the accident at the shop. He serves the complaint by having his investigator, Poirot, deliver a copy of the complaint and summons to Marlowe at the shop. Is service proper?

9.    Herrick sues Marlowe in Massachusetts federal district court for the injuries suffered in the accident at the shop, and Marlowe decides to implead Daniel under Fed. R. Civ. P. 14, on the theory that Daniel, as a joint tortfeasor, is liable to pay half of any judgment Herrick obtains against him. Marlowe serves the complaint on Daniel under Fed. R. Civ. P. 5, by mailing a copy to him at his home in Boston. Is service proper?

10.   Assume that Marlowe has incorporated his business in Massachusetts, as Poetic Truck Repair, Inc. Herrick decides to sue the corporation for his injuries suffered on its premises. He serves the complaint by having Poirot deliver copies of the summons and complaint to Daniel at the shop. Is service proper on the corporation?

## Crossing State Lines

11.   Philips sues Datarama Corp., a Texas corporation doing business in Texas, for violation of the federal antitrust laws. Unlike most federal statutes, the antitrust laws specifically authorize nationwide service of process but do not specify how such service is to be made. See 15 U.S.C. §22, which provides in part that "all process in such cases may be served in the district of which it [the corporate defendant] is an inhabitant, or wherever it may be found." If Philips sues Datarama in Massachusetts federal court, may she serve the complaint on Datarama by the mail/acknowledgment procedure in Rule 4(c)(2)(C)(ii)?

## Harder than You Think

12.   Philips sues Datarama, among others, under the Federal Interpleader Act, which also authorizes nationwide service of process. See 28 U.S.C. §2361, which provides (in part) that process in such actions "shall be . . . served by the United States marshals for the respective districts where the claimants reside or may be found." Philips serves Datarama by mailing copies of the summons and complaint to it at its Texas headquarters, certified mail, return receipt requested. Is service proper?

13. Suppose that Philips sues Boswell in the federal district court for the District of Massachusetts under 28 U.S.C. §1983 for violation of her federal civil rights. Boswell is from Connecticut and cannot be served in Massachusetts. Philips searches the United States Code but finds no special provision governing service of process in such cases. She therefore serves Boswell under Rule 4(c)(2)(C)(ii) by mailing copies of the summons and complaint and the notice/acknowledgment forms, with a return envelope, to Boswell in Connecticut. Is service proper?

## Easier than You Think

14. Recall question 10, in which Herrick sues Poetic Truck Repair, Inc. in Massachusetts federal court. Suppose that Poetic is incorporated in New York, where it does most of its business, but also has a small truck repair shop in Revere, Massachusetts. May Herrick serve Poetic under the mail/acknowledgment procedure?

15. Review the introductory memo in the Schulansky case, infra pp. 323-325. What methods could Schulansky's attorney use for service of process on Ronan and Ronan Construction Company in that case?

# ANALYSIS

## A Comedy of Errors

1. Service is improper because Marvell has only delivered a copy of the complaint itself. Rule 4(d) requires both the summons and the complaint to be served on the defendant. See also Rule 4(a) and 4(c)(2)(A), (B), and (C), which all refer to service of the summons and complaint.

This requirement makes sense. The complaint is simply the plaintiff's introductory pleading, stating the nature of the case and the relief sought. It is designed to inform the defendant of the events that gave rise to the plaintiff's claim and the nature of his claim. The summons, on the other hand, is an official court document, issued by the court and signed by the court clerk (see Fed. R. Civ. P. 4(b)), commanding the defendant to respond to the accompanying complaint. Look, for example, at the *Schulansky* summons, which warns the defendant that "[y]ou are hereby summoned and required to serve . . . an answer to the complaint which is herewith served upon you." It is the court itself, not the plaintiff, that has the authority to compel the defendant to respond to the complaint, and it is the summons by which the court exercises that power.

2. This time Marvell has served the right documents but has done it in the wrong manner. Presumably, he is proceeding under Fed. R. Civ. P. 4(d)(1), which authorizes personal service on in-state defendants. However, buried back in Rule 4(c)(2)(A) is the provision authorizing service by any person who is not a party and is not less than 18 years of age. Marvell is a party; the

rule bars him from serving the summons and complaint himself, presumably on the theory that such service might lead to immediate (but distinctly nonjudicial) settlement of the parties' differences.

Prior to the most recent amendments of Rule 4 in 1983, service could only be made by a United States marshal or a person specially designated by the court to serve process. The revised rule eliminates use of the marshals for routine service of process but preserves a limited role for them in special circumstances. See Rule 4(c)(2)(B).

3.    *Technicalities, technicalities.* Herbert has apparently relied again on subsection 4(d)(1) of the federal rule but has not fulfilled the requirements of that subsection. *First,* it is doubtful that Donne's summer house constitutes his "dwelling house or usual place of abode"; it is apparently a vacation home. *Second,* the rule requires the process server to leave the summons and complaint with a person of suitable age and discretion residing therein. Herbert has clearly failed to meet this requirement.

Herbert might claim that service was proper under Mass. R. Civ. P. 4(d)(1). Remember that under Fed. R. Civ. P. 4(c)(2)(C)(i), he has the option to serve under the state service rules. Mass. R. Civ. P. 4(d)(1), unlike its federal counterpart, does not require that the summons and complaint be left with anyone. However, it does require them to be left at the "last and usual place of abode," which probably does not include a seasonal home. In addition, under the Massachusetts rule service must be made by a sheriff or other official process server. Mass. R. Civ. P. 4(c). Service is therefore improper under either rule.

4.    It is difficult to fault Marple here, but Donne will probably win this round too. Here again, Herbert has apparently tried to comply with Rule 4(d)(1) of the Federal Rules. That rule allows him to leave the summons with a person other than the defendant but only if that person is of suitable age and discretion *and* resides at the defendant's dwelling house or usual place of abode. Presumably, Sister Donne has just flown in for the marathon and would not be held to "reside" at Donne's Boston home.

You well might ask, "How is Marple to know that Sister Donne doesn't live in the house?" Perhaps Sister will tell her if she asks; most people are fairly trusting and not expecting the process-server. If not, Marple takes a risk by serving in this manner. She might do better, time permitting, to serve the defendant personally or by mail under Fed. R. Civ. P. 4(c)(2)(C)(ii).

5.    *He who laughs last laughs best.* Although Herbert's latest attempt is insufficient under Fed. R. Civ. P. 4(d)(1) (because not left with a person of suitable age, etc.), that is not his only option. Fed. R. Civ. P. 4(c)(2)(C)(i) authorizes service under the Massachusetts provisions as well. Mass. R. Civ. P. 4(d)(1) allows service by leaving a copy of the summons and complaint at the defendant's last and usual place of abode. The state rule does not include a requirement that it be left with a family member or with any person at all.

Thus, having the alternative of service under state law proves useful to effect service on the elusive defendant such as Donne.[5]

Service is proper here, unlike in question 4, because the papers were left at the defendant's last and usual place of abode, and they were served by the sheriff. The Massachusetts rule may be more liberal on the methods of service, but it is more restrictive on the issue of who serves it. This is certainly appropriate if service is to be allowed without personal delivery. A sheriff or constable is a neutral party with a professional reputation to protect. His or her certification that service was actually made by leaving the papers at the last and usual place of abode is more trustworthy than that of a party or someone working for the party.

6. Service is improper here. Although Herbert got off to a good start by using the new mail/acknowledgment procedure in Fed. R. Civ. P. 4(c)(2)(C)(ii), he failed to follow it through properly. Under the explicit terms of the mail/acknowledgment procedure, if the plaintiff chooses to use the mail procedure and the acknowledgment is not returned, the plaintiff is required to then serve the defendant "in the manner prescribed by subdivision (d)(1) or (d)(3) [of Federal Rule 4]." Since Donne is an individual defendant, Rule (d)(1) applies; that subsection does not authorize service by simply leaving the papers at Donne's home. Ironically, Herbert's second effort would have been sufficient under Rule 4(c)(2)(C)(i), if he had used it initially (see question 5), but is improper as a follow-up to mail service. See *Billy v. Ashland Oil Inc.*, 102 F.R.D. 230, 233-234 (W.D. Pa. 1984); but see *Humana Inc. v. Avram A. Jacobson, M.D., PA*, 804 F.2d 1390 (5th Cir. 1986) (approving service under state law despite the language of the statute).

## Variations

7. Since nothing in this question indicates that Marlowe's business is incorporated, we will assume that he is doing business as an individual and that Herrick is suing him individually. Apparently, Herrick's argument is that service is proper under Fed. R. Civ. P. 4(d)(1) because Daniel, as Marlowe's general manager, is his agent for service of process. The argument fails, however, because 4(d)(1) (and its Massachusetts counterpart) only authorize service on an agent "authorized by appointment or by law to receive service of process." Daniel may act generally for Marlowe in the shop, but this general authority to conduct his business is not the same as being specifically appointed to receive service of process.

---

5. While it is clear that leaving copies of the summons and complaint at the last and usual abode is sufficient under Mass. R. Civ. P. 4(d)(1), as incorporated by Fed. R. Civ. P. 4(c)(2)(C)(i), it is questionable whether such service is constitutionally sufficient. See *Greene v. Lindsay*, 456 U.S. 444, 452-456 (1982) (service in eviction proceeding by posting on door of apartment invalid under due process clause).

This provision is meant to reach cases in which the defendant has specifically empowered another person to accept notice of suits. It does not apply to an employee of the defendant who acts generally for him in the conduct of his business. 2 Moore's at ¶4.12. Specific appointments to accept process are sometimes made in contracts, where one of the parties seeks to insure that he will be able to sue the other in a particular state. See, e.g., *National Equipment Rental v. Szukhent*, 375 U.S. 311 (1964) (approving service on agent for service appointed in contract between the parties). They may also occur by operation of law. For example, Massachusetts law provides that a nonresident who does business in any Massachusetts city or town appoints the clerk of that city or town his agent for service of process in actions arising out of business conducted there. Mass. Gen. Laws ch. 227, §5A. In such a case, service on the city clerk would satisfy the provision in Rule 4(d)(1) for service on an agent "authorized . . . by law to receive service of process."

8.   This raises a fairly obvious issue but one that is not explicitly answered by the rule. Service is proper on Marlowe in this case but not on Daniel. Every defendant is entitled to direct notice of suits against him, under the provisions of Rule 4. Just as the law refuses to presume that a general agent of Marlowe would inform him of a suit, it also refuses to rely on one defendant to inform others (who, in many cases, he may not even know) that they have been sued. Each defendant is entitled to proper service under the Rules. Herrick will have to serve Daniel separately under one of the provisions of Rule 4.

9.   By now you may be wondering how these rules can be so intricate yet leave so many questions unanswered. In this case, the defendant has brought in a new party, who clearly must be informed of the suit. It would appear that Rule 4 should apply since it governs service of summonses and complaints, and Rule 14(a) requires the impleading party to serve a summons and complaint on the third party. However, Rule 5(a) provides that "every pleading subsequent to the original complaint" shall be served on all parties, and Rule 5(b) authorizes such service by ordinary mail, which is insufficient under Rule 4.

While the Rules themselves are not explicit on the point, the policies that underlie service suggest that the third-party complaint, like an original complaint, should be served under Rule 4. The purpose of Rule 4 is to insure adequate notice to parties who do not yet know that they have been sued. Rule 5, by contrast, is designed to provide a simple method for exchange of the many subsequent pleadings and papers that are filed in the case. It trades a little bit of certainty (under the stricter procedures of Rule 4) for a great deal of efficiency (under the ordinary mail provision of Rule 5). The rationale for doing so is that the defendant is already aware of the suit and will stay in touch with subsequent developments. That rationale does not apply to the new third-party defendant; as to him, the third-party complaint is his first notice of the action, and he has the same right to notice of it under the due process clause as an original defendant. See *Adams Dairy Co. v. National Dairy Products Corp.*, 293 F. Supp. 1164, 1165 (W.D. Mo. 1968) (Rule 4 makes exclusive provision for service of all summonses and complaints, including third-party complaints); 3 Moore's at ¶14.18[2] (once motion to implead is granted, the third-party plaintiff should obtain summons from the clerk and have it served in accordance with Rule 4).

10. Service on in-state corporations is governed by Rule 4(d)(3) rather than (d)(1). Subsection (d)(3) authorizes service on a "managing or general agent" of the corporation as well as various officers or appointed agents. Therefore, whether service on Daniel will suffice turns on whether his functions as service manager for the truck repair business make him a managing or general agent. This will depend on the specifics of Daniel's duties, but it is likely that he will satisfy this requirement. The rationale for allowing service on a general agent for a corporation is that an employee with general responsibilities is likely to realize the importance of the summons and complaint and inform the appropriate officers of the corporation of service. A service manager (once again, no pun intended) for a business that solely does repair work is likely to have that kind of general responsibility and awareness.

Note that under Rule 4(d)(3) service on a managing agent is sufficient, although question 7 indicates that it is not under Rule 4(d)(1). This distinction reflects the policy of the rule that when an individual is sued he should personally be informed unless he has specifically consented to service on another on his behalf. A corporation, however, is not a flesh-and-blood defendant; it cannot be "personally" informed of the action. Instead, the Rule authorizes service on corporate employees sufficiently highly placed to make it probable that the corporate officers who must respond to the suit will learn of it.

Service on Daniel in this case might also be proper under Mass. R. Civ. P. 4(d)(2). Use of state procedure is proper for service on corporations as well as individuals. Fed. R. Civ. P. 4(c)(2)(C)(i). Mass. R. Civ. P. 4(d)(2) authorizes service on a domestic corporation by service on the person in charge of the corporate business at its principal place of business in the state. Depending on the particular facts, Daniel might well satisfy this provision.

## Crossing State Lines

11. As explained in the introduction, service on out-of-state defendants is governed by Rule 4(e) rather than 4(c) and (d). Thus, the mail/acknowledgment procedure under Rule 4(c)(2)(C)(ii) is not directly applicable; it can only be used if Rule 4(e) incorporates it by reference. Under Rule 4(e) service may be made in the manner prescribed by a federal statute, or if such a statute authorizes out-of-state service but makes no provision as to how it is to be done, service may be made in a manner authorized by Rule 4. The statute at issue here authorizes nationwide service ("wherever it may be

found") but prescribes no method for service. Service may therefore be made under any of the three basic methods available for in-state service ("a manner stated in this rule"), that is, personal service (4(d)(1)), mail/acknowledgment (4(c)(2)(C)(ii)), or state in-state service methods (4(c)(2)(C)(i)). Philips's method is therefore proper.

## Harder than You Think

12. In this case the federal statute does prescribe, at least in part, the method for service of process: It must be served by the United States marshal for the district where service is made. Philips has disregarded that requirement. Instead, she has served Datarama under one of the provisions for out-of-state service under Massachusetts law. See Mass. R. Civ. P. 4(e)(3). This is proper under the second sentence of Fed. R. Civ. P. 4(e), which authorizes service on nonresident defendants in the manner prescribed in a state statute or rule. The important point here is that the state methods authorized under the second sentence are an *alternative* to the federal methods under the first. See 2 Moore's at ¶4.01[21]. Even if, as here, a federal statute applies and prescribes a particular method of service, the plaintiff has the option to use state out-of-state procedures instead.

13. Service is improper here because the first sentence of Rule 4(e) does not apply at all. It is true that the last part of that sentence authorizes service by the methods in Federal Rule 4 (including the mail/acknowledgment procedure), but that only applies where a federal statute authorizes service on nonresident defendants ("Whenever a statute of the United States or an order of court thereunder provides for service . . .") but fails to specify a method of service. When there is no federal statute authorizing such service, the only provision authorizing out-of-state service is the second sentence of the rule, which authorizes service in the manner provided for out-of-state service under the law of the state where the court sits. Mail/acknowledgment is not proper under Mass. R. Civ. P. 4(e), governing out-of-state service in actions in the Massachusetts courts, and is therefore not authorized here. Got that?!

## Easier than You Think

14. The crux of the matter here is that while Poetic is a foreign corporation (i.e., incorporated outside the state), it is doing business in Massachusetts. Consequently, Rule 4(e), which applies to parties "not inhabitant of or found within the state," does not apply. Poetic is "found within the state" and may be served under the provisions governing in-state service, including the mail/acknowledgment procedure under Rule 4(c)(2)(C)(ii). Although the subsection does not specify where the summons and complaint are to be sent in such cases, it does authorize service on a managing or general agent. There-

fore, service on Daniel as Poetic's "managing agent" in the state would be proper.

This conclusion is reinforced by the provisions of Fed. R. Civ. P. 4(d)(3). That provision, which details one method for serving in-state defendants, specifies that service can be made under its provisions on a domestic *or foreign* corporation. The clear implication is that a "foreign" corporation (that is, one incorporated in another state) can be served under in-state procedures if it is found within the state.

Many states, including Massachusetts, have provisions for substituted service on a state official in actions against foreign corporations. See Mass. Gen. Laws ch. 181, §§3, 3A (foreign corporation doing business in Massachusetts must designate Commissioner of Corporations as its agent for service of process in actions against it). Such statutes include a requirement that notice of the action be forwarded to the defendant corporation. See Mass. Gen. Laws ch. 181, §4 (providing for notice to be mailed to the corporation of all actions in which substituted service is made upon the commissioner).

15. The defendants in *Schulansky* are both out-of-state defendants, one an individual and the other a corporation. The claims against them are common-law negligence and breach of contract claims; no federal statute governs service of process in such cases. Consequently, the first sentence of Rule 4(e) does not apply at all, and the plaintiff's only option for service upon them is under the second sentence of that subsection, which authorizes service in the manner prescribed by Massachusetts law for service on out-of-state defendants. Those provisions are set forth in Mass. R. Civ. P. 4(e) and include any method for service on an in-state defendant, any manner prescribed by the law of the state where service is made (i.e., New Hampshire's provisions for *in-state* service), any form of mail requiring a signed receipt, or any method ordered by the court. The simplest method will probably be service by certified mail, return receipt requested.

The provision for service under the law of the state where service is made is a little confusing. Fed. R. Civ. P. 4(e) incorporates the methods for service under Massachusetts law, which allows Schulansky to look to Mass. R. Civ. P. 4(e). Subsection (2) of Massachusetts Rule 4(e) specifically allows the plaintiff to look to the methods provided for service in the state where service is to be made.

And you thought you wanted to be a litigator.

# 5

---

# *Diversity Jurisdiction: When Does Multiplicity Constitute Diversity?*

## Introduction

A major premise underlying our Constitution is that the states function quite well in most respects and that federal interference should be confined to those areas where there is a special need for national policy. For example, in 1787, when the Constitution was drafted, every state already had its own system of courts. The Framers saw no need to abolish those courts in favor of federal courts administered by the national government. Instead, the Framers authorized the creation of a separate federal court system (see Article III, §1), but only authorized those courts to hear limited categories of cases that, for one reason or another, involved a particular national interest. Article III, §2. Jurisdiction of all other cases was left to the courts of the states.

One of the major categories of cases that the Framers authorized federal courts to hear is the so-called diversity jurisdiction, described in Article III, §2 as cases "between citizens of different states." In diversity cases, as in some others enumerated in Article III, §2, the subject matter jurisdiction of the federal courts is defined by who the parties to the suit are, rather than the subject matter of the underlying dispute.[1] The plaintiff in a diversity case may

---

1. Other such examples in Article III are cases to which the United States is a party; cases involving ambassadors, ministers, and foreign citizens; and cases between states.

seek recovery on a battery theory, a fraud claim, a right created by state statute, or any other state law cause of action. So long as she sues a diverse defendant and the claim is for more than $10,000, the federal court will have subject matter jurisdiction on the basis of diversity.

The Framers' apparent reason for singling out diversity cases for federal jurisdiction was a fear that out-of-state citizens would suffer prejudice if they were forced to litigate against local citizens in the local state courts. That rationale has been long disputed by the scholars,[2] and repeated efforts have been made to abolish diversity jurisdiction, but reports of its death, in the words of Sam Clemens, have been greatly exaggerated.

Although Article III authorizes jurisdiction over diversity cases, it does not directly confer the diversity jurisdiction, or any other category of jurisdiction, on the lower federal courts. Rather, it authorizes Congress to create lower federal courts, and to confer jurisdiction upon them to hear the types of cases enumerated in Article III, §2. This important additional requirement is succinctly explained by Judge Sirica in one of his Watergate opinions:

> [F]ederal courts may assume only that portion of the Article III judicial power which Congress, by statute, entrusts to them. Simply stated, Congress may impart as much or as little of the judicial power as it deems appropriate and the Judiciary may not thereafter on its own motion recur to the Article III storehouse for additional jurisdiction. When it comes to jurisdiction of the federal courts, truly, to paraphrase the scripture, the Congress giveth, and the Congress taketh away.[3]

Thus, a plaintiff invoking federal jurisdiction must always be prepared to show that her case is not only within the constitutional bounds of Article III, but also within some congressional grant of jurisdiction as well.

In the case of diversity jurisdiction, Congress has granted to the federal courts some, but not all, of the Article III diversity jurisdiction. The statutory grant, in 28 U.S.C. §1332, is narrower than Article III, for example, in that it includes an amount-in-controversy requirement, while Article III authorizes jurisdiction over all diversity cases, regardless of the sum in dispute. Chief Justice Marshall further narrowed the reach of the statute in *Strawbridge v. Curtiss*, 7 U.S. 267 (1806). *Strawbridge* holds that a case is not within the statutory grant of diversity jurisdiction unless there is "complete diversity" between the parties, that is, all plaintiffs in a suit are from different states from all defendants at the time suit is brought.

As a result of these restrictions, many cases within "the Article III storehouse" may not be brought in federal court as diversity cases. This relationship between the constitutional and statutory requirements is reminiscent of the separate limits on personal jurisdiction in the fourteenth amendment and

---

2. For a review of the debate, see Wright, Federal Courts §23 (4th ed. 1983) (hereinafter cited as Wright).

3. *Senate Select Committee v. Nixon*, 366 F. Supp. 51, 55 (D.D.C. 1973).

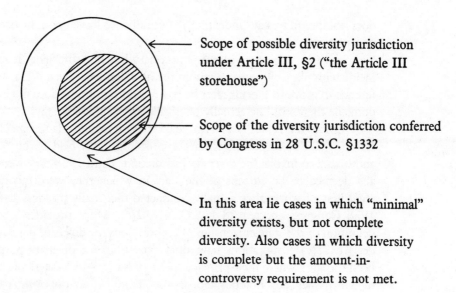

Scope of possible diversity jurisdiction under Article III, §2 ("the Article III storehouse")

Scope of the diversity jurisdiction conferred by Congress in 28 U.S.C. §1332

In this area lie cases in which "minimal" diversity exists, but not complete diversity. Also cases in which diversity is complete but the amount-in-controversy requirement is not met.

**Fig. 5–1**

long-arm statutes. See Chapter 2, pp. 19-21. Here, as there, the legislature may grant less than all of the constitutionally available jurisdiction but not more. See Figure 5-1.

Constitutions establish grand principles but seldom explain exactly how to apply them. In the area of diversity jurisdiction, for example, it has been left to the courts to determine what it means to be "citizens of different states." For natural persons (that is, human beings), the courts have equated state citizenship for diversity purposes with the common law concept of domicile. A person's domicile is generally defined as the state where she has taken up residence with the intent to reside indefinitely. Under this definition, residence is not equivalent to domicile; it is necessary but not sufficient to establish a domicile for diversity purposes. If Hawes owns houses in Missouri and Wyoming and spends a good deal of time in both states, he will still have only one domicile. Which state it is depends on his subjective intent — sometimes almost impossible to ascertain — to make one particular state his "home." See Wright at 147.

It is not necessary to irrevocably decide to live forever in a state to establish domicile there, but you must be physically present there, without any fixed intention at the time to leave that state to make your home somewhere else. If Hawes quits his job and goes to Florida in hopes of finding a good job, he establishes a new domicile, even though he may leave if the job market proves unpromising. However, if Hawes goes to Florida for a few months as an undercover agent for the FBI, with the intent to return to his home in Missouri when the case is closed, he remains domiciled in Missouri, even if the exact length of time it will take to crack the case is unknown. Although the exact date of his departure from Florida is unknown, Hawes does not intend to stay "indefinitely" but rather to leave upon the occurrence of a particular event.

Similarly, subjective intent is necessary but not sufficient: It must coincide with physical presence within the new domicile. Even if Hawes firmly intends to move to Florida after he retires next month, he does not acquire a domicile there until he actually physically arrives there to stay.

Although it is hardly a foregone conclusion from the language of Article III and §1332, corporations have consistently been held to be "citizens" authorized to invoke the diversity jurisdiction. Until 1958 they were generally deemed to be citizens of the state in which they were incorporated, regardless of where they actually conducted their daily business activity. In 1958 Congress enacted 28 U.S.C. §1332(c), which provides a statutory definition of the state citizenship of corporations for diversity purposes. Under §1332(c) corporations have dual citizenship for diversity purposes in both the state where their principal place of business is located and the state in which they are incorporated. Consequently, if an opposing party is a citizen of either of those states, diversity does not exist.

The "principal place of business" provision in §1332(c) has created some interpretive problems. In many cases corporations carry on their business totally or predominately in one state, so it is clear that they are citizens of that state for diversity purposes. In other cases, however, particularly cases involving very large corporations or corporations whose business involves commerce or transportation among numerous states, it will be difficult to point definitively to one state as the corporation's principal place of business. If there is a definable center of the productive activities of the corporation, that is, the manufacturing or other profit-making activity that the corporation is engaged in, most courts tend to choose that state. The term "place of business," after all, connotes the place where you do what you exist to do, and the term "principal" place of business suggests the place where you do the most of it. See, e.g., *Kelly v. United States Steel Corp.*, 284 F.2d 850 (3d Cir. 1960).

However, the day-to-day activities of some corporations may be so dispersed as to make it artificial to characterize one state as the center of their productive activities. In such cases, the courts have sometimes looked to the so-called nerve center of the corporation, the central location or home office from which the corporate activities are coordinated, as the principal place of business. See, e.g., *Egan v. American Airlines, Inc.*, 211 F. Supp. 292 (E.D.N.Y. 1962). In some cases the center of operations and nerve center tests may both point to a single state.[4]

---

4. Like so many procedural issues, however, this one is not entirely settled. The Seventh Circuit uses the nerve center test alone to establish a corporation's principal place of business. *Wisconsin Knife Works, Inc. v. National Metal Crafters,* 781 F.2d 1280, 1282-1283 (7th Cir. 1986).

Assume in answering the following questions that all actions are brought in federal court, that the amount-in-controversy requirement is met in each case, and (unless otherwise specified) that each case is based on state law.

# QUESTIONS
## The Basic Diversity Requirements

1.  Is there diversity between the parties in the following cases:
    a.  Marlowe, from California, sues Archer, from California, in a federal district court in Illinois.
    b.  Carella, from New York, sues Marlowe (Cal.) and Archer (Cal.).
    c.  Carella (N.Y.) sues Marlowe (Cal.) and McGee, a Floridian, in a federal district court in California.
    d.  Carella (N.Y.), McGee (Fla.), and Spenser (Massachusetts), sue Marlowe (Cal.), Archer (Cal.), and Meyer (New York).
    e.  Marlowe (Cal.) sues Carella (N.Y.) and Marple, an Englishwoman.
    f.  Same facts as (e), except that Marple, still an Englishwoman, lives in California.
    g.  Spenser (Mass.) sues the state of New York for revoking his private investigator's license. (Compare Article III, §2 with §1332).

2.  Marlowe (Cal.) sues Archer (Cal.) in a federal court in California for damages under a federal firearms control statute. May the court hear the case?

3.  Marlowe (Cal.) sues McGee (Fla.) and Archer (Cal.). His claim against McGee is for defamation, a state law claim. His claim against Archer arises from the same incident but is based on federal law. Will the federal court have jurisdiction?

4.  Marlowe (Cal.) sues McGee (Fla.) for libel. He subsequently learns that Archer (Cal.) co-authored the offending article and amends his complaint to assert a libel claim against Archer as well. Will the federal court have jurisdiction over the action?

5.  Carella (N.Y.) collides with McGee (Fla.) during a car chase in New York City. Carella is disabled in the accident, retires to Florida, and sues McGee in a federal district court in Florida. Is the suit proper?

6.  Meyer, a New Yorker, decides to move to Arizona. He buys an Audi from Isola Volkswagen, a New York dealership, and sets off with his family for Arizona. While driving through Oklahoma, he is involved in an accident and hospitalized.
    a.  Four months later, while still in the hospital, he files suit against Isola in an Oklahoma federal court. May the court entertain the action?
    b.  While in the hospital, Meyer receives an offer to stay in Oklahoma and work as a detective for an oil company. He accepts and several

months after beginning work sues Isola in federal court. Is the suit proper?

## Corporate Diversity

7. Carella (N.Y.) sues Underworld, Inc., incorporated in Delaware, doing business in every state, with its principal place of business in Florida. Suit is brought in the federal district court for the Northern District of Florida. Does the court have jurisdiction?

8. McGee (Fla.) sues Underworld in a New York federal court. Is the suit proper?

9. Marlowe (Cal.) sues Gamblers International, Inc., a corporation incorporated in Nevada. Gamblers has two casinos, one very large casino in Reno, which grosses $40 million per year, and another casino in California, which does $35 million in business each year. The corporate offices are in Reno. Is there diversity jurisdiction in Marlowe's suit?

10. Prior to the 1958 amendment that provided for dual citizenship of corporations for diversity purposes, corporations were considered citizens of their state of incorporation only. Did the amendment expand or contract corporate access to federal court?

# *Aggregation of Damages*

Congress has limited the diversity jurisdiction of the federal courts to cases "where the matter in controversy exceeds the sum or value of $10,000, exclusive of interest and costs." 28 U.S.C. §1332(a). It has been up to the courts to flesh out the meaning of that limitation. The paradox of the amount-in-controversy requirement is that it is impossible to know the value of the plaintiff's claim until the court has adjudicated it. The plaintiff may ask for $50,000 but only recover $3,000 or lose the case entirely after trial. How is the court to determine its power to hear the case without hearing the case?

This paradox has been resolved by the very sensible rule announced in *St. Paul Mercury Indemnity Co. v. Red Cab Co.*, 303 U.S. 283 (1938). Under that case, the plaintiff's good faith claim in her complaint for damages in excess of $10,000 controls, unless it appears to a legal certainty that the plaintiff will not be able to recover that amount. 303 U.S. at 288-289. In many cases in which the plaintiff seeks intangible damages, such as pain and suffering, loss of business good will, or emotional distress, it will be virtually impossible to demonstrate that she could not meet the amount requirement, because it is difficult to predict how a jury will value such losses. Thus, while the *St. Paul Mercury* rule is sensible from an administrative point of view, it greatly reduces the effectiveness of the requirement as a limit on diversity cases in federal court.

The courts have also been left to evolve rules to deal with aggregation of claims, in situations where one or more plaintiffs assert multiple claims. The basic rules, for better or worse, are that a single plaintiff may aggregate any claims she has against a single defendant to reach the required sum, but may not aggregate claims against different defendants, except in those rare situations where the defendants share a common undivided interest in the subject matter of the suit. See Wright at 197-198. Each plaintiff must also independently satisfy the amount requirement. For a full (but skeptical) discussion of aggregation, see Wright at 196-201.

The following questions will help you to apply the aggregation rules, if not to appreciate them.

# QUESTIONS

## Aggravation of Damages

11. Is the amount-in-controversy requirement met in each of the following cases? (Assume that diversity is otherwise proper and that there is no common undivided interest involved in the suit.)

  a. Hammer sues Holmes for $6,000 for his personal injuries suffered in an auto accident and $6,000 for damage to his car in the same accident.

  b. Hammer sues Holmes to recover $7,000 on a loan he made to Holmes and $8,000 for an unrelated libel.

  c. Hammer sues McGee for $12,000 for fraud, based on a business deal, and also seeks $4,000 in the same suit from Carella for losses suffered in the same deal.

  d. Hammer and Marlowe sue McGee together for losses suffered in the business deal. Hammer seeks $9,000 in damages and Marlowe seeks $5,000.

## Adding Insult to Injury

  e. McGee sues Spenser for causing $7,000 worth of damage to McGee's houseboat. His complaint contains two counts. Count One seeks $7,000 from Spenser for negligently ramming the boat while docking in Fort Lauderdale. Count Two seeks $7,000 from Spenser on the theory that he intentionally damaged the boat.

  f. McGee's $15,000 houseboat is completely destroyed in a collision with boats piloted by Spenser and Carella. He claims that both Spenser and Carella were negligent and sues them both to recover for the damage to the boat.

  g. McGee sues Spenser for $7,000 for intentionally injuring his boat and for $10,000 in punitive damages.

# ANALYSIS

## The Basic Diversity Requirements

1a. Marlowe and Archer are both from California. You can't get any less diverse than this, under any definition of diversity. The fact that Marlowe has sued in an Illinois federal court is irrelevant. No matter which district he chooses, the parties are from the same state. Don't be thrown off the track by the suit being brought in a third state. For diversity purposes (unlike personal jurisdiction purposes), the crucial question is where the parties live, not where they sue.

b. This is a proper diversity case even though both defendants are from California. The *Strawbridge* rule requires that all defendants be from different states from all plaintiffs; parties on the same side of the "v" may be co-citizens. While this might not satisfy one's intuitive notion of "complete diversity," it is diverse enough to satisfy Chief Justice Marshall and §1332.

c. This is the completest of all possible diversities because all parties are from different states. It is therefore a proper diversity case. Once again, the place of suit is irrelevant to the diversity analysis (although sometimes crucial to the other two rings, personal jurisdiction and venue). Carella's choice of the defendant's home forum does not destroy diversity, just as the choice of forum could not create it in question 1a.

d. There is no diversity jurisdiction here. While there are diverse citizens on both sides of the "v," there are also New Yorkers on both sides, which violates the *Strawbridge* rule. This is an ironic result: Why should a New York state court jury be any less prejudiced against Marlowe and Archer, simply because Meyer has been sued as well? Indeed, might not the jury shift the blame from the in-state defendant to the out-of-staters? It is easy to poke holes in the *Strawbridge* rule in cases like this; indeed, Chief Justice Marshall is said to have regretted the decision himself. Wright at 141.[5] But any effort to amend the diversity statute to revise the *Strawbridge* rule would probably lead to an expansion of diversity jurisdiction. In an age when diversity is in disrepute such an amendment is unlikely.

Note the various ways in which the plaintiffs could restructure this suit to use the federal courts. All three plaintiffs could sue Marlowe and Archer, or McGee and Spenser could sue all three defendants. In either case, diversity would exist, but some part of the controversy would have to be heard separately in state court.

e. This is a suit between diverse citizens with an additional party who is an alien (a harsh-sounding term for a person who is a citizen or subject of another country). Article III, §2 does not specifically provide for this kind of

---

5. On the other hand, this application of the rule is not entirely irrational. Carella could not sue Meyer in federal court alone, since they are both from New York. Why should he be able to do so simply by joining other defendants who are diverse?

case, but it does separately authorize jurisdiction over cases between citizens of different states and cases between citizens and aliens ("between a State, or the Citizens thereof, and foreign States, Citizens or Subjects"). It is a fair inference that a combination of the two is also proper. Congress has expressly made that inference in 28 U.S.C. §1332(a)(3).

f. Marple is an alien whether she is currently living in California or England. She cannot become a state citizen without first becoming a United States citizen. Thus, even if she is domiciled in California, this is a proper diversity case. See, e.g., *Mas v. Perry,* 489 F.2d 1396 (5th Cir. 1974). For an interesting variation on this case, see *Twentieth Century-Fox Film Corp. v. Taylor,* 239 F. Supp. 913 (S.D.N.Y. 1965), in which Elizabeth Taylor was sued for various claims arising out of the filming of the movie "Cleopatra." Although Taylor was an American citizen at the time suit was filed, she was domiciled abroad. Consequently, she was not subject to suit in federal court under the diversity statute since she was not a citizen of any state, nor was she an alien since she had not relinquished her American citizenship. Id. at 914 n.2.

g. Jurisdiction is improper in this case even though Article III, §2 appears to authorize jurisdiction over a case such as this, between a state and a citizen of another state. As Judge Sirica points out, the constitutional authority will not suffice without a Congressional grant of jurisdiction as well. If you look carefully at 28 U.S.C. §1332, you will see that it does not include jurisdiction over this type of case.

2.    This question is meant to dispel one potential source of confusion. It is only necessary to have one basis of federal jurisdiction to sue in federal court. Here, Marlowe's suit is brought under a federal statute. It is a case "arising under federal law," a separate basis for federal subject matter jurisdiction authorized by Article III and 28 U.S.C. §1331. It is therefore irrelevant that the parties are from the same state.

3.    This suit is proper even though Archer and Marlowe are both from California. Marlowe has a federal claim against Archer, a separate basis for suing him in federal court. To ascertain whether diversity exists, you need only consider the parties who are being sued on that jurisdictional basis even if there are other parties to the action. Clearly, on the facts Marlowe could sue McGee and Archer in separate actions in federal court, one based on federal question jurisdiction and the other on diversity. It would hardly make sense to allow him to do that, but not to allow him to sue them in a combined action.

4.    The federal court would be forced to dismiss this action for lack of diversity jurisdiction. Marlowe's amendment has "destroyed diversity" by adding a party from his home state. Even though the court had jurisdiction over the action as originally filed, it must dismiss once the nondiverse party is added. Otherwise, the plaintiff would be able to gain access to federal court by suing diverse parties in the initial action and adding home-state defen-

dants later on. See *Owen Equipment & Erection Co. v. Kroger,* 437 U.S. 365 (1978).

As a practical matter, Marlowe will not offer this amendment if he wishes to remain in federal court and knows that his amendment will destroy diversity. He will sue Archer separately in state court. If unified litigation is more important than access to federal court for part of his claim, he will bring a separate action against both defendants in state court and dismiss his federal suit against McGee.

**5.** Although the parties were diverse at the time of the incident that gave rise to Carella's claim, they no longer are at the time of the suit: Carella has apparently changed his domicile by retiring to Florida. Although it is unclear from the statute, courts have held that the magic date for determining diversity is the date of filing suit. *Hawes v. Club Equestre El Comandante,* 598 F.2d 698, 701 (1st Cir. 1979). If the parties are not diverse on that date, there is no jurisdiction. If they are, it does not matter that they were from the same state when the claim arose. Nor is the fact that the accident took place in New York of any help; the place of the underlying events in suit, like the place where the plaintiff brings the action, is irrelevant to the determination of diversity.

**6a.** If you have already studied personal jurisdiction, you will recognize this hypo as a slightly modified version of the facts in *World-Wide Volkswagen v. Woodson,* 444 U.S. 286 (1980). The case could not properly be brought as a diversity case, since Meyer is still a New Yorker. Even though he intends to settle in Arizona, and has left New York, perhaps never to return, he has not yet established a domicile in Arizona. To do so, he must physically arrive in the state with the intent to remain indefinitely.

Nor may Meyer argue that he is domiciled in Oklahoma, based on his four months' stay there. He has arrived there and established a "residence" of sorts,[6] but so far as we know has not changed his intent to go on to live in Arizona. Residence in Oklahoma without the necessary intent is just as ineffective to create a new domicile as intent to live in Arizona without residence there. Until the two coincide in a new state, Robinson remains a New York domiciliary.

**b.** A frequent mistake in applying the domicile rule is to conclude that intent and residence must coincide when a person originally arrives in the state. Not so; as long as the two coincide at some time while she is there, a new domicile is established. In this case, Meyer does not intend to stay in

---

6. Establishing a residence for domicile purposes need not entail purchasing a house or leasing an apartment. Even an overnight stay in a hotel, or a night spent in the family camper may suffice. See Restatement (Second) of Conflicts of Laws §12, illustration 2; cf. *T.P. Laboratories v. Huge,* 197 F. Supp. 860, 863 (D. Md. 1961). Some authorities state the requirement as one of "physical presence" rather than residence. See, e.g., *Holmes v. Sopuch,* 639 F.2d 431, 433 (8th Cir. 1981).

Oklahoma when he arrives but forms that intent later, while residing there. That is sufficient to make Oklahoma his domicile, and this is consequently a proper diversity case.

## Corporate Diversity

7.  Diversity jurisdiction is proper here, since Carella is not from either Underworld's state of incorporation or the state where it has its principal place of business. The fact that Underworld does business in New York, the plaintiff's home state, does not affect diversity as long as New York is not Underworld's principal place of business. Distinguish personal jurisdiction over the corporation, which may be established (in appropriate cases) in a state where the corporation does business, even though it does a great deal more business in other states. See Chapter 1, question 8.

8.  There is no diversity jurisdiction here because the plaintiff is from the same state as Underworld's principal place of business. McGee may not claim diversity on the ground that he is from Florida and Underworld from Delaware: Underworld is *also* from Florida under §1332(c). Neither the corporation nor the opposing party may pick and choose between these two states in order to establish diversity. The corporation is from both states and therefore complete diversity is lacking.

9.  In this case, the defendant has very large facilities in two states, both of which might ordinarily be deemed "principal" places of business. While it may seem artificial to designate either as more "principal" than the other, §1332(c) has been consistently interpreted to mean that a corporation can have only one principal place of business for diversity purposes. See 28 U.S.C. §1332(c) ("*the* state where it has its principal place of business") (emphasis supplied). Thus, the court will have to choose California or Nevada; since the corporate headquarters and the larger casino are both in Nevada, it will likely conclude that Gamblers's principal place of business is Nevada. Thus, it will be a citizen of Nevada on this basis as well as based on incorporation there and will be diverse from Marlowe. In many cases, as in this one, corporations will be citizens of only one state under §1332(c) because they are incorporated in the state where their principal place of business is located.

10. The amendment restricted corporate access to the federal courts by increasing the number of cases in which it will share the same state citizenship with opposing parties. For example, a mining corporation might incorporate in Delaware, for tax or legal reasons, but do all its mining business in Colorado. Under the earlier interpretation, it was diverse from a Colorado citizen and could invoke federal jurisdiction even though, in day-to-day reality, it functioned as a local Colorado corporation. Under §1332(c), however, that corporation is deemed a citizen of Colorado as well and confined to the state courts in suits against local citizens.

## Aggravation of Damages

11a. Hammer may aggregate his claims against Holmes, a single defendant, to reach the required jurisdictional amount. Since the two claims combined exceed $10,000 the amount-in-controversy requirement is met.

b. Aggregation is proper because the plaintiff may aggregate her claims against a single defendant even if, as here, they are totally unrelated.

c. Hammer satisfies the amount requirement against McGee but not against Carella. He may not bootstrap his $4,000 claim against Carella to his claim against McGee; aggregation only allows the plaintiff to aggregate claims against a single defendant. Hammer's claim against Carella will be dismissed for lack of jurisdiction.

For an interesting decision applying this rule to class actions, see *Zahn v. International Paper Co.*, 414 U.S. 291 (1973). In *Zahn,* the named plaintiffs claimed more than $10,000 in damages, but many members of the class they sought to represent did not. The Court stuck to its guns on the traditional aggregation rules and held that the class members' claims had to be dismissed for failure to meet the amount-in-controversy requirement.

d. Both of these claims will be dismissed. Just as Hammer was precluded from aggregating claims against separate defendants, he is also precluded from aggregating his claims with those of another plaintiff to reach the $10,000-plus threshold.

## Adding Insult to Injury

e. If you thought carefully about this case, you should have concluded as a matter of common sense that the amount-in-controversy requirement is not met. The rule that the plaintiff may aggregate her claims against a single defendant applies to claims for *separate losses,* such as those asserted in question 11b, not to demands for the same relief based on different theories. McGee has only suffered $7,000 in damages; that is what he is suing to recover. Granted, he has two possible theories of relief, but he will clearly not recover $7,000 on both theories. Spenser could not have been negligent *and* intentionally caused the damage. If McGee wins at all, he will win on only one theory and only recover the amount of his loss.

Indeed, even in cases where a plaintiff might recover on both theories, she will not be awarded more than her actual damages, absent a claim for punitive damages. For example, McGee might sue an auto dealer for breach of contract and breach of implied warranty to recover for a car worth $6,000 less than he paid for it. Even if the court finds for McGee on both counts, he will still recover only the $6,000 he has lost; no court will give him double damages simply because he advanced two theories for relief.

f. In this case McGee is claiming that both defendants' negligence contributed to cause the loss of his boat. If it turns out that only Spenser was at fault, McGee would recover the entire $15,000 from him, or from Carella if he caused the collision. If they are held jointly negligent, the law in most states would allow McGee to collect the full $15,000 from either, assuming that McGee was not negligent himself. (It would then be up to the defendant who had paid to seek "contribution" from the other.) Thus, since both defendants are at risk for the entire $15,000, the amount-in-controversy requirement is satisfied against both.

g. Here, McGee's actual damages are $7,000, but he may recover more than his actual damages if the law of the state allows recovery of punitive damages. If the state does allow punitive damages in the kind of action McGee brings, the amount requirement is likely met. Under *St. Paul Mercury,* the plaintiff's demand controls unless it appears to a legal certainty that he could not recover the jurisdictional amount. It is extremely difficult to say for sure that McGee will not recover $3,000 in punitive damages, since punitive damages turn on a jury's subjective assessment of the extremity of the defendant's conduct and at the time the defendant challenges the sufficiency of the amount sought the court will have little familiarity with the underlying facts of the case.

However, if the relevant state law bars punitive damages, the amount-in-controversy requirement will not be met and the case will be dismissed, since the only allowable damages do not amount to more than $10,000.

# 6

---

# *Personal and Subject Matter Jurisdiction Compared: The First Two Rings*

## Introduction

Much of the civil procedure course is devoted to the fundamental issue of choosing the proper court in which to bring a lawsuit. As you probably already know, there is quite a choice: Each of the 50 states has its own court system, not to mention the District of Columbia and other territories. In addition, there is a separate system of federal courts, established and administered by the federal government but geographically located throughout the United States. Thus, in any particular state there will be both the local state courts and one or more "branches" or districts of the federal court system.

The plaintiff is not free to choose indiscriminately among the various federal and state courts in the 50 states. There are three basic requirements that limit the proper courts for any lawsuit. *First* is the need to find a court that can exercise personal jurisdiction over the defendant. *Second,* not all courts can hear all types of cases: The plaintiff must choose a court that has "subject matter jurisdiction" over the kind of case he wishes to litigate. *Third,* the chosen forum must be a proper "venue" under the applicable venue statutes. I call these the three rings of civil procedure and visualize them as in Figure 6-1.[1] As a rule, courts can only hear those cases that satisfy

---

1. I am indebted to Professor Abram Chayes of Harvard Law School, my own civil procedure teacher, for this helpful diagram.

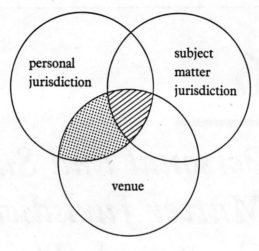

Fig. 6–1

all three rings (the shaded area on the diagram). Frequently, a case will satisfy one or two of these prerequisites but fail the third. For example, the plaintiff may have chosen a court that has personal jurisdiction over the defendant and is a proper venue under the relevant venue statute (see the dotted area in the diagram), yet the court will still have to dismiss the action if the third ring, subject matter jurisdiction, is not met.

This chapter compares the first two rings, personal and subject matter jurisdiction. Each of these requirements serves a distinct purpose, yet they are related, and students understandably confuse them initially. Personal jurisdiction, as Chapter 1 explains, is a geographical limitation intended to prevent courts from hauling defendants into the state to defend suits unless the defendant has previously established a relationship to the state that makes it fair to require him to do so.

Because personal jurisdiction turns in each case on the relationship of the suit or the parties to the state where the court is located, jurisdiction may be proper in one state for a particular action but not in another. For example, if Gable sues Leigh, a Texan, for assault arising out of threats Leigh made during a stunt at a Hollywood movie opening, it would be unreasonable to force Leigh to defend the action in Minnesota. She has (presumably) no relation to Minnesota, did not make the threats in Minnesota, and had no reason to expect that any suit arising from the incident would be brought in Minnesota. However, it would be fair to require her to defend the assault action in California, since she made the statements there and can reasonably expect them to injure Gable there.

Similarly, the courts of a single state may have jurisdiction over one suit between particular litigants but not another between the same parties, if the second suit is unrelated to that state. Although Gable's first assault action could not be brought in Minnesota, he might well be able to sue Leigh there for another assault if Leigh repeats her threatening statements at a Minneapolis opening.[2]

Subject matter jurisdiction, by contrast, concerns the generic nature of the case before the court. State court systems, for example, will frequently have specialized courts that only hear certain types of disputes, such as landlord/tenant cases (a housing court) or family and inheritance matters (a probate court). Each state also has a set of courts of "general jurisdiction" that have subject matter competence over a wide range of the usual types of suits, such as torts, contracts, property, and other common claims.[3] These general trial-level courts have different names in different states. In California they are called the Superior Courts; in Pennsylvania, the Courts of Common Pleas; in New York, perversely, the Supreme Courts.

By contrast, the subject matter jurisdiction of the federal district courts, the trial level courts of the federal judicial system, is quite limited. Those courts were not created to displace the preexisting state systems, but only to provide a federal forum for specific categories of cases of federal concern. The federal courts have jurisdiction over cases arising under federal law, cases between citizens of different states (the so-called diversity jurisdiction), and other more limited categories of cases. United States Constitution Article III, §2. By contrast, they have no jurisdiction over most common types of suits, such as tort suits, contract actions, or actions seeking recovery under state statutes (unless the suit also meets the requirements for diversity or some other category of federal jurisdiction).

## Sources of Confusion

A number of factors conspire to make these differing concepts difficult to sort out. First, although Article III, §2 of the Constitution confers jurisdiction over various categories of cases on federal courts, it does not withdraw jurisdiction over those cases from the state courts. The state courts have "concurrent jurisdiction" over cases within the federal judicial power unless Congress has conferred exclusive jurisdiction on the federal courts by stat-

---

2. As Chapter 2 demonstrates, satisfaction of the personal jurisdiction "ring" requires an analysis of both the constitutional limits of the due process clause and the applicable statutory limits on personal jurisdiction in the state where suit is brought. Gable will have to consider both tiers of this analysis to obtain personal jurisdiction over Leigh.

3. When the legislature creates a specialized court for a certain type of claim, it may or may not withdraw jurisdiction over such claims from the trial courts of general jurisdiction. For example, in a state with a special housing court for landlord/tenant cases, the plaintiff may have the option to bring a landlord/tenant case in the superior court as well. In other states, the state housing court may have "exclusive" jurisdiction of such claims.

ute.[4] Thus, a state court may hear many claims arising under federal law, such as federal civil rights cases, even though the plaintiff would have the option to bring the action in federal court as well. By contrast, the federal courts do not have concurrent jurisdiction over state law actions (unless the parties are diverse); they may only hear those cases specifically provided for in Article III of the United States Constitution and by jurisdictional statutes passed by Congress.

The Framers of the Constitution made the situation particularly confusing by creating the diversity jurisdiction (see Article III, §2), which authorizes the federal courts to hear cases between citizens of different states. In most situations, subject matter jurisdiction is defined by the nature of the controversy (such as housing cases, probate cases, or tax cases), but here the Framers chose to confer upon federal courts the power to hear cases on the basis of who the parties are. Despite this focus on the domicile of the parties, this is *not* personal jurisdiction; it does not focus on the geographical relationship of the events giving rise to the suit to the state where suit is brought but broadly grants subject matter jurisdiction to any federal court, no matter where located, so long as the case is between citizens of different states. For example, if Flynn, from Oregon, sues Peck, from Maryland, for a breach of contract arising in Montana, the case is a proper diversity case (assuming the amount in controversy exceeds $10,000). Any federal district court will have subject matter jurisdiction over it, though many will not have personal jurisdiction over Peck.

Another potential source of confusion arises from the fact that the concept of domicile is relevant to both personal and subject matter jurisdiction. A natural person (that is, a human being-type defendant) is subject to personal jurisdiction in the state where he is domiciled, that is, the last state where he has established a residence with the intent to reside indefinitely. See Restatement (Second) of Conflicts of Law §27 (1971). An individual's state citizenship for purposes of determining diversity jurisdiction is also determined by this same domicile concept. But in applying the concept to determine personal jurisdiction, the court will ask whether the defendant's domicile is in the state where suit is brought. When invoking this concept to determine subject matter jurisdiction based on diversity, the court will simply compare the plaintiff's domicile to the defendant's to make sure they differ.

For the purposes of this chapter, it is necessary to touch briefly on a problem that puzzles lawyers as well as law students — the reach of personal jurisdiction in the federal courts. As a matter of *constitutional power*, the federal courts' power to exercise personal jurisdiction is not limited by the fourteenth amendment due process analysis of the *International Shoe* line of

---

4. An example of such a statute is 28 U.S.C. §1338(a), which makes federal jurisdiction over patent and copyright cases exclusive.

cases, but instead by the due process clause of the fifth amendment. Under fourteenth amendment analysis, state courts may only exercise personal jurisdiction over parties who have formed a relationship to that state. By contrast, under the fifth amendment a defendant need only have an appropriate relationship to the United States — such as being found or domiciled in the United States or having minimum contacts here that give rise to the claim — in order to be subject to personal jurisdiction in a federal court. Thus, it is generally held that Congress has the power to authorize federal courts to exercise nationwide jurisdiction, that is, to require parties found anywhere in the United States to respond to suits brought in any federal district court. See generally Casad at ¶5.01.[5]

In some types of actions, Congress has authorized nationwide jurisdiction in the federal courts through special jurisdictional provisions governing particular types of actions. An example is 28 U.S.C. §2361, which authorizes nationwide service in interpleader actions. Unless such a special provision applies, however, the authority for federal courts to serve process outside the state where they sit is restricted by the Federal Rules of Civil Procedure. Under Fed. R. Civ. P. 4(e), a federal court is authorized to serve process out of state "under the circumstances and in the manner" prescribed by state law, that is, to exercise personal jurisdiction only to the extent it could be exercised by the courts of the state in which the federal court sits. Thus, if Gable sues Leigh in federal court in California, and Congress has not authorized broader jurisdiction for the type of suit involved, the court will only exercise personal jurisdiction over Leigh if the California courts could do so under the California long-arm statute and the due process clause of the fourteenth amendment.

This is really a very sensible rule. By generally confining the reach of personal jurisdiction in the federal court to that of the state courts of the same state, the Rules eliminate a potential ground for "forum-shopping" based on purely procedural considerations. As indicated above, in many cases plaintiffs will have a choice of state or federal court because both systems have concurrent subject matter jurisdiction over many types of suits. If the reach of personal jurisdiction were generally broader in federal court, plaintiffs would frequently choose to bring suit there for this reason alone, even though state court would otherwise be a more appropriate forum.

---

5. A frequent argument in support of this conclusion is that Congress did not have to create separate federal courts in each state. It might have created regional courts or a single court located at the seat of the federal government. Had Congress taken this course, it would obviously have been necessary to authorize such a court to exercise broad jurisdiction over defendants from all over the country. Since such nationwide jurisdiction might well have been necessary, it would be incongruous to hold that it is constitutionally impermissible. See, e.g., *Briggs v. Goodwin,* 569 F.2d 1, 8-10 (1st Cir. 1977), rev'd on other grounds sub nom. *Stafford v. Briggs,* 444 U.S. 527 (1980).

The following questions should help you to sort out these related concepts. Assume in all cases that the relevant long-arm statute authorizes exercise of all constitutionally permissible jurisdiction. See the California statute supra p. 20.

# QUESTIONS

## Four Basic Cases

1.  Stewart, a California citizen, wishes to sue Cagney, also a Californian, for battery, to recover for injuries he suffered in a fight between them on a Los Angeles street. Stewart prefers to sue Cagney in California.

    a.  Would a California state court have personal jurisdiction over Cagney?

    b.  Would a California federal court have personal jurisdiction over Cagney?

    c.  Would a California state court have subject matter jurisdiction over the action?

    d.  Would a California federal court have subject matter jurisdiction over the action?

2.  Assume that Cagney is from New York and attacked Stewart while visiting California to make a movie. Stewart, a California citizen, prefers to sue Cagney in California.

    a.  Would the California state court have personal jurisdiction over Cagney?

    b.  Would the California federal court have personal jurisdiction over Cagney?

    c.  Would a California state court have subject matter jurisdiction over the action?

    d.  Would a California federal court have subject matter jurisdiction over the action?

3.  On the facts of question 2, could Stewart have sued Cagney in either a state or federal court in New York?

4.  On the facts of question 2, could Stewart have sued Cagney in either a state or federal court in Nevada?

## Some Variations

5.  One more variation on the facts of question 2. Assume that after the Los Angeles battery but before bringing suit Cagney moves to California.

    a.  May Stewart sue him in federal court in California?

    b.  May Stewart sue him in a New York state court?

6.  Colbert sues Hepburn in the federal district court for the Southern District of California for breach of a contract to star in a movie. Both parties

are domiciled in New York, the contract was made there, and the movie was to be made there. However, Colbert prefers to sue in California where she is currently working and also prefers to sue in federal court. Hepburn, who is currently working in Arizona, does not object to the California court hearing the case. May it do so?

7.    Colbert sues Kojak in New York for a violation of her federal civil rights. Suit is brought under 42 U.S.C. §1983, the statute that authorizes suits for such violations. The claim arises out of events taking place in New York, and Kojak is domiciled there.

    a.    May Colbert bring the suit in a New York state court?

    b.    May she bring the suit in a California federal court?

    c.    Assume, on the same facts, that Colbert is from California. Could she bring the action in a California federal court?

8.    May Colbert sue Hepburn in a New York state court for violation of a copyright she holds on a book about the golden age of the movies? See 28 U.S.C. §1338(a).

# ANALYSIS

## Four Basic Cases

1a.    The California state court will have personal jurisdiction over Cagney on several bases. First, the California court may exercise personal jurisdiction over Cagney on the basis of his California domicile. Domicile in the forum state has been held an adequate basis for asserting personal jurisdiction, even if the claim sued upon did not arise in the state. *Milliken v. Meyer*, 311 U.S. 457 (1940). A person who has chosen the state as his domicile may fairly be said to have submitted himself generally to the judicial power of that state's courts, as a quid pro quo for enjoying the benefits and protections of living within the state.

In addition, Cagney has (allegedly) committed an in-state tortious act by assaulting Stewart in California. Virtually every state's long-arm statute authorizes personal jurisdiction over defendants for claims arising out of torts committed within the state, and this assertion of jurisdiction is clearly constitutional under *International Shoe*. Where Cagney has entered the state and consciously committed an act intended to harm Stewart in California, it is both fair and foreseeable to require him to respond to a California suit arising out of those in-state acts. See Chapter 1, question 3.

b.    As stated in the introduction, the federal district courts' reach of personal jurisdiction is restricted in most cases to that of the courts of the state. Fed. R. Civ. P. 4(e); *De Melo v. Touche Marine, Inc.*, 711 F.2d 1260, 1264-1266 (5th Cir. 1983). Rule 4(e) requires the federal court to look to the statutes or court rules governing personal jurisdiction in the state where the federal court sits. For example, the Idaho federal court will look to the

Idaho long-arm statute. If the statute authorizes the assertion of jurisdiction, and such an exercise of jurisdiction would not exceed the due process limits on *state* court jurisdiction, the federal court will have personal jurisdiction. Similarly, the California federal court will look to the California jurisdiction statutes as well as the constitutional limits on state jurisdiction. Since the California state court would have personal jurisdiction over Cagney, the federal court will too.

One interesting consequence of this rule is that the reach of personal jurisdiction may vary from one federal court to another because each exercises jurisdiction to the extent permitted in the state in which it sits, and the reach of long-arm statutes varies from state to state.

c. Every state court system has a set of courts that has broad subject matter jurisdiction over state law claims, including battery claims. These courts of "general jurisdiction" are the workhorses of the state court systems because they are the basic trial courts for most types of claims. In California, they are called the superior courts, and their jurisdiction includes tort claims such as the battery alleged in *Stewart v. Cagney*. Note that the analysis here for subject matter jurisdiction focuses on the nature of the case Stewart is asserting, rather than the relationship of the underlying events to the state of California, as in the personal jurisdiction analysis.

d. The California federal district court will not have subject matter jurisdiction over this case. The federal courts are not courts of general jurisdiction, but are limited to the types of cases listed in Article III, §2 and the federal statutes, such as 28 U.S.C. §§1331 and 1332, that directly confer subject matter jurisdiction on the federal courts. Since nothing in Article III grants federal courts jurisdiction over battery cases, Stewart's suit may not properly be brought in federal court.

It is true that cases involving state claims, such as battery, negligence, or breach of contract may be brought in federal court if there is diversity between the parties. The Framers, in their wisdom, saw fit to allow even cases based on state theories of recovery to be brought in federal court, if the parties are from different states. But here they are not, so there is no basis for federal subject matter jurisdiction. Only the California state court has both personal and subject matter jurisdiction over Stewart's suit; if venue is also proper, it may proceed to hear the case.

2a. On these facts Cagney is not subject to personal jurisdiction in California on the basis of his domicile, but the minimum contacts analysis in question 1a remains unchanged. Cagney has still committed a tortious act in California likely to injure Stewart there. He will be subject to "specific" in personam jurisdiction there for suits arising out of this in-state tortious act. Even though it may be extremely inconvenient for Cagney to return to California to defend the action, under due process analysis the California court may require him to do so. See, e.g., *Elkhart Engineering Corp. v. Dornier Werke*, 343 F.2d 861, 865-868 (5th Cir. 1965) (approving jurisdiction in

Alabama over German corporation for tort claim arising out of single transaction in the state).

b. As suggested above, the federal court under Fed. R. Civ. P. 4(e) will exercise personal jurisdiction to the same extent as the state court. Since the California state court may require Cagney to return and defend, the federal court may as well.

c. The answer here is the same as question 1c; the California superior court is a court of general subject matter jurisdiction that may hear tort claims. Thus, as in question 1, the California state court satisfies both rings; if venue is proper, it may hear this case.

d. It is still true, as in question 1d, that the federal courts have no subject matter jurisdiction over battery cases because nothing in Article III bestows jurisdiction of common law tort claims on the federal courts. However, Article III does authorize federal courts to hear cases between citizens of different states, regardless of the nature of the underlying dispute between them, and Congress has conferred that jurisdiction on the federal district courts in 28 U.S.C. §1332, subject to the amount-in-controversy requirement. Since Cagney and Stewart are now diverse, the federal court has subject matter jurisdiction over the suit between them if Stewart seeks more than $10,000 in damages. So here too the two rings intersect: Stewart will have a choice of California state or federal court for this suit, assuming that he can satisfy the third ring, venue, in both courts.

3.    Stewart may sue Cagney in state or federal court in New York. Here, there is no minimum contacts basis for personal jurisdiction, but Cagney is subject to personal jurisdiction there because New York is his domicile. When jurisdiction is based on domicile it is irrelevant that the cause of action did not arise there. See Chapter 1, p. 6. Thus, the state courts in New York may exercise personal jurisdiction over him, and a New York federal court may do so as well, under Fed. R. Civ. P. 4(e).

Subject matter jurisdiction is also proper in the state or federal court in New York. The state trial courts of New York, the inaptly named supreme courts, have general subject matter jurisdiction over battery cases, including battery cases that arise in other states. The federal court in New York also has subject matter jurisdiction based on diversity since Stewart and Cagney are still diverse. Notice that Cagney's New York domicile is essential to establish a basis for personal jurisdiction over him there. For subject matter jurisdiction, however, he need only be domiciled in some state other than California. The fact that he happens to be domiciled in the state where suit is brought is not essential for establishing diversity. Forty-eight other states would do as well.

4.    If Stewart sues in Nevada, the subject matter analysis is the same as question 3. Nevada's trial level courts (called district courts) have general jurisdiction over tort claims. And, the federal district court in Nevada will

have diversity jurisdiction over this case; Stewart and Cagney are just as diverse there as they are anywhere else.

The personal jurisdiction analysis differs, however, because Cagney has no minimum contacts with Nevada that gave rise to this claim, and he is not domiciled there. Absent consent, or perhaps service of process on Cagney in Nevada, neither the Nevada state court nor the federal court sitting in that state will have the power to require Cagney to come to Nevada to defend this particular suit. Here Stewart will come up at least one ring short.

Note in particular that the existence of diversity here does not substitute for personal jurisdiction; diversity is a separate requirement for a separate purpose. To rephrase the old song, you *can* have one without the other.

## Some Variations

5a.  Cagney and Stewart were diverse at the time of the events giving rise to the suit but, as a result of Cagney's move, no longer are. Since the relevant date for determining diversity is the date suit is filed (*Smith v. Sperling*, 354 U.S. 92, 93 n.1 (1957)), the federal court lacks subject matter jurisdiction over the action.

b.  The problem with suing in a New York state court is that this claim arises out of events that took place in California. Since the claim is unrelated to New York, the only possible basis for personal jurisdiction is Cagney's domicile. Cagney was domiciled in New York at the time of the assault but isn't at the time of suit.

The rationale for allowing a state to exercise personal jurisdiction on the basis of domicile is that a party living in the state is so integrally related to the state that it is fair to require him to appear in its courts. *Milliken v. Meyer*, 311 U.S. at 463. In addition, it is unlikely to be inconvenient to defend in the state of one's domicile. This rationale suggests that domicile jurisdiction should apply (as it does) to domicile at the time of suit, not at the time of the events that led to the suit. *Nichols v. Inglimo*, 421 N.E.2d 1014, 1016-1017 (Ill. App. 1981). The New York court therefore lacks personal jurisdiction over Cagney.

Minimum contacts (specific in personam) jurisdiction provides an interesting contrast. Cagney can be required to return to defend a California suit arising out of the assault there, even if he has had no contact with the state since then. The rationale underlying minimum contacts jurisdiction is that performing certain acts in a state carries with it predictable consequences, including a duty to return to defend those acts in court. The defendant cannot avoid those consequences by subsequently avoiding the state. If he could, minimum contacts jurisdiction would be meaningless.

6.  This question highlights an important distinction between personal and subject matter jurisdiction. The California court lacks any basis for personal

jurisdiction over Hepburn on this claim. However, personal jurisdiction is deemed a privilege of the defendant, which will be waived if he fails to assert it. *Rauch v. Day & Night Manufacturing Corp.*, 576 F.2d 697, 701 (6th Cir. 1978). Consequently, a court that lacks personal jurisdiction over a case may still hear it, if the defendant does not object. Since Hepburn is willing to litigate the claim in California, she will presumably waive her objection by failing to raise it. See Fed. R. Civ. P. 12(b)(2), 12(g), 12(h).

However, the California federal court also lacks subject matter jurisdiction over this action. Nothing in Article III, §2 or the federal jurisdictional statutes gives the federal courts jurisdiction over state contract claims between nondiverse citizens. Hepburn's willingness to have the federal court hear the case is irrelevant: The parties cannot confer subject matter jurisdiction on the court. Subject matter jurisdiction allocates governmental power among different tribunals. That allocation is made by the Constitution and Congress, not the parties. Consequently, even if neither party objects to the federal court hearing the case, it will refuse to do so.

7a. This suit is proper in state court in New York. Personal jurisdiction is satisfied because the claim arises out of alleged deprivations of rights taking place in New York. Under the minimum contacts test, Kojak could fairly be required to defend a suit arising out of these in-state acts in a New York court. In addition, he is subject to personal jurisdiction in New York on the basis of his domicile in the state.

Subject matter jurisdiction is also proper in the New York state court, even though this is a case arising under federal law. As a rule, the general trial courts of each state have subject matter jurisdiction of almost any kind of case, unless it has been exclusively delegated to a specialized state court or (for some cases within the federal subject matter jurisdiction) to the federal courts. Even though federal civil rights cases arise under federal law and are therefore properly brought in federal court under 28 U.S.C. §1331, Congress has not made federal jurisdiction over such cases exclusive. Consequently, the state courts retain concurrent jurisdiction to hear such claims.

b. Because the case arises under federal law, the California federal court will have subject matter jurisdiction. 28 U.S.C. §1331. However, the facts do not indicate any relationship of this claim to the state of California. The California courts therefore lack personal jurisdiction over Kojak, since there are no "minimum contacts" among the claim, Kojak, and the forum state; under Rule 4(e), the federal court will not exercise personal jurisdiction if the California state court could not do so.

c. Moving Colbert's domicile to California creates some distinctions from the prior case, but distinctions without any relevant difference. Colbert's California domicile would be an adequate basis for personal jurisdiction over *her*, were she the defendant, but it does not alter the due process requirement that the defendant, the party being unwillingly haled before the court, must have minimum contacts with the state that is doing so. Kojak lacks any such contacts, at least for this claim. Personal jurisdiction is therefore lacking.

The other difference here is that the parties in this case are diverse. This gives the court an alternate source of subject matter jurisdiction (which is unnecessary, since it is a federal question case anyway), but it does not affect the lack of personal jurisdiction. Innumerable first-year exam answers notwithstanding, diversity is *not* a substitute for personal jurisdiction.

8.   Although the general rule is that jurisdiction over cases arising under federal law is concurrent, Congress has the power to make federal jurisdiction over cases within the Article III power exclusive. It has done so for copyright cases, presumably because of the specialized nature of these suits and the national scope of the protection conferred by the copyright laws. See 28 U.S.C. §1338(a). Consequently, the state court lacks subject matter jurisdiction over this case.

# 7

# *Second-Guessing the Plaintiff's Choice of Forum: Removal*

## Introduction

The traditional rule in American courts has been (and largely, still is) that the plaintiff chooses the forum in which to try a suit, subject to the limitations of personal jurisdiction, subject matter jurisdiction, and venue. She may choose the geographical place of suit, by suing in the courts of the state she prefers. She may also choose the court system in which to litigate by starting the action in either a federal or state court. In this respect, and in others, it is said that "the plaintiff is master of her claim."

Removal is an exception to this rule, however. The federal removal statutes allow the defendant, after the plaintiff has chosen a state court, to "second-guess" that choice by "removing" some types of cases from the state court to a federal court. Once properly removed the case becomes a federal case, and the state court loses jurisdiction over the action. Both pretrial litigation and trial will take place in the federal court.

The rationale for removal is that defendants as well as plaintiffs should have the option to choose federal court for cases within the federal jurisdiction. That jurisdiction is intended to protect both parties and therefore both should have access to it. If a federal court is particularly qualified to decide cases arising under federal law, then a defendant should be able to ask it to do so, just as a plaintiff may. Similarly, if an out-of-state defendant may suffer prejudice from litigating in a state court, she should have the same right as an out-of-state plaintiff to avoid that prejudice by invoking federal diversity jurisdiction.

A natural corollary of this rationale is that removal jurisdiction should be available to the defendant only in cases that the plaintiff could have commenced in federal court. Removal is not meant to expand federal jurisdiction, merely to make it available to defendants. Therefore, 28 U.S.C. §1441(a) only authorizes removal of state court actions "of which the district courts of the United States have original jurisdiction." If the plaintiff could not have chosen to bring the action in federal court initially, the defendant cannot remove it. For example, if Oakley sues Cody, a fellow Kansan, on a state law contract claim, she could not sue in federal court, since there is neither diversity nor a federal question. Consequently, her action against Cody in state court will not be removable. By contrast, if she sued Cody under a federal age discrimination statute, or if they were citizens of different states, Cody could remove because Oakley could have chosen to sue him on that claim in federal court.

A caution is in order here, however. While it is generally true that a defendant may not remove if the federal court would not have had original jurisdiction, the converse proposition is not so ironclad. In some cases, removal is barred even though the plaintiff could have commenced the action in federal court. Section 1441(b), for example, bars removal of a diversity case if any defendant in the action is a citizen of the state where the action is brought. Even though a diversity case against an in-state defendant may be filed initially in federal court, Congress did not see fit to authorize removal of such cases.

Interestingly, there is no explicit authority in the Constitution for snatching cases out of the hands of state courts by removal to federal court. Yet the First Congress provided for removal in the Judiciary Act of 1789, and it has been with us in one form or another ever since. The courts have consistently upheld the constitutionality of the removal procedure. See Wright at 209. Because removal only applies to cases that could have been brought *originally* in federal court, there seems little constitutional distinction between allowing the plaintiff to choose the federal court in a case within the federal court's jurisdiction and allowing the defendant to do so by removing a state court action.[1]

While removal jurisdiction depends on the scope of original jurisdiction of the federal courts, it also perversely depends on the jurisdiction of the *state* court in which it was brought. The federal court's removal jurisdiction is said to be "derivative" (Wright at 212) of the state court's, so that it can only properly acquire jurisdiction of a removed case if that case was properly commenced in the state court. For example, if the plaintiff brings a claim for patent infringement in state court and the defendant removes it, the federal court will have to dismiss the case. Patent cases are within the exclusive

---

1. However, §1441(c), the enigmatic provision for removal of "separate and independent" claims, may be an exception to this principle.

jurisdiction of the federal courts. 28 U.S.C. §1338(a). Consequently, the state court had no jurisdiction over the action initially, and the federal court cannot acquire "derivative" jurisdiction over the suit. Thus, because only a federal court can hear the case, the federal court can't hear it. However, if the plaintiff is not too bewildered to press on, she will be free to commence an *original* action in federal court on the patent claim.

Even if a state court case satisfies the jurisdictional requirements for removal, there are drastic limits as to which court it may be removed *to*. You can't remove to another state court or to a state court in a different state. You can't remove to a federal court in another state or even in another district in the same state. There is only one lonely court that can host a removed action: the federal district court "for the district and division embracing the place where such action is pending [in the state court]." 28 U.S.C. §1441(a). Thus, in the Schulansky case (see Part Five) Ronan may only remove the suit to the federal district court for the District of Massachusetts, because Plymouth County, where the suit was initiated, falls within that district. In addition, removal is a one-way street: A defendant sued in federal court may not remove the action to state court.

The usual federal venue rules do not apply in removed actions. If the suit was properly brought in the state court, under applicable state venue rules, it may be removed to the appropriate federal district court, even though it could not have been started in that federal court under 28 U.S.C. §1391. Stated somewhat differently, the proper venue in a removed case is the federal district that encompasses the place where the state suit is commenced, not the various choices in the venue statutes governing actions filed initially in federal court. Thus, removal only partially displaces the plaintiff's choice: She still gets to choose the state where the action will be litigated, even if she ends up in federal court in that state due to removal by the defendant.

It may be helpful to compare removal under §1441 with transfer of venue under 28 U.S.C. §1404(a). Section 1404(a) provides for geographical transfer from one district court within the federal system to another in a different state or district. See Jones's motion to transfer venue in the Schulansky case, infra Chapter 27. Removal, by contrast, authorizes transfer from the state court system to the federal system within the same state. Transfer displaces the plaintiff's geographical choice for litigation, while removal displaces the plaintiff's choice of the state court system in favor of a federal court within the same geographical area. As the *Schulansky* papers suggest, it may be possible to use both devices in a single suit. For a case that was removed and then transferred (and then dismissed for forum non conveniens!), see *Piper Aircraft Co. v. Reyno,* 454 U.S. 235 (1981).

The right to remove applies to cases, not claims: When the defendant properly removes a suit to federal court, the defendant's entire suit is removed, including not only the specific claim that gives rise to removal jurisdiction, but also any related claims that the federal court has the power to hear under pendent or ancillary jurisdiction. Suppose, for example, that Colter sues Bridger (a citizen of the same state) for violation of his federal civil rights (a claim based on federal law that state courts as well as federal courts may hear), and asserts a claim for relief on a state law battery theory as well. If Bridger removes, the federal court acquires jurisdiction of the entire action, including the civil rights claim that provides the basis for federal court jurisdiction and the pendent state law claim. Neither the plaintiff nor the defendant can dissect a single case and send only parts of it to the federal forum.

After removal, a case proceeds in federal court under the Federal Rules. See Fed. R. Civ. P. 81(c). Essentially, that court picks up the ball in mid-air and continues to juggle it. The state court complaint and answer (if one has been filed before removal) will be filed with the removal petition. 28 U.S.C. §1441(a). See the petition for removal in *Schulansky v. Ronan*, infra p. 347. The court may order the parties to file discovery material and other filings from the state court in the federal court for use in the action. 28 U.S.C. §1447(d). If the state court has entered any orders prior to removal, such as a preliminary injunction or a protective order concerning discovery, those orders remain in effect in the federal court, unless modified by the federal judge. 28 U.S.C. §1450. It's a little like the Red Sox being whisked out of Fenway Park to Dodger Stadium in the fourth inning and being told to just finish the game under the National League rules.

The following questions illustrate the substantive limits on removal jurisdiction. The second set of questions deals with removal procedure. For purposes of this chapter, I have stubbornly ignored the murky mysteries of §1441(c) dealing with removal of "separate and independent" claims (see generally Wright at §39); you should do the same in answering the questions.

# QUESTIONS

## The Power to Remove

1. Earp, from Kansas, sues Dillon, also a Kansan, in a state court in Kansas. His claim is based on violation of the federal civil rights laws. May Dillon remove?

2. Suppose Earp (still from Kansas) sues Carson, from Colorado, in the Colorado state court on a state law assault claim. May Carson remove?

3. Assume the same facts as question 2, but Earp sues a second defendant, Hickok, as well. Hickok is from Missouri. Can the defendants remove?

4. Consider the same facts again, with another twist: Earp, from Kansas, sues Carson (Col.) and Hickok (Mo.) on the assault claims, in a Kansas state court. Can the defendants remove?

5. Chester, from Iowa, sues Carson, a Coloradan, and James, a Kansan, in state court in Kansas, on a federal civil rights claim.

    a.   May Carson remove?

    b.   If so, to which court or courts?

6.    Recall that old chestnut case, *Louisville and Nashville R.R. v. Mottley,* 219 U.S. 467 (1911), in which the Supreme Court dismissed for lack of subject matter jurisdiction because the federal question in the case arose as a defense. Suppose that the plaintiffs in that case sued the (nondiverse) railroad for breach of contract in state court. Ten days later the railroad answered, raising the defense that the federal statute precludes it from renewing the Mottleys' passes. Ten days after answering, the railroad removes the case to federal court. Is removal proper?

## Some Refinements

7.    Suppose, on the facts of question 4, that Carson wants to remove, but Hickok likes the state court. Can Carson remove the case? See 28 U.S.C. §1441(a).

8.    Earp sues James, a fellow Kansan, on a state law assault claim. Six months later Earp's lawyer decides, on the basis of his further knowledge of the case gleaned from discovery, that Earp also has a claim against James for a federal civil rights violation arising out of the same facts. He amends to assert the federal claim. May James now remove?

9.    Earp, a Kansan, sues Bean, a Texan, on a state law abuse-of-process claim. He brings suit in state court in Iowa, seeking $12,000 in damages. Bean removes to federal court. Subsequently, Earp amends to add James, a fellow Kansan, as a second defendant. Should the federal court remand the case to state court?

10.  On the facts of question 9, suppose that Earp has claims against Bean and James for abuse of process. Earp deliberately decides to sue them jointly in a single action in state court in order to avoid removal to federal court. Is this permissible? Will it work?

11.  Suppose, on the facts of question 9, that Earp sues Bean in state court. Anticipating removal, he seeks only $8,000 in damages, leaving out a demand for consequential damages worth $4,000. May Bean remove?

12.  James sues Earp, his fellow Kansan, on an assault claim. Earp counterclaims for damages for violation of his federal civil rights, arising out of the same encounter. (See Rule 13(a)). Does §1441 allow James to remove?

## Unlucky Number 13

13.  Dillon (a Kansan) sues Greeley (a New Yorker) for $25,000 for breach of a contract under which Dillon licensed Greeley to manufacture electrical circuits upon which he held a patent. He also sues in a second count for infringement of the patent itself (that is, manufacturing the circuits without

permission from the patent holder). The suit is brought in a Kansas state court. Greeley removes to the federal district court for the District of Kansas. Is the removal proper? See 28 U.S.C. §1338(a).

# The Procedure for Removal

The procedure for removal, set forth in §1446, is relatively straightforward. The defendant (or defendants) must file a petition for removal in the appropriate federal district court, together with all pleadings, process, and other papers on file in the state action and a bond. 28 U.S.C. §1446(a). The petition must be filed within 30 days of receiving the plaintiff's pleading in the state suit. 28 U.S.C. §1446(b). Once the petition is filed and the state court is notified, that court loses control of the case automatically. It may not proceed with discovery, try the case, or issue orders to the parties. 28 U.S.C. §1446(e). The Schulansky case in Part Five provides a full example of the removal process.

Although the state court loses power over the case once it has been removed, the removal decision is not irrevocable. If the plaintiff contends that the case is not removable, her recourse is to move in the federal court to remand for lack of jurisdiction. 28 U.S.C. §1447(c). Thus, the decision whether the federal court has jurisdiction will be made, quite properly, by the federal court. If that court concludes that the case was improperly removed, it will remand the case to the state court, which will once more pick up the ball and run with it.

In many cases, the right to remove will not be clear from the face of the complaint. For example, most states do not require the plaintiff to allege the citizenship of the parties because state court jurisdiction does not depend upon it. Compare Fed. R. Civ. P. 8(a)(1); see p. 336. Thus, a defendant who claims the right to remove on the ground of diversity may have to ascertain the citizenship of the plaintiff and allege in her removal petition that diversity exists. Section 1441(a) explicitly allows the removing defendant to allege in the removal petition any such facts that are necessary to demonstrate the right to remove.

# QUESTIONS

## Some Technicalities

 14. Chester, an Iowa citizen, sues Holiday, of Kansas, for malpractice in a leg operation. Suit is brought in an Iowa state court. His complaint does not state a dollar demand for relief (some states don't require it; others don't even allow it). Holiday wants to remove. Can he?

15. Suppose the Long Branch Saloon, a corporation, sues Holiday in Nebraska to collect $15,000 rent due on Holiday's office above its Dodge City, Kansas saloon. Several months later Holiday discovers, much to his surprise,

that the Long Branch Saloon in Dodge City is the smallest of three such establishments run by Long Branch. Its principal place of business and state of incorporation is Colorado. Holiday removes on the basis of diversity. Can he do so?

16. James sues Earp on a federal claim in Kansas state court. Earp plans to remove. Assume that under the Kansas rules of civil procedure Earp must answer within 15 days.

    a.  Should Earp answer in the state court prior to removal?

    b.  If Earp removes before answering, when should he answer in federal court?

17. Assume that Earp removes James's suit against him within 30 days. However, James disputes the right to remove since he claims that his action is based on state law rather than federal law.

    a.  James moves in the state court to have the case remanded for lack of removal jurisdiction. The court agrees that removal was improper. What should it do?

    b.  James moves for remand in the federal court. That court agrees that removal was improper. What should it do?

18. Masterson sues Hickok, Earp, and Dillon for violation of federal fire-arms regulations. He serves Hickok on June 1 and Earp on June 15. As of June 25 Dillon has not yet been served. If Earp wants to remove, what should he do? See 28 U.S.C. §1441(b).

## Two Bemusing Variations on Question 18

19. Assume that Earp and Hickok remove the case on June 27. On July 12 Dillon is served. If he prefers state court, does he have any recourse? Should he?

20. Assume that Earp and Hickok do nothing. On July 12 Dillon is served. If he wants to remove, what should he do?

## A Final, Fundamental Point

21. Chester sues Holiday in an Iowa state court. Holiday removes. Three days later he moves to dismiss the complaint, on the ground that the court lacks personal jurisdiction over him. Is this motion permissible?

# ANALYSIS

## The Power to Remove

1. Earp has asserted a right to relief arising under federal law. Had he chosen to do so, he could have commenced this case in federal court under 28 U.S.C. §1331. Thus, the case satisfies the requirement of §1441(a) that the

federal courts have original jurisdiction over the action (or, more accurately, *would* have had original jurisdiction over it had it been brought in federal court).

However, §1441(b) must also be considered since it places some further restrictions on removal jurisdiction. That section does not restrict removal of Earp's suit. It provides that cases "founded on a claim or right arising under the Constitution, treaties or laws of the United States shall be removable without regard to the citizenship of the parties." Since Earp's claim is based on a federal question, it is irrelevant that the parties are not diverse and that there is an in-state defendant in the action. Removal is proper.

2.    Assuming that the amount-in-controversy requirement in 28 U.S.C. §1332 is satisfied, this is a straightforward diversity case. A federal district court would have original jurisdiction over the case, but this is one of those situations where the federal courts' removal jurisdiction is narrower than their original jurisdiction. Section 1441(b) provides that actions based on diversity ("[a]ny other such action") cannot be removed if any defendant is from the forum state. Under this provision Carson is barred from removing this case.

The logic behind this limitation is that diversity jurisdiction was intended to protect out-of-state parties from local prejudice, so there is no need to extend it to cases where suit is brought in the defendant's home state. (Of course, that rationale would support a similar restriction on *original* diversity jurisdiction but there is no such restriction: Logic has its limits.)

3.    This question makes one narrow point: §1441(b) precludes removal of a diversity case if *any* defendant is from the state where the state court action is brought ("only if none of the parties . . ."). Carson is still in the case; ergo, no removal. Here again, Earp could have initiated the action in federal court as a diversity action in Colorado or elsewhere, but removal is narrower.

4.    Moving the case back to Kansas changes the result. The case is still within the federal court's diversity jurisdiction, but now no defendant is from the forum state, so they may remove under §1441(b). Note that this configuration, with the Kansas plaintiff using the Kansas state courts to recover from two non-Kansas defendants, presents the strongest risk of prejudice to the defendants and therefore is the best candidate for removal jurisdiction.

5a.    This case, like that in question 1, is a federal question case and still removable as such. Here, however, there is also diversity of citizenship, a separate basis for federal jurisdiction. The interpretive problem raised is whether it is removable "without regard to the citizenship or residence of the parties" (§1441(b)) when there is *both* a claim under federal law and diversity. If not, removal would be barred due to the presence of an in-state defendant, James. The answer is "yes"; the case may be removed because it is just as squarely founded on a claim under federal law when there is diversity as when there is not.

b. Carson would clearly prefer to remove to the Colorado district court, to get the benefit of the home forum. However, removal is not meant to give the defendant a geographical choice of forum, only a choice to use the federal court system. The action can only be removed to the federal district court for the District of Kansas. If there were more than one federal district in Kansas (as there is in New York, for example), Carson would only be able to remove to the district in which the state court where Chester brought suit is located.

6. On the facts given here, there is no original federal jurisdiction because it is a state law claim between nondiverse parties. Of course, when the railroad answers the complaint in the state court, raising the federal statute as a defense, it becomes clear that a federal issue exists in the case. However, that does not make it a case that arises under the laws of the United States. Jurisdiction is determined by looking at the plaintiff's complaint, to determine if he seeks recovery under federal law. The Mottleys did not. The only difference between this hypo and *Mottley* is that in the hypo we *know* the railroad will raise a federal defense at the time when removal is sought. But it is a defense nonetheless, and it does not convert the Mottleys' contract action into a federal question case. Since the federal issue does not arise on the face of the well-pleaded complaint, there is no original federal jurisdiction. No original jurisdiction, no removal jurisdiction.

A number of commentators have suggested that this rule, like *Mottley* itself, makes little sense because the assertion of the federal defense clearly indicates that the case involves federal issues. See, e.g., American Law Institute, Study of the Division of Jurisdiction Between State and Federal Courts §1312(a)(2) and accompanying commentary (1969).

## Some Refinements

7. The answer to this question depends on the meaning of §1441(a), which provides that the "defendant or defendants" may remove. Although it is not a foregone conclusion from the language of the statute, the courts have held that the alternative reference to the "defendants" means that, in a multi-defendant case, all defendants must join in the removal petition. See *Chicago, Rock Island & Pacific Railway Co. v. Martin*, 178 U.S. 245 (1900); *Tri-Cities Newspapers, Inc. v. Tri-Cities Printing Pressman and Assistants' Local 349*, 427 F.2d 325, 326-327 (5th Cir. 1970). Carson will be stuck in state court, even though he may be subject to prejudice as an out-of-stater. While this is a reasonable interpretation of the statute, it prevents removal in cases in which the policy underlying diversity jurisdiction would support it.

8. Again, removal jurisdiction turns on original jurisdiction. In this question there was no original federal jurisdiction over the case when it was filed; the claim was based on state law and between nondiverse parties. However, once Earp amends to assert a federal claim, the case looks different. Earp is now relying on federal law as a basis for relief. If the case had been brought in

this amended form in federal court, the court would have had jurisdiction under 28 U.S.C. §1331.

The removal statute specifically provides for removal in cases like this, when the case becomes removable after the filing of the original complaint. See 28 U.S.C. §1446(b) second paragraph, which gives the defendant 30 days from the amendment to file a removal petition. This approach is clearly necessary; otherwise plaintiffs could avoid removal by suing in state court on a state law theory alone, and later amending to assert their federal claims.

Note that once the case is removed, both the federal claim and the related state assault claim will be heard in the federal court. If the combined action had been brought originally in federal court, the court could have heard the state law claim under principles of pendent jurisdiction. See infra Chapter 12, pp. 159-160. Consequently, the court may also do so in a removed action.

9.   Whatever answer you come up with for this question is troubling. By adding a Kansas defendant after removal, Earp has "destroyed diversity." If he had started this case in federal court and later added James, the court would have dismissed for lack of subject matter jurisdiction. *Owen Equipment & Erection Co. v. Kroger,* 437 U.S. 365, 373-374 (1978). On the other hand, if Earp can win a remand by this device after Bean removes, it allows him to defeat the right to removal by his subsequent choice of defendants, a choice he was not inclined to make until the defendant invoked the removal jurisdiction.

Because the addition of the nondiverse party destroys the basis for subject matter jurisdiction, the court will have to remand the case if the amendment is allowed. In some cases, when the amendment was apparently offered for the sole purpose of defeating removal, courts have simply refused to allow the amendment, thus preserving diversity jurisdiction. *Boyd v. Diebold Inc.,* 97 F.R.D. 720, 722-723 (E.D. Mich. 1983). In other cases, however, in which the nondiverse party was added in good faith for independent reasons, such as efficiency, courts have allowed the amendment and then remanded the case to state court under 28 U.S.C. §1447(c). See, e.g., *McIntyre v. Codman & Shurtleff, Inc.,* 103 F.R.D. 619, 621-623 (S.D.N.Y. 1984).

10.   There is nothing improper in Earp's choice here. It will work, so long as he really does have colorable claims against both defendants. The joinder rules in most states allow Earp to choose to sue the defendants together. The fact that he has exercised that option in part to secure the forum of his choice is a permissible form of "forum-shopping." However, were he to assert a frivolous claim against James for the sole purpose of avoiding removal, he would violate the procedural rules governing pleadings as well as his professional responsibility as an officer of the court.

11.   Here again Earp has structured his lawsuit to prevent removal by seeking damages that do not satisfy the amount-in-controversy requirement of

§1332. This is permissible even if Earp could have sought higher damages. If Earp is willing to pay the price — foregoing his other $4,000 claim — to buy a state forum, he may do so. *St. Paul Mercury Indemnity Co. v. Red Cab Co.,* 303 U.S. 283, 294-295 (1938).

12. The issue here is whether a plaintiff can remove. James could not have started in federal court because he had no basis upon which to invoke federal jurisdiction. However, if Earp had started the litigation by suing on the civil rights claim first, James could have removed. Shouldn't James have the same right to remove, whether as the original defendant or as the "defendant" on the counterclaim? The Supreme Court says no, as a matter of statutory interpretation. Section 1441(a) authorizes removal by "the defendant or defendants." In *Shamrock Oil and Gas Corp. v. Sheets,* 313 U.S. 100 (1941), the Court concluded that only the original defendant satisfied this language, so that a plaintiff may not remove under the statute. See generally 1A Moore's at ¶0.157[7].

## Unlucky Number 13

13. Despite the fact that federal courts have exclusive jurisdiction over patent claims, this action is removable in part. Dillon asserted two claims against Greeley, one for patent infringement and one for breach of contract. Even though the contract involved a license to manufacture circuits covered by a patent, Dillon is still seeking recovery under the contract in the first count of his complaint. This is a state law cause of action and was therefore properly before the state court. Cf. *Aronson v. Quick Point Pencil Co.,* 440 U.S. 257, 262 (1979) (states free to regulate contracts relating to patent properties). Since the parties are diverse, the amount requirement is satisfied, and no defendant is from Kansas, this part of the case is removable.

The patent infringement claim was never properly before the state court, since the federal courts have exclusive jurisdiction over such claims under 28 U.S.C. §1338(a). The federal court must dismiss it. However, once the breach of contract claim is removed, Dillon will be able to amend under Fed. R. Civ. P. 15(a) to assert this claim in the removed action.

## Some Technicalities

14. The problem for Holiday here is that removal turns on original federal jurisdiction, in this case, diversity jurisdiction. The federal court only has diversity jurisdiction if more than $10,000 is in dispute, but the court can't tell from the complaint whether this prerequisite is met, and Holiday must remove within 30 days or waive his right to do so. Under these circumstances §1446(a) allows Holiday to put in his petition for removal any facts that are not shown in the pleadings but are necessary to demonstrate his right to remove. He might, for example, state that Chester sent him a demand letter

seeking $30,000 in damages, or that the medical bills resulting from Chester's treatment alone exceed $10,000.

15. The smart aleck answer to this question is "yes": You can always remove, even if you have no valid ground, by filing a petition, which automatically removes the action whether it is within federal jurisdiction or not. But of course it will be remanded on the plaintiff's motion if that jurisdiction is lacking.

The more meaningful answer is that Holiday's motion comes too late. If a case is removable as originally filed, the removal petition must be filed within 30 days after the complaint is served on the defendant. 28 U.S.C. §1446(b). Although there was no way to know it from the original pleadings, this case was removable from the beginning. The system puts the burden on the defendant to *find out* if the case is within the removal jurisdiction within the 30-day period. Holiday's plea "but I didn't realize we were diverse!" will fall on deaf ears.

16a. The fact that this case may be removable does not relieve the defendant of his obligation to comply with state court rules of procedure, so long as the case is in state court. If Earp waits more than 15 days to remove, he should answer the complaint. Alternatively, he may remove before the answer is due; a defendant may remove "within thirty days" (1441(b)) of service of the complaint, so there is nothing to prevent her from removing before 15 days have elapsed. Once the case has been removed, the state rules no longer apply.

In some circumstances, courts have held that a defendant waives the right to remove by taking defensive action in the state court, such as filing a permissive counterclaim or cross-claim. The rationale for these decisions is that the defendant has demonstrated her willingness to have the state court adjudicate the case by taking affirmative steps in the state court. However, simply filing an answer required by the state rules does not constitute such voluntary submission and does not waive the right to remove. *Haun v. Retail Credit Co.*, 420 F. Supp. 859, 863-864 (W.D. Pa. 1976).

b. If Earp removes before the answer is due, he must answer within five days of filing the removal petition or within 20 days after the original complaint was served upon him, whichever is longer. Fed. R. Civ. P. 81(c).

17a. Although the state court is convinced that it alone has jurisdiction over the case, it can do nothing to help Earp. Once the case is removed the state court loses all power over it even if it was improperly removed. 28 U.S.C. §1446(e). The court should advise Earp to lodge his objection in the proper forum, the federal court.

b. Here, Earp has followed the proper procedure for objecting to removal, a motion in the federal court to remand the action to the state court. The federal court will hear the motion and resolve any factual issues necessary to determine its jurisdiction. If it concludes that jurisdiction is lacking, it will remand the case to the state court. Note that it does *not* dismiss the case but remands it. The plaintiff need not refile, pay a new fee, or worry about the statute of limitations, since the original suit continues its wobbly way in the state court.

18. The problem here is that §1441(a) has been interpreted to require all defendants to join in the removal petition. *Chicago, Rock Island & Pacific Ry. Co. v. Martin,* 178 U.S. 245, 247-248 (1900). Dillon has not even been informed of the suit yet; do the other defendants have to find Dillon, tell him the bad news, and convince him to join in the petition?

Although it is not entirely clear from the statute, the cases hold that only the defendants actually served need join in the removal petition. See 28 U.S.C. §1441(b) (parties "joined and served as defendants" must join in removal petition); *DiCesare-Engler Productions Inc. v. Mainman Ltd.,* 421 F. Supp. 116, 120 (W.D. Pa. 1976). But see the next two questions as to what happens when the last defendant is served.

## Two Bemusing Variations

19. If all defendants are served at the same time, each will have the power to prevent removal by refusing to join in the removal petition. In this case, however, Dillon finds himself in federal court without having had the chance to forestall removal by refusing to join in the petition. It appears that Dillon may still prevent the case from being heard in federal court by moving to remand on the ground that he does not consent to removal. Cf. *Hutchins v. Priddy,* 103 F. Supp. 601, 607 (W.D. Mo. 1952) (subsequently served defendant may move to remand to state court).

20. This is an interesting twist. Here, Hickok and Earp did not choose to remove, but Dillon would like to. Even if he can convince them to join in the petition, it is too late: They have waived their right to removal by failing to file within 30 days. This result is unfair to Dillon. Hickok and Earp may be entirely indifferent on the removal issue. Had Dillon been timely served, he could have convinced them to join and obtained the federal forum. By serving him late the plaintiff has essentially defeated Dillon's right to remove. The cases hold that Dillon is out of luck in this situation, at least where there is no evidence of a deliberate attempt on the part of the plaintiff to defeat removal by staggered service on successive defendants. See *Brown v. Demco, Inc.,* 792 F.2d 478, 481-482 (5th Cir. 1986).

## A Final, Fundamental Point

21. The motion is proper. Holiday does not waive his objection to personal jurisdiction just because he prefers to litigate in federal court. Indeed, he may have removed precisely because he believes that a federal judge will take a more objective view of the jurisdiction question. Removal does not affect

Holiday's right to raise any objections or defenses he may have; it only changes the court in which they will be presented. On the other hand, had Holiday waived his personal jurisdiction objection by answering in state court before removal but failing to raise the defense (compare Fed. R. Civ. P. 12(b), (g), (h)) removal would not revive it.

# 8

---

# *Proper Venue in Federal Courts: A Rough Measure of Convenience*

## Introduction

Earlier chapters have considered personal and subject matter jurisdiction, two crucial restrictions on the forums in which a lawsuit may be brought. Frequently, these "first two rings" will dramatically limit the plaintiff's choice of forum. For example, if Jones comes to Alabama, Smith's home state, and is injured there in a collision with Smith, she will likely be able to obtain personal jurisdiction over Smith only in Alabama.

However, personal and subject matter jurisdiction will not always significantly limit the plaintiff's choice of forum. For example, historically (and it may still be true) it has been permissible to obtain personal jurisdiction over an individual defendant by serving him personally within the forum state.[1] Thus, a plaintiff might bring suit in any judicial district in which the defendant can be served with process, even though neither the parties nor the events involved in the suit had any relationship to that district.

In order to assure that suits are tried in a place that bears some sensible relationship to the claims asserted, all court systems have venue provisions that restrict the plaintiff's choice of forum. Venue requirements are imposed

---

1. As to the continuing viability of such "transient jurisdiction," see Chapter 27, p. 385; Casad at ¶2.04[2][c].

by statute and represent the legislature's attempt to allocate cases to particular courts, based on connections of the parties or the events in suit to the place of trial. Common venue provisions allow cases to be brought where one of the parties resides or does business, where the claim arose, or where property in dispute is located. Such requirements form a third ring, apart from and in addition to personal and subject matter jurisdiction, which must be satisfied (or waived) in order to proceed in a particular court.

The basic federal venue provisions are found in 28 U.S.C. §1391. That section makes venue proper in diversity cases in the judicial district where all plaintiffs or all defendants reside or where the claim arose. 28 U.S.C. §1391(a). In federal question cases venue is restricted to the district where all defendants reside or where the claim arose. 28 U.S.C. §1391(b). There is no logical reason why venue should be more restrictive in federal question cases; indeed, logic suggests that access to federal court should be broader in these cases in which the federal courts have more expertise and more interest. The disparity is apparently the result of a historical accident, which has never been corrected by Congress. See Wright at 240-241.

As in so many other areas of civil procedure, the venue provisions in §1391 include ambiguous terms that the courts have had to elucidate. For example, the term "reside" in §1391(a) and (b) has spawned contradictory holdings. Some courts have equated it with the state citizenship/domicile analysis used in the diversity context, while others have concluded that residence is a broader term, so that a plaintiff with houses in two districts could sue in either, even though only one would qualify as his domicile for diversity purposes. The trend of authority favors the former interpretation. See, e.g., *Lee v. Hunt,* 410 F. Supp. 329, 332 (M.D. La. 1976). Professor Wright explains the difference in wording on the ground that the venue statute restricts suit to the *district* in which the party is domiciled and that Congress simply used "reside" to avoid awkward references to "citizens" of a district. Wright at 243-244.

Prior to 1966 §1391 only provided for venue on the basis of the parties' residence. Consequently, in many multiparty cases suit could not be brought in federal court at all. For example, if Jones, an Oregon citizen, sued Smith, an Idaho citizen and Brown, from California, on a federal question claim, she could not sue in any federal district because §1391(b) explicitly limited venue to districts where "all defendants" reside, and the statute made no provision for suit where the claim arose. Congress alleviated this problem to some extent in 1966, by amending §1391 to authorize venue in the district where the claim arose. This provision assures that in every case venue will be proper in at least one federal district.

However, courts have so far failed to formulate a consistent definition of "where the claim arose" under §1391(a) and (b), for cases arising out of activities in a number of states. For example, an action for violation of the federal trademark laws may involve (1) a decision made in one state to market the goods, (2) sales of the goods by the defendant in several different states, and (3) harm to the plaintiff's business in one or more other states. Some courts have held that a claim arises in any state that has "significant contacts" with the claim. See, e.g., *Data Disc, Inc. v. Systems Technology Associates, Inc.,* 557 F.2d 1280 (9th Cir. 1977). However, the Supreme Court has indicated that the "claim arose" language should be more strictly interpreted, with an emphasis on the acts of the defendant that gave rise to the claim. *Leroy v. Great Western United Corp.,* 443 U.S. 173 (1979). After *Leroy* it may not be sufficient to base venue solely on the fact that the plaintiff suffered injury in a particular district or on minor contacts with the district when the contacts of the claim with other districts are much more substantial.

Keep in mind that venue analysis, unlike personal jurisdiction, focuses on districts not states. If Yancey, from Alabama, sues Seward, who lives in Manhattan, for a libelous statement made in Manhattan, venue is proper (on the basis of the defendant's residence and also because it is where the claim arose) in the Southern District of New York, which encompasses Manhattan, but not in other districts in New York. Personal jurisdiction, by contrast, would be proper in any court in New York State, based on the fact that the claim arose in the state or that Seward is domiciled there.

Venue, like personal jurisdiction, is considered a personal privilege of the defendant, which may be waived. See *Neirbo Co. v. Bethlehem Shipbuilding Corp.,* 308 U.S. 165, 168 (1939). Under the Federal Rules of Civil Procedure, the defendant waives his objection to venue by failing to raise it when he responds to the plaintiff's complaint. See Fed. R. Civ. P. 12(b), (g), & (h); Chapter 14, p. 189. Parties may even agree in advance to a particular venue for suits that may arise between them. Many contracts contain such "forum selection clauses," and these have generally been held enforceable in the federal courts, even if they lay venue in a district that would not be proper under §1391. Cf. *The Bremen v. Zapata Off-Shore Co.,* 407 U.S. 1, 9-19 (1972) (approving enforcement of forum selection clause in absence of showing of unfairness).

Section 1391(a) and (b) broadly cover all diversity and federal question claims "except as otherwise provided by law." An important caveat is in order, based on this exception. Specialized venue provisions govern many types of claims that appear to be covered by §1391(a) and (b). For example, you would reasonably conclude from §1391(b) that patent infringement claims, which arise under federal law, may be brought wherever the defendant resides or the claim arose. Not so; lurking elsewhere in the Code is 28 U.S.C. §1400(b), which restricts venue in patent infringement actions to the district where the defendant resides or where he committed acts of infringement *and* has a regular and established place of business. Special venue provisions also govern copyright suits, interpleader actions, actions against federal officials, and others. See generally 15 Wright and Miller, Federal Practice and Procedure §§3810-3825 (hereinafter cited as Wright and

Miller). There is no way to guard against such pitfalls other than a careful search of the statutes prior to bringing suit.[2]

For the following cases, assume all actions are brought in federal court, subject matter jurisdiction is proper, and no special venue statute applies.

# QUESTIONS

## The Basic Venue Provisions

1.    Grant, from Ohio, sues Lee, from Virginia, for a breach of contract that took place in Tennessee. What federal venues are proper?

2.    Grant (Ohio) sues both Lee (Va.) and Jackson, a West Virginian, on the same breach of contract claim. What venues are proper?

3.    Grant's partner, McClellan, a Pennsylvania citizen, joins as a co-plaintiff in Grant's suit against Lee and Jackson. Where may the suit be brought?

4.    Suppose that McClellan (Pa.) and Grant (Ohio) are determined to bring suit in federal court but not in Tennessee. What would you advise them to do?

5.    Grant (Ohio) sues Lee (Va.) and Jackson (W. Va.) on two claims, for breach of contract and for violation of a federal trademark statute. May he bring suit in Ohio?

6.    Lincoln, from Illinois, sues Davis on a federal claim that arose in Iowa. Davis is a Mississippi state legislator representing the region around Tupelo, Mississippi. He has a home in Tupelo (in the Northern District of Mississippi) where his family stays and an apartment in the state capitol, Jackson, in the Southern District of Mississippi. Where may the suit be brought?

## Abroad and at Home

7.    Peele, a British subject living in Maryland, sues Lee (Va.) and Jackson (W. Va.) for a breach of contract that took place in Tennessee. What federal venues are proper?

8.    Assume that Lee (Va.) beats Peele (U.K.) to the punch by suing him first for breach of the same contract. What venues are proper?

9.    Suppose that Lee (Va.) sues *both* Peele (U.K.) and Grant (Ohio) on the contract claim. In what districts is venue proper? (If you think hard about this one, you will be in danger of getting it wrong. Consider carefully the policy underlying §1391(b).)

---

2. Similar traps for the unwary may await the state court plaintiff. In Massachusetts, for example, there is a general venue statute, Mass. Gen. Laws ch. 223, §1, analogous to 28 U.S.C. §1391, but an ancient venue statute provides that an action in replevin "shall be brought in the county where the goods or beasts are detained." Mass. Gen. Laws ch. 223, §4.

# Corporate Venue

For many years corporations were considered to "reside" for venue purposes only in the state where they were incorporated. Under this rule, if Ace Corporation were incorporated in Delaware but did all of its business in Florida, Brett could not sue Ace in Florida on the basis of the corporation's "residence," even though, as a practical matter, it was more at home there than in any other state.

This result was changed by a 1948 amendment to §1391, which added a new subsection dealing specifically with corporate venue. Under §1391(c), a corporation is deemed a citizen for venue purposes of its state of incorporation and of all states where it is licensed to do business or is doing business. Thus, in the example above, venue would be proper in at least one district in Florida, since Ace does business in Florida.

True to form, several interpretive issues have arisen under the statute. First, a question arose as to whether §1391(c) constituted a separate, exclusive provision governing venue in cases involving corporations or whether it was merely intended to define corporate residence for purposes of applying §1391(a) and (b). Suppose, for example, that Brett is from Arkansas and wants to sue Ace Corporation at home. Section 1391(a) authorizes suit where all plaintiffs reside in diversity cases, but §1391(c) speaks of suing corporations where they are incorporated, do business, or are licensed to do business. If §1391(c) is intended to operate independently of (a) and (b), Brett will have to go to Ace. However, if §1391(c) simply defines the term "reside" in subsections (a) and (b) for cases involving corporations, Brett may sue Ace in Arkansas under §1391(a) on the basis of his own residence there. Most cases have held that §1391(c) defines corporate residence in §1391(a) and (b) rather than providing separately for venue in cases involving corporations. Therefore, §1391(a) still applies to diversity cases against corporations, and Brett may sue Ace in Arkansas, his home state. See, e.g., *Strick Corp. v. A.J.F. Warehouse Distributors, Inc.,* 532 F. Supp. 951, 960-961 (E.D. Pa. 1982).

It has also been held that §1391(c) only applies to actions in which corporations are defendants, not to actions brought by corporations as plaintiffs. This is hardly clear from the statute, and many of the earlier cases concluded that §1391(c) applied to corporate plaintiffs and defendants. See, e.g., *Wear-Ever Aluminum, Inc. v. Sipos,* 184 F. Supp. 364, 366 (S.D.N.Y. 1960). The more limited view of the statute is now fairly well settled, however, apparently on the rationale that it was added to make it easier to sue corporations, not to make it easier for them to sue. Thus, when corporations are plaintiffs they are still deemed to reside only in their state of incorporation for venue purposes. *American Cyanamid v. Hammond Lead Products, Inc.,* 495 F.2d 1183, 1184-1185 (3d Cir. 1974).

# QUESTIONS

## Applying §1391(c)

10. Grant (Ohio) sues Dixie Corporation, incorporated in South Carolina and doing business in South Carolina, Virginia, and West Virginia. Grant's claim is for a libelous statement made by an officer of the corporation in the Eastern District of Pennsylvania. May Grant sue in the Eastern District of Pennsylvania? yes

11. What districts other than the Eastern District of Pennsylvania would be proper venues in Grant's action in question 10?

12. Assume that Dixie Corporation's principal place of business is South Carolina and that only 5 percent of its business is done in Virginia. Grant sues Dixie in the Eastern District of Virginia on the libel claim. Is venue proper?

13. Suppose Dixie does business in all 50 states. What venues are proper in Grant's libel claim against it?

14. Dixie Corp. and Lee (Va.) sue Grant (Ohio) for a breach of contract that took place in Indiana. Where is venue proper?

(NY)   NY  < NC (all states)
              SC (general)

## Variations

15. Greeley (a New York citizen) sues Southern Corporation (incorporated in North Carolina and doing business in all southern states) on a state law misrepresentation claim. He also joins Calhoun, a South Carolina citizen, as a co-defendant. His claim against Calhoun arises under federal law. Both claims arise out of an act which took place in New York. What venues are proper?

16. Assume that Greeley (N.Y.) had sued Lee, residing in the Eastern District of Virginia, and Southern, which does business in the Western District of Virginia but not the Eastern District. Is venue proper anywhere in Virginia?

17. Lee (E.D. Va.) and Burnside (from the Western District of Virginia) sue Greeley (N.Y.) on a state tort claim arising in New York. Can they sue in Virginia?

18. Assume that Greeley fails to object to venue in the case just described. Can the judge dismiss the case sua sponte?[3]

19. Chase, from Ohio, sues Breckenridge, from Kentucky, on a contract claim arising in Maryland. Breckenridge impleads Greeley (from New York) claiming that he was also at fault and should pay half of any damages Chase recovers. Is venue proper in Kentucky?

---

3. "Sua sponte" means on the judge's own initiative, without being requested to do so by the parties.

**20.** Chase (Ohio) sues Breckenridge (Ky.) on a federal claim in the Kentucky district where Breckenridge resides. Three months later he amends his complaint to add Calhoun, from South Carolina, as a second defendant on the same claim. Is venue proper?

# ANALYSIS

## The Basic Venue Provisions

**1.** Because this is a diversity case, venue is governed by §1391(a). Under that subsection venue is proper in the judicial district in Ohio in which Grant resides, the district in Virginia in which Lee resides, or in the district in Tennessee where the breach of contract took place (assuming that the "claim arose" where the breach took place).

**2.** This is still a diversity case governed by §1391(a). Here, however, "all defendants" are not from the same district, so that basis for venue is eliminated. The only proper venues will be Grant's district in Ohio and the district in Tennessee where the claim arose.

**3.** As you have probably noticed, these questions successively whittle away at Grant's venue choices. Since the phrase "where all plaintiffs or all defendants reside" has been construed to mean exactly what it says, there is no proper venue in this action based on the residence of the parties because there is no state where all plaintiffs or all defendants reside. Consequently, the only proper venue in this case is the district where the claim arose, presumably the appropriate district within Tennessee.

As discussed in the introductory note, the district where the claim arose was not a proper venue prior to 1966. Thus, on these facts there was no proper federal venue and the plaintiffs would have had to sue in state court, despite the existence of complete diversity.

**4.** Grant and McClellan can restructure their suit in several ways to sue in federal court. Each may sue separately in his home district:

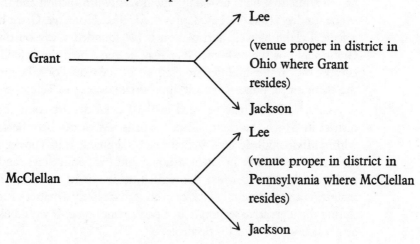

Or, they may join as plaintiffs in federal court actions against the defendants individually:

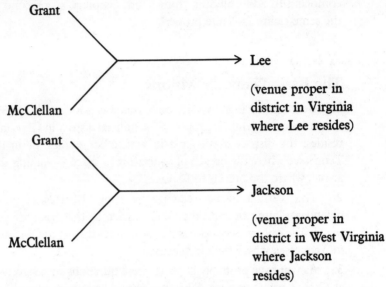

Grant

McClellan

Lee

(venue proper in
district in Virginia
where Lee resides)

Grant

McClellan

Jackson

(venue proper in
district in West Virginia
where Jackson
resides)

The result only makes limited sense: Grant and McClellan may drag Jackson to Ohio and Pennsylvania to defend separate actions, but not to Virginia to defend one. Jackson is protected from distant litigation if he is sued by two plaintiffs but not if he is sued by one. As the title of the chapter suggests, §1391 is a shotgun provision that provides at best a "rough measure" of convenience.

5.    The answer to this question turns on whether §1391(a) or §1391(b) applies. Subsection (a) governs cases founded "solely on diversity," while subsection (b) provides more limited venue options in cases not founded "solely on diversity." The plaintiff may not pick and choose his jurisdictional basis in order to have wider venue choices. Here, for example, Grant would like to argue that he is invoking only diversity jurisdiction and that venue is proper under §1391(a), based on his residence. However, Grant has asserted a federal claim as well; jurisdiction is *not* founded solely on diversity and Grant may not sue at home. Nor may he sue where the defendants reside because they reside in different districts. Venue would only be proper where the claim arose, presumably the appropriate district in Tennessee.

6.    Clearly, Davis may be sued in the federal district court for the Iowa district in which the claim arose, but it is less clear where he can be sued within Mississippi. It appears that Davis's domicile is in Tupelo, the district he represents, where he owns a home and his family stays, and where he undoubtedly returns when the legislature is out of session. Although he maintains an apartment in Jackson, this is more likely a matter of convenience during the legislative session than a permanent home. It would likely qualify as a residence but not his domicile.

The answer to the question, then, will turn on the meaning the court ascribes to the term "resides" in §1391(b). Under the majority view that a person resides only in the district where he is domiciled, Davis may be sued in the Northern but not the Southern District of Mississippi.

This concept is confusing because we generally think of parties being domiciled for diversity purposes in the entire state where they live, not just a particular city or district. While Davis's Tupelo domicile makes him a citizen of the state of Mississippi for diversity purposes, venue analysis focuses more specifically on the particular judicial district in which his home is located. Venue is not proper in this case in the Southern District of Mississippi merely because Davis is domiciled somewhere within the state. Under the majority view, he only "resides" for venue purposes in the Northern District of Mississippi, the district in which he is domiciled.

## Abroad and at Home

7.   I started to answer this question by stating that this is a diversity case governed by §1391(a). A little research revealed, however, that strictly speaking, a case between an alien and a citizen is not a diversity case (a case "between citizens of different states") but an alienage case. See *Prudencio v. Hanselman*, 178 F. Supp. 887, 888-891 (D. Minn. 1959); 15 Wright and Miller at §3810. This makes sense when you think about it (*really* think about it), but it is certainly excusable to conclude that it is a diversity case, since jurisdiction over cases involving aliens is conferred by §1332, entitled "Diversity of Citizenship."[4]

If this isn't a diversity case, and there is no special venue provision that applies,[5] it is governed by §1391(b). Since the defendants reside in different states, the action may only be brought in the Tennessee district where the claim arose.

Even if my original assumption that this case was a diversity case covered by §1391(a) were correct, it would not change the result. Peele is an alien. If residence under the venue statute is equated with state citizenship, as most courts conclude, he cannot "reside" in any state, since he can't be a citizen of a state without first being a citizen of the United States. See 15 Wright and Miller at §3810; compare Chapter 5, question 1f. The result is that an alien plaintiff is at a disadvantage in using the federal courts. Even if he is domiciled in a state, he cannot sue "at home" under the venue statute.

---

4. A number of decisions have missed or disregarded this distinction, however. See, e.g., *Fleifel v. Vessa*, 503 F. Supp. 129, 130 (W.D. Va. 1980). Indeed, as eminent an authority as Supreme Court Justice William Brennan has discussed such cases as a species of diversity jurisdiction. See *Atascadoro State Hospital v. Scanlon*, 105 S. Ct. 3142, 3157 (1985) (dissenting opinion).

5. Section 1391(d) does not apply because it only applies to suits against aliens.

8.    Lee may sue Peele in any judicial district in the United States. 28 U.S.C. §1391(d). Isn't it satisfying, once in a long while, to come across a clear, unambiguous rule of law? You can't get much clearer than this: Venue is proper in any district in the country. Of course, this does not mean that Lee will really be able to sue Peele anywhere he chooses: The personal jurisdiction ring will likely limit him considerably.

9.    Here is the way I originally analyzed this hypo: The case is not founded solely on diversity because Peele is an alien, so §1391(b) must apply. Under that provision, suit may be brought wherever all defendants "reside" or the claim arose. We just decided that an alien cannot reside in any district for venue purposes because he is not a United States citizen. Therefore, "all defendants" do not reside in any district and suit may only be brought in the district in Tennessee in which the claim arose.

Wiser heads reject this literal analysis, however. Wright and Miller suggest that because an alien can be sued in any district, venue should be proper in the district where all the other (U.S. citizen) defendants reside. 15 Wright and Miller at §3810. The "all defendants" provision in §1391(b) is intended to protect defendants from being dragged into a district where they couldn't be sued alone. Since aliens may be sued anywhere, this limitation was not intended to protect them, and they should not be considered in applying it. While this is a less literal reading of the statute, on balance it seems like a more sensible one. If it is accepted by the court, venue will be proper in both the Ohio district in which Grant resides, and the district in Tennessee in which the claim arose.

## Applying §1391(c)

10.    Grant's suit is proper because the claim arose in the Eastern District of Pennsylvania. As the introduction points out, §1391(c) provides the definition of corporate "residence" to be used in applying §1391(a) and (b); it does not displace those sections in cases involving corporations. Section 1391(a) still authorizes suit in diversity cases in the district where the claim arose.

11.    Grant could also sue in the Ohio district where he resides, in the District of South Carolina (based on Dixie's incorporation there or business done there), and in the districts within Virginia and West Virginia where Dixie does business. These districts are proper venues, even though the business Dixie does there has nothing to do with the claim that Grant asserts. The venue statute only requires that the corporation do business in the district, not that the claim arise out of the business done there. Don't confuse this requirement with long-arm statutes, which confer personal jurisdiction only for claims arising out of the business done within the forum state. Compare Chapter 2, question 2a.

12.    Venue is proper here. The statute simply requires that the corporation do business in the district, not a large part of its total business. The fact that

Dixie's principal place of business is in South Carolina does not change the fact that it does business in Virginia. If that business is done in the Eastern District, venue is proper there.

Be careful not to import the principal place of business concept into venue analysis. It is crucial to the subject matter/diversity analysis, under §1332(c), but irrelevant to venue under §1391(c). Venue is based on doing business, not doing most of your business, within the district.

Of course, the fact that venue is proper in this district does not by itself make suit proper there. Since this claim arose in Pennsylvania, and Dixie does little business in Virginia (thus making general in personam jurisdiction unlikely), Grant may have trouble satisfying the personal jurisdiction ring in Virginia. Even if jurisdiction could be found in Virginia, the court might order the case transferred under 28 U.S.C. §1404(a).

13. Venue is proper in those districts within each of the 50 states in which Dixie does business as well as the district where Grant resides and where the claim arose. It is quite possible that Dixie does business in some districts within a state but not others. For example, it may deal with retailers in Atlanta, but none in other parts of Georgia. If so, it could be sued in the Northern District of Georgia but not the middle or southern districts in that state. Thus, it is not necessarily true that a corporation can be sued anywhere under the venue statute simply because it does business in all 50 states.[6]

14. Since this is a diversity case, venue is governed by §1391(a). Venue is proper under that section where all plaintiffs reside. Lee resides in Virginia. When Dixie is a defendant, it resides there for venue purposes under §1391(c) because it does business there. However, as the introduction indicates, most cases now hold that corporate *plaintiffs* "reside" only where they are incorporated, in Dixie's case, South Carolina. Venue is therefore proper only in the Ohio district where Grant resides or the Indiana district where the claim arose.

## Variations

15. In this case, Greeley's claim against Southern is based "solely" on diversity, but it is joined with a federal question claim against another defendant. Therefore, the "action" as a whole is not founded solely on diversity, and §1391(b) applies. Cf. *Applegate v. Scott,* 581 F. Supp. 735, 736 (D.N.J. 1984) (§1391(b) applies where plaintiff brings action based on diversity but subsequently amends to add claims based on federal law). Under that provi-

---

6. On the other hand, corporations that do substantial business in a state will usually be licensed by the state. Such licensing provisions generally authorize the conduct of business throughout the state. Thus, Dixie may be "licensed to do business" (28 U.S.C. §1391(c)) in judicial districts where it is not in fact doing business. There is a split of authority on the issue of whether venue is proper in those districts as well. See Moore's at ¶0.142[5.-1-3], n.31.

sion, venue is proper in the New York district where the claim arose. In addition, venue is proper in the district where all defendants reside. Calhoun resides in the District of South Carolina (it has only one) and so does Southern, under §1391(c), because it does business there. Venue is proper in that district as well.

16. Section 1392(a) allows Greeley to bring this action in either district in Virginia, apparently on the theory that it is not that inconvenient for a defendant to defend in another district within the same state. For the defendant doing business in San Diego who is forced to defend a suit in San Francisco, this theory may have little intuitive appeal. A rough measure of convenience indeed!

A similar provision applies to defendants from different divisions within the same judicial district. Some districts are subdivided, for administrative purposes, into two or more divisions. In such districts, suit must be brought in the division where the defendants reside. 28 U.S.C. §1391(a). If they reside in different divisions within a single district, suit may be brought in either division. 28 U.S.C. §1393(b).

17. Although §1391(a) applies, the plaintiffs do not all reside in the same district. And there is no provision analogous to §1392(a) allowing plaintiffs from different districts in the same state to sue in either district. The apparent result, then, is that neither district in Virginia is proper. See Wright at 240.

A nice question is whether plaintiffs from different divisions within a district may sue together in either division. Section 1393(b) authorizes defendants to do so but again there is no similar provision for multidivision plaintiffs. Yet §1391(a) clearly authorizes them to sue somewhere in the district, since they both reside there. I have not researched this pithy issue, but assume that either division will do.

18. At least one court has held that the judge cannot dismiss an action sua sponte for improper venue because venue is a privilege of the defendant, which he may waive. *Concession Consultants Inc. v. Mirisch,* 355 F.2d 369, 371 (2d Cir. 1966); see also 15 Wright and Miller at §3826 (p.257). Further reflection suggests that it may well be appropriate for the court to exercise some control over venue even if the parties are satisfied. Venue also serves the interests of the judicial system by allocating business to courts with some connection to the case. See *Gulf Oil Corp. v. Gilbert,* 330 U.S. 501, 508-509 (1947). Where no such connection exists, the public interest suggests that a court should have the power to send the parties elsewhere. Such power is provided, however, by §1404(a), authorizing the court to transfer cases to other districts. Perhaps this adequately protects the system's interest.

19. In this case, venue is proper in the appropriate district in Kentucky if you only consider the residence of the original parties, since the defendant is a Kentucky citizen. But Breckenridge has brought in another party, the third-party defendant Greeley:

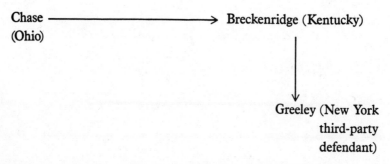

Chase ⎯⎯⎯⎯⎯⎯⎯⎯⎯⎯⎯→ Breckenridge (Kentucky)
(Ohio)

Greeley (New York
third-party
defendant)

Is he considered in determining whether all defendants are from the same district?

If he were, it might encourage defendants to implead third parties from other districts to defeat venue. Or, if the court refused to allow them to bring in third parties if venue would be affected, it would undermine the liberal joinder provisions of the Federal Rules. See Fed. R. Civ. P. 14. Most courts have concluded that only the original parties to the action should be considered in applying the venue statute. Subsequent claims, such as third-party claims, counterclaims, and cross-claims do not affect venue. Thus, venue would lie in the Kentucky district where Breckenridge resides.

20. This case is a bit different from the last. Here, the new party is added by the plaintiff. If he is allowed to lay venue where one defendant resides and then add a defendant from another district by amendment, he might evade the terms of the venue statute by suing some defendants and adding others later. Therefore, Calhoun's residence must be taken into account, and venue is rendered improper under §1391(b) by the amendment. If the defendants made a timely objection to venue, the case would have to be dismissed. As a practical matter, however, the court would likely refuse the amendment (or allow the plaintiff to withdraw it) to avoid the venue problem.

# 9

# *Choosing a Proper Court: The Three Rings Reconsidered*

## Introduction

A major purpose of this book is to introduce procedural concepts, such as personal and subject matter jurisdiction and venue, and to illustrate their operation through a variety of examples. However, an equally important goal is to help you to see the interrelatedness of things, to explore how these procedural doctrines interact to form a rather elegant system for adjudication of law suits. This chapter reconsiders the three rings analyzed in earlier chapters in order to emphasize how these separate constraints operate together to circumscribe the plaintiff's choice of a proper forum.

As a preliminary matter it is important to reemphasize that all three of these prerequisites must be satisfied in order to bring suit in a particular forum. It is no answer to an objection to personal jurisdiction that diversity (or some other basis for subject matter jurisdiction) is present, or that the venue provisions of 28 U.S.C. §1391 are satisfied. Each of the three doctrines has a different legal source, serves a distinct purpose, and employs a different standard. The limits on federal subject matter jurisdiction are found in Article III, §2 of the Constitution, which authorizes federal jurisdiction over certain limited types of cases. Personal jurisdiction, on the other hand, arises from due process limitations in the fifth and fourteenth amendments, and limits the power of states to require out-of-state defendants to defend suits in their courts. The third ring, venue, does not have a constitutional source: It is a statutory limit that imposes separate constraints on the place of trial to protect parties from inconvenient litigation.

While the three rings are distinct in theory, the potential for confusing them is great because the standards that govern personal jurisdiction, subject matter jurisdiction, and venue are closely related. For example, the concept of domicile may be relevant to analysis of all three rings. Courts use the domicile test to determine the state citizenship of individual parties (that is, natural persons) under 28 U.S.C. §1332(a)(1), the basic diversity provision. Domicile in the forum state is also a proper basis for exercising personal jurisdiction over an individual defendant. *Milliken v. Meyer*, 311 U.S. 457 (1940). Last, domicile is relevant (with a twist) to the determination of proper venue because most courts hold that individual parties "reside" for purposes of the venue statute in the judicial district where they are domiciled. Wright at 243-244. The "twist" is that venue is only proper in the particular district within the state in which the party has her domicile, not in the entire state.

The concept of domicile, in the traditional common law sense of a place of residence where one intends to remain indefinitely, does not apply to corporations because they cannot have intent in the same sense that individuals do. However, the analogous doctrines of corporate citizenship or presence within the state are relevant to several branches of the three-ring analysis. For the purpose of establishing subject matter jurisdiction on the basis of diversity, a corporation is deemed to be a "citizen" of the state of its principal place of business, as well as the state where it is incorporated. 28 U.S.C. §1332(c). To establish personal jurisdiction over corporations, however, the courts invoke the separate but confusingly similar concept of general in personam jurisdiction. Under general in personam jurisdiction analysis, a corporation is subject to personal jurisdiction in states in which it conducts substantial and continuous business activities. See Chapter 1, p. 6. The state in which a corporation is incorporated and the state of its principal place of business would almost certainly satisfy this standard, but other states may satisfy it as well.

For example, a major airline would be subject to general in personam jurisdiction in many states, due to the volume of flights it operates from those states and the facilities and employees it maintains there. Yet only one state will be its "principal place of business" for diversity purposes under 28 U.S.C. §1332(c). Thus, both of these related inquiries consider the amount of business activity in the state, but the two standards do differ, and the states that meet the standards will overlap but may not be exactly the same.

Venue in suits against corporations requires yet another related but distinct analysis. Under 28 U.S.C. §1391(a), venue in a diversity case will lie in any judicial district in which all the plaintiffs or all the defendants "reside." For individuals, residence for venue purposes is generally equated with domicile, but, as explained above, corporations do not have a domicile in the common law sense of the term. Instead, corporate "residence" for venue purposes is defined in the venue statute. It differs from both the corporation's state citizenship for diversity purposes and the standard for general in personam jurisdiction over the corporation. Under 28 U.S.C. §1391(c), a corporate defendant[1] resides for venue purposes in all judicial districts in which the corporation does business, is incorporated, or is licensed to do business.

Thus, corporate activity or presence in the district is relevant to determining venue in cases against corporate defendants, just as it is relevant to determining their state citizenship for diversity purposes and their amenability to personal jurisdiction. However, a much smaller quantum of corporate activity will satisfy the venue requirement than is needed to establish a corporation's "principal place of business" for diversity purposes or "substantial and continuous activities" for general in personam jurisdiction. Under §1391(c) the corporation need only be "doing business" or "licensed to do business" in the state; obviously, a corporation may do business or be licensed to do business in numerous states that are not its principal place of business under 28 U.S.C. §1332(c) and where its activities are not sufficiently substantial and continuous to satisfy general in personam jurisdiction analysis.

## *Relation of the Claim to the Forum*

Another understandable source of confusion in applying the three-ring analysis is the fact that one of the rings may require a relationship between the state in which the suit is brought and the claim the plaintiff asserts, while that relationship is irrelevant to applying the other rings. Suppose, for example, that Santini, a California high-wire artist, sues Robinson Shows, Inc., a Virginia corporation with its principal place of business in Virginia. If Santini brings suit in an Alabama federal court for a negligence claim that arose in Missouri, it is irrelevant to diversity analysis that the claim did not arise in Alabama. Diversity jurisdiction turns on a comparison of the citizenship of the parties, not on the relationship between the parties or the claim and the forum state. So long as the parties are from different states (and the amount-in-controversy requirement is met) diversity is satisfied.

Similarly, the fact that Santini's claim did not arise in Alabama may be irrelevant to the venue analysis. If Robinson does business in Alabama, venue will be proper there under 28 U.S.C. §1391(c) even though the claim does not arise out of the business done in the state. There is no requirement in §1391(c) that the claim must arise out of the in-state business, only that the defendant be "doing business" in the district where suit is brought. However, if Robinson does not do business in Alabama, the relationship of the claim to the forum state could be crucial in establishing venue because venue is also

---

1. Most courts have held that §1391(c) only applies to corporate defendants. A plaintiff corporation resides only in its state of incorporation for venue purposes. See Chapter 8, p. 107.

proper under §1391(a) in the district where the claim arose, regardless of the residence or general business activities of the parties.

The relation of the claim to the forum state may even be irrelevant to personal jurisdiction. If the circus does sufficient business in Alabama, it will be subject to general in personam jurisdiction there. If so, it may be sued there for any cause of action, regardless of whether it arises out of Robinson's contacts with Alabama. See Chapter 1, p. 6. However, absent such pervasive contacts with the forum state, Santini will probably have to rely on minimum contacts analysis to establish personal jurisdiction over Robinson. Under that analysis, it is crucial that the claim arise out of the defendant's deliberate contacts with the state where suit is brought. In addition, when personal jurisdiction is based on minimum contacts, the applicable long-arm statute will also require that the claim arise out of those contacts. See, e.g., Uniform Interstate and International Procedure Act §1.03(a), (b), supra at p. 23 (limiting jurisdiction to claims arising from the enumerated in-state contacts).

When personal jurisdiction is based on minimum contacts, the long-arm statute may provide an additional source of confusion. Most long-arm statutes authorize jurisdiction over claims that arise out of the defendant's "transacting business" in the forum state, a phrase dangerously reminiscent of the "doing business" provision in §1391(c). Many courts have interpreted this "transacting business" language broadly, to authorize a court to exercise specific in personam jurisdiction over a defendant for claims that arise out of a single transaction related to the forum state, even though the defendant has no other contacts with the state. See Chapter 2, question 8. Yet there is considerable debate in the cases as to whether a single transaction in the district is sufficient to satisfy the "doing business" provision of §1391(c), so as to make that district a proper venue. Some courts have equated these two standards and concluded that venue is proper under the "doing business" clause of §1391(c) if the corporate defendant is subject to personal jurisdiction under the "transacting business" language of the state's long-arm statute and the minimum contacts test. See, e.g., *Stith v. Manor Baking Co.*, 418 F. Supp. 150, 155 (W.D. Mo. 1976). Others, however, conclude that the venue statute was intended to restrict suits to forums that will be reasonably convenient for the defendant and that a higher quantum of activity should be required to satisfy this language in the venue statute. See, e.g., *Johnson Creative Arts Inc. v. Wool Masters, Inc.*, 743 F.2d 947, 951-955 (1st Cir. 1984).[2]

Thus, it may not always be true that venue will be proper under the "doing business" provision of §1391(c) in states where a corporate defendant

---

2. For a review of the debate, which remains unresolved by the Supreme Court, see Note, Federal Venue Over Corporations Under Section 1391(c): Plaintiff Corporations, The Judicial District Limitation, and Doing Business, 12 Ga. L. Rev. 296, 308-321 (1978).

is subject to specific in personam jurisdiction under a "transacting business" long-arm provision. You would think, however, that the reverse *would* be true, that if the defendant's contacts with the state are sufficient to satisfy the (possibly stricter) standard for "doing business" under §1391(c), they must be sufficient to support specific in personam jurisdiction under the minimum contacts test. Alas, not even this is invariably true. As indicated above, the business that supports venue under §1391(c) need not relate to the claim in suit. Thus, a corporate defendant might be "doing business" in the state under §1391(c) but not satisfy the "transacting business" requirement in the long-arm statute since the claim did not arise from the in-state activities.

The subtlety of these interrelations suggests that they were deliberately designed to intimidate first year law students. However, the situation is not really so bad once you have worked with the related doctrines in the context of specific examples. The following questions will help you to sort out the various rings. Assume, unless the question specifies otherwise, that the relevant long-arm statute is like California's (see supra p. 20), which authorizes the exercise of all constitutionally permissible jurisdiction, and that all suits are brought in federal court. You may wish to refer to 28 U.S.C. §133 (found in most of the civil procedure supplements), which lists the federal judicial districts in each state.

# QUESTIONS

## Into the Rings

1.   Barnum, a citizen of Maine, sues Ringling Brothers, Inc. for injuries suffered when Leo, a trained lion, escaped from the circus train near Bangor, Maine. Ringling Brothers is incorporated in Wisconsin with its principal place of business in New York. The circus winters in Florida, has permanent facilities for training performers in Ohio, and performs for three weeks to a month in every state on the eastern seaboard.[3]

   a.   Could the suit be brought in federal district court in Maine? (Maine has only one judicial district.)

   b.   Could the suit be brought in the Northern District of New York?

   c.   Could the suit be brought in any federal district court in Ohio?

   d.   Could the suit be brought in any federal district court in New Jersey?

2.   Barnum sues Ringling Brothers and Kelly, the clown who let the lion escape from the train. Barnum claims that Kelly left Leo's cage unlocked while the train was refueling in Bangor. Kelly is domiciled in Florida.

---

3. For those whose geography is rusty, the eastern seaboard states include Maine, New Hampshire, Massachusetts, Connecticut, Rhode Island, New York, New Jersey, Delaware, Maryland, Virginia, North Carolina, South Carolina, Georgia, and Florida.

a.   May Barnum sue in federal district court in Maine?

b.   May he sue in a Florida federal district court?

c.   May he sue in a New York federal district court?

## A Circus Trick

3.   Suppose the circus sues Kelly, from Florida, and Rice, a Vermont citizen, for allowing Leo to escape. The circus alleges that Rice was negligent in failing to lock the cage when the train left Rutland, Vermont, and that Kelly was negligent in failing to check the lock when the train stopped to refuel in Bangor. The suit is brought in Maine.

a.   Will the Maine federal district court have subject matter jurisdiction over the action?

b.   Will the court have personal jurisdiction over the parties?

c.   Is Maine a proper venue?

4.   Beatty, an Arizona citizen, sues the Bailey Circus Corporation for an injury suffered when Elmer, a willing but occasionally clumsy elephant, fell on him while he (Beatty) was watching a circus performance in Phoenix, Arizona. At the time that the accident occurred in 1983 Bailey was incorporated in Delaware with its principal (and only) place of business in Phoenix. Since 1983, however, the circus has prospered. As of 1986 when suit was brought its principal place of business was California, although it still performed extensively in Arizona as well. May Beatty bring suit in federal court in California?

## Procedural Acrobatics

5.   Suppose that Beatty brought the suit against Bailey and Stenk, Elmer's trainer. Stenk is from New Mexico. In 1986, Beatty brings his suit in the New Mexico district court, the *state* court of general jurisdiction in New Mexico. Assume that the relevant New Mexico venue statute authorizes venue in the county where any defendant resides and that the suit is brought in the county where Stenk resides.

a.   Is the suit properly before the court?

b.   May the defendants remove to federal court?

## A Two-Ring Circus

6.   A representative of Ringling Brothers visits Adler, a retired clown who lives in Cedar Rapids, Iowa, in the Northern District of Iowa. The agent explains that the circus wishes to get Adler's permission to use a famous poster of Adler in promoting the circus, for a small royalty. Adler agrees. Ringling Brothers uses the picture in advertising in New York, but does not pay Adler. Adler decides to sue Ringling Brothers for breach of contract and

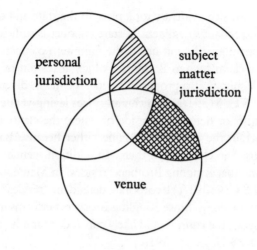

**Fig. 9–1**

federal copyright infringement. (Assume, contrary to fact, that the general venue statute applies to copyright claims.)

    a. Can you think of a court or courts that fall in the shaded area of Figure 9-1, that is, in which personal jurisdiction and subject matter jurisdiction are satisfied but venue is not? (The relevant facts concerning Ringling Brothers' business activities are found in question 1.)

    b. Can you think of a court or courts that would fall in the hatched area of Figure 9-1, in which venue and subject matter jurisdiction are proper, but the court would not have personal jurisdiction over Ringling Brothers?

# ANALYSIS

## Into the Rings

**1a.** As pointed out in the introduction, the suit may only be brought in those federal courts that satisfy all three rings of the analysis for choosing a proper court. There is clearly no problem with subject matter jurisdiction. Barnum is a Maine citizen, and Ringling Brothers is a citizen of Wisconsin and New York under 28 U.S.C. §1332(c). As long as Barnum's claim is for more than $10,000 the requirements for federal subject matter jurisdiction based on diversity are met. The fact that Barnum is a citizen of the state where suit was brought is unnecessary to the diversity analysis; that analysis is satisfied as long as he and Ringling Brothers are citizens of different states, regardless of which states those are.

    The Maine court will also have personal jurisdiction over Ringling Brothers in this action. The claim arises out of a negligent act by its employee, which evidently took place in the state and caused injury in the state. The defendant's negligent in-state conduct is sufficient to support specific in personam jurisdiction under the minimum contacts test, that is, jurisdiction over a claim such as Barnum's, which arises out of the in-state act itself.

Venue is also proper in Maine. Venue in diversity cases is governed by 28 U.S.C. §1391(a), which authorizes laying venue in the district where the plaintiffs or defendants reside or where the claim arose. Venue is therefore proper in the District of Maine either because Barnum lives in Maine or because the claim arose there. In addition, venue would be proper on the ground that Ringling Brothers "resides" in Maine for venue purposes. Under 28 U.S.C. §1391(c) a corporate defendant "resides" in every district in which it does business. Since Ringling Brothers performs in Maine for several weeks each year, the court would likely conclude that it is "doing business" in Maine under 28 U.S.C. §1391(c).

b. This suit could certainly be brought in some district in New York, but we don't have enough facts to decide whether it can be brought in the Northern District.

The analysis of the court's subject matter jurisdiction is exactly the same as in question 1a. A diversity case is a diversity case is a diversity case: If the parties are from different states and the amount-in-controversy requirement is satisfied, any federal court will have subject matter jurisdiction on the basis of diversity.

Personal jurisdiction over Ringling Brothers is almost certainly proper in New York because it has its principal place of business there, which in virtually every case will establish the type of substantial and continuous contacts necessary to support general in personam jurisdiction over a corporation. Be careful, however, to distinguish this personal jurisdiction analysis from the diversity analysis. For personal jurisdiction, the question is whether Ringling Brothers' activities in the state are so substantial and continuous as to make it fair to subject it to personal jurisdiction for any claim. By contrast, whether the corporation is a citizen of the state for diversity purposes turns on whether that state is the one state in which the corporation's business activities are centered under the various tests for determining a corporation's principal place of business. See Chapter 5, p. 66.

Venue in Barnum's suit is proper in those judicial districts in New York in which the circus is "doing business" or licensed to do business. It does not matter that the claim did not arise out of the business the circus does in New York, because 28 U.S.C. §1391(c) makes any judicial district a proper venue if the corporation does business in that district, without regard to whether that business gave rise to the claim. Presumably, the theory is that litigation in that state is not inconvenient for the corporation if it is already conducting activities in the forum and that this will be true even if the activities are unrelated to the claim.

However, it is not clear from the facts that Ringling Brothers does business or is licensed to do business in all judicial districts in New York. Perhaps New York is its principal place of business because its corporate offices are located in Manhattan, in the Southern District of New York, but it does not perform or conduct any other business in other judicial districts in the state. If that is true, then the Southern District will be the only proper venue in New York State. If, however, it also does business in the Northern District of New York (such as performing there on a regular basis) or is licensed to do business throughout the state of New York, suit will be proper there as well. (Recall that amenability to personal jurisdiction, unlike venue, goes by state, not judicial district. If Ringling Brothers is subject to personal jurisdiction in any court in the state, it is subject to personal jurisdiction in all of them.)

Even if Barnum has filed suit in a forum where all three rings intersect, it is still not certain that the suit will be heard there. The court has the power under 28 U.S.C. §1404(a) to transfer cases "for the convenience of parties and witnesses in the interest of justice," including cases in which the plaintiff has properly chosen that court under the three-ring analysis.

c. Suit would also be proper in Ohio for this claim, on much the same reasoning as question 1b. Subject matter jurisdiction is no problem since, as indicated above, the parties are just as diverse if suit is brought in Ohio as they are if suit is brought anywhere else. Note that Ringling Brothers is not a "citizen" of Ohio for diversity purposes even though it has substantial business activities there that would subject it to general in personam jurisdiction in that state.

Venue would also be proper in the judicial district within Ohio in which Ringling Brothers' training facility is located. Although the claim did not arise in Ohio, the circus "does business" in that district under 28 U.S.C. §1391(c). However, venue would not be proper in any other district in Ohio, unless the circus is licensed to do business in the entire state. (Since corporations that do substantial business in a state are usually required to be licensed, and the license usually authorizes the conduct of business throughout the state, this is a good possibility. See Chapter 8, n.6.)

Last, general in personam jurisdiction would probably be proper over Ringling Brothers in Ohio because they have a substantial, continuous presence in the state, due to their permanent training facility there. Presumably, they own or rent property there and have regular employees in the state, contacts that frequently support general in personam jurisdiction.

If Barnum brings suit in Ohio, the circus will have a good case for transfer of venue under 28 U.S.C. §1404(a) because the claim did not arise in Ohio, and the defendant's activities in the forum, though substantial, are completely unrelated to the cause of action before the court.

d. At last we have happened upon a forum where this law suit cannot be brought. Although diversity still exists, and venue could be premised on the fact that Ringling Brothers "does business" in New Jersey by performing there annually, there is no basis for personal jurisdiction over Ringling Brothers in New Jersey for this claim. The claim does not arise out of any contacts of the defendant with New Jersey, so minimum contacts jurisdiction is not appropriate under *International Shoe*. And, the three-week tour that the circus makes in the state is unlikely to satisfy the substantial and continuous contact requirement for general in personam jurisdiction.

The circus could consent to personal jurisdiction in New Jersey or waive its objection under Fed. R. Civ. P. 12 by failing to assert it. See Chapter 14, p. 189. If it did so, the court would have the authority to entertain the suit under our tripartite analysis but might still transfer, on its own motion, to the district of Maine.

2a. This suit may properly be brought in Maine. Complete diversity is present: Barnum is a citizen of Maine; Kelly is a citizen of Florida; and Ringling Brothers is a citizen of New York and Wisconsin. Personal jurisdiction is proper over both defendants under minimum contacts analysis, based on the negligent act of Kelly in allowing Leo to get loose. This is a minimum contact of Kelly personally, since she actually did the negligent act in the state. It is also a minimum contact of the corporation because Kelly's negligence was in the course of her work for the circus, and the contacts of the corporation's agents while acting on its behalf will be attributed to the corporation.

Venue is also proper under §1391(a) because the claim arose in Maine as well as because the plaintiff resides there. The fact that all defendants do not reside in Maine is irrelevant if one of these other bases for venue is satisfied. Since there is only one district in Maine there is no need to focus more specifically on where the claim arose within the state.

b.   Barnum will also have the option to sue in Florida under the three-ring analysis. Diversity is still present; here again it is irrelevant to diversity analysis that one of the parties (Kelly) is from the forum state. Personal jurisdiction is also likely to be proper over both defendants in Florida. Kelly is subject to jurisdiction there because she is domiciled there, and the circus is subject to general in personam jurisdiction there if it has its permanent winter quarters in Florida.

Venue is more complicated. Under 28 U.S.C. §1391(a), venue is proper in the districts where all defendants reside. Kelly "resides" in Florida because that is her domicile, but the cases have generally held that individuals reside for venue purposes only in the district within the state where they have their home. See Chapter 8, question 6. If Kelly's home is in the Northern District of Florida, she does not "reside" in the Southern District. Similarly, if Ringling Brothers' winter quarters is in the Southern District, it "resides" there under §1391(c) (even sitting out the winter and getting ready for the new season is part of the circus's business) but not in the Northern District. On these facts, venue would be improper under §1391(a) because "all defendants" do not reside in the same district. However, this situation is addressed by a special venue statute, 28 U.S.C. §1392(a), which authorizes suit in *either* district under these circumstances. Alternatively, if Kelly is domiciled in the district where the circus has its winter quarters (or a district in which it performs on a regular basis), venue will be proper in that district under §1391(a), on the ground that "all defendants" reside there.

    c. Suit will not be proper in New York because personal jurisdiction could not be asserted over Kelly in New York, under either minimum contacts analysis or general in personam analysis. It might be possible to serve the summons and complaint on Kelly while she is in New York to perform, but even if in-state service is still sufficient to establish personal jurisdiction, venue would not be proper in New York because 28 U.S.C. §1391(a) makes venue proper where "all defendants" reside and only one of them, Ringling Brothers, "resides" in New York for venue purposes.

## A Circus Trick

3a. The Maine federal court, like any federal court, will have subject matter jurisdiction in this case, since there is complete diversity. Of course, the amount-in-controversy requirement will have to be met, but my guess is that a lot more than $10,000 goes into your basic trained lion. If Leo falls in love with a moose and never returns, the circus will be able to make a good faith argument that the requirement is met.

    b. Personal jurisdiction presents a more difficult issue. Since neither defendant is domiciled in Maine, the circus will have to rely on specific jurisdiction, based on minimum contacts analysis. Kelly is clearly subject to jurisdiction in Maine under the *International Shoe* analysis because the claim arose from her negligent act in Maine. However, Rice's alleged negligence arose in Vermont, and it is doubtful that the mere foreseeability that the door would swing open in another state is sufficient to support jurisdiction over Rice there. Compare Chapter 1, question 5. Absent personal service in Maine or consent by Rice, the court will not have personal jurisdiction over her.

    c. It is not entirely clear whether the District of Maine would be a proper venue in this action. Venue may not be based on the fact that Ringling Brothers does business there because §1391(c) does not apply to corporate plaintiffs, only corporate defendants. See Chapter 8, p. 107. The only possible basis for venue, then, is that the claim arose in Maine. This is clearly true as to the claim against Kelly, but at least debatable as to Rice, whose negligent act took place in Vermont and who clearly will be inconvenienced by a suit in Maine. See *Leroy v. Great Western United Corp.*, 443 U.S. 173, 183-185 (1979) ("where the claim arose" provision should be construed in relation to the convenience of the defendant and the witnesses).

4. The interesting aspect of this question is that none of the three rings would have been satisfied if Beatty had brought suit immediately after the injury. At the time of the accident, the parties were not diverse, but have

become diverse in 1986, due to the change in Bailey's principal place of business. It is settled that diversity jurisdiction turns on the state citizenship of the parties when the suit is filed. See Chapter 5, question 5. Diversity jurisdiction is therefore proper in this case if the amount in controversy exceeds $10,000. In a case as weighty as this, that sounds likely.

Similarly, Bailey would not have been subject to personal jurisdiction in California in 1983. Since the claim arose in Arizona, Bailey was not (and still is not) subject to specific jurisdiction in California for this claim. Nor was Bailey subject to general in personam jurisdiction in California in 1983. Bailey had no contacts with California at the time this claim arose; its continuous and substantial business in California has all developed afterwards. May it be sued there in 1986 based on general in personam jurisdiction, even if it was not subject to such jurisdiction at the time the claim arose?

Logically, it should not matter that the corporation was not subject to general in personam jurisdiction in California when the claim arose. No one was trying to assert jurisdiction over it then. The rationale underlying general in personam jurisdiction is that extensive corporate presence within the state reduces the inconvenience of litigation and affiliates the corporation with the state in such a substantial way as to make it fair to sue it there for any claim. If that presence exists at the time the suit is brought, the rationale for subjecting the corporation to jurisdiction is satisfied. In addition, any inconvenience to the corporation from litigating in the state occurs when the litigation takes place, and at that time Bailey had a substantial presence in the forum state.

Venue will also be proper in those federal districts in California where Bailey does business. Nothing in 28 U.S.C. §1391(c) suggests that the corporation had to be "doing business" in the district when the claim arose. Here again, the rationale, based on convenience to the defendant, supports the conclusion that the statute should be applied as of the time when suit is brought.

## Procedural Acrobatics

5a.  This chapter deals primarily with the choice of a proper federal forum. The same three rings must also be satisfied if suit is brought in state court, but the standards for meeting those tests differ in a state suit. All states have a trial court that exercises broad subject matter jurisdiction over most types of claims, including negligence claims. In New Mexico, these courts of general jurisdiction are called district courts. They have subject matter jurisdiction over garden variety tort claims such as Beatty's, as well as a broad range of other common law and statutory causes of action. There is no need to consider the state citizenship of the parties, since the diversity requirements of 28 U.S.C. §1332 apply to subject matter jurisdiction of the federal courts, not that of the state courts.

Venue analysis also differs in state court actions. Each state has its own statutes defining proper venue for claims brought in its courts, which may vary considerably from the federal venue provisions. Here, the New Mexico statute is satisfied if Stenk "resides" (whatever that may mean under the New Mexico statute) in the county where the suit is filed. By contrast, venue would not be proper in this example under 28 U.S.C. §1391.

Personal jurisdiction analysis, however, is likely to be the same whether the suit is brought in state or federal court. As indicated in Chapter 6, the federal courts generally exercise personal jurisdiction only to the extent that it would be exercised by the state courts in that state, under Fed. R. Civ. P. 4(e), (f). See pp. 80-81. In this case, jurisdiction would be proper over Stenk, on the basis of her New Mexico domicile, but not over Bailey, since the claim did not arise in New Mexico and the facts do not indicate that Bailey would be subject to general in personam jurisdiction there.

b. By now you may wish you had run away and joined the circus instead of going to law school. Taming lions or swallowing swords might not be so bad after all.

The personal jurisdiction analysis will not be affected by the defendant's decision to remove, since both courts apply the same statutory and constitutional standards for exercising personal jurisdiction (unless a specific federal statute authorizes the federal courts to exercise broader jurisdiction). Fed. R. Civ. P. 4(e). Defendants do not waive their right to object to personal jurisdiction by removing to federal court. See Chapter 7, question 21. Bailey could seek dismissal on this ground in the federal court after removal.

Venue and subject matter jurisdiction, however, require further analysis. Venue would not be proper under §1391 because all defendants do not reside in Arizona and the claim did not arise there. However, the usual federal venue provisions do not apply in removed actions. For removed cases, the applicable provision is 28 U.S.C. §1441(a), which requires that the case must be removed to the district and division embracing the place where the state action was brought. See *Polizzi v. Cowles Magazines,* 345 U.S. 663, 665 (1953). Thus, as long as the defendants file their removal petition in the federal district that includes the county where the state action was filed, venue will not be a problem.

The subject matter jurisdiction analysis requires a two-level inquiry. First, the removal statute requires that the case have been within the original subject matter jurisdiction of the federal court. 28 U.S.C. §1441(a). Assuming that suit was brought after Bailey moved its principal place of business to California, that requirement would be met. However, even if a case satisfies the basic diversity requirements, §1441(b) bars removal if any defendant is a citizen of the forum state. Since Stenk is a citizen of New Mexico, the case is not removable.

## A Two-Ring Circus

6a. It is possible that both the Northern and Southern Districts of Iowa fall into this area on the diagram, where both subject matter and personal jurisdiction are proper but venue is not. Federal subject matter jurisdiction is proper in either of these districts because Adler plans to assert a federal claim, and pendent jurisdiction will apply to his related breach of contract claim. (The court would also have independent jurisdiction over the contract claim on diversity grounds.) Personal jurisdiction is likely to be upheld in any Iowa court since the claim results, at least indirectly, from Ringlings' deliberate contact in going to Iowa to make the royalty agreement with Adler. This would likely suffice for specific in personam jurisdiction under the *International Shoe* minimum contacts test and satisfy the Iowa long-arm statute as well, assuming it has a "transacting business" provision similar to the Uniform Interstate and International Procedure Act. See supra p. 23. Since personal jurisdiction goes by state, not district, Ringling Brothers would be subject to specific in personam jurisdiction in the Southern District as well as the Northern.

However, venue would not be proper in the Southern District of Iowa because the facts do not indicate that Ringling Brothers does any business there and the claim certainly did not arise there. It may even be improper in the Northern District. Although the claim does arise out of the contract made in that district, in the general sense that it results from a breach of that contract, it is doubtful that this is sufficient to satisfy the "where the claim arose" language in 28 U.S.C. §1391(b). The court might conclude, based on the rationale that the venue provisions primarily protect defendants, that the claim arose where the pictures were used without permission. The court might also conclude that Ringling Brothers is not "doing business" in the Northern District of Iowa under 28 U.S.C. §1391(c), if the negotiation of this contract is the only contact it has had with that district. As the introduction suggests, single or isolated contacts with the state may not satisfy the "doing business" language in §1391(c), even if it would constitute "transacting business" under a state long-arm statute. Last, venue would not be proper on the basis of Adler's residence because the case is not founded solely on diversity. See 28 U.S.C. §1391(b).

b. This one is easy. Subject matter jurisdiction is proper in this case in any court in the federal system based on the analysis in part a above. Venue will be proper in any district in which Ringling Brothers does business, a wide choice considering what we know of its activities. However, personal jurisdiction over the circus will only be proper in Wisconsin, New York, Florida, and Ohio (on the basis of substantial and continuous contacts) and in Iowa and New York on the basis of minimum contacts giving rise to the claim. In each of the states where the circus tours for a few weeks but has no other contacts, there will be no basis for asserting personal jurisdiction over it for this claim, even though it is "doing business" there under the venue statute and the diversity requirements for subject matter jurisdiction are met.

# PART TWO

## *The Scope of the Action*

# 10

## *Sculpting the Lawsuit: The Basic Rules of Joinder*

## Introduction

A great deal of time is spent during the first year of law school analyzing decided cases, doing post mortems on past lawsuits. But every lawsuit also has a beginning, and at the beginning someone must make important tactical decisions about the scope of the lawsuit, that is, whom to sue and which claims to assert. The traditional rule in American courts has been, and largely still is, that "the plaintiff is master of his claim," that it is up to the plaintiff (or his lawyer) to decide who the parties to the suit will be and which claims will be asserted in the action.

An example may help to frame the problem. Assume that Wright is the main contractor on a construction job in Erie, Pennsylvania. The electrical subcontractor is Edison Electric. While driving to the construction site, Edison's site manager, Volt, collides with Wright's cement truck and with a private vehicle driven by Ellsworth. All three drivers are injured, and the two trucks are heavily damaged.

If Volt decides to bring suit against Wright to recover for his injuries, he will have to decide whether to sue alone, or to bring a combined action along with Edison Electric, which will seek to recover for the damage to its truck. Ellsworth may also wish to join as a plaintiff to recover for her personal injuries and property damage. Alternatively, Volt may wish to sue both Wright and Ellsworth on the theory that each was negligent or, for whatever reason, to sue one tortfeasor but not the other.

133

Volt's options as to which defendants he may sue and which potential plaintiffs he decides to sue with are defined by the rules of "joinder of parties." In the federal courts, initial joinder of parties is governed by Fed. R. Civ. P. 20(a), which authorizes plaintiffs to sue together if (1) they assert claims arising out of the same transaction or occurrence and (2) their claims against the defendant or defendants will involve a common question of law or fact. In Volt's suit, for example, Volt and Edison may join as plaintiffs because their claims arise out of the same accident and the factual issue of whose negligence caused the accident is common to both their claims.

Similarly, Rule 20 allows the plaintiff to sue multiple defendants in a single action if the same criteria are met. Volt could sue Ellsworth and Wright as codefendants in the same action, since he claims relief from each arising from the same accident, and there will be a common question as to whose negligence caused the accident. Here are some configurations that would be permissible under the rule:

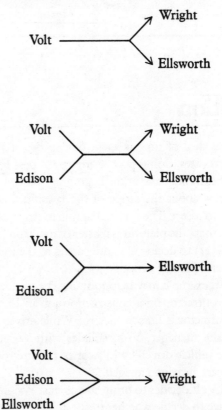

It makes good sense to allow parties to join as plaintiffs or sue defendants jointly in a single action if the criteria in Rule 20(a) are met. When a number of claims involve a single transaction or occurrence, and the same issue or issues will have to be litigated to resolve each claim, it is more efficient to litigate those issues once, in a combined action, rather than repeatedly in separate suits. In addition, resolving those issues in a single action avoids the possibility of inconsistent judgments on the same issue. For example, if Volt sues Ellsworth and recovers, but Edison sues her and loses, the two juries must have disagreed on whether Ellsworth was negligent (barring any contributory negligence defense). Such inconsistent results reflect unfavorably on the judicial system and are best avoided where possible. If Volt's and Edison's claims are tried together there will be no inconsistent verdicts since there will be only one finding on Ellsworth's negligence.

Interestingly, however, Rule 20(a) does not require parties to be joined whenever the criteria in the rule are met. At least initially, the joinder decision is left to the plaintiffs. If they choose to sue some, but not all defendants in one action, they may sue the others in a separate action or never sue them at all. If they choose not to join in a suit by other plaintiffs against the defendant, they remain free to pursue their own claims in separate suits.

## An Early but Sensible Question

1. Since it promotes efficiency and consistency to litigate related claims such as Volt's and Edison's together, why doesn't Rule 20(a) *require* joinder of parties where the two criteria in the rule are met?

_____

You should be careful to distinguish Rule 20, which governs joinder of *parties,* from Rules 18 and 13, which authorize parties, once they are properly joined in a law suit, to assert additional *claims* against opposing parties. Rule 13 authorizes a defending party in a suit to assert claims back against a party who has claimed against him. Such counterclaims come in two shapes, compulsory (Rule 13(a)) and permissive (Rule 13(b)). If the defending party's counterclaim arises from the same transaction or occurrence as the claim against him, it is compulsory, which essentially means that he must assert it in the original action or lose it. For example, if Volt sues Ellsworth for his injuries arising out of the accident, and Ellsworth suffered injuries in the same accident that she attributes to Volt's negligence, she must assert her claim for these injuries in Volt's action. This rule makes sense; it forces parties who are already adversaries to litigate all claims arising from the same set of facts in a single action.

## Another Impromptu Question

2. Under Rule 20(a), the parties are never forced to bring parties into a particular suit. Rule 13(a), by contrast, compels a party to assert some claims at a time and place not of his choosing. Why did the rulemakers choose to force parties to assert compulsory counterclaims?

_____

Defending parties may also assert counterclaims that are completely unrelated to the original claim under Rule 13(b). This cannot be justified on efficiency grounds, since (by definition) a permissive counterclaim will involve different events from the main claim, and the court will almost certainly order separate trial of the permissive counterclaim. See Rule 42(b). But the rule at least allows a defendant, once brought before the court, to settle all his claims against his opponent, without having to initiate a separate lawsuit.

Yet another type of claim is addressed in Rule 13(g), which provides for assertion of *cross-claims* arising out of the same transaction or occurrence as the main claim. A cross-claim is a claim asserted by one party against a co-party; that is, someone on the same side of the "v" as the claimant. Again, suppose that Volt sues Wright and Ellsworth for injuries suffered in the accident. If Wright suffered injuries as well and believes that the accident was Ellsworth's fault, she may cross-claim against Ellsworth for her injuries. This is called a cross-claim, rather than a counterclaim, because it is asserted by one defendant against a codefendant, not against an opposing party. The configuration would look like this:

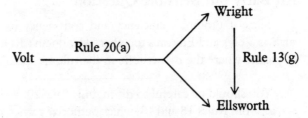

(Volt joins Wright and Ellsworth as defendants under
Rule 20(a); Wright cross-claims against Ellsworth
under Rule 13(g))

Here again, allowing assertion of these claims in the main action promotes efficiency and consistency because the same underlying facts will be litigated on the main claim and the cross-claim. Yet here again, the rule makes joinder optional, leaving Wright free to sue separately on her claim against Ellsworth if she prefers to do so.

The various joinder rules may also work in tandem. For example, the counterclaim rules, Rules 13(a) and (b), both authorize "a pleading" to assert a claim against an "opposing party." Once again the rulemakers have chosen the language of the rule with care. This language authorizes any defending party — not just an original defendant — to assert counterclaims against a party who has claimed against him. In the last diagram, Ellsworth is a defending party on Wright's cross-claim. Rule 13 applies to any claim she may have against Wright. If she has a claim against Wright for her injuries in the collision, she must assert it as a compulsory counterclaim once Wright has asserted a claim against her. If she has any unrelated claims against Wright, she may assert them, but is not required to, under Rule 13(b).

Rule 18(a) is the last and broadest of the basic joinder rules. Unequivocally, it provides that a party seeking relief from an opposing party may join with his original claim any additional claims he has against that opposing party. Suppose, for example, that Volt exchanges words with Wright after the accident and a fight ensues. Rule 18(a) allows Volt to assert his claim for assault in the same action with the negligence claim. It would also allow Volt to add a completely unrelated claim against Wright for libel, or trespass, or anything else: Unlike Rule 20(a), there is no common transaction or occurrence requirement in Rule 18(a).

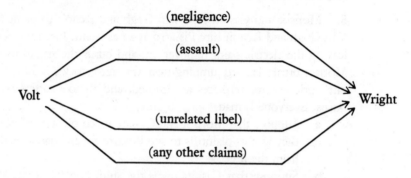

(Rule 18(a) authorizes joinder of all
these claims, related and unrelated)

Rule 18(a), like Rule 13, authorizes "a pleader" to assert as many claims as she has against an opponent. This applies not only to the original plaintiff, but to any party seeking relief against another party, whether on a counterclaim, cross-claim or third-party claim. Suppose, for example, that Volt sues Ellsworth and Wright for negligence, based on the collision at the construction site, and Ellsworth cross-claims against Wright for her damages arising out of the accident. Rule 18 authorizes Ellsworth, as a party seeking relief, to add on any claim, related or unrelated, which she may have against Wright:

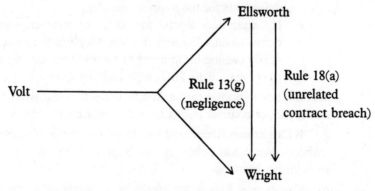

Here, Rule 18(a) authorizes Ellsworth to assert a second claim against Wright for breach of contract even though the second claim is unrelated to the main claim and therefore would not be a proper Rule 13(g) cross-claim in this action if brought alone.

In puzzling out the following examples, start by identifying the party asserting the claim as a plaintiff or defendant and then consider, given the particular posture of the claim, which of the rules applies. Assume that all suits are brought in federal court.

# QUESTIONS

## An Artistic Disaster

3.    Morisot and Cassatt hire Van Gogh and Renoir to paint their studio. Van Gogh and Renoir hire Pissarro as an assistant. Pissarro goes for coffee, leaving the electric paint remover on, and burns the studio to the ground. Morisot breaks her leg jumping from the third-story window, three of Cassatt's priceless masterpieces are burned, and Renoir suffers second-degree burns. Everyone is mad.

    a.   Suppose that Morisot and Cassatt are co-owners of the studio. May they join as plaintiffs to sue Pissarro for the damages to the studio from the fire?

    b.   Suppose that Cassatt owns the studio on her own. May she and Morisot join as plaintiffs to sue Pissarro for his negligence, if Cassatt seeks recovery for damage to the building and Morisot seeks damages for her broken leg?

    c.   Assume that Van Gogh and Renoir are liable for the negligence of Pissarro under the law of respondeat superior, if he acted in the scope of his employment in leaving the heat gun on. May Morisot sue Van Gogh, Renoir, and Pissarro in a single action to recover for her broken leg?

    d.   Could Cassatt sue Van Gogh and Renoir for breach of contract for burning down her studio in the process of painting it, and Morisot join as a co-plaintiff, asserting a negligence claim against the same defendants for the injury to her leg?

    e.   If Cassatt sues Renoir for breach of contract, may Renoir assert claims against Pissarro and Van Gogh in the same suit for negligently causing his injuries? (To answer this question, you will have to compare Rule 20(a) with Rule 14(a).)

4.    If Cassatt chooses to sue Renoir alone, may she assert both negligence and breach of contract claims against Renoir for her losses in the fire?

5.    If Cassatt sues Renoir and Van Gogh for breach of contract, do the rules authorize her to add a claim against Renoir for breach of a separate contract to paint her house?

6.    Cassatt sues Renoir for breach of the studio painting contract. Later, after losing on that claim, she sues Renoir for a previous breach of the unrelated contract to paint her house. Can she do that?

## The Tables Turned

7.  Assume that Morisot owned the studio and contracted with Renoir and Van Gogh to paint it. Morisot sues Renoir for negligence and breach of contract as a result of the studio fire. Renoir asserts a claim against Morisot in the same action for payments due for part of the painting that had been completed before the building burned. Is Renoir's claim properly joined?

8.  Following up on the last question, assume that Renoir also has a claim against Morisot for injuries suffered in an auto accident two months after the fire but before the suit was commenced. Can he assert this claim as well?

9.  Suppose on the same facts that the only claim Renoir had against Morisot was for the unrelated auto accident. Could he assert it in this action?

10. If Morisot sues Renoir for her fire losses, may Renoir assert his claim against Morisot for breach of the studio painting contract and also bring in Cassatt (a co-signer of the contract) as a codefendant on that claim?

## Acting at Cross-Purposes

11. Suppose that Cassatt sues Renoir, Van Gogh, and Pissarro jointly. She seeks recovery from Pissarro for his negligence and from Renoir and Van Gogh as Pissarro's employers, under the doctrine of respondeat superior. Renoir wishes to assert a claim against Pissarro for indemnification (that is, reimbursement for any damages he must pay) if he is found liable to Cassatt since it was Pissarro's negligence that actually caused the damage to the studio.

    a.  May Renoir assert this claim against Pissarro in the same suit?

    b.  Why is this claim *not* a counterclaim?

12. On the facts of question 11, could Renoir assert a claim against Pissarro for his own injuries suffered in the fire?

13. If, as in question 11, Cassatt sues Renoir and Van Gogh for their negligence in allowing the studio to burn, may Renoir assert a claim against Van Gogh for his failure to pay him half of the money they earned on another paint job?

14. Another variation on the theme of question 11: Suppose that Cassatt sues Renoir and Van Gogh, and Renoir wishes to assert claims against Van Gogh for his own injuries due to the fire *and* for the money owed him for the other paint job. May he do so?

15. Van Gogh and Renoir may not see eye-to-eye as to who caused the fire. If Renoir asserts a cross-claim against Van Gogh for indemnification for any damages he must pay Cassatt, may Van Gogh turn around and assert a claim against Renoir on a similar theory? (For example, each partner might claim that the other's faulty instructions to Pissarro actually caused the fire and that while he may be liable to the plaintiff for his partner's negligence, he should be indemnified by the negligent partner.) Would this claim be proper?

### Last Impressionists

16. One final question to make a particular point. Suppose Morisot (from Massachusetts) sues Renoir (from Maine) and Van Gogh (from Massachusetts) for their negligence in burning down the studio. Is the suit proper?

# ANALYSIS

### An Early but Sensible Question

1. While it would serve several goals of our procedural system to force all parties to join in a single action if their claims arise out of the same events, it would raise other serious procedural difficulties. Suppose that Volt and Ellsworth want to sue in federal court, but Edison prefers the state court? Suppose that Volt prefers to sue in Maine, but the others prefer New Hampshire? What if Edison wants to bring suit immediately, but Volt prefers to attempt a settlement first? Will Volt's lawyer represent all parties or will each have his or her own lawyer? Who will plan litigation strategy? What if they can't agree? Suppose that some of the potential plaintiffs are also potential defendants: Who will decide which side of the "v" to put them on?

In addition to these possible differences of opinion as to tactical choices, the jurisdictional problems would be even more serious. The right to join parties under the Federal Rules does not confer subject matter jurisdiction on the court. Fed. R. Civ. P. 82. For example, suppose that Volt is from Maine, Ellsworth from New Hampshire, and Wright, the intended defendant, from Maine. If Volt and Ellsworth were forced to sue together, the suit could not be brought in federal court because there would be no complete diversity. Under permissive joinder, if Ellsworth prefers federal court she may preserve the option to sue there by *not* joining as a coplaintiff with Volt. Alternatively, assume that Volt wishes to sue Wright, from Maine, and Ellsworth, from New Hampshire, for damages that took place in the Pennsylvania accident. Under Rule 20(a), which allows Volt to sue each defendant separately, he will at least be able to sue Wright at home in Maine because the Maine court will have personal jurisdiction over Wright on the basis of her domicile. If Volt were forced to join both defendants, he would have to sue in Pennsylvania, the one state where he could obtain personal jurisdiction over both defendants.

Obviously, a compulsory joinder rule would raise a host of procedural problems, which would undermine rather than further the goal of efficiency. The rulemakers wisely chose to stick with the old adage that "the plaintiff is master of his claim," rather than to create a whole new set of procedural complexities.

### Another Impromptu Question

2. Although forcing joinder of parties raises many problems, most of these do not apply to the joinder of an additional *claim* between parties who are

already properly before the court. The subject matter jurisdiction problems referred to in the analysis of question 1 will not arise in the compulsory counterclaim situation since there is usually ancillary jurisdiction over compulsory counterclaims. See Chapter 12, question 4. Nor will personal jurisdiction bar assertion of the claim: The plaintiff, by initiating suit, submits to jurisdiction for counterclaims arising out of the transaction or occurrence that is the subject of his claim. 6 Wright and Miller at §1416. Nor does compulsory joinder of the counterclaim pose uncertainties as to who must be joined since no new parties are brought into the suit by the assertion of the counterclaim.

The only substantial argument against making counterclaims compulsory is that it violates the longstanding common law principle that the plaintiff (or, in this case, the defendant) is master of his claim, free to choose where and when to assert any claim he may have. The rulemakers evidently concluded that this was insufficient to outweigh the obvious advantage of litigating the same facts and issues between the same parties in a single action. Some state rulemakers have weighed these policies differently, however, and refused to make any counterclaims compulsory. See Friedenthal, Kane, and Miller, Civil Procedure 350 n.15 (1985).

## An Artistic Disaster

3a. This question presents the simplest example of parties who wish to join as coplaintiffs in a single lawsuit. Rule 20(a) allows it, so long as they are asserting claims arising out of the same transaction or occurrence and their claims will involve at least one common question of law or fact. These criteria are met here because Morisot and Cassatt both seek relief arising out of the fire and both claims involve a common question of fact, whether Pissarro was negligent.[1]

b. The only difference between this example and the first is that the two plaintiffs seek compensation for different injuries. However, that does not affect their right to sue together. Rule 20(a) does not require that the plaintiffs seek recovery for exactly the same injuries or on a joint interest. In fact, the rule specifically provides that any one plaintiff "need not be interested in obtaining . . . all the relief demanded." It only requires that the underlying transaction or occurrence be the same and that the two plaintiffs' claims share a common question of law or fact. Those criteria are met here, and joinder is proper under the rule.

This result is appropriate, given the efficiency and consistency goals of Rule 20(a). As long as the claims will require resolution of common issues, joint litigation in a single suit will save time for the parties, the witnesses, and the court.

---

1. Indeed, they may even be required to join as plaintiffs, under Fed. R. Civ. P. 19.

c. Rule 20(a) applies not only to plaintiffs bringing suit together, but also to one or more plaintiffs bringing suit against multiple defendants. Here, Morisot seeks relief from all three defendants on claims arising out of the same fire, and her right to recover on each claim will require litigation of the negligence issue. Joinder is proper.

d. This example involves multiple plaintiffs and defendants. While Rule 20(a) does not explicitly authorize suit by multiple plaintiffs against multiple defendants, it does specifically authorize suits by multiple plaintiffs and (in the subsequent sentence) against multiple defendants. It is a fair inference that both types of joinder may be used in the same suit. It is proper, therefore, for some or all of the potential plaintiffs to join to sue all of the potential defendants or to sue selected defendants.

The other difference in this example is that the two plaintiffs are proceeding on different theories: Cassatt for breach of contract and Morisot for negligence. Compare question 1b, in which the plaintiffs proceeded on the same theory but for different damages. Nothing in Rule 20(a) requires the plaintiffs to proceed on the same theories in order for joinder to be proper. The idea behind the joinder rule is that there is efficiency and consistency to be gained from litigating the same facts in a single action. These goals are served by joinder criteria that allow a single action even though the plaintiffs are proceeding on different theories.

However, the criteria of the rule must still be met. In this case the "same transaction or occurrence" test clearly is met since all claims arise out of the fire. The "common question of law or fact" requirement will likely be met as well: Both Morisot and Cassatt will have to prove that Pissarro's acts caused the fire in order to recover from Van Gogh and Renoir on their respective theories. So long as some such common question exists, joinder is proper, even though many issues will be totally different.

e. In this case, it is the defendant who has joined multiple parties in the action, not the plaintiff:

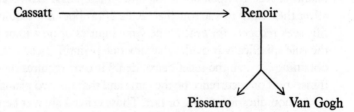

The general language of the second sentence of Rule 20(a), if read in isolation, might be interpreted to allow a defendant to join new parties as "defendants" in the original action. However, a look at Rule 14(a) indicates that this type of situation, a defendant bringing new parties into the suit (whom the plaintiff did not choose to sue), is separately dealt with in that rule, which allows joinder only in much more limited circumstances than Rule 20(a). See Chapter 11.

By contrast, Rule 20(a) only applies to joinder of parties by the original plaintiffs. The rulemakers' meticulous language confirms this: Rule 20(a) speaks specifically of "plaintiffs" and "defendants" rather than "parties claiming a right to relief" or similarly general language. Compare Rules 18 and 13, which are deliberately phrased more generally in order to apply more broadly.

4.   This example is typical of the myriad cases in which plaintiffs assert a number of claims against a single defendant for the same injuries but based on different theories of relief. The question here is joinder of claims, not parties, since Cassatt is seeking relief from a single party on two separate claims. Rule 18(a) establishes a refreshingly broad rule for joinder of claims: Once Cassatt decides to sue Renoir, she may join whatever claims she has against Renoir in the suit. Thus, joinder of the negligence and contract claims is proper.

5.   The answer to this question involves application of both Rules 20 and 18. Rule 20 allows Cassatt to sue Renoir and Van Gogh together for breach of the studio-painting contract. Compare question 3c. Rule 18 allows Cassatt, once she has properly asserted a claim against Renoir, to assert her unrelated contract claim against Renoir as well, even though it arises out of a completely separate incident. Visually, the case looks like this:

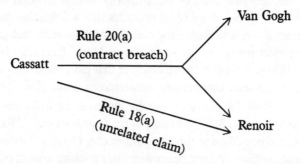

This compound effect of the rules is confusing. It seems to contradict the limitations on joinder established in Rule 20(a) since it allows Cassatt to inject into the case a claim that is completely unrelated to the transaction or occurrence that gave rise to the joint claim she has against the two defendants. After all, if she sued Van Gogh on the studio claim and joined Renoir on the unrelated claim only, joinder would not be proper under Rule 20(a) . . . *n'est-ce pas?* That is true, but the Rules take the position that once you *have* properly gotten the two of them into court, you may add any claims you have against either defendant, related or unrelated. Presumably, the theory is that once the parties become proper adversaries in a lawsuit they ought at least to have the opportunity to resolve all their differences in one suit.

6.   This question is meant to emphasize one point about Rule 18(a): that it is permissive. Cassatt may assert unrelated claims against Renoir under Rule 18(a), but is not obligated to do so. Thus, she could bring separate actions

against Renoir on these two unrelated contract claims in whatever order she chose.

One note of caution should be added. While Rule 18 may not force a plaintiff to join all his claims against a defendant in a single action, the rules of res judicata will (at least under federal res judicata principles), if the claims arise out of a single transaction or occurrence. If Morisot sues Renoir for breach of the painting contract and for negligently causing the fire that led to her leg injuries, these would constitute a single "claim" for res judicata purposes that must be litigated in one action, despite the permissive language of Rule 18(a). See Chapter 19, which compares the joinder rules with the principles of res judicata and especially question 2b, which specifically addresses the Rule 18 issue. However, because the two claims asserted here are completely unrelated, separate suits will be permissible under res judicata analysis as well as Rule 18(a).

## The Tables Turned

7.     Morisot's joinder of Renoir and Van Gogh as codefendants is proper here under Rule 20(a). Renoir's claim against Morisot is a counterclaim under Rule 13(a), that is, a claim by a defending party against the party suing him. Not only do the rules authorize Renoir to assert this claim, they require him to do so. Rule 13(a) provides that a defending party's pleading "shall" state as a counterclaim any claim he has that arises out of the same transaction or occurrence as the main claim. Here, Renoir's claim arises out of the performance of the same contract that gave rise to one of Morisot's claims. It is therefore a compulsory counterclaim under Rule 13(a).

8.     Rule 13 provides for the assertion of both compulsory (13(a)) and permissive (13(b)) counterclaims. In this example, Renoir has properly asserted one of each: the compulsory claim against Morisot based on the painting contract and the permissive counterclaim arising out of his auto accident with Morisot. The difference between the two is the source of the claim: The contract claim, which arises out of the same transaction as the original claim, is compulsory, while the claim arising from unrelated events is permissive.

9.     Yes, Renoir is free to assert his unrelated counterclaim, even though it is the only claim he has against Morisot. Rule 13(b) authorizes the assertion of unrelated counterclaims without restriction.

This may seem illogical. Why drag claims into the lawsuit that will have no factual relation to the main claim? It hardly seems likely to promote efficiency to join the painting contract claim with the auto accident claim, which will present completely different factual and legal issues. The rules allow joinder of such claims, however, on the theory that a defendant, once forced into court by the plaintiff, ought at least to have the option to settle all disputes with that plaintiff in a single action. That way, the defendant can save the cost of filing a new action and serving process on the defendant in a separate action and perhaps lower the cost of discovery as well. If a single trial does not make sense, the court may order separate trials. Fed. R. Civ. P. 42(b).

10. Here Renoir asserts a counterclaim against Morisot and wants to add an additional party to the counterclaim. Cassatt is not yet a party to the action. Although the plaintiff is ordinarily "master of his claim," to include or exclude possible parties, this is a situation where the defendant also gets some control over the parties. Under Rule 13(h), Renoir is authorized to bring in an additional party on the counterclaim, so long as the requirements of Rule 20(a) (same transaction or occurrence and common question of law or fact) are met. They are met here, so the joinder of Cassatt as an additional party to the counterclaim against Morisot is proper.

## Acting at Cross-Purposes

11a. This is the first example in which one defendant seeks to recover against a codefendant. Rule 13(g) authorizes assertion of such "cross-claims" if they arise out of the same transaction or occurrence as the original claim. Renoir's claim qualifies because it arises out of the fire.

   b. Be careful to distinguish cross-claims from counterclaims. Counterclaims are asserted against a party who has asserted a claim against you. Cross-claims are asserted against a coparty, that is, a party to the action who is on the same side of the "v" as the cross-claimant. Renoir's claim is not a counterclaim, since Renoir is not claiming against Cassatt, who sued him, but against Pissarro, his codefendant.

12. This is also a valid cross-claim under Rule 13(g). It differs from the last example because the cross-claimant here seeks recovery for his own injuries, not indemnification for damages he may have to pay the plaintiff. Either type of claim is permissible so long as it arises out of the transaction or occurrence that gave rise to the main claim. See the second sentence of Rule 13(g), which deals with the situation in question 11 but not question 12, and provides that a cross-claim may be for indemnification but need not be.

13. This attempt at joinder is improper. As already stated, Rule 13(g) requires that the cross-claim arise out of the same transaction or occurrence as the main claim; this completely unrelated claim is therefore improper. Under the efficiency rationale of the joinder rules, this result is appropriate. Because the claims involve completely separate transactions, there will be little efficiency gained from litigating them together. Similarly, these claims pose no risk of inconsistent judgments because the judgments rendered on them will not involve the same issues. To add the unrelated claim, on the other hand, could make the litigation confusing and disorganized.

14. After the answer to the last question, you may be somewhat frustrated by the answer to this one. Joinder of both claims is proper here. Renoir's claim for his own injuries is a proper cross-claim, as in question 12. And,

once a proper cross-claim has been asserted against Van Gogh, Renoir may add on any other claims he has against Van Gogh, under Rule 18(a).

It is crucial to understand the difference between the role of Rule 18(a) in questions 13 and 14. Although Rule 18(a) appears on its face to authorize any party to assert any claim he has against an opposing party, the rule actually requires a party to assert one claim that is proper under the other joinder rules before he can add others to it under Rule 18(a). Thus, once Renoir has properly asserted a cross-claim against Van Gogh under Rule 13(g), he may add others under Rule 18(a). Similarly, if Renoir asserted a third-party claim against Pissarro under Rule 14(a), he could add others under Rule 18(a). But Rule 18(a) is not a general hunting license to assert any claim against any party; if it were, all the other rules discussed in this chapter would be unnecessary.

Admittedly, it does not seem logical to allow Renoir to assert the unrelated claim if he asserts a related one (as here), but not if he asserts it alone (as in question 13). Yet that is just what the rules do. Perhaps the rationale is that once Renoir and Van Gogh become adversaries by the assertion of a proper cross-claim, they might just as well resolve all their differences in a single suit. Once again, the court has the discretion to order a separate trial of the unrelated claim if there is no efficiency to be gained from joint litigation.

15. Not only may Van Gogh assert this claim, he *must* do so under Rule 13(a). When Renoir claims against him, Van Gogh becomes a defending party subject to the counterclaim rules of 13(a) and 13(b). Visually the case looks like this:

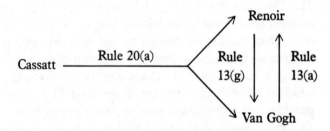

Remember that the counterclaim rules are written in general language to apply to all defending parties, not just original defendants. Since Van Gogh's claim for indemnification from Renoir arises out of the same transaction or occurrence as the cross-claim, it is a compulsory counterclaim and must be asserted in this action or lost.

## Last Impressionists

16. The point of this question is so important that I have devoted an entire chapter to it. See Chapter 13, Jurisdiction vs. Joinder: The Difference between Power and Permission. Fundamentally, the problem here is that Mori-

sot has the right under Rule 20(a) to join Van Gogh and Renoir as codefendants on the claim, but the court lacks subject matter jurisdiction because there is neither complete diversity nor a federal claim. The joinder rules do not provide a basis for subject matter jurisdiction, they only govern who may properly be made parties if the court has jurisdiction. Thus, this case is not properly before the court even though the joinder rules are satisfied.

# 11

## Into the Labyrinth: Joinder of Parties under Rule 14

## Introduction

A persistent civil procedure theme explored in the earlier chapters is the right of the plaintiff or plaintiffs to sculpt the lawsuit by their choice of the forum and their initial decisions to join parties as plaintiffs or defendants. An equally persistent theme, however, is the various ways in which the plaintiff's well-laid plans may go awry. For example, she may end up in a different court if the defendant removes or seeks a change of venue. Or she may end up *defending* a claim if another party asserts a cross-claim or counterclaim against her.

Rule 14 provides another example of the complexities that await the unwary plaintiff who disregards Dickens's famous advice.[1] Rule 14 gives a defendant a limited right to *implead* (that is, bring into the suit) strangers against whom she has claims related to the main action. Under the rule the defendant may bring in a person not yet a party to the suit who may be liable to her, the defendant, for all or part of any recovery the plaintiff obtains on the main claim.

In many tort cases third parties are impleaded for *contribution,* that is, to obtain a judgment that the third party is liable to pay the main defendant part of the damages she is ordered to pay the plaintiff. For example, suppose that Napoleon sues Wellington for tortious injuries arising out of a polo match.

---

1. "Suffer any indignity that can be done you rather than come [to the courts of chancery]." Charles Dickens, Bleak House 7 (Norton ed. 1977).

Wellington claims that Robespierre, riding a third horse, was also negligent. Under the traditional rules of contribution among joint tortfeasors, Wellington would be entitled to recover from Robespierre half of any damages Wellington pays Napoleon, if he can prove that Robespierre was also negligent. On these facts Wellington may implead Robespierre under Rule 14 since he may be liable to Wellington for part of any damages that Wellington is ordered to pay Napoleon. The case looks like this:

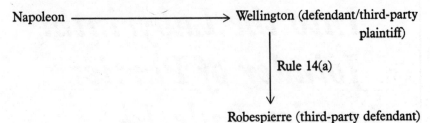

Napoleon ——————————————→ Wellington (defendant/third-party plaintiff)

Rule 14(a)

Robespierre (third-party defendant)

In other cases the defendant may claim that the third party is liable to her for all damages that she may have to pay the plaintiff. In the Schulansky case, for example, the last claim for relief in Ronan's third-party complaint alleges that Jones is liable to *indemnify* him for any damages that Schulansky recovers from Ronan because his negligence allegedly caused the damage that led to the action against Ronan. (See infra p. 378.) Another common example of a proper impleader claim is a claim for indemnity against an insurer. If Wellington is insured against negligence with Lloyds of London, he may implead Lloyds for indemnity. In this example Wellington claims that if he is held liable to Napoleon, Lloyds should reimburse him as it has contractually agreed to do in the insurance agreement. In both of these examples the defendant seeks to pass on all of his liability, not a part as in the contribution example. This also satisfies the requirement in Rule 14 that the impleaded party may be liable to the defendant for "all or part" of the plaintiff's claim against the defendant.

It is crucial to distinguish these cases from the situation in which the defendant contends that another person is directly liable to the plaintiff but not to her. Suppose that Wellington's polo match took place in a jurisdiction that did not allow contribution between joint tortfeasors. In that case Robespierre might still be liable to Napoleon directly, but Wellington could not implead him because Robespierre would not be liable to him at all. He can't offer up Robespierre as an alternative defendant to Napoleon, saying, "Here, Napoleon, you sued me, but you really should have sued us both, so here's Robespierre; go at him." That would allow the defendant to dictate to the plaintiff whom to sue where, in defiance of the conventional doctrine that the plaintiff is master of her claim.

To further illustrate this point, assume that a police officer assaults Dillinger in the course of arresting him for robbery. Dillinger sues Officer Hayes, a six-foot-two, red-headed policeman, for the assault. Hayes claims mistaken identity: it was actually Officer Kelly, another six-foot redhead, who arrested Dillinger. Hayes cannot implead Kelly. He has no claim that Kelly is liable to him. Either one or the other assaulted Dillinger; one or the other will be solely liable to him. Hayes contends of course that Dillinger should have sued Kelly instead of him, but this gives him no right to substitute another defendant or to add one under Rule 14. That rule does not allow defendants to suggest new targets for the plaintiff. Rather, it allows defendants to bring in targets of their own if they may be able to pass on liability to the impleaded party.[2]

It follows from this central requirement of Rule 14 that the third-party defendant's liability depends on the outcome of the main claim. If Napoleon does not recover from Wellington, Wellington will have no right of contribution against Robespierre. Robespierre can hardly be asked to contribute if Wellington doesn't have to pay. Nor would Lloyds be liable to indemnify Wellington unless Wellington has to pay a judgment, or Jones to pay Ronan if Schulansky loses on the main claim. The impleaded party may escape liability by defeating either the plaintiff's original claim or the defendant's derivative claim against her. Consequently, the rule allows her to assert defenses to both. See Rule 14(a), fourth sentence (defenses to third-party claim) and fifth sentence (defenses of the defendant to the plaintiff's claim).

The impleader claim is treated like an original suit for pleading, service, and other purposes. The defendant, as "third-party plaintiff," must file a third-party complaint against the impleaded "third-party defendant." The complaint must comply with the pleading requirements of Rules 8-11 and must be served under Rule 4. The third-party defendant must respond under Rule 12 and has the same options to answer or move to dismiss. The third-party defendant may also file counterclaims against the third-party plaintiff and may implead further parties under Rule 14. That rule also allows the plaintiff and the third-party defendant to assert claims against each other if they arise out of the same transaction or occurrence as the main claim. See Rule 14, sentences six and seven.

Under Rule 14 a defendant may implead a third party within ten days of answering the complaint, without obtaining leave of court. This automatic

---

2. At one time, Rule 14 did allow defendants to add new parties who might be liable directly to the plaintiff. That provision created serious problems that led to the elimination of this option:

> [I]n some cases plaintiff declined to press his claim against the third-party defendant and could not be compelled to amend his complaint in order to do so. When that occurred, the third-party action would have to be dropped since no one had alleged a claim against the third-party defendant. In other cases, an amendment to assert a direct claim against the third-party defendant, if allowed, would have destroyed diversity of citizenship as the basis of federal jurisdiction. For these reasons the rule was amended in 1948 to eliminate defendant's right to implead persons directly liable to plaintiff.

6 Wright and Miller at 200.

impleader provision suggests that the court must hear the third-party claim if it is filed within the ten-day period. However, the cases establish that it is always within the court's discretion to refuse to entertain the impleader claim. See generally 3 Moore's at ¶14.05[2]. Factors favoring impleader include the efficiency of hearing the related claims together and avoidance of repeated suits or inconsistent judgments. Factors suggesting denial of impleader include undue delay in seeking it, complication of the issues in the main action, and potential prejudice to the plaintiff from impleading a sympathetic third party. In some cases the court may be able to address these concerns by allowing the impleader but separating the main suit and the third-party suit for trial. See Rule 14, sentence eight; 6 Wright and Miller at §1443.

Two further important points concerning the relation of impleader claims to our three-ring analysis should be mentioned. First, in determining whether diversity jurisdiction is proper, the citizenship of the third-party defendant is irrelevant; only the citizenship of the original parties is considered. Suppose, for example, that Napoleon is from Maine, Wellington from Connecticut, and Robespierre from Maine:

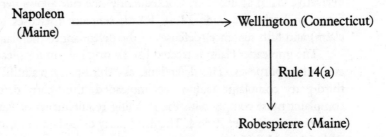

This case is properly before the court even though the third-party defendant is from the same state as the plaintiff. The same is true if Robespierre is from Connecticut. Subject matter jurisdiction over the third-party claim itself will usually be proper under ancillary jurisdiction, at least in diversity cases. See Chapter 12, question 8.

The third party's citizenship is also irrelevant in determining whether venue is proper. The case in the illustration could properly be brought in Connecticut ("where all the defendants reside," 28 U.S.C. §1391(a)) despite the fact that the third-party defendant resides in Maine, not Connecticut. 6 Wright and Miller at §1445, p.240. If the third party's citizenship were counted, defendants would be able to defeat federal jurisdiction in many cases in which the plaintiff had properly invoked it initially by selectively impleading defendants from the right (that is, the wrong) states.

The questions below may help to dispel some of the darkness that engulfs this murky rule. In answering them, assume that all cases are brought in federal court and that subject matter jurisdiction is proper in each case. In addition, focus on whether the claim would satisfy the requirements of Rule 14, not whether the court (assuming the rule is satisfied) would exercise its discretion to hear the impleader claim.

# QUESTIONS

## Basics of the Rule

1.   Ali sues Bellefonds, the engineer on a canal construction project, for negligence arising out of faulty engineering calculations in planning the canal. May Bellefonds implead Le Pere, another engineer whom he claims was also negligent in making the calculations?

2.   Ali sues Bellefonds for his faulty engineering calculations. Bellefonds impleads Le Pere, alleging that it was actually Le Pere who did the calculations. Is the impleader proper?

3.   France sues DeLesseps, a general contractor, for faulty canal construction. DeLesseps claims that if there was a breach it was actually the fault of Said, the dredging subcontractor on the job, and that Said should therefore bear the loss. Can he implead Said?

4.   Suppose that DeLesseps is unclear as to whether the defective construction work resulted from Said's dredging work or faulty concrete work done by another subcontractor, Ismail. May he implead both?

5.   Assume that France sues DeLesseps on the canal contract, and DeLesseps wishes to recover from Said, his subcontractor, for certain camels Said took away when he left the job. May he implead Said?

6.   In the same contract action, could DeLesseps implead Said and assert both the indemnification claim described in question 3 and the camel-trover claim in question 5?

## Variations on a Theme

7.   Suppose that DeLesseps is sued by France for breach of the canal contract. He impleads Said for faulty subcontract work, and Said wants to assert a claim against France for intentional interference with his contract with DeLesseps. May he do so?

8.   Notice that the language of the Rule (always *so* carefully chosen by the Solomons of civil procedure) does not call Said's claim against France in the last question a counterclaim. Why isn't it a counterclaim?

9.   Think of three ways in which a counterclaim could insinuate itself into this suit.

10.   Assume that DeLesseps impleads Said for indemnification on the theory that his faulty dredging work caused the contract breach. Said claims that his insurer, Cairo Casualty and Indemnity Co., has a duty to pay any damages resulting from his breach. May Said assert a claim against Cairo in the same action?

11.   If Said is impleaded, may France assert a claim against Said for shoddy construction on an unrelated job Said did for France?

12.   Suppose that DeLesseps counterclaims against France, to collect the contract price for the canal work. May France implead Disraeli, who co-

signed the contract along with France and is therefore also contractually bound to pay DeLesseps for the contract work?

## Another Unlucky Number 13

13. Assume that France is from California, DeLesseps from Texas, and Said from Arizona. The canal work was done in Colorado. France sues DeLesseps in Texas, and DeLesseps impleads Said. Is the impleader proper?

## A Last Brainteaser for the Rules Enthusiast

14. Along the same general lines as the earlier questions, assume that France sues DeLesseps and he impleads Said. Said wishes to assert a claim against France for interference with his contract with DeLesseps. He also claims that Porte (an agent of France not yet a party to the suit) took part in the intentional interference. Can he add Porte as an additional party to his interference with contract claim against France? Visually the hypo looks like this:

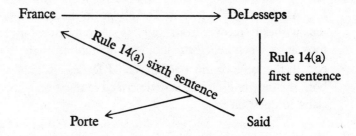

# ANALYSIS

## Basics of the Rule

1.   Here, Bellefonds seeks to implead Le Pere, not yet a party to the suit, to recover part of any judgment Ali recovers from Bellefonds. Assuming that the relevant state law authorizes contribution among joint tortfeasors, this is a proper impleader claim. Le Pere is a new party who "is or may be liable to him [Bellefonds] for all or part of the plaintiff's claim against him [Bellefonds]." If Bellefonds is found liable to Ali, and Le Pere is also found negligent, Bellefonds will be entitled to recover half of the damages he pays Ali from Le Pere. Note that at the time he impleads Le Pere, it is not clear that Le Pere will be liable to contribute. That depends on whether Bellefonds is found negligent, whether Le Pere is found negligent, and whether Bellefonds pays more than half of the judgment. But the rule only requires that Le Pere "may" be liable to him; Le Pere's liability need not follow automatically from Bellefonds's, nor must Bellefonds have already been adjudged liable before he can implead Le Pere.

2.   As stated in the introduction, impleader under Rule 14 cannot be used to foist alternate defendants on the plaintiff. Ali chose to sue Bellefonds, not Le Pere. If Bellefonds didn't do the faulty calculations, Ali will lose his suit against him. Maybe he will then sue Le Pere or maybe he won't. That's his choice. But Bellefonds may not bring Le Pere in on the mere allegation that he is liable to Ali. He may only implead Le Pere to recover from him part of the damages Bellefonds must pay Ali. If liability is an either/or proposition, Bellefonds has no such claim against Le Pere and impleader should be denied.

Ali could have chosen to join Bellefonds and Le Pere as codefendants under Rule 20(a). See Chapter 10, p. 134. Or Bellefonds may defend against Ali's claim on the ground that Le Pere was the offending party instead of him. But he can't use Rule 14 as a backdoor means of forcing Ali to sue Le Pere, which Rule 20(a) allows but does not require Ali to do.

3.   This is a proper impleader claim. DeLesseps, as the general contractor, will be liable to France if the work does not meet the contract specifications even though it was a subcontractor's negligence that caused the breach. However, he will surely have a contractual right under his separate contract with Said to indemnity for damages caused by Said's faulty subcontract work. Thus Said "may be liable to him [DeLesseps] for all . . . of the plaintiff's claim against him [DeLesseps]," and DeLesseps may properly implead him under the first sentence of Rule 14(a).

4.   In this case Said is unclear as to whether he should be indemnified by one subcontractor or the other or both. Although the rule is not explicit on the point, there is no reason why a defendant should have to limit his impleader claims to one third party when several may be liable to him. As long as the provisions of Rule 14 are satisfied, a defendant may implead multiple third-party defendants, claiming either joint or alternate liability.

5.   This is not a proper impleader claim. Here, DeLesseps has a claim against Said arising out of the same transaction (the construction of the canal) as the main claim, but Said's liability to DeLesseps is not derivative of the main suit. DeLesseps has a totally independent claim against Said, which he could assert whether France wins or loses on the main claim or never sues at all.

It might make sense to design the rules of procedure to allow the defendant to expand the lawsuit in this way, but it would certainly introduce many tangential claims sharing few witnesses or factual or legal issues with the main claim. That would be the case here since the claim for the missing camels is clearly distinct from the faulty construction claim. The rule-makers decided to confine the defendant's options more narrowly, by use of the "may be liable to the defendant for all or part of the plaintiff's claim" language. But see, with some perplexity, the following question.

6.   Curiously, despite the answer to question 5, Rule 18(a) expressly allows DeLesseps, once he has forced Said into the suit on a proper impleader claim,

to add on this independent claim. Presumably the rationale for this is that once the third-party defendant is in the case the Rules might as well allow the defendant to settle all her differences with the third-party defendant in a single action. Visually the suit looks like this:

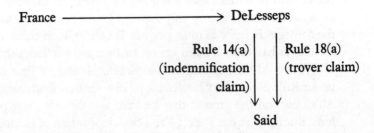

However, Rule 18(a) alone does not allow DeLesseps to bring Said into the suit. To do that, DeLesseps must first assert a claim complying with Rule 14. Rule 18 only allows him to add related (or unrelated) claims once he has properly impleaded Said under Rule 14.

## Variations

7.   In this example, Said has been properly impleaded and seeks to assert a related claim against the original plaintiff. The sixth sentence of Rule 14(a) explicitly authorizes Said to do so. The suit now looks like this:

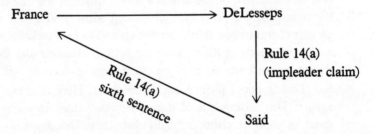

But Said cannot assert any claim he has against France. Under Rule 14(a), his claims against plaintiff are limited to those that satisfy the same transaction or occurrence test encountered in Rule 20. Assuming the court takes a reasonably broad view of that test, this claim will satisfy it.

8.   A counterclaim is defined in both Rule 13(a) and (b) as a claim against an "opposing party." Before Said asserts a claim against France they are not opposing parties. France has a claim against DeLesseps, not Said. Although France and Said are locked in the same litigious dance, they are not yet partners.

9.   Counterclaims may be asserted by any defending party against her opponent. Rule 13(a). Obviously, DeLesseps may have some against France. Said, once impleaded, may assert counterclaims against DeLesseps. See Rule 14(a), fourth sentence. Indeed, he *must* assert them if they satisfy the Rule

13(a) test for compulsory counterclaims. For example, he may have a claim against DeLesseps for the subcontract price for his services. This claim arises out of the same transaction as DeLesseps's claim against him and must be asserted in the impleader action under Rule 13(a).

Lastly, once Said has asserted a claim against France, they become opposing parties as well. If France has any claim against Said arising from the canal construction, he must assert it. If he has any other claim against Said, he may assert it as well under Rule 13(b). Thus, hydra-like,[3] the suit may grow:

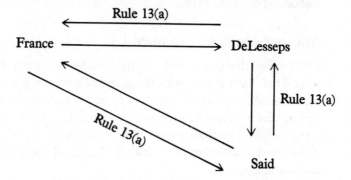

10. Said may indeed implead Cairo under Rule 14(a). The ninth sentence of that rule allows the third-party defendant to assert such telescoping third-party claims against further parties. The suit now looks like this:

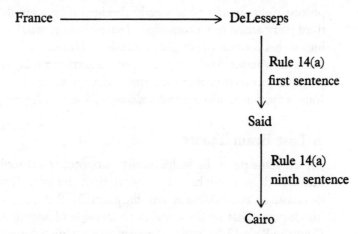

Imagine the title of Cairo's answer to this claim: "Fourth-Party Defendant's Answer to the Third-Party Defendant/Fourth-Party Plaintiff's Fourth-Party Complaint"!?

11. France's claim here does not arise out of the same transaction or occurrence as the main claim. The seventh sentence of Rule 14 authorizes joinder

---

3. The hydra, a Greek beast, was reputed to sprout two heads for each lopped off by its unfortunate adversary.

of claims the plaintiff has against the third-party defendant, if those claims satisfy the same transaction or occurrence test. By implication the rule excludes unrelated claims, so this one fails. As well it should; there has to be some limit to the introduction of unrelated matters into the action, lest it become completely unmanageable.

12. This is an example of a plaintiff, now a defendant on a counterclaim, impleading a party who may be liable to her (the plaintiff) for all or part of a judgment the counterclaiming defendant obtains from her. It is explicitly authorized by Rule 14(b).

## Another Unlucky Number 13

13. The fact that you were given the states for each party should have tipped you off that there is some jurisdictional problem here. It can't be diversity: As the introduction points out, the third party's citizenship is irrelevant to determining diversity, and besides, there is complete diversity anyway. It can't be venue either. The third party's state is disregarded in determining proper venue. Here, "all defendants" reside in Texas, although Said, the third-party defendant, does not.

It must be personal jurisdiction. Indeed it is, or may be. *Whenever* a party is brought into a suit, whether as an original defendant, third-party defendant, additional party to a counterclaim, whatever, the court must have the power to require that party to appear and defend in that state. Said's due process rights would be as clearly abridged if he were forced to defend a third-party action in a forum with which he lacks contacts as if he were forced into such a court as the original defendant. Therefore, the court will have to consider whether Said has minimum contacts with Texas or is subject to personal jurisdiction there for this claim on some other basis. Compare Jones's motion to dismiss in *Schulansky v. Ronan,* Chapter 27.

## A Last Brain Teaser

14. At some point the hydra must be stopped, and it seems that the Rules intend to draw a limit here. Rule 14(a), sixth sentence, allows the third-party defendant to assert claims against the plaintiff if they arise out of the underlying dispute. That sentence makes no mention of adding additional parties. Compare Rule 13(h), which expressly allows adding parties to counterclaims and cross-claims. Nor does Rule 20(a) apply here; that rule only applies to the joinder of original defendants. For these more abstruse variants you have to find explicit authority in one of the other joinder rules, and it appears that by providing no such authority the rules stop short of allowing this claim.

# 12

# *Jurisdictional Fellow Travelers: The Basics of Pendent and Ancillary Jurisdiction*

## Introduction

You have already read — and you will hear it repeated ad nauseum for the rest of your professional life — that the subject matter jurisdiction of the federal courts is limited to the categories of cases enumerated in Article III, §2 of the Constitution. However, in a number of important cases the Supreme Court has appeared to violate that fundamental precept by upholding federal jurisdiction over claims that clearly fall outside these categories when those claims are joined in a single suit with a jurisdictionally sufficient claim.

Historically, two independent doctrines evolved to support jurisdiction over such related claims in federal court. The first, *pendent jurisdiction,* was typically invoked when a plaintiff asserted a claim against one or more defendants under federal law and added a second claim under state law. Visually the classic pendent case looks like this:

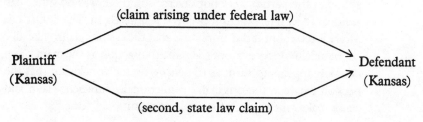

159

In such cases the federal court has jurisdiction over the federal law claim but frequently does not have jurisdiction over the state law claim since there is no diversity between the parties.

In *United Mine Workers v. Gibbs*, 383 U.S. 715 (1966), for example, the plaintiff asserted a federal claim against the defendant under the Labor Management Relations Act and a second claim under state law for interference with contractual relations. Since there was no diversity between the parties in *Gibbs* and the interference claim arose under state law, it was clear that Article III, §2 did not authorize Gibbs to sue the union in federal court on the interference claim alone. Yet the *Gibbs* court held that the federal court had "pendent" jurisdiction over the state law claim because it was joined with the federal labor law claim.

The *Gibbs* court resolved this paradox by holding that Article III grants jurisdiction over entire "cases," not just over particular claims or issues in a case. So long as a case involves a claim that is jurisdictionally sufficient under Article III, the argument goes, the court has constitutional power to hear the entire dispute between the parties, not just the claim that is expressly provided for in Article III, §2. Thus, so long as the plaintiff asserts a claim based on federal law, diversity, or some other proper federal ground, the federal court has the power — at least the *constitutional* power — to hear all his claims arising out of the same "common nucleus of operative facts." In *Gibbs*, for example, the case was properly before the federal court because the plaintiff asserted a claim under the federal labor laws. The constitutional "case," however, was broader than the federal claim, encompassing all of Gibbs's claims arising out of the same nucleus of operative facts, the opening of the new mine.

A somewhat similar approach evolved under the rubric of *ancillary jurisdiction* to deal with a different set of cases in which related claims were asserted by defendants or other additional parties. The typical ancillary jurisdiction case involved a jurisdictionally sufficient claim by a plaintiff against a defendant (under either federal question or diversity jurisdiction), which triggered a further state law claim by a defending party that did not satisfy any independent ground of federal subject matter jurisdiction.

The classic example is *Moore v. New York Cotton Exchange*, 270 U.S. 593 (1926), in which the plaintiff sued the defendant under the federal antitrust laws, and the defendant asserted a compulsory counterclaim against the plaintiff under state law. The court upheld jurisdiction over the state law claim, although the parties were not diverse and there was no other basis for independent federal jurisdiction over the counterclaim. The Court's discussion in *Moore* is terse, but it did emphasize that the counterclaim (like all compulsory counterclaims) arose out of the same transaction as the main claim. Thus, the decision appears to turn, as did *Gibbs*, on the conclusion that the close connection between the original, jurisdictionally sufficient claim and the added claim makes them part of a single constitutional "case."

From the seed of the *Moore* case, the courts extended ancillary jurisdiction to many claims that bear a "logical relationship" to the main claim. For example, third-party claims under Rule 14 have consistently been held ancillary. Suppose, for example, that Ace, a New Yorker, sues Queen, from California, for Ace's injuries suffered in an auto accident, and Queen impleads Jack (also from California) under Rule 14 for contribution on the theory that he was a joint tortfeasor. The federal court has jurisdiction over the main claim on the basis of diversity, but there is no independent jurisdiction over the claim between Queen and Jack since there is no diversity between them and the claim is not based on a federal question. The federal courts have taken ancillary jurisdiction over such impleader claims, however, since they are by definition "logically related" to the main claim: The third-party plaintiff can only recover from the third-party defendant if the plaintiff recovers from the third-party plaintiff. Fed. R. Civ. P. 14; see, e.g., *Dery v. Wyer*, 265 F.2d 804, 807-808 (2d Cir. 1959).

On a similar rationale ancillary jurisdiction was extended to cross-claims under Rule 13(g) and intervention as of right under Rule 24(a). But the same logic dictated denial of ancillary jurisdiction for permissive counter-claims and permissive intervention because by definition such claims lacked a close logical relation to the main claim. See generally Friedenthal, Kane, and Miller at §2.14.

# A New Layer of Analysis

All of this was complex enough for courts to apply or civil procedure students to learn. Unfortunately (but probably justifiably), the Court has multiplied these woes by introducing a more sophisticated analysis of the limits of such supplemental jurisdiction in several cases since *Gibbs*. In *Aldinger v. Howard*, 427 U.S. 1 (1976) and *Owen Equipment & Erection Co. v. Kroger*, 437 U.S. 365 (1978), the court reiterated one of the basic principles of federal jurisdiction: that federal jurisdiction is not only limited by the Constitution but also must be conveyed to the federal district courts by Congress in one of the jurisdictional statutes. (Recall Judge Sirica's well-phrased comments on the "Article III storehouse," supra p. 64.) Consequently, courts confronted with both ancillary and pendent jurisdiction cases must look to the jurisdictional statute on which the main claim is based to determine whether it expressly or impliedly negates or supports jurisdiction over related state law claims.

In *Aldinger*, for example, the plaintiff brought suit against several individual defendants under a federal statute, 28 U.S.C. §1983, and attempted to append a second state law claim, based on the same incident, against a county. The claim against the individual defendants was clearly authorized by a special jurisdictional statute applicable to civil rights cases, but that statute had not been interpreted to authorize jurisdiction over counties since at the time[1] they were not subject to suit under §1983. *Aldinger* at 5. The Court concluded that even though the claim could be viewed as part of a single constitutional case under the *Gibbs* analysis, adding a state law claim against the county would be inconsistent with the apparent intent of Congress to limit federal civil rights claims against counties.

Similarly, in *Kroger* the Court appeared to accept the constitutional case analysis of *Gibbs*, but went on to consider whether the relevant jurisdictional statute, 28 U.S.C. §1332, indicated congressional intent to grant the federal courts ancillary jurisdiction over a claim asserted by the plaintiff against a nondiverse third-party defendant. Although the Court concluded that the claim at issue was part of the same constitutional "case," it refused to extend ancillary jurisdiction to the claim because such an extension would be inconsistent with the long-standing interpretation of §1332 requiring complete diversity between the parties.

In light of *Kroger* and *Gibbs*, it appears that pendent and ancillary jurisdiction are converging toward a single doctrine of supplemental jurisdiction, which requires a three-part analysis. First, the court must consider whether there is a constitutional basis for the exercise of jurisdiction over the related but jurisdictionally insufficient claim. This analysis, set forth in the first part of the *Gibbs* opinion, requires the court to consider first whether the plaintiff has asserted a substantial claim within the federal court's jurisdiction and second whether the state law claim is part of the same constitutional case. The jurisdictionally sufficient federal claim need not arise under federal law; a diversity claim or one based on another statute, such as the Federal Tort Claims Act, will also meet the threshold requirement of a proper federal claim. Once a proper federal claim has been asserted, all claims arising out of the same nucleus of operative facts as the federal claim will satisfy the one constitutional case requirement.

If the court concludes that it may constitutionally assert jurisdiction over the entire case, including the state law claims, it must then analyze the congressional intent behind the statute that grants jurisdiction over the proper federal claim. If anything in the statute or its legislative (or judicial) history suggests that Congress has "expressly or by implication negated" (*Aldinger* at 18) jurisdiction over the related, jurisdictionally insufficient claim, then it must refuse to hear it. If, on the other hand, the legislative history of the statute suggests congressional intent to confer broad jurisdiction over the

---

1. When *Aldinger* was decided, counties were not considered "persons" subject to suit under §1983. *Monroe v. Pape*, 365 U.S. 167, 187-191 (1961). After *Aldinger* was decided, however, the Supreme Court overruled this aspect of *Monroe*. See *Monell v. Department of Social Services*, 436 U.S. 658, 690-691 (1978). Thus, if the same case arose today, it is not at all clear that the Court would hold that the claim against the county was barred.

entire "case," including the added claims, then the court at least has power to entertain all the claims in the case.

Lastly, if the added claims pass the first two parts of the test so that the court has jurisdictional authority to hear them, it must then decide whether it should exercise that jurisdiction. This discretionary decision rests on the various prudential factors discussed in *Gibbs*. 383 U.S. at 726. Interestingly, the ancillary jurisdiction cases prior to *Kroger* did not suggest that a court had discretionary power *not* to hear ancillary claims. Once the courts determined that the claim was ancillary, they usually took jurisdiction, without any discussion of prudential factors that might caution against the exercise of that jurisdiction. However, *Kroger*'s endorsement of the *Gibbs* analysis suggests that federal judges may refuse to exercise ancillary jurisdiction if the prudential factors discussed in *Gibbs* counsel against it, and some cases have so held. See, e.g., *Waste Systems, Inc. v. Clean Land Air Water Corp.*, 683 F.2d 927, 930-931 (5th Cir. 1982) (concluding that jurisdiction over cross-claims was permissible under the first two prongs of the *Gibbs/Kroger* test but declining to exercise it as a matter of discretion).

The Supreme Court has described ancillary and pendent jurisdiction as "two species of the same generic problem" (*Kroger* at 370) and doubted whether any "principled distinction" (*Aldinger* at 12) remains between them. However, in analyzing the following cases, you may find it useful to compare the configurations of the parties to the cases you have read to see whether they resemble traditional pendent or ancillary cases. Then consider, based on the Court's analysis in *Gibbs* and *Kroger*, whether the court has jurisdiction to entertain the state law claim under Article III and the relevant jurisdictional statute. (For the moment don't worry about the third, discretionary level of the analysis.)

In working through these questions, be very careful not to confuse permission to join claims under the Rules with power to take jurisdiction of such claims under the *Gibbs/Kroger* analysis. For example, the Rules authorize joinder of permissive counterclaims (Rule 13(b)), but ancillary jurisdiction does not extend to them. This crucial distinction is the subject of the next chapter.

You will have to read and digest the *Kroger* and *Gibbs* cases to adequately understand the questions that follow. A little treatise reading would also help; I recommend Friedenthal, Kane, and Miller at §§2.12-2.14 for a good, short discussion. For more detail, there is an excellent discussion on these doctrines in Note, A Closer Look at Pendent and Ancillary Jurisdiction: Toward a Theory of Incidental Jurisdiction, 95 Harv. L. Rev. 1935 (1982). You may also find it helpful to draw quick diagrams of the configurations of the parties to illustrate who is a plaintiff, defendant, or other creature and who is on the receiving end of each of the asserted claims. Assume in each case that suit is brought in federal court.

# QUESTIONS

## Basic Cases

1.   Keats, from Minnesota, is arrested by Shelley, a Minnesota police officer, for disturbing the peace. During the arrest, Shelley forcibly restrains Keats, and Keats resists. Keats claims that Shelley used excessive force in making the arrest. He sues Shelley under the federal civil rights statute, 42 U.S.C. §1983. Keats also seeks to recover from Shelley on a state law claim for battery based on the scuffle that took place during the arrest.

   a.   Does the court have the power to hear the battery claim?
   b.   Assume that the court concludes that it lacks power to hear the battery claim. What should it do with the $1983 claim?
   c.   Assume that the court declines in its discretion to hear Keats's battery claim. What will happen to the federal claim?
   d.   Assume for this question only that there is no such doctrine as pendent jurisdiction. What would Keats have to do in order to recover on both of his claims?

2.   Apparently there was some prior history to the Keats/Shelley altercation. Shelley owed Keats $50 at the time of arrest as payment for work that Keats had done on his house. Keats was upset because he had not been paid and tempers flared, leading to the arrest. Keats therefore asserts a third claim for the debt in his action against Shelley. Does the court have the power to hear it?

3.   Browning, Blake, and Wordsworth are involved in a three-car collision on Route 192, near Dayton, Ohio. Browning, a New Yorker, sues Blake and Wordsworth, both from Ohio, for $20,000 for her personal injuries. Blake asserts a cross-claim against Wordsworth for his own injuries arising from the same collision. Does the court have jurisdiction over the cross-claim?

4.   Suppose, on the facts of question 3, that Blake (Ohio) asserts a counterclaim against Browning (N.Y.) for $5,000 dollars for his injuries. Does the court have jurisdiction to hear the counterclaim?

5.   May Blake assert a $5,000 counterclaim against Browning in the accident case for a trespass on his property four months prior to the accident?

6.   Please reconsider the Keats/Shelley debacle in question 1. Would the court in that action have jurisdiction over a counterclaim by Shelley against Keats for battery based on Keats's acts in resisting the arrest?

## Important Question, Requiring Thought

7.   Now please reconsider question 3, in which Browning sued Blake and Wordsworth for her injuries in an auto accident. In that case could Blake (Ohio) assert a counterclaim against Browning (N.Y.) for an unrelated

breach of a patent Blake holds? Assume that the counterclaim is for $7,000 in damages.

8. Suppose that Browning (N.Y.) sues Blake (Ohio) for her injuries from the collision, and Blake impleads Wordsworth (Ohio) for contribution if he is found liable to Browning. Is there jurisdiction over the impleader claim?

9. Assume that there is jurisdiction over Blake's claim in question 8. Does the court have discretion to decline jurisdiction over the impleader claim?

10. Assume for this question only that the doctrines of pendent and ancillary jurisdiction never developed. Blake (Ohio) impleads Wordsworth (Ohio) for contribution in Browning's suit. Would the court have jurisdiction over Blake's impleader claim against Wordsworth anyway?

## An Important Caveat

11. Browning (N.Y.) sues Blake (Ohio) in New York on the auto accident case. Blake answers the complaint, denying negligence and impleading Wordsworth (Ohio). What will be the problem with the New York court taking jurisdiction over the impleader claim?

## Complex Variations

12. If Blake (Ohio) impleads Wordsworth (Ohio), and Browning, the New York plaintiff, then asserts a claim directly against Wordsworth, will the court have the power to hear it?

13a. If Blake (Ohio) impleads Wordsworth (Ohio), and Wordsworth asserts a claim against Browning (the N.Y. plaintiff) for $5,000, for his own injuries in the accident, will the court have the power to hear it?

b. Suppose that Wordsworth is impleaded and claims against Browning, and Browning then asserts a $5,000 claim against Wordsworth arising from the collision?

14. Coleridge claims injury from medical malpractice by Brontë, a doctor employed by the federal government. Under the Federal Tort Claims Act, he may sue the United States for his injuries but only in federal court. 28 U.S.C. §1346(a). Coleridge brings a federal suit against the United States and also asserts a negligence claim against Brontë (a citizen of the same state as Coleridge) in the same action. Is jurisdiction proper?

15. If Browning, from New York, sues Blake, from Ohio for $30,000 as a result of her injuries in the auto accident, may Wordsworth (Ohio) join as a coplaintiff to recover from Blake for his injuries in the same accident?

16. On the facts of the last question, could Cowper, a New York passenger in Browning's car, join as a coplaintiff to recover $5,000 for damage to his car?

## Poetic Injustice: A Last Trick Question

17. Coleridge, from Oregon, sues Brontë, from Texas, for libel. He claims $15,000 damages. Brontë impleads Cowper (a New York citizen and co-author of the offending essay) for contribution. Brontë also seeks an additional $6,000 from Cowper for an unrelated loan she had made to him. Does the court have jurisdiction over Brontë's loan claim against Cowper?

# ANALYSIS

## Basic Cases

1a. This is the most common type of pendent jurisdiction, in which the plaintiff asserts a federal question claim against the defendant and a related state law claim against the same defendant. It is exactly analogous to *Gibbs*, which established the modern criteria for the exercise of pendent jurisdiction. The case clearly satisfies *Gibbs*'s criteria for a single constitutional case: The plaintiff has asserted a colorable claim under federal law (the §1983 claim) and the state law battery claim arises out of the same "nucleus of operative facts," the arrest.

After *Kroger*, the court must presumably ask as well whether there is anything in the relevant jurisdictional statute that suggests congressional intent to restrict pendent claims in §1983 cases. There is no reason for you to be able to answer that question at this stage of law school; the important point is to recognize the need to analyze the jurisdictional statute as well as the scope of the constitutional case under *Gibbs*.

That statutory analysis would go something like this: §1983 is a remedial statute, intended to encourage plaintiffs to bring actions to recover for civil rights violations. If Congress thought about the pendent jurisdiction problem at all when it enacted §1983 (and the correlative jurisdictional provision, 28 U.S.C. §1343), it probably intended to provide plaintiffs with an opportunity for full redress in a single action by joining in their federal action all their claims against the defendant based on the same facts. Courts routinely take pendent jurisdiction over state law claims in §1983 actions, at least claims against the same defendant. Compare *Aldinger* (discussed at pp. 161-162), in which the state law claim was asserted against a new party, which at the time was not considered subject to suit under §1983.

Of course, the court will still have discretion to decline to hear the battery claim if it involves sensitive issues of state law, if the federal claim is resolved early in the litigation, or for the other reasons discussed in *Gibbs*.

b. If the court lacked jurisdiction over the related state law claim, it would have to dismiss it. But it could not dismiss the federal claim: It has jurisdiction over that claim, and (absent some extraordinary situations not discussed here, such as federal abstention) it has a duty to exercise that jurisdiction by hearing and deciding the §1983 claim.

c. The same result follows if the court concludes that it has jurisdiction over the battery claim but declines to hear it as a matter of discretion. The plaintiff is still entitled to a federal forum on his federal claim even though the related state claim will be heard in state court. Of course, if the court declines to hear the state law claim, the plaintiff might decide to dismiss the federal suit and file in state court, in order to have all claims heard in a single proceeding.

d. If the Supreme Court had not discovered pendent jurisdiction embedded in the Framers' broad language in Article III, Keats would not have been able to join his battery claim in the federal suit. Consequently, he would have had two choices. He could have brought two lawsuits, one in federal court on the §1983 claim and the other in state court on the battery claim. Alternatively, he could have brought a single action in state court seeking relief on both claims, since state courts have concurrent jurisdiction over federal claims unless Congress specifically makes federal jurisdiction over particular types of cases exclusive. Thus, a state court could decide Keats's §1983 claim, and, of course, it could also decide his state law claim as well.

These alternatives for Keats illustrate the importance of pendent jurisdiction. Without it, parties would be encouraged to sue in state court in order to have their entire case resolved in one proceeding. Thus, many important federal cases ("federal" in the sense that they contain heady issues of federal law), would be heard in state rather than federal courts even though a primary purpose of federal courts is to expound and develop federal law. Because pendent and ancillary jurisdiction assure that many of these cases will be brought in federal court, Professor Arthur Miller views it as a kind of "protective" jurisdiction. Miller, Ancillary and Pendent Jurisdiction, 26 S. Tex. L.J. 1, 4 (1985).

2. This example fails at the first level of the analysis, the same constitutional case requirement discussed in *Gibbs* and apparently endorsed in *Kroger*. *Gibbs* holds that jurisdictionally insufficient claims are part of the same case and therefore within the Article III grant of federal jurisdiction if they arise out of the same nucleus of operative facts as the federal claim. Here, the assault claim does, but the debt claim does not. Although there may be a causal relationship between the debt and the eventual arrest and assault, it is too attenuated to make them part of the same nucleus of facts.

It is not clear whether the reach of a "common nucleus of operative facts" is the same as the "same transaction or occurrence test" used in the federal joinder rules. One scholar suggests that since the transaction or occurrence test was well established when *Gibbs* was decided, the court must have meant something different — and probably broader — when it formulated the common nucleus test in *Gibbs*. See Matasar, A Pendent and Ancillary Jurisdiction Primer: The Scope and Limits of Supplemental Jurisdiction, 17 U.C.D.L. Rev. 103, 130 (1983). It is probably safe to assume that the *Gibbs* test is satisfied if the related state claim arises out of the same transaction or occurrence as the federal claim but that it might also be satisfied in some more loosely related situations. Compare the formulation used in the earlier ancillary jurisdiction cases, which required only a "logical relationship" between the two claims.

3.    This is a cross-claim by a defending party against another defendant arising out of the events that gave rise to the original claim. Prior to *Kroger,* the courts routinely took ancillary jurisdiction over cross-claims between codefendants. Because a cross-claim by definition arises out of the same transaction or occurrence as the main claim (see Rule 13(g)), it was considered to bear a "logical relationship" to the main claim sufficient to make it part of the same "case." Therefore, if, as here, there was jurisdiction over the main claim, the court would hear the cross-claim as well.

Cross-claims are probably still ancillary in diversity cases after *Kroger.* First, the Court in *Kroger* appears to endorse *Gibbs*'s common-nucleus test for constitutional jurisdiction, and Blake's cross-claim satisfies that because it arises out of the accident that gave rise to the main claim.

On the statutory level, the *Kroger* Court appears to find implicit authority in §1332 for entertaining ancillary claims by defending parties. Kroger at 375-376. The Court distinguished such cases from the facts of *Kroger* on the ground that the defendant is unwillingly before the court, while the plaintiff in *Kroger* had deliberately chosen the more restrictive federal forum over the state court, which could have heard all her claims in a single action. It is also unlikely that cross-claims pose the risk of collusion that the Court saw in allowing the plaintiff v. third-party claim in *Kroger.* It hardly seems likely that defendants will solicit suit against them by diverse plaintiffs in order to assert cross-claims against codefendants in federal court.

However, the *Kroger* court in rejecting jurisdiction over Mrs. Kroger's claim against the third-party defendant also pointed out that her claim, while it arose from the same incident, lacked the "logical dependence" on the main claim that an impleader claim under Rule 14 requires. Kroger at 376. Liability in an impleader action is derivative; that is, the third-party plaintiff only recovers from the impleaded party if the plaintiff recovers against him. If that kind of dependence is crucial to ancillary jurisdiction, Blake's cross-claim should not qualify since Blake could recover from Wordsworth even if Browning loses on the main claim. However, the cases suggest that even after *Kroger,* the courts will disregard this implication, focus instead on the defensive posture in which the added claim is asserted, and conclude that cross-claims are still ancillary in diversity cases. See 3 Moore's at ¶13.36.

4.    This is the classic ancillary jurisdiction situation addressed in *Moore v. New York Cotton Exchange,* 270 U.S. 593 (1926). Blake's counterclaim is compulsory here because it arises from the same accident as the main claim. Yet the court lacks independent jurisdiction over it because it does not satisfy the amount-in-controversy requirement. Prior to *Kroger,* compulsory counterclaims were consistently held ancillary. By definition (see Fed. R. Civ. P.

13(a)) they arise from the same transaction as the main claim and therefore bear a "logical relation" to the main claim.

Under the *Gibbs/Kroger* analysis, there is no doubt of the court's constitutional power to hear the added claim since it arises out of the same incident as the main claim. The next question then, as above, is whether the diversity statute expressly or impliedly negates the exercise of jurisdiction over this related but jurisdictionally insufficient claim. As in question 4, the claim lacks the logical dependence on the main claim that an impleader claim must have. But it is asserted by a defending party, unwillingly before the court, and it does not present the anomaly of the *Kroger* case of two nondiverse parties litigating in federal court. Thus, even after *Kroger,* the courts will likely continue to hold that compulsory counterclaims are ancillary in diversity cases.

5.   Because this claim does not arise out of the same transaction or occurrence as the main claim, there is no basis for ancillary jurisdiction over it. It founders on the *Gibbs* constitutional analysis, which only extends ancillary jurisdiction to claims that arise from the same nucleus of operative facts as the main claim. Consequently, there is no basis for the court, under Article III, to append it to the other claim.

Thus, this claim will have to be dismissed for lack of subject matter jurisdiction unless there is an independent ground for subject matter jurisdiction. Although Blake and Browning are diverse, the amount in controversy requirement is not met so there is no independent subject matter jurisdiction over the counterclaim. It will have to be dismissed.

6.   The case is much like question 4, a counterclaim that is jurisdictionally insufficient, though compulsory. The only difference is that the main claim in this case is brought under federal question jurisdiction, not diversity. The constitutional analysis should be the same, but the statutory analysis must focus on 28 U.S.C. §§1331 and 1343 (which confer federal jurisdiction over civil rights cases) rather than on §1332. Nothing in those statutes suggests congressional intent to limit ancillary claims in civil rights cases, and the same solicitude for the defendant "haled into court against his will" applies here as in diversity cases. This claim would almost certainly be held a valid ancillary claim.

## Important Question, Requiring Thought

7.   This hypo isn't that hard, but it is very important. This case is like question 5, except for one crucial difference. In this case there *is* a separate, independent ground for jurisdiction over the counterclaim. While the court could not take ancillary jurisdiction over the claim under the *Gibbs/Kroger* analysis, it has direct jurisdiction over the patent claim since it is a claim arising under the federal patent laws, which the federal court may hear under 28 U.S.C. §1338. Thus, there is no need to invoke ancillary jurisdiction here.

8.   This claim is analogous to the Power District's third-party claim against Owen in *Kroger*. While this claim was not in issue in *Kroger*, the Court's discussion clearly indicated approval of ancillary jurisdiction over impleader claims, at least in diversity cases. The Court distinguished third-party impleader claims from Mrs. Kroger's claim against Owen on the ground that impleader claims are asserted by defendants and are logically dependent on the outcome of the main claim. See *Kroger* at 376. On the constitutional level, if the impleader claim satisfies the requirements of Fed. R. Civ. P. 14, the court suggests that it will have a sufficiently close relationship to the main claim to satisfy the same case requirement of *Gibbs*.

9.   A short answer to this is that the court has discretion under Rule 14(a) itself to decline to entertain an impleader claim, completely apart from possible discretion built into the ancillary jurisdiction test. However, since this chapter is on jurisdiction, the thrust of the question is clearly whether once a court has concluded that a claim is ancillary it has discretion to refuse to hear the claim for the various prudential reasons discussed in *Gibbs*.

The concept of discretion to refuse to hear related state law claims was introduced in *Gibbs*, a pendent jurisdiction case. The ancillary jurisdiction cases prior to *Kroger* did not include a discretionary step: If the claim was logically related to the main claim, the court took jurisdiction. As discussed in the introduction, however, a number of the post-*Kroger* cases suggest that the unified three-part analysis for incidental jurisdiction does include discretion to decline jurisdiction in typical ancillary situations.

10.  The point here is fundamental, but by no means obvious. The impleaded third party, Wordsworth, is diverse from the plaintiff but not from the defendant who impleaded him. Whom do you count in measuring diversity over the third-party claim?

The answer is that the third-party action by Blake against Wordsworth is viewed separately for purposes of determining subject matter jurisdiction. Since Blake and Wordsworth are from the same state there is no independent ground for jurisdiction over the impleader claim. If ancillary jurisdiction were unavailable this claim could not be joined. The fact that Wordsworth is diverse from Browning avails him not. Conversely, if Wordsworth were from New York there would be independent subject matter jurisdiction even though he was *not* diverse from the plaintiff.

## An Important Caveat

11.  A persistent theme of this book is the interrelatedness of the various procedural doctrines studied in civil procedure. The procedure devotee is always trying to juggle a variety of concepts at the same time. Here, for example, the problem is personal jurisdiction, not subject matter. While Blake has apparently consented to personal jurisdiction in New York (by answering to the merits without objecting to jurisdiction), there is no indica-

tion that Wordsworth has done so or that the claim arose out of any minimum contacts he has with New York. Ancillary jurisdiction provides a basis for subject matter jurisdiction over this case, but it does not establish personal jurisdiction over the third-party defendant. Whenever a court takes jurisdiction over a claim against an original defendant, third-party defendant, or whatever, it must have a ground for forcing the defending party to appear and defend in that court. Ancillary jurisdiction is no substitute for personal jurisdiction; be careful to keep your rings straight! See *Doebler v. Stadium Productions Ltd.,* 91 F.R.D. 211, 213-214 (W.D. Mich. 1981).

If, however, Wordsworth answers without objecting to personal jurisdiction, the court may hear the action since ancillary jurisdiction provides a subject matter basis for the court to proceed and the lack of personal jurisdiction may be waived.

## Complex Variations

12. If you diagrammed this case, you will have noticed that it is the same configuration as *Kroger* with the plaintiff asserting a claim against the third-party defendant. *Kroger* clearly holds that there is no ancillary jurisdiction over such a claim in a diversity case. However, in this case there may be independent subject matter jurisdiction over the claim. The plaintiff and the third-party defendant here are diverse; if Browning's claim is for more than $10,000 the court will have jurisdiction over it.

13a. This configuration is the reverse of *Kroger,* a claim by the third-party defendant against the plaintiff. There is no independent jurisdiction over the claim because the amount in controversy requirement is not satisfied. It is difficult to predict whether the Supreme Court will extend ancillary jurisdiction to this type of claim in diversity cases. On the one hand, this is a state law claim which does not satisfy s. 1332(a), just as Mrs. Kroger's claim was. On the other, the claim here is asserted by the defending party, who has not chosen the forum and is hardly likely to collusively induce his own joinder in order to claim against the plaintiff. At least one case has interpreted *Kroger* to authorize ancillary jurisdiction in a similar situation. See *Finkle v. Gulf & Western Mfg. Co.,* 744 F.2d 1015, 1018-1019 (3d Cir. 1984).

b. Of course this had to be the next question. Here, the third party has claimed against the plaintiff, and that makes the plaintiff a defending party who must assert any counterclaim she has arising out of the same incident. Fed. R. Civ. P. 13(a). But doesn't it directly contradict *Kroger* to allow ancillary jurisdiction over the plaintiff's claim? Can subject matter jurisdiction over this claim depend on whether the plaintiff asserts the claim first or in response to the third-party defendant's claim? Yet there is also an argument for allowing Browning to do it since she is now a defending party. Wouldn't it be crazy, from an efficiency point of view, to hear Wordsworth's claim but not Browning's counterclaim?

Any line the court draws here will be a thin one, difficult to defend in close cases. It is hard to argue that there is a jurisdictionally significant difference between this case and *Kroger*, but the Court has favored defending party claims, and there is certainly less likelihood of collusion here. The *Finkle* court upheld jurisdiction over this type of claim as well, and I'd say their guess is as good as any.

14. In this example Coleridge asks the court to take "pendent party" jurisdiction over the claim against Brontë. His claim against the United States is jurisdictionally sufficient because §1346(b) authorizes (in fact, requires) him to sue the United States in federal court. However, Coleridge has attempted to assert a new claim against a new party, an extension of the concept of supplemental jurisdiction. Compare *Aldinger v. Howard*, 427 U.S. 1 (1976).

Such an attempt was rejected by the Supreme Court in *Aldinger* since the relevant jurisdictional statute in that case implied a limitation on the joinder of the additional claim. See *Aldinger* at 15-17. Here, however, the statute that confers jurisdiction over the main claim creates exclusive federal jurisdiction: Coleridge cannot sue the United States in state court. Consequently he must assert his related claim against Brontë in the federal action or else bring separate suits against the two defendants, one in federal court and the other in state court. Several courts have inferred that Congress must have intended broad joinder of claims and parties in Federal Tort Claims Act cases in order to insure an effective remedy without requiring a multiplicity of actions. See, e.g., *Lykins v. Pointer Inc.*, 725 F.2d 645 (11th Cir. 1984); cf. *Ortiz v. United States*, 595 F.2d 65 (1st Cir. 1979).

If jurisdiction is upheld in these cases, the plaintiff will be allowed to sue a nondiverse defendant on a state law claim, just because he has also sued another defendant on another claim arising from the same incident. Although this may be consistent with the *Gibbs* Court's broad reading of Article III, §2, it obviously departs from *Kroger* on the statutory level of the analysis based on the difference between the Federal Tort Claims Act and the diversity statute.

15. Here, a nondiverse plaintiff seeks to append his claim against the defendant to the jurisdictionally sufficient claim of another diverse plaintiff. Allowing this would directly contradict §1332 as interpreted in *Strawbridge v. Curtiss*, 7 U.S. 267 (1806), and *Kroger*. If complete diversity means anything, it means that this cannot be done.

16. Here, both plaintiffs are diverse from the defendant, but only the first satisfies the amount in controversy requirement. Constitutionally, this may be "one case" under *Gibbs*, but the second plaintiff runs afoul of the second, statutory level of the analysis. Section 1332 has always been interpreted to require each plaintiff to separately satisfy the amount in controversy requirement. See *Zahn v. International Paper Co.*, 414 U.S. 291, 292-296 (1973); Chapter 5, p. 69. Allowing Cowper to pile on here would essentially overrule

that interpretation of the statute, which both Congress and the Supreme Court have refused to do. For a case directly on point, see *Hixon v. Sherwin-Williams Co.*, 671 F.2d 1005, 1007-1009 (7th Cir. 1982).

## Poetic Injustice

17. In this case, Brontë impleads Cowper on two claims, neither of which satisfies the amount in controversy requirement. (Her contribution claim is for $7,500, half of the plaintiff's claim against her, and her separate claim is for $6,000.) There would be ancillary jurisdiction over the contribution claim alone since it is a derivative claim arising out of the same underlying facts as the main claim. There would not be ancillary jurisdiction over the loan claim if sued on alone since it is unrelated and therefore not part of the same "constitutional case."

However, when the two claims are joined against Cowper, they add up to more than the required $10,000.01. Since a plaintiff (presumably including a third-party plaintiff) may aggregate unrelated claims to satisfy the amount requirement, Brontë has an independent basis for subject matter jurisdiction over both her claims against Cowper so both may be heard.

I warned you it was tricky.

# 13

## Jurisdiction vs. Joinder: The Difference between Power and Permission

## Introduction

Concepts such as ancillary jurisdiction and joinder of parties are difficult enough to grapple with individually. Yet these doctrines do not exist in isolation; they interact to create a system[1] that lawyers must understand as a whole in order to litigate effectively. The real challenge (and fascination) of civil procedure is to try to see how the various pieces of the puzzle fit together into an interrelated, consistent framework for adjudication.

The last three chapters have separately analyzed the rules governing joinder of claims and parties, on the one hand, and the doctrines of pendent and ancillary jurisdiction on the other. However, a particular suit is proper only if both the joinder rules and related jurisdictional doctrines are satisfied. This chapter will explore the interrelations of these affiliated doctrines.

As the earlier chapters on joinder demonstrate, no party may assert a claim against another party in the federal courts unless one of the joinder

---

1. Some lawyers, those unfortunates who have never been captivated by the symmetry and logic of it, might call it a maze, a net, or a trap.

rules — Rules 13, 14, 18, 20, and 24 — authorizes assertion of that claim. However, the fact that the Rules authorize joinder of a particular claim is not sufficient to assure that the federal court may hear the claim. The court must also have a basis for exercising subject matter jurisdiction over the claim. The federal courts have only limited jurisdictional power; if there is no basis in Article III, §2 to hear a claim, "permission" to join a claim under the Rules can not substitute for it.

An example may help. If Nimitz is injured in an auto accident involving two other drivers, Spruance and Halsey, Rule 20(a) allows him to sue them both in a single suit. Nimitz's claims against both arise out of a single occurrence and will both involve the common factual issue of whose negligence caused the accident. However, if Halsey and Nimitz are both from Texas, the suit will be dismissed for lack of subject matter jurisdiction since there is no complete diversity.

This need for both power and permission follows from basic constitutional doctrine. All jurisdiction must be found in the "Article III storehouse," and it is up to Congress to confer all or part of that jurisdiction on the lower federal courts. See Judge Sirica's comments, p. 64. The Federal Rules, on the other hand, are promulgated by the Supreme Court. While the Court has the power to make rules to assure the orderly conduct of business in the federal courts (see 28 U.S.C. §2072), the Court may not use its rule-making power to expand the jurisdiction of those courts. Thus, though the Court has broadly authorized joinder of claims and parties under the Federal Rules, the need for subject matter jurisdiction provides an implicit limitation on joinder in every case. The Court itself reaffirmed this limitation in Fed. R. Civ. P. 82, which provides in part that "[t]hese rules shall not be construed to extend or limit the jurisdiction of the United States district courts or the venue of actions therein."

Although joinder cannot substitute for jurisdiction, it would often make life easier if it could. There is a tension between the Rules, which encourage broad joinder of related claims to promote efficiency, and the strict Article III limits on federal court jurisdiction. In cases such as the Halsey example above, it would make eminent good sense to hear the related claims together since the witnesses and much of the evidence will be the same, the legal issues will overlap, and the plaintiff is the same in both claims. The joinder rules encourage and sometimes even require such sensible litigation practice, but good sense may be thwarted at times by the limitations on federal subject matter jurisdiction.

The Supreme Court struggled with this tension in *Owen Equipment & Erection Co. v. Kroger,* 437 U.S. 365 (1978). In *Kroger,* joinder of Mrs. Kroger's claim against Owen, the third-party defendant, was permissible under Rule 14. It certainly would have made sense to hear that claim in the same action with the main claim and the third-party claim: The parties were all before the court already, much of the evidence would have been the same, and the judge was already familiar with the case. But the Court balked at extending ancillary jurisdiction to provide a basis for subject matter jurisdiction over the claim. Absolutes are absolutes, and subject matter jurisdiction is as absolute as you get in the civil procedure business.

In many cases pendent and ancillary jurisdiction *will* provide a jurisdictional base for additional claims. Indeed, these doctrines were crafted to do just that, as an accommodation to the needs of modern litigation practice. For example, the Court indicated in *Kroger* that ancillary jurisdiction would support the third-party claim by the Power District (the original defendant) against Owen, the third-party defendant. In other cases when ancillary jurisdiction will not apply, there may be a separate basis for subject matter jurisdiction. For example, if Mrs. Kroger had been from Colorado, there would have been independent diversity jurisdiction over her claim against Owen. Since joinder was proper under Fed. R. Civ. P. 14(a), both power and permission would have been proper. Yet other cases may fall between the cracks, either for lack of jurisdiction or, conversely, because the joinder rules do not authorize assertion of the claim.

The questions below will help you to grasp the distinction and the interrelations between these two problems. In analyzing these cases, assume that all are brought in federal court and that personal jurisdiction is proper.

# QUESTIONS

## Some Basics

1.  Nimitz, a citizen of Texas, sues Bradley, from Missouri, and Patton, from California. Nimitz claims that each defendant libeled him, though on different occasions. He claims $30,000 in damages from each. Is the case properly before the court?

2.  Nimitz (Tex.) sues Bradley (Mo.) for the libel claim and an unrelated breach of contract. He seeks $5,000 dollars in damages on the contract claim and $30,000 on the libel claim. Can the court entertain the claims?

3.  Nimitz (Tex.) brings suit against Bradley (Mo.) and Clark, a Texas citizen. Nimitz asserts that the two defendants violated his federal civil rights by arresting him under an invalid warrant. Does the federal court have power and permission to hear the claims?

4.  Suppose that Nimitz (Tex.) sued only Clark (Tex.) on the federal civil rights claim and a state law battery claim arising from the same arrest. Are power and permission both present?

## Mixing Apples and Oranges

5.  Assume that Nimitz (Tex.) sues Clark (Tex.) and Bradley (Mo.). He asserts his civil rights claim against Clark and a state law battery claim against Bradley, arising from the same arrest. Is the case properly before the court?

6.  Suppose, on the facts of the last question, that Clark counterclaims against Nimitz for $15,000 due on a loan he made to Nimitz six months

prior to the arrest? Does the court have both power and permission to hear the claim?

7.  Instead of counterclaiming against Nimitz (Tex.), Clark (Tex.) cross-claims against Bradley (Mo.) to recover on a $15,000 loan to him. Is the claim properly before the court?

8.  Nimitz (Tex.) sues both Bradley (Mo.) and Gavin, also from Missouri, for violation of his federal civil rights. Could the federal court entertain a cross-claim by Bradley against Gavin, alleging that Gavin assaulted him (Bradley) in the course of the arrest?

## A Few Mazes, Nets, or Traps

9.  Halsey, a New Jersey citizen, sues MacArthur, from Arkansas, for injuries arising out of a boating accident. MacArthur impleads Spruance, from Arkansas, who was piloting a third boat involved in the collision. MacArthur seeks contribution from Spruance, as well as recovery for libel arising out of a newspaper article in which Spruance deprecated his leadership skills. Can a federal district court in Arkansas entertain the entire suit?

10.  Suppose on the facts of question 9, that MacArthur (Ark.) impleaded Spruance (Ark.) for contribution, and *Halsey* (N.J.) then asserted a libel claim against Spruance. Is Halsey's claim properly before the court?

11.  Assume that Halsey (N.J.) sues MacArthur (Ark.) alone on his claim arising out of the boating accident, and MacArthur counterclaims against Halsey and Spruance (Ark.) for his own injuries in the collision. Can the federal court hear the counterclaims?

12.  Halsey (N.J.) sues MacArthur (Ark.) for his injuries in the accident, and Spruance (Ark.) intervenes in the suit to assert a claim against MacArthur for his injuries. May the court hear Spruance's claim?

## A Too Hard Hypothetical

13.  King, a citizen of California, enters into a contract in California to purchase a parcel of land in Kansas from Eisenhower, a Kansan, and Patton, a Californian. Eisenhower and Patton held title to the parcel jointly. King subsequently discovers, to his surprise and contrary to the representations of the sellers, that the parcel is dead flat, quite useless for his intended ski resort. He sues Eisenhower in California to rescind the sale. Patton moves to intervene as a defendant. May the court hear the suit?

# ANALYSIS

## Some Basics

1.  Power: Yes    Permission: No

This case in its present form would have to be dismissed. Jurisdiction is proper in the action since there is complete diversity and the amount in

.controversy apparently exceeds $10,000 against each defendant. However, Nimitz's joinder of Patton and Bradley is improper under the joinder provisions of the Federal Rules. Rule 20(a), which governs joinder of multiple defendants, only authorizes joinder if the plaintiff's claims against both defendants arise out of the same transaction or occurrence. Nimitz alleges libel on two separate occasions; although his theory of liability is the same against each, his claims are based on separate historical occurrences. Thus, joinder under the Rules is not satisfied, though jurisdiction is proper.

Although Nimitz's case can't be heard in its present form, it need not be dismissed in its entirety either. Under Fed. R. Civ. P. 21, the court may drop either Patton or Bradley from the action, eliminating the joinder problem. Nimitz will presumably then file a separate suit against the dropped defendant, perhaps in the same court, that will proceed independent of the original case.

**2.  Power: Yes     Permission: Yes**

The court in this case has an adequate basis for joinder and jurisdiction. Rule 18(a) authorizes a single plaintiff to join any claims she has against an opposing party, regardless of whether they arise from a single transaction or occurrence. Rule 18(a) is the ultimate in permissiveness: Whatever you have, based on whatever historical events, may be joined, so long as the various claims are asserted against a single defendant.

Jurisdiction is also satisfied here because the parties are diverse and the amount in controversy requirement is satisfied by aggregation of Nimitz's two claims against Bradley; aggregation of a single plaintiff's claims is allowed against a single defendant but not against multiple defendants. See Chapter 5, p. 69.

**3.  Power: Yes     Permission: Yes**

This case may properly be brought in federal court. Joinder is proper here, unlike in question 1, because the same transaction or occurrence requirement of Rule 20(a) is met; Nimitz seeks damages against both defendants based on the same underlying real-world event. The second requirement of Rule 20(a), that Nimitz's claims against the two defendants must share a common question of law or fact is also clearly met since Nimitz must presumably prove many of the same facts (for example, the invalidity of the warrant) to prevail on both claims.

Jurisdiction is also satisfied in this suit since Nimitz asserts a federal claim against each defendant. 28 U.S.C. §1331. The lack of complete diversity is therefore irrelevant.

**4.  Power: Yes     Permission: Yes**

This is an easy case. Rule 18(a) authorizes joinder of the two claims, even though they are based on different sources of law. It would similarly authorize joinder of any other claims which Nimitz's creative genius (tempered, of course, by the ethical constraints of Rule 11) might come up with, regardless of whether they arose from the arrest or any other incident.

Jurisdiction over the federal civil rights claim is proper under 28 U.S.C. §1331. Jurisdiction over the state law claim is proper (but discretionary) under pendent jurisdiction since it arises from the same nucleus of operative facts as the federal claim. See Chapter 12, question 1.

## Mixing Apples and Oranges

5.  Power: Yes    Permission: Yes

The problem here is clearly not on the joinder issue; Rule 20(a) authorizes joinder of these claims since they both arise out of the same arrest and will likely involve common questions of fact, such as who injured Nimitz.

Jurisdiction is more difficult. Jurisdiction is proper over Nimitz's claim against Clark because it arises under federal law. However, his claim against Bradley is based on state law; it must have a separate basis for federal jurisdiction. Nimitz and Bradley are diverse . . . but Nimitz and Clark are not. However, since there is a separate basis for jurisdiction over Clark, his citizenship need not be considered in measuring diversity even though he is a party to the action. See Chapter 5, question 3. Consequently, Clark does not destroy diversity. If Nimitz seeks more than $10,000 from Bradley the suit is proper.

There is a possible alternate basis for jurisdiction here as well. Nimitz might argue that *pendent party* jurisdiction should extend to his claim against Bradley. This is a very complex issue in light of *Aldinger v. Howard,* 427 U.S. 1 (1976), *Owen Equipment & Erection Co. v. Kroger,* 437 U.S. 365 (1978), and 28 U.S.C. §1331. Luckily, due to the presence of the first basis for jurisdiction, we (like the Supreme Court) do not have to reach the issue.

6.  Power: No    Permission: Yes

Here, the federal court lacks power to hear the counterclaim, although the Rules grant permission to hear it. Clark's counterclaim is permissive because it arises from a transaction unrelated to the main claim. Rule 13(b) authorizes (but does not require) Clark to assert it in this action.

However, there is no independent basis of subject matter jurisdiction over this claim because it is a state law claim between nondiverse parties. Clark would have to rely on ancillary jurisdiction to support this claim. However, the counterclaim here does not bear the "logical relationship" to the main claim that is necessary to support ancillary jurisdiction. A Rule 13(b) permissive counterclaim, by definition, is totally unrelated to the main claim. Consequently ancillary jurisdiction does not extend to it, and the court lacks subject matter jurisdiction over it. See Chapter 12, question 5.

**7. Power: Yes    Permission: No**

Clark will have to save this claim for another day as well. Jurisdictionally, the claim passes muster since there is diversity between Clark and Bradley (the only opposing parties on the cross-claim) and the amount in controversy is sufficient. But the Rules don't authorize assertion of this claim in the Nimitz lawsuit: Rule 13(g) limits cross-claims to those arising out of the same transaction or occurrence as the main claim.

This result makes good sense. There is no relationship between the factual or legal issues relevant to the main claim and those relevant to the cross-claim and therefore no efficiency to be gained from allowing them to be heard in the same suit.

**8. Power: Yes    Permission: Yes**

This is a nice contrast to question 7. Here, unlike question 7, joinder is proper under Rule 13(g) since the cross-claim arises out of the same incident as the main claim. Jurisdiction is supplied by the doctrine of ancillary jurisdiction because the cross-claim arises out of the same nucleus of facts as the main claim, and the Supreme Court at least implied in *Kroger* that ancillary jurisdiction still extends to cross-claims. See Chapter 12, question 3.

## A Few Mazes, Nets, or Traps

**9. Power: In part    Permission: Yes**

The Rules authorize joinder in this case, but jurisdiction is only proper over part of the case. First of all, I asked whether an *Arkansas* federal district court could hear the action. Really, this was just to blow a little smoke. Personal jurisdiction and venue are satisfied because both defendants are domiciled in Arkansas. *Milliken v. Meyer*, 311 U.S. 457 (1940); 28 U.S.C. §1391(a). And the particular federal district in which the suit is brought is irrelevant to determination of subject matter jurisdiction.

Joinder is also proper in this action under Rules 14 and 18. MacArthur properly brought in Spruance under Rule 14(a) since he is seeking to recover from Spruance part of any damages that Halsey may recover against Mac-Arthur. MacArthur's claim for contribution satisfies this requirement because he is asking Spruance to pay him half of any judgment Halsey wins, by way of "contribution" to the judgment. MacArthur's libel claim is also proper: Under Rule 18(a) MacArthur may assert any additional claims he has against Spruance, once he has asserted one claim against him that is proper under the Rules. MacArthur could not have impleaded Spruance on the basis of his libel claim since it is a separate, independent claim that does not satisfy the "may be liable to him for all or part of the plaintiff's claim" requirement of Rule 14(a). But once he impleads Spruance on a proper Rule 14(a) claim, he can pile on any claims he has against Spruance.

So much for permission. The claims must also be analyzed individually as to jurisdictional power. There is ancillary jurisdiction over MacArthur's third-party claim against Spruance for contribution since it is a derivative claim that depends on the outcome of the main claim between Halsey and MacArthur. The Supreme Court's reasoning in *Kroger* appears to endorse this exercise of ancillary jurisdiction. But ancillary jurisdiction does not extend to the libel claim since it is unrelated to the main claim. Nor is there an independent basis for subject matter jurisdiction since it is a state law claim between nondiverse parties.

## 10. Power: Yes    Permission: No

This question involves a state law claim between diverse parties; if the claim is for more than $10,000, it is within the court's diversity jurisdiction. However, the Rules do not authorize joinder of this claim. The only rule that authorizes claims by plaintiffs against third-party defendants is Rule 14(a), which limits such claims to those arising from the same transaction or occurrence as the main claim. Halsey's claim is independent of the boating accident and therefore must be sued upon separately.

Curiously, if Halsey asserted a claim against Spruance for injuries arising from the boating accident, he could then pile on the unrelated libel claim under Rule 18(a). Jurisdiction and joinder would both be satisfied and the court would be able to entertain the claim. However, it would likely be severed for trial under Rule 21(b) and proceed effectively as a separate action anyway.

## 11. Power: Yes    Permission: Yes

Both joinder and jurisdiction are satisfied in this case. Joinder is proper under Rule 13(h); Spruance is an additional party to a compulsory counterclaim. Visually the case looks like this:

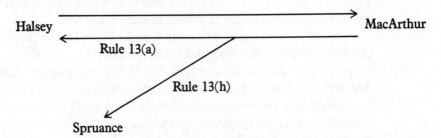

As to the power question, ancillary jurisdiction applies to compulsory counterclaims in diversity cases, and that power apparently extends as well to added parties to such counterclaims, like Spruance. Wright and Miller at §1436. Thus, even if complete diversity is lacking, or MacArthur claims less than $10,000 from Spruance and Halsey, the court may hear the counterclaims.

The irony here is that MacArthur may assert a counterclaim that he could not have asserted as an original claim. If he had sued Halsey and Spruance together, the case would have been dismissed for lack of diversity. While this result is ironic, it is not entirely illogical since the policy underlying ancillary jurisdiction is to allow defendants hauled into court against their will broad opportunities to settle all claims arising out of the events that give rise to the litigation.

## 12. Power: No    Permission: Yes

Permission to join Spruance's claim is provided here by Rule 24(b), which allows a party to intervene if her claim shares a question of fact or law with the main claim. Here, Spruance and Halsey will both seek to prove that MacArthur was negligent, thus satisfying the Rule 24(b) standard. (Of course, intervention under Rule 24(b) is always at the discretion of the court.)

However, the general rule is that ancillary jurisdiction does not extend to permissive intervenors' claims. Absent ancillary jurisdiction, this claim is improper because it is based on state law and Spruance and MacArthur are from the same state.

This case presents a situation in which it would make a lot of sense to take ancillary jurisdiction. The claims arise out of the same nucleus of operative facts, thus satisfying the constitutional test for a single case. In terms of efficiency there is as much justification for hearing this claim as there is for hearing a third-party impleader claim, for example. But if Spruance were allowed to intervene in this case, it would essentially allow him to evade the complete diversity requirement. Instead of suing with Halsey, which would be improper under *Strawbridge v. Curtiss,* 7 U.S. 267 (1806), he could simply allow Halsey to start the suit and then achieve the same result by intervening.

If Spruance met the standard for intervention as of right under Rule 24(a), his claim would be ancillary. *Curtis v. Sears, Roebuck and Co.,* 754 F.2d 781, 783 (8th Cir. 1985). But the Rule 24(a) standard is not met simply because he was injured in the same accident. To intervene under Rule 24(a), Spruance would have to show that his ability to protect his own rights would be compromised if the Halsey/MacArthur suit went forward without him. Since Spruance could sue MacArthur separately, he probably cannot meet this standard unless MacArthur's funds are limited and might be exhausted by Halsey's claim.

## A Too Hard Hypothetical

### 13. Power: Yes and No    Permission: Yes and No

*First,* just to clear away the underbrush a little, this suit is not precluded because it is brought in California rather than Kansas. A suit to rescind a contract for the sale of land is a transitory action, which may be maintained wherever personal jurisdiction is proper over the defendants. The California court may well have jurisdiction over the defendants on the basis of negotiations or representations that took place in California. (By contrast, a "local" action may only be brought where the disputed land lies; an example would be an action by King to quiet title to the Kansas parcel, which would have to be brought in Kansas. See generally 3A Moore's at ¶0.142[2-1].)

*Second,* joinder is proper here, in one sense, under Rule 24(a). Patton claims an interest in the transaction in issue since rescission of the sale would return part ownership to him. As a practical matter an order of the court in the King/Eisenhower suit would affect his interest. For example, if King is still making payments on the sale to Eisenhower and Patton, he will presumably cease doing so after an adjudication that he is entitled to rescission. On the facts, it is not clear whether Patton's interest is adequately represented by Eisenhower, but it may well not be, and the burden to establish this third factor under Rule 24(a)(2) is minimal.

The problem here is that the *original* suit is improper under Rule 19. In a suit for rescission of a contract, joint sellers are generally considered indispensable parties under Rule 19(b) since their interests will inevitably be affected by a judgment in their absence. Since Patton is indispensable but could not be joined as an original party (because his presence would destroy diversity), the case has to be dismissed.[2] Otherwise, the complete diversity requirement could be evaded in indispensable parties cases by leaving out the nondiverse indispensable party, and letting that party intervene as of right.

The irony here is that ordinarily there is ancillary jurisdiction over the claims of intervenors as of right. If Patton were not an indispensable party, he *could* intervene as of right, despite the fact that he and King are both Californians, and the suit would be jurisdictionally proper. However, because Patton absolutely has to be there, the court can't let him in: There is no jurisdictionally proper basic lawsuit to which to append his ancillary claim. See 7 Wright and Miller at §1610, pp. 98-101.

Don't blame me. I didn't make the rules.

---

2. In some cases the court may retain jurisdiction of the original action even though the absentee is indispensable if it can craft the judgment to avoid prejudice to the absentee. See Fed. R. Civ. P. 19(b). Such shaping of the judgment will be problematic in this case, however.

# PART THREE

# *Steps in the Litigation Process*

# 14

## Getting Off Easy: The Motion to Dismiss

## Introduction

The defendant usually responds to the plaintiff's complaint by filing an answer as provided in Fed. R. Civ. P. 12(a). (For an example, see the answer to the Schulansky complaint, Chapter 24.) However, the rules provide a second option in limited circumstances: If the defendant has certain preliminary objections to the suit, he may avoid answering immediately by filing a motion to dismiss the complaint instead under Fed. R. Civ. P. 12(b). See Jones's motion to dismiss in *Schulansky*, infra pp. 389-390.

Two important points about such "pre-answer motions" should be made at the outset. *First*, filing a pre-answer motion under Rule 12(b) is an *alternative* to answering the complaint. A defendant who moves to dismiss under Rule 12(b) need not answer the complaint until after the motion is decided. See Rule 12(a), last sentence. If he prevails on the motion, he may never have to answer. This can be a strong tactical advantage since filing an answer may require the defendant to admit damaging allegations in the complaint or, at a minimum, reveal much of his litigation strategy.

*Second*, filing a pre-answer motion is entirely optional. Defendants are not required to use it to raise the defenses listed in Rule 12(b); each may be raised in the answer instead. See Fed. R. Civ. P. 12(b), which provides that the listed defenses may, "at the option of the pleader" be raised by pre-answer motion. What, then, is the point of providing a separate device for raising these particular defenses?

Essentially, the Rules provide this device in order to short-circuit the usual litigation process in cases in which the defendant has a valid defense, evident from the outset, to the court proceeding with the case. These defenses come in two kinds. Some of the 12(b) defenses are immediately fatal to the plaintiff's case. For example, if the court lacks subject matter jurisdiction over the action (Rule 12(b)(1)), it has no power to render a valid judgment; it would be a useless charade for it to go any further with the action. The same is true if the court is not a proper venue (Rule 12(b)(3)) or lacks personal jurisdiction over the defendant (Rule 12(b)(2)). A defendant should not even be required to answer the allegations in the complaint if the case has been brought in the wrong court. To protect the defendant from such inappropriate suits, Rule 12(b) provides an avenue to secure immediate dismissal in cases where the court is powerless to do anything else.

Other defenses under Rule 12(b) raise defects in the procedure by which the plaintiff has initiated the action. The defense of insufficiency of service of process (Rule 12(b)(5)), for example, attacks the manner in which the complaint was served. Similarly, the Rule 12(b)(7) defense of failure to join an indispensable party asserts a defect in the scope of the suit as the plaintiff has framed it. Generally, these are curable defects that will not require dismissal of the suit but will have to be remedied before the case proceeds. If service of process was insufficient, for example, the court will order proper service of the complaint before proceeding. Similarly, if an indispensable party has not been joined, the court will not automatically dismiss the case but will order joinder of the indispensable party if feasible.[1] In these cases the Rule provides a mechanism to flush out preliminary problems and resolve them before getting into the substantive work of the lawsuit.

The 12(b)(6) dismissal, unlike the other pre-answer defenses, challenges the substantive merits of the complaint. The defendant who moves to dismiss "for failure to state a claim upon which relief can be granted" asserts that even if the plaintiff were to prove all the allegations in the complaint, he would still not be entitled to any relief. It hardly makes sense for the court to entertain the action and decide the facts if the law will not provide any relief to the plaintiff even if he proves everything alleged in the complaint. An example would be a suit for infliction of emotional distress, in a jurisdiction that does not recognize a right to recover for emotional suffering alone, unaccompanied by physical injury. In such a case the court might just as well dismiss at the outset since the plaintiff will not be entitled to relief if he is allowed to proceed with the suit.

---

1. In some cases these defects may not be curable. For example, joinder of an indispensable party might destroy diversity, thus undermining the federal court's subject matter jurisdiction. In such cases the court may have to dismiss.

Although the 12(b)(6) motion is unique in attacking the substantive merits of the plaintiff's claim, it is akin to the "fatal" defenses under 12(b)(1), (2), and (3) in that it can lead to dismissal if it is upheld by the court. However, in all federal courts, a plaintiff whose *complaint* has been dismissed under Rule 12(b)(6) will be given at least one opportunity to amend the complaint to state a compensable claim, before his *case* is dismissed.[2] If the defect in the original allegations was simply a matter of improper pleading, the plaintiff can amend the complaint to state a compensable claim once the defect is brought to his attention. On the other hand, if the plaintiff is unable to state a claim after amending because the defect was one of substance, then the case will be dismissed. The Rule 12(b)(6) motion is explored in more detail in Chapter 15.

So much for the consequences of raising 12(b) defenses. The more puzzling aspect of the rule is the consequences of *not* raising them. Rules 12(g) and (h), which govern those consequences, appear Byzantine at first but are more easily understood once their rationale is clear. Essentially, those subsections of the rule, read together (very carefully), provide that four of the 12(b) defenses will be waived if not raised in the defendant's first response to the complaint. If the defendant objects to personal jurisdiction, venue, the form of the process, or the method of service of process he must raise those defenses in the pre-answer motion or (if he does not make a pre-answer motion) in the answer. If he fails to raise any of these preliminary defenses in his initial response he has waived that defense for all time.

This result, hard though it may be to extract from the language of these subsections, makes good sense. If the defendant has suffered any prejudice from these preliminary defects, he should become aware of it when the complaint is served upon him. It is not unreasonable to put the burden on him to raise these defects right away; otherwise the court and the parties might proceed to adjudicate the suit, only to learn down the road that the court has no right to do so. To avoid this waste of resources the rule provides that the defendant must raise these defenses immediately or waive them by his failure to do so.

These rules may seem fussy and technical to you, but it is well worth your while to learn them now. Many a lawyer has re-read these rules in a cold sweat to find out if he has unwittingly waived his client's rights. It is one thing to lose a case by doing the wrong thing, but it is all the more embarrassing to lose it by doing nothing. Under Rule 12 the decision to do nothing is fraught with consequences for your client.

---

2. Some circuits hold that the plaintiff has an absolute right to amend under Fed. R. Civ. P. 15(a). See, e.g., *Car Carriers, Inc. v. Ford Motor Co.*, 745 F.2d 1101, 1111 (7th Cir. 1984). Others allow such amendments as a matter of discretion. *Triplett v. Leflore County*, 712 F.2d 444, 446 (10th Cir. 1983).

# QUESTIONS

## Traps for the Unwary

1.   David files a complaint for assault against Goliath. Goliath files a timely motion to dismiss for insufficient service of process. Several months later, the judge denies the motion to dismiss and so notifies the parties.

May Goliath, after being notified of the denial of his motion:
   a.   move to dismiss for lack of personal jurisdiction?
   b.   answer, raising the defense of lack of personal jurisdiction?
   c.   move to dismiss for failure to state a claim upon which relief can be granted?
   d.   answer, raising the defense of failure to state a claim upon which relief can be granted?
   e.   move for a more definite statement under Rule 12(e)?
   f.   move to dismiss for lack of subject matter jurisdiction?

2.   After the court denies his motion to dismiss for insufficient service of process, Goliath answers the complaint. May he include in his answer:
   a.   a defense of improper venue?
   b.   a claim that the court lacks subject matter jurisdiction over the action?
   c.   a defense that David has given him a signed release from liability on all claims arising out of the alleged assault?

3.   Suppose that Goliath decides to answer David's complaint instead of filing a Rule 12(b) motion to dismiss or any other pre-answer motion. May he include in his answer:
   a.   a defense of insufficiency of service of process?
   b.   a defense that the complaint fails to state a claim upon which relief can be granted?
   c.   a motion for a more definite statement?
   d.   a defense that the court lacks subject matter jurisdiction over the action?

4.   Assume that Goliath's first response to the complaint is to move for a more definite statement. The judge grants the motion and orders David to file a clearer complaint within ten days. David complies. After Goliath receives the more definite statement, may he:
   a.   move to dismiss for insufficiency of service of process?
   b.   move to dismiss for failure to state a claim upon which relief can be granted?
   c.   answer, raising the defense of insufficiency of service of process?
   d.   answer, raising the defense of failure to state a claim upon which relief can be granted?

5.   If Goliath responds to the complaint by moving to dismiss for insufficiency of service of process, may he move at the same time to dismiss for improper venue and lack of personal jurisdiction?

6. What is the difference between the defense of insufficiency of service of process (Rule 12(b)(5)) and insufficiency of process (Rule 12(b)(4))? See Rule 4(b).

## Permutations

7. Assume that Goliath answers the complaint and includes in his answer a counterclaim against David, seeking damages from David for calling him a bully. David contends that the counterclaim does not state a claim upon which relief can be granted. What should he do?

8. David files his claim for assault. Goliath moves to dismiss it under Rule 12(b)(3). David wishes to amend his complaint to add a claim for battery. May he do so without leave of court? (You will need to consider Rules 15(a), 7(a), and 7(b) to answer this question.)

9. David sues for assault, and Goliath files an answer, denying that he intentionally assaulted David. Several months later, he realizes that the court lacks personal jurisdiction over him and seeks to amend his answer, with leave of court, under Rule 15(a), to raise this defense. May he do so?

## Taking Logic to Its Extreme

10. One more variation, and then we will banish David and Goliath back to antiquity. David sues Goliath; Goliath answers and counterclaims; David moves to dismiss the counterclaim. May Goliath amend his answer to include the defense that the court lacks personal jurisdiction over him?

## A Useful but Audacious Exercise

11. Students always express frustration with Rules 12(g) and (h), saying they are unreadable and hypertechnical legalisms. If you agree, try to rewrite those two subsections in clearer terms without changing their meaning.

# ANALYSIS

## Traps for the Unwary

1a. No. Rule 12(g) provides that a defendant who chooses to make a pre-answer motion must include in that motion all the 12(b) defenses he has at the time. Any of the listed defenses that are omitted from the motion are waived with the exception of the defenses preserved by Rule 12(h)(2) and (3). Here, Goliath must have known, if he received the complaint at all, that he was being ordered to appear before a court that might not have jurisdiction over him. Since that defense was "available to him" at the time he filed his first motion to dismiss, it could have been consolidated in the first motion. Rule 12(g), first sentence. Since Goliath omitted it, Rule 12(g) provides that he cannot make a second motion to dismiss on this ground.

This provision prevents the defendant from nickel and diming the plaintiff to death by repeated motions to dismiss on different grounds. Otherwise, Goliath might make three or four successive motions, each on a single ground, and delay the proceedings unduly.

b. No again. Here, Goliath seeks to raise in his answer a defense that he could have included in his pre-answer motion. Rule 12(g) does not cover this; it only bars Goliath from making a second pre-answer motion on this ground. However, Rule 12(h)(1)(A) does prevent him from raising it because he made a pre-answer motion but omitted this defense from it. Goliath does not have to file a motion to dismiss at all, but if he decides to the combination of Rules 12(g) and (h) forces him to put all four of these defenses in the motion or waive the ones he omits.

Don't be fooled by Rule 12(h)(1)(B), which appears to imply that these four defenses can be raised in either the motion to dismiss or the answer. That subsection provides that these defenses are waived if *not* raised by one device or the other. It does not authorize the defendant to leave it out of a motion and then insert it in his answer.

c. Probably not. Since Goliath has made a pre-answer motion to dismiss, Rule 12(g) requires him to include in that motion all 12(b) defenses "then available to him." The second sentence of the rule states that he cannot make a new pre-answer motion based on such defenses.

This does not mean, however, that Goliath has waived his right to raise this defense entirely. Rule 12(g) only prevents him from making another pre-answer motion on this ground. Rule 12(h)(2) allows him to raise it in his answer or later in the case. The defense of failure to state a claim is fundamental; no defendant should be held to waive it by the mere failure to raise it at the beginning of the suit. If the system so provided we would be back to the rigidities of the common law, which forced the parties to stick to their original pleadings even if subsequent investigation uncovered new facts or theories that made those pleadings obsolete. The four disfavored defenses are distinguishable since these objections should be apparent to the defendant as soon as he receives the summons and complaint.

I said above that Goliath would "probably not" be allowed to move to dismiss on this ground. It is possible that his objection to service of process was that no copy of the complaint was served on him. If that were the case he would not have known what the complaint alleged and could not have had grounds to move to dismiss under 12(b)(6). On those facts he *would* be able to file a second pre-answer motion raising this defense since the 12(b)(6) defense was not "available to him" when he filed the first one. The fact that the judge denied the first motion makes this unlikely, however.

d. Yes. The 12(b)(6) objection may be raised in the answer, even though it was omitted from an earlier pre-answer motion. Rule 12(h)(2) expressly provides that this defense may be raised "in any pleading permitted or ordered under Rule 7(a)." An answer is clearly permitted (indeed, required) by Rule 7(a).

e. Probably not. The motion for a more definite statement raises the defense that the complaint is so unclear that the responding party cannot frame a meaningful response to it. This defense will be "available" to the pleader as soon as the complaint is served on him and therefore should be raised in the first pre-answer motion. Note that the carefully chosen language of Rule 12(g) requires consolidation of this 12(e) defense as well as the various 12(b) defenses.

There is a possibility, as in question 1c, that Goliath never received a copy of the complaint. If so, then he could hardly be expected to know that it would be incomprehensible when he did get it. If this were the case, the defense would not have been available to Goliath when he filed his first pre-answer motion, and he would be allowed to file a second motion on this ground.

f. Yes. Although Rule 12(g) requires consolidation of all 12(b) defenses in the first motion, Rule 12(h)(3) provides an explicit exception for this one. That subsection provides that "[w]henever" it appears by "suggestion of the parties or otherwise," that subject matter jurisdiction is lacking, the court shall dismiss the action. Presumably, "whenever" includes before an answer but after a pre-answer motion and presumably "suggestion of the parties" may be by motion. Because no court can act beyond its subject matter competence, a court should — and will — dismiss whenever the lack of jurisdiction is called to its attention.

2a. No. As soon as the complaint was served on Goliath, he was in a position to object to venue. Here Goliath made a pre-answer motion, and Rule 12(g) requires him to include his venue defense in his pre-answer motion or waive it. Because he did not include the venue defense in his first response to the complaint, it is lost, waived, gone forever.

Actually, it may not always be that easy for defendants to determine from the complaint that they have an objection to venue or other preliminary defenses, such as personal or subject matter jurisdiction. It may not be clear, for example, whether a corporate defendant "does business" in a state under 28 U.S.C. §1391(c). The defendant may not be able to tell from the complaint whether all defendants are from the same state or pinpoint where the claim arose. See 28 U.S.C. §1391(a), (b). Yet the rule requires immediate assertion of the defense. Clearly, if there is doubt as to the propriety of venue the defense should be raised, subject to the ethical restraints on pleading in Rule 11. If more time is needed to investigate before responding, counsel may move for an extension of time to file a response under Fed. R. Civ. P. 6(b).[3]

b. Yes. As previously stated in question 1f, Rule 12(h)(3) authorizes either party to raise this defense at any time.

_____

3. Although the motion to dismiss for improper venue will be waived if not raised in the answer or pre-answer motion, a motion to transfer venue to another federal district under 28 U.S.C. §1404(a) can be made at any time.

c. Yes. This is not one of the preliminary defenses singled out in Rule 12(b) for special treatment. It is an affirmative defense on the merits to the plaintiff's claim, which properly should be raised in the answer. Indeed, it could not be raised in a pre-answer motion even if Goliath wished to: Rule 12(b) provides that all Goliath's defenses, except the seven listed in 12(b) itself, must be presented in the answer.[4] Since this defense may not be raised before answering, it is certainly appropriate to put it in the answer.

3a. Yes. Rule 12 does not require Goliath to raise his defense of improper service in a pre-answer motion. It only requires that if he makes such a motion, he include all his preliminary defenses. He may simply file an answer including this defense, and it will be considered by the court in the same manner as if it had been raised by pre-answer motion. (See the answer in the Schulansky case, infra p. 362, which asserts an objection to personal jurisdiction that could have been presented by pre-answer motion under Rule 12(b)(2) instead.) The real difference is a tactical one: If Goliath answers, he must respond to the substantive allegations in the complaint. He must make his admissions and denials under Rule 8(b), raise his affirmative defenses under Rule 8(c), and assert his counterclaims under Rule 13. If he moves to dismiss, he may avoid, at least temporarily, the need to answer the plaintiff's allegations.

b. Yes. As in the previous answer, Goliath has the choice to raise this in the answer instead of by pre-answer motion. Indeed, he may raise it in the answer even if he omitted it from a pre-answer motion. See question 1d.

c. No. The purpose of the motion for a more definite statement is to provide the defendant with a sufficiently clear statement of the plaintiff's allegations so that he can meaningfully respond to it, either by filing a pre-answer motion or by answering the complaint. Consequently, Rule 12(e) requires the defendant to make this motion "before interposing his responsive pleading."

d. Yes. Rule 12(b) allows this to be raised by motion, but Rule 12(h)(3) makes clear that whether or not a pre-answer motion was made, this basic defense may be raised in the answer or at any other time as well.

4a. No. The defense of insufficiency of service challenges the manner in which the complaint and summons were served upon the defendant. Goliath should have been aware of any defects in the method of service as soon as the papers were served upon him even if the complaint itself was indecipherable. Since the defense was available to him when he filed the motion for a more definite statement, he should have joined it in that motion. Rule 12(g), read very carefully, says so; Rule 12(h)(1)(A) says that the defense is now waived.

b. Yes. This defense was presumably not "available" to Goliath when he filed his motion for a more definite statement because he couldn't figure out

---

4. However, the defense of release could be raised by a motion for summary judgment even before answering. See generally Chapter 15. See also Fed. R. Civ. P. 12(c).

what the plaintiff's complaint was trying to allege. It is only after Goliath receives the clearer complaint that he is able to ascertain whether the plaintiff's allegations state a claim. Because this defense was not previously available, Rule 12(g) does not preclude Goliath from subsequently asserting it in another pre-answer motion despite the usual command of Rule 12(g) that all pre-answer defenses be raised together.

c. No. Goliath should have been aware of defects in the method of service at the time he was served with the complaint. As in question 4a, this defense was available to him when he filed the earlier motion, and Goliath has waived it by failing to raise it there.

d. Yes. *First*, the defense was not available at the time the first motion was made. See question 4b. *Second*, this defense can be raised in the answer whether or not it was omitted from a pre-answer motion. Rule 12(h)(2).

5.  I threw this question in to see if you would stick to your guns and answer "absolutely." The defendant is not required to stake his case on one of these defenses if others may also be available to him. Not only may he assert multiple objections under Rule 12(b), he *must* do so to avoid waiving them. That is the purpose of Rules 12(g) and (h).

6.  The Rule 12(b)(4) motion challenges the adequacy of the summons itself, the court document served on the defendant ordering him to respond to the complaint. Rule 4(b) details the requirements of a proper summons. (For an example of a summons, see Chapter 23.) A motion to dismiss under Rule 12(b)(4) might allege that some requirement of that rule was omitted, such as the clerk's signature or the court seal.

By contrast, the Rule 12(b)(5) motion for insufficiency of service of process challenges the manner in which the complaint and summons were delivered to the defendant. See Chapter 4 concerning proper methods of serving process in the federal courts. A Rule 12(b)(5) motion by Goliath might be based, for example, on the ground that it was not left at his cave with a person of suitable age and discretion (see Rule 4(d)(1)) but at a neighbor's instead.

## Permutations

7.  Rule 12(b) governs not only an original defendant's options in responding to a complaint but also those of other defending parties. Rule 12(b), first sentence. Here, David, as a defending party on Goliath's counterclaim, may present his defense of failure to state a claim by a motion to dismiss or in his answer to the counterclaim just as the original defendant may. The same would be true of a defendant responding to a cross-claim or a third-party complaint.

8.  Rule 15(a) allows a party to amend his pleading once "as a matter of course," that is, without leave of court, before his opponent files a responsive pleading. Is Goliath's motion to dismiss a responsive pleading? No. Rule 7(a)

enumerates permissible pleadings, including complaints, answers, and re-plies; motions are provided for in a separate subsection (7(b)). See *Car Carriers Inc.*, 745 F.2d at 1111. Since a motion is not a pleading, Goliath has not yet filed a responsive pleading, and David is free to amend without the court's permission. Indeed, if the court is slow to decide the motion, this period for amendments as of right may go on for some time.

9.   Goliath's train of thought here is obvious. He has run afoul of the rule by failing to include the jurisdictional defense in his answer. Under Rule 12(h)(1), therefore, he has waived the personal jurisdiction defense. When Goliath realizes his oversight, he tries to get it into the answer by amendment under Rule 15, asking the court to accept the amendment and treat it as though it had been included in the original answer.

If this worked, it would provide an easy end run around the waiver provisions of Rule 12, at least if the judge granted the motion. It won't work. Rule 12(h)(1)(B) provides that the defense is lost if it is left out of a pre-answer motion or a responsive pleading "or an amendment thereof permitted by Rule 15(a) to be made as a matter of course."[5] As usual, the rulemakers thought about this possibility, and impliedly rejected Goliath's tactic by limit-ing the use of amendments to cure such omissions to those filed as a matter of course. Goliath only had 20 days to amend as of right (Rule 15(a)); since several months have elapsed he has waived his objection to personal jurisdic-tion. Even if the judge were willing to grant leave to amend, it would be inconsistent with the limitation in Rule 12(h)(1)(B) to allow the defendant to do so. *Morgan Guaranty Trust Co. of New York v. Blum*, 649 F.2d 342, 345 (5th Cir. 1981).

## Taking Logic to Its Extreme

10. Apparently Goliath may make this amendment even if months have elapsed since David's motion. Rule 12(h)(1)(B) by implication allows Goli-ath to amend his original answer to allege additional 12(b) defenses, so long as the amendment is allowable "as a matter of course." Under Rule 15(a) a defendant may amend as a matter of course at any time before a responsive pleading is filed, if one is permitted. Because Goliath has included a counter-claim in his answer, a responsive pleading (a reply, see Rule 7(a)) is required, but David hasn't filed it yet since he chose to file a pre-answer motion instead. *Ergo,* Goliath is allowed to amend as of right and may still raise the objection to personal jurisdiction.

Upon reflection, this seems a hypertechnical interpretation of Rule 15(a). The intent behind the rule was probably to allow a defendant extra time to amend his *counterclaim* if a reply has not yet been served, not to leave

---

5. Amendments as a matter of course may only be made before a responsive pleading is served or within 20 days of filing the pleading. Fed. R. Civ. P. 15(a).

open indefinitely the opportunity to raise preliminary objections to the original complaint. If this is so, Goliath should be limited to 20 days to amend the answer itself.

## A Useful but Audacious Exercise

11. If you made a real effort to rewrite these subsections, you will have developed some grudging respect for the work of the rule-makers. Their version is elegant and precise, although difficult to understand without considerable study. Here is my rewrite; it may be clearer in some respects but I still like their version better.

> **12(g).** A party who makes a motion under this rule may join with it any other motions authorized by this rule that the party then has available to him. If a party makes a pre-answer motion under this rule, he must include in it any defense he has under Rule 12(b)(2), (3), (4), or (5), or 12(e). Any of these defenses is waived if it was available and omitted from a pre-answer motion.
>
> **12(h)(1).** If a party does not make a pre-answer motion, he must include any defense he has under Rule 12(b)(2), (3), (4), or (5), or 12(e) in his responsive pleading or in an amendment to it permitted by Rule 15(a) as a matter of course. If he fails to do so, the omitted defenses are waived.
>
> **12(h)(2).** A defense of failure to state a claim upon which relief can be granted or failure to join a party indispensable under Rule 19 may be raised by pre-answer motion under Rule 12(b). If omitted from a pre-answer motion, it may be raised in any pleading permitted or ordered under Rule 7(a) or by a motion for judgment on the pleadings or at the trial on the merits.
>
> **12(h)(3).** The defense of lack of subject matter jurisdiction may be raised in a pre-answer motion, in a responsive pleading, or at any time by suggestion of the parties or the court. Whenever it appears by suggestion of the parties or otherwise that the court lacks jurisdiction over the subject matter, the court shall dismiss the action.

My version sounds more like a civil procedure class than a provision of the Rules. In addition, if you read my version carefully, you will find a few cases that aren't adequately dealt with.

# 15

---

# *Defective Allegation or Insufficient Proof? Dismissal for Failure to State a Claim Compared to Summary Judgment*

## Introduction

### *Rule 12(b)(6):*

One major theme of the civil procedure course is "The Perils of Plaintiff" or "all the ways you can bring a lawsuit and never get to trial." We have already explored a variety of purely *procedural* defects that may bring the suit to an untimely end, such as lack of jurisdiction, improper venue, and improper service of process. However, there are also several devices that defendants may use to challenge the merits of the plaintiff's case before trial, which may foreclose a trial if the court agrees with the defendant's objections. The principal devices for such pretrial resolution are the motion to dismiss for failure to state a claim upon which relief can be granted, or "12(b)(6) motion," and the motion for summary judgment under Rule 56. This chapter will examine these two motions in turn and offer some examples to help you distinguish them.

Under Rule 12(b)(6) of the Federal Rules (and the similar "demurrer" device in code pleading jurisdictions) a defendant may move to dismiss the plaintiff's complaint on the ground that it fails to state a claim that entitles the plaintiff to any form of relief. The gist of the defendant's objection in making the motion is that the "wrong" that the plaintiff describes in her complaint is not recognized as a violation of the plaintiff's legal rights. If that's true, the court would not be able to grant her damages or other relief even if she can prove all the facts alleged.

Suppose, for example, that Ferraro sues Gramm for voting Republican, after he promised Ferraro that he wouldn't. The law does not currently recognize a right to have promises performed unless consideration, estoppel, or some other additional acts make the promise binding. Even if Ferraro proves that Gramm made the promise, a court could not grant her any relief for Gramm's failure to keep it. Since there is no right to relief on Ferraro's claim, it would simply place a pointless burden on the court and the parties to proceed with the action. On these facts Gramm could move to dismiss the complaint for failure to state a claim upon which relief could be granted.

Because the purpose of the Rule 12(b)(6) motion is to test whether the plaintiff's allegations (assuming they can be proved) state a claim for which a court might grant relief, the *only* appropriate question posed by the motion is whether the complaint itself states a legally sufficient claim. Consequently, the court does not consider any other pleadings or evidence in deciding the motion. It only addresses a purely legal question: whether, if the plaintiff can prove the allegations in the complaint, she will have established a cause of action entitling her to some form of relief from the court. In cases like Ferraro's, dismissal on the basis of the complaint alone is appropriate under this test. Since Ferraro's complaint does not state a legal wrong for which the court could grant her redress, allowing her to litigate the allegations through discovery and trial would be a waste of both the parties' and the court's time.

Dismissal of a suit for failure to state a claim is a drastic measure. If the court dismisses, the plaintiff will never have the opportunity to prove her case or to gather evidence through the discovery process that might demonstrate that she has suffered a legally cognizable injury. Consequently, courts give every benefit of the doubt to the plaintiff in deciding the motion. The Supreme Court has held that a complaint should not be dismissed under Rule 12(b)(6) "unless it appears beyond doubt that the plaintiff can prove no set of facts in support of his claim which would entitle him to relief." *Conley v. Gibson*, 355 U.S. 41, 45-46 (1957). The court may not consider the likelihood that the plaintiff will be able to prove her factual allegations; it must assume for purposes of deciding the motion that the plaintiff *can* prove them. The pleadings must also be liberally construed in favor of sustaining the complaint. Thus, if the allegations in the complaint are susceptible of two constructions, one of which would support relief while the other would not, the court must construe the complaint in favor of the pleader. For example, a complaint that alleges that the defendant "swerved and ran into me on Bleecker Street" might be construed to allege either negligent driving or an unavoidable accident. The court, under *Conley,* would likely infer that the plaintiff (who, after all, is suing the defendant) is alleging that the collision resulted from the defendant's negligence.

In many cases a complaint will be vulnerable to dismissal under Rule 12(b)(6) because the plaintiff has sought relief for acts that are simply not proscribed under current law, as in the Ferraro case. In other cases, however, the complaint may be defective because the plaintiff (or her lawyer) has simply failed to allege the necessary elements of a claim that, if properly pleaded, would state a sufficient claim. Suppose, for example, that Berlin sues Porter for malicious prosecution, alleging that Porter filed a criminal complaint against him without cause, and that as a result he suffered damage to his reputation. To recover for malicious prosecution a plaintiff must allege that the original proceeding (in this example, the criminal case) was terminated in her favor. See 52 Am. Jur. 2d, Malicious Prosecution §6 (1971). If Berlin's complaint does not allege favorable termination, Porter may move to dismiss for failure to state a claim on the ground that Berlin has failed to allege all the necessary elements of a claim for malicious prosecution. Berlin's failure to plead favorable termination may simply be an oversight. If so, the court will allow Berlin to amend the complaint to add this allegation, and the suit will proceed.[1] However, if Berlin cannot allege favorable termination (if, for example, he was actually convicted or the case was continued), then his complaint is fatally defective and should be dismissed.

Before comparing the Rule 12(b)(6) motion with the motion for summary judgment, a few examples may help to clarify the function of the motion to dismiss for failure to state a claim. In considering the examples below, assume that all actions are brought as diversity actions in federal court, that there is no problem with personal or subject matter jurisdiction, and that state substantive law applies.

# QUESTIONS

## Threshold Challenges

1.   While Gershwin and his wife, Comden, are jogging in Central Park in New York City, a car driven by Hart careens off the road and hits Gershwin. Comden witnesses the accident. She is not injured but suffers severe emotional distress from seeing Gershwin seriously injured. She sues Hart, alleging the above facts in her complaint, and claiming a right to damages for

---

1. When a complaint is dismissed, the court will virtually always give the plaintiff at least one opportunity to amend to cure defects in the original complaint. See 3 Moore's at ¶15.10.

negligent infliction of emotional distress. Hart moves to dismiss under Rule 12(b)(6).

    a.   How would you phrase the issue posed by Hart's motion?

    b.   Assume that New York law does not recognize a right to relief for negligent infliction of emotional distress unless the plaintiff also suffered direct physical injury from the defendant's negligence. Will Hart's motion be granted?

**2.**   On the same facts as question 1, Comden sues for her emotional injuries and her husband joins as coplaintiff to recover for his physical injuries. If Hart moves to dismiss Comden's claim, will the motion be granted?

**3.**   Assume that Comden makes the same allegations but also includes in her complaint an allegation that there is a right to relief under New York law for negligent infliction of emotional distress. Hart moves to dismiss for failure to state a claim. Should the motion be granted?

**4.**   Assume, for purposes of this question only, that the right to recover for negligent infliction of emotional distress under New York law is not quite so clear. Early cases rejected such recovery, but recent appellate cases have granted a right to relief for intentional infliction of emotional distress, and Comden can make a fair argument that those cases effectively overrule prior law and recognize a right to relief for negligently inflicted emotional injuries as well. Is a motion to dismiss for failure to state a claim a proper means for Hart to challenge the complaint?

**5.**   Suppose that Hart claims that it was not his car that hit Gershwin. May he move to dismiss under Rule 12(b)(6) on this ground?

## Void for Vagueness?

**6.**   Assume that New York law bars recovery for emotional injuries without accompanying physical impact but that Comden words her complaint more generally. She alleges that Hart negligently drove his automobile in Central Park on the day in question and that Hart's negligence proximately caused personal injuries to Comden, for which she claims damages. Hart moves to dismiss for failure to state a claim. Will the motion be granted?

**7.**   Rogers, an employee of Broadway, Inc., hits Kern on Fifth Avenue while driving a Broadway truck used to deliver theatrical scenery. Kern sues Rogers and Broadway for negligence. In his complaint he alleges that Rogers's negligence caused the accident and that Rogers works for Broadway and was driving Broadway's delivery truck at the time of the accident. Although Kern's complaint does not say so, his claim against Broadway is evidently based on the doctrine of respondeat superior, which makes employers liable for the torts of their employees committed in the scope of their employment. Assume that Broadway would be liable for Rogers's acts under New York law if he was in the course of his deliveries for Broadway when the accident took place but not if the collision occurred while he was on a side trip for his own purposes, even though he was driving a Broadway truck.

    a. Broadway moves to dismiss Kern's claim against it for failure to state a claim upon which relief can be granted. Should the motion be granted?

    b. Broadway claims that Rogers was not delivering scenery at the time but had borrowed the truck to run up to the Met to see the new Renoir show on his lunch hour. Broadway moves to dismiss for failure to state a claim. Will its motion be granted?

8. Assume, on the facts of question 7, that Broadway answers the complaint, denying that Rogers was acting in the scope of his employment at the time of the accident. Subsequently, it files a motion to dismiss for failure to state a claim, on the ground that Rogers was on a side trip at the time of the accident.

    a. Is Broadway's motion procedurally proper?

    b. Will the motion be granted?

# Summary Judgment Distinguished:

The first part of this chapter suggests that the plaintiff does not bear a heavy burden in avoiding dismissal under Rule 12(b)(6). She need not prove any facts nor even allege them in detail so long as the court can infer that she is alleging the elements of a proper claim. The motion offers no assistance in weeding out cases in which a proper cause of action has been alleged but the plaintiff cannot prove her claim. Yet some device is necessary to eliminate such cases to save the expense and inconvenience of trying cases that clearly must fail for lack of any evidence on a crucial element of the claim.

The motion for summary judgment under Fed. R. Civ. P. 56 is designed to allow early resolution of such cases. *Summary* judgment means judgment without trial, the entry of judgment by the court in favor of either the plaintiff or the defendant. Such resolution of the case by the judge, over the opposing party's objection, is appropriate only if the evidence before the court demonstrates that there are no disputed issues of material fact and that the moving party is entitled to recover on the undisputed facts. Fed. R. Civ. P. 56(c).

Suppose, for example, that Berlin, the malicious prosecution plaintiff introduced above, properly alleges that the prior criminal action was terminated in his favor (as well as all the remaining elements of a claim for malicious prosecution), but Porter knows that the case was continued[2] by the

---

2. In some states, many minor criminal cases are "continued" for a period of time rather than dismissed or tried. Under this procedure the court can impose conditions on the defendant in exchange for suspending the prosecution, but the defendant does not plead guilty or acquire a criminal record. Since this practice is routinely used in cases in which the defendant's guilt is clear, it is doubtful that the court would hold that such a continuance constitutes "favorable termination" under the common law of malicious prosecution. At least one case has held that it does not. *Van Arsdale v. Caswell,* 311 S.W.2d 404 (Ky. 1958).

court, rather than dismissed. Under Rule 56, Porter may challenge Berlin's ability to prove favorable termination by moving for summary judgment, supported by admissible evidence to prove that the case was continued. Porter's supporting evidence suggests that Berlin can not prove an essential element of his claim and challenges Berlin to respond to the motion by producing admissible evidence that would tend to prove that element.

If Berlin has such opposing evidence, he must submit it to avoid summary judgment. Fed. R Civ. P. 56(e). He might, for example, submit evidence that there were two charges against him and that one was continued but the other was dismissed. He might submit evidence that the continuance the defendant relies on was simply to postpone the hearing and that the case was subsequently dismissed. Such evidence would demonstrate that there is a "genuine issue of material fact" as to whether the prior proceeding was terminated in Berlin's favor.

If Berlin makes such a showing, summary judgment must be denied. Summary judgment can never be used to try the facts but only to determine whether there are genuinely contested issues of material fact. Thus, the burden of the party opposing summary judgment is slight: She need only show that she has some evidence upon which a jury could resolve the factual issues in her favor. If there is a genuine dispute as to the relevant facts, it is the jury's role to resolve it. The judge's role on summary judgment is only to determine whether the parties' evidence reveals such a factual dispute. If Berlin's action against Porter were allowed to go to a jury without any evidence to support Berlin's claim that the original action had terminated in his favor, the jury would have no legitimate means of finding for Berlin. A verdict for him could only reflect irrational decision-making. Summary judgment avoids this risk as well as the delay and expense of trying unprovable cases.

## Some Interim Questions

9.    Assume that Berlin has alleged that the prior suit was terminated in his favor but has no evidence to prove it. Could Porter obtain dismissal of Berlin's claim under Rule 12(b)(6) at the outset of the case?

10.  Why might Berlin have filed the action if the case was continued indefinitely rather than dismissed? Isn't he wasting his time and money and flaunting the ethical constraints on pleading in Rule 11?

---

Rule 56 provides that a motion for summary judgment may be supported by affidavits, depositions, answers to interrogatories, or other admissible evidence. Fed. R. Civ. P. 56(c), (f). As a general rule, admissible evidence includes sworn testimony (in the form of sworn affidavits, depositions, answers to interrogatories or requests for admissions, or in-court testimony taken at a hearing on the motion) or reliable documentary or physical evidence. (For several examples of appropriate evidence in support of a motion for summary judgment see the deposition excerpt and affidavit that Ronan's lawyers prepared in *Schulansky v. Ronan,* Chapter 28.) Allegations in the pleadings, which represent the parties' *assertions* as to what they can prove, are not admissible evidence.[3]

## Another Interim Question

11. Why do you think the rule requires that the evidence presented in support of a motion for summary judgment be evidence that would be admissible at trial?

———————

If a party moves for summary judgment and supports the motion with admissible evidence the opposing party must generally respond with countervailing evidence in order to avoid the entry of judgment against her. Fed. R. Civ. P. 56(e). It is not sufficient for the opposing party to respond by simply reiterating that she disagrees with the moving party's proffered evidence. At the summary judgment stage the court wants to see what evidence the parties have to put before the jury if a trial is held, not a rehash of their positions in the pleadings. Otherwise, the motion would simply occasion a renewed swearing match between the parties that would not probe their ability to prove their cases.

In some cases summary judgment is an effective means of resolving cases because the parties agree on the underlying facts but disagree as to the legal implications of those facts. Suppose, for example, that Kern, in the negligence case described in question 7, sues Rogers and Broadway and alleges that Rogers was acting in the scope of his employment for Broadway. Broadway denies that allegation. Kern takes Rogers's deposition, and Rogers testifies that he was driving Broadway's delivery truck, that he was on his way to deliver scenery but planned to stop at the Met on his way, that the trip to the Met did take him off of his usual route, and that the accident took place on that side trip. He further testifies that he had his supervisor's permission to stop there. The parties may agree on these facts, but disagree as to whether, as a matter of law, Broadway can be held liable in these circumstances. If so, Broadway could obtain a resolution of this issue by moving for summary judgment and submitting Rogers's deposition in support of its motion. Presumably, Kern will not submit opposing evidence, since he agrees with this

———————

3. Although the court will not consider the parties' allegations as evidence, it will view any admissible evidence submitted in the light most favorable to the party opposing the motion. If the evidence offered by the party opposing summary judgment could give rise to two inferences, for example, one of which would support the opposing party's case, the court will assume that the jury would make that inference, and deny summary judgment. *Anderson v. Liberty Lobby, Inc.,* 106 S. Ct. 2505, 2513 (1986).

statement of the facts but will argue that on the established facts Broadway *could* be held liable and therefore is not entitled to judgment.

## One More Pause

12. How would you phrase the issue posed by Broadway's motion?

---

In the Broadway hypo immediately above, summary judgment could have been sought by Kern as well as Broadway, on the ground that the undisputed facts establish his right to recover. Indeed, in cases where the facts are agreed and the issue is whether the applicable law allows relief, it is common for both parties to file "cross motions" for summary judgment. The motion can also be used to resolve parts of cases; in the hypo above, for example, summary judgment in Broadway's favor would eliminate it as a defendant but not Rogers. Similarly, a party might obtain summary judgment on some claims in a multiclaim lawsuit but not others. Fed. R. Civ. P. 56(c), (d). See the motion in *Schulansky,* infra pp. 407-408.

Perhaps the following cases will help you to understand a device that is hard to describe in the abstract but fairly straightforward in operation.

# QUESTIONS

## No Genuine Issue

13. Recall the situation in question 6, involving Comden's claim against Hart for negligent infliction of emotional distress. In that example, Comden pleaded generally that she had suffered "personal injuries" and the complaint therefore survived a motion to dismiss.
    a.  Assuming again that New York law does not recognize a right to relief for negligent infliction of emotional distress, could Hart obtain dismissal of this case on a motion for summary judgment?
    b.  If he seeks summary judgment, what supporting materials might he submit?

14. Suppose, on the same facts, that Hart moves for summary judgment against Comden supported by an excerpt from Comden's deposition in which Comden admitted that she suffered no physical injury. Comden responds with an affidavit that states in detail the emotional injuries she sustained and details lost earnings that resulted from her emotional reaction to the accident. She also submits authenticated bills for resulting psychiatric care. Should the motion be granted?

15. In Kern's action against Rogers and Broadway, assume that Kern alleges that Rogers hit him while driving the delivery truck up Fifth Avenue and that he was acting in the scope of employment. Broadway answers, denying that Rogers acted in the scope of his employment and subsequently moves for summary judgment, attaching an excerpt from Rogers's deposition. In the

deposition, Rogers testified that he was driving the truck and that he had a load of scenery to deliver uptown but that he did plan to make a short detour to stop at the Met on his way. Kern opposes the motion but does not submit any supporting materials. Should the motion be granted?

16. Assume that Broadway's motion is supported instead by a sworn affidavit of Rogers's supervisor, stating that no deliveries were scheduled for that day and that Rogers took the truck solely to visit the Met.

    a. Kern submits no opposing evidence but argues in opposition to the motion that he has alleged in his complaint that Rogers acted in the scope of his employment, thus placing that fact in dispute. Should the motion be granted?

    b. Kern submits his own affidavit in opposition to the motion, in which he states under oath that Rogers was "acting in the scope of his employment at the time of the accident." Should the motion be granted?

    c. Kern submits an opposing affidavit that states that Broadway's shop is on 58th Street, south of the museum, and that the accident took place on 96th Street, well north of it. He further states that Rogers told him that he was in a hurry because he had to deliver scenery for a show that night. Should the motion be granted?

## Mixed Motions

17. Suppose that Porter, our malicious prosecution defendant in questions 9 and 10, moved to dismiss under Rule 12(b)(6) and attached a certified copy of the docket in the criminal action that showed that the case had been continued rather than dismissed. Berlin opposes the motion but submits no supporting evidence. Is the motion proper?

# ANALYSIS

## Threshold Challenges

1a. The issue posed by the motion is "whether a party who suffers emotional distress from witnessing negligently caused injury to another but suffers no direct injury herself, has a right to recover damages from the negligent party." Note that the issue is not whether Comden actually suffered the injury or whether Hart was negligent but only whether, assuming all the pleaded facts to be true, the law authorizes an award of damages for such injuries.

    b. This motion should be granted. It is clear from the allegations in Comden's complaint that she is claiming relief based solely on emotional distress. If New York law does not recognize a right to relief for acts that only cause emotional distress to the defendant, Comden has asked for relief that the court cannot grant. If the court allowed Comden to proceed to trial, and Comden proved at trial that Hart was negligent, and that she did suffer emotional distress as a result of Hart's negligence, the court would still be unable to grant Comden's demand for damages. The claim Comden has alleged is simply not recognized under the applicable law as a legal wrong entitling her to compensation. If that is true, there is no reason to proceed to trial. In such cases, the court can short-circuit the process by dismissing the case at the outset. That's what Rule 12(b)(6) is designed to do.

2.    In this case, Comden's claim is joined with Gershwin's negligence claim for his physical injuries suffered in the accident. Under any state's law, his allegations of physical injuries resulting from the defendant's negligence will entitle him to relief from the court, if he can prove that those injuries were caused by Hart's negligence. Comden's claim, however, is still solely for emotional distress. The fact that her co-plaintiff has alleged a compensable claim does not save her claim. The court can dismiss some claims from a suit even though other compensable claims are stated, either by the same plaintiff or by another. Nor is Comden's claim saved by the fact that another plaintiff alleges physical injuries. The rule stated in the question allows recovery for emotional suffering only if *that* plaintiff also suffered physical injury.

3.    Comden's train of thought here is creative, though unavailing. If the court must assume the truth of the allegations in the complaint, why not allege that the law allows relief for emotional distress? Unfortunately, Comden is singing the wrong tune. The court only accepts the *factual* allegations of the complaint as true for purposes of the motion. The legal issue is exactly what the motion is intended to resolve. Rule 12(b)(6) would be useless if the plaintiff could simply allege that she has stated a compensable claim and thereby prevent the court from deciding whether she has.

4.    In this problem, it is difficult to determine whether Comden has stated a claim for relief because the state of the law on the crucial issue in the case is not definitively settled by the cases. If the recent cases have effectively overruled the old doctrine, Comden has stated a compensable claim and must be allowed a chance to prove her allegations. If, on the other hand, the old rule remains valid (perhaps because the recent cases limited the right to recover to emotional distress caused by intentional acts) Comden has not stated a claim.

Although the motion here requires close analysis of the relevant case law, Hart's motion to dismiss is still a proper means to challenge the sufficiency of Comden's complaint. The Rule 12(b)(6) motion is available to resolve difficult issues of law as well as clear ones and whether Comden has stated a claim depends on a question of law. If the court determines that the recent New York cases have established a right to recover for negligent infliction of emotional distress, it should deny the motion and allow Comden to go forward to try to prove the allegations on which her recovery depends. On the other hand, if the court concludes that the recent cases are limited to intentional acts, it should dismiss since Comden's allegations are based solely on negligence.

Admittedly, some courts may be reluctant to grant motions to dismiss if the state of the law is unsettled. The court may sense that the issue is a close one that could be better decided on a full record after discovery or trial. The judge may also prefer to have the state of the law clarified by an appellate court, the court primarily responsible for developing common law principles, and therefore allow the case to proceed to trial and hence to resolution on appellate review. But if the court is convinced that the law does not allow recovery, it has the power to dismiss under Rule 12(b)(6) since the issue, though difficult, is one of law for the court.

5.   Be careful to distinguish the issue of the legal sufficiency of the alleged cause of action from the factual proof that the allegations are true. Hart in this case has really asked the judge to determine the facts, not the legal sufficiency of the allegations. This is beyond the purview of the Rule 12(b)(6) motion, which only asks the court to determine whether the plaintiff's complaint states a claim upon which relief can be granted, not whether the allegations in that complaint are true. On such motions, the court assumes the truth of the plaintiff's factual allegations in order to protect the plaintiff's right to have a jury decide the facts. Indeed, at this stage of the case the court has absolutely no basis to determine whether it was Hart's car that hit Gershwin because it has no evidence before it. Hart's assertion is a defense that should be raised in the answer; the motion will be denied, with annoyance.

## Void for Vagueness?

6.   Comden has phrased her allegations here so generally that the court cannot tell from the complaint that the "personal injuries" she has suffered are solely emotional. You and I may know it from the facts described in question 1. Hart may know it since he knows full well his car only hit Gershwin. But for purposes of the motion to dismiss, the court only "knows" what is in the complaint. Under *Conley v. Gibson*, the court must ask whether the plaintiff, on the allegations of the complaint, could prove any set of facts that would entitle her to relief. On these general allegations, Comden might prove that the "personal injuries" she suffered were physical injuries, clearly compensable under traditional negligence law. Thus, the complaint states a claim upon which relief may be granted, and the motion must be denied.

If this tactic will avoid dismissal, and pleading this generally is sufficient under *Conley v. Gibson*, you may well ask why plaintiffs would ever plead a questionable cause of action more specifically. One answer is that a more specific complaint is more helpful to the court and also will trigger more specific responses from the defendant in her answer. See Chapter 25, p. 366. In addition, the plaintiff may prefer to put the difficult legal issue on the table from the beginning. After all, if the case will ultimately turn on the legal question, it may be desirable to resolve it at the outset rather than vigorously litigating the truth of the factual allegations only to discover down the line that proving them will still leave the plaintiff without any right to relief.

On the other hand, in many cases plaintiffs *do* plead their claims very generally, as *Conley v. Gibson* allows, in order not to reveal weaknesses in their cases or simply to avoid giving the opposing party any "free discovery." In some cases such generality may at least postpone the day of reckoning, but as we shall see, the defendant may frequently be able to obtain equally prompt dismissal of the action by moving for summary judgment.

7a. Although Broadway's liability will turn on whether Rogers was acting in the scope of employment at the time of the accident, Kern has not explicitly pleaded that Rogers was doing so. However, he has pleaded that he was driving Broadway's delivery truck. In ruling on the motion to dismiss, the court must resolve any ambiguities in the pleadings in favor of the nonmoving party. If the court, looking at the complaint, can reasonably infer that the plaintiff is stating a valid cause of action, it must deny the motion to dismiss.

In this case the court can infer from the plaintiff's allegations that Rogers worked for Broadway and was driving Broadway's truck, together with the fact that he has sued Broadway, that the plaintiff is claiming a right to relief under respondeat superior for a tort committed by Rogers in the course of his employment for Broadway. Kern's pleading certainly would have been more artful if he had explicitly alleged that Rogers was driving the truck in the course of his employment for Broadway, but there is enough there for a court to conclude under the liberal pleading standard of *Conley v. Gibson* that Kern may have a compensable claim. Perhaps a judge who loves her rules will require Kern to amend, but no court should dismiss the action on these pleadings.

b. In this case, Broadway does not claim that Kern could not recover even if he proved that Rogers injured him while driving in the course of his employment for Broadway. Rather, Broadway denies that Rogers was acting in the scope of employment when he injured Kern since he was on a "frolic and detour" at the time of the accident. This denial should be raised in the answer rather than by motion to dismiss. The motion should be denied.

8a. Broadway's motion is procedurally proper. Rule 12(h)(2) authorizes the defendant to raise the objection of failure to state a claim in any pleading, by motion for judgment on the pleadings,[4] or even at trial. Essentially, the rules allow this objection to be raised throughout the suit because it is pointless for a court to proceed if it cannot ultimately provide the plaintiff with any relief.

---

4. A judgment on the pleadings is authorized by Fed. R. Civ. P. 12(c). It may be used either as a delayed motion to dismiss, that is, a challenge to the sufficiency of the complaint standing alone, or to challenge the sufficiency of the complaint in light of particular defenses raised in the answer. See generally 2A Moore's at ¶12.15.

b. The motion will be denied here just as it should be in question 7 in which it was raised before answering. The only difference between this case and question 7 is that the defendant's answer clearly places in issue the question of whether Rogers was acting in the scope of his employment. However, the objection of failure to state a claim, whether made before or after the answer is filed, still challenges only the legal sufficiency of the plaintiff's claim. Broadway's denial does not change the fact that if Kern proves that Rogers was acting in the scope of his employment Broadway may be liable. Whether he actually was within the scope of employment is a factual issue to be resolved later in the suit.

## Some Interim Questions

9.  Even if he knows that Berlin cannot prove his claim for malicious prosecution, Porter will not be able to obtain dismissal under Rule 12(b)(6). On a 12(b)(6) motion the court only considers whether the plaintiff has alleged the elements necessary to state a claim. Here, the facts state that Berlin alleged in his complaint that the original action terminated in his favor. The court cannot look beyond the plaintiff's allegations in deciding the Rule 12(b)(6) motion; therefore, such a motion would have been denied since Berlin has alleged all the elements of the claim. Porter needs to "pierce the pleadings," that is, go beyond the allegations in the complaint in order to convince the court that although Berlin has *alleged* a proper claim for malicious prosecution, he cannot *prove* the favorable termination element of his claim.

10.  People file lawsuits for many reasons. Berlin may have been unclear as to the necessary elements of the claim, or he may have had grounds to believe that under the applicable law a continuance is sufficient to satisfy the favorable termination requirement. He may have hoped to induce Porter to settle the claim despite some doubt as to its legal sufficiency. He may even have had little hope of winning, yet filed suit as a means of venting his anger or embarrassing the defendant. In some cases such suits may violate the ethical limitations on pleading in Fed. R. Civ. P. 11 or the Code of Professional Responsibility as a misuse of court process. In others, however, they may simply reflect the uncertainties inherent in the application of general legal principles to particular cases.

For whatever reason, many suits are filed that, when tested on the merits, prove fatally defective. Summary judgment provides a means to probe for such defects without going to trial on all issues in the case.

## Another Interim Question

11.  The point of the summary judgment motion is to demonstrate to the court that there are factual issues for a jury to decide. "Admissible" evidence is evidence that is deemed sufficiently reliable, under long established rules of

evidence, to allow a jury to hear and consider it in reaching a decision on the facts. If the party opposing summary judgment has no admissible evidence to prove her case (or any crucial element of the case), the jury would have no basis upon which to render a verdict for her and trial would consequently be unnecessary.

## One More Pause

12. The issue posed is whether an employer is liable under respondeat superior for an employee's tort when the employee causes injury while on a diversion from her duties with the employer's permission.[5] This is an issue of law that may be resolved by the court. Broadway has framed this issue for the court by offering admissible evidence — Rogers's sworn testimony — to establish the underlying facts. Since Kern has not submitted any opposing evidence as required by Rule 56(e), the court can assume the truth of these facts and resolve the legal issue without trial.

Note that here, as on the motion to dismiss under Rule 12(b)(6), the case ultimately boils down to a legal issue. However, in the procedural posture of this case, a 12(b)(6) motion would have been denied because Kern had properly alleged that Rogers acted in the scope of his employment in driving the truck. Even if Broadway denies it, Kern's complaint states a claim upon which relief can be granted. In order to properly pose the legal question for the court, it is necessary for Broadway to do more than challenge the sufficiency of the complaint itself. It must either present evidence in support of the motion or point to evidence already on file in the action, which demonstrates that Kern cannot prove his allegation that Rogers acted within the scope of his employment. See *Celotex Corp. v. Catrett*, 106 S. Ct. 2548, 2552-2555 (1986).

## No Genuine Issue

13a. This is exactly the type of situation in which summary judgment allows parties to obtain judgment without trial, despite the fact that the plaintiff's complaint alleges a proper claim for relief. Here, Hart knows that Comden cannot prove a compensable claim under New York law, but he has to show the court that this is true by challenging Comden to produce evidence to support her claim. By moving for summary judgment supported by admissible evidence that Comden suffered no physical injuries, Hart will flush out the fatal weakness in Comden's case. Presumably, Comden will be unable to counter Hart's evidence since it is true. The motion will therefore demonstrate that there is "no genuine issue" (Fed. R. Civ. P. 56(c)) as to whether

---

5. I assume the court would answer this question "no" since the fact that an employee has permission to deviate from her duties doesn't make the deviation part of her master's business.

Comden suffered physical injuries and that Hart is entitled to judgment as a matter of law since psychic injuries do not give rise to a right to recover under applicable law. Id.

b. Hart may use any admissible evidence to support his motion. A party's answers to interrogatories, for example, are sworn statements that would be admissible at trial. Hart could send interrogatories to Comden asking whether she suffered physical injury in the accident. Comden will presumably answer "no," and that answer could be submitted in support of the motion. Hart could offer Comden's testimony in her deposition or an affidavit of Hart stating that his car did not hit Comden and that he observed Comden after the accident and that she had no physical injuries. Sworn affidavits of other witnesses would also constitute proper supporting evidence or a police report in which Comden stated that she suffered no physical injury or other evidence, so long as the evidence is admissible under the rules of evidence and tends to prove the underlying fact.

14. Assuming that New York law does not allow recovery for purely emotional injuries, Comden's claim will again end on a sour note. Hart has submitted admissible evidence in support of his motion that indicates that Comden did not suffer physical injury. Comden has filed an opposing affidavit, but the affidavit does not demonstrate that there is any issue as to whether she suffered physical injury. Her evidence goes to prove the severity of her psychic injury, but that is not enough to entitle her to take her case to a jury. She may be totally incapacitated and prove it by the testimony of 20 unimpeachable witnesses, but she will still not be entitled to relief if the law requires accompanying physical injury.

This example illustrates an important point. It is not enough to show that there is a dispute in the evidence on *some* fact; the dispute must be on an issue that is material to the right to recover. Here, Comden's opposing affidavits indicate that she can prove facts, but facts that are irrelevant under the governing law. Thus, there is no dispute of *material* fact (see Fed. R. Civ. P. 56(c)), and Hart is entitled to judgment as a matter of law.

15. You may have concluded that Broadway's motion should be granted on the purely procedural ground that Kern has filed no affidavits or other evidence in opposition to the motion. Rule 56(e) appears at first blush to require this result since it provides that a party opposing summary judgment may not simply rest on the allegations in her pleading but is required to come forward with evidence in support of those allegations.

That conclusion, while understandable from an initial reading of Rule 56(e), is wrong. Summary judgment should only be granted under Rule 56(e) "if appropriate." It is never "appropriate" to grant the motion if the moving party's evidence itself supports differing interpretations of the facts. It is only where the moving party's materials establish that party's version of the facts that the burden shifts to the opposing party to introduce contrary evidence.

In this example, Rogers's deposition indicates that he planned to take a side trip to the Met. If the accident happened while he was on that side trip, Broadway would not be liable (under our assumption that respondeat superior does not apply to such detours under New York law) since that part of the trip would not be in the scope of employment. However, the deposition does not indicate exactly where the accident took place; Rogers's testimony does not preclude the possibility that it took place a hundred yards from Broadway's office while Rogers was still on his delivery route. If that were true, presumably Broadway would be liable. Thus, Broadway's supporting evidence does not demonstrate that there is no genuine issue of fact as to whether Rogers acted in the scope of employment.[6] Since Broadway has not carried its burden to establish a version of the facts that will entitle it to summary judgment, the motion should be denied even without any contrary submissions by Kern.

Of course, it is hardly advisable for Kern to rest solely on the argument that there is ambiguity in Broadway's evidence. The better course in this case would be for Kern to offer positive evidence to support his contention that Rogers was in the scope of employment rather than rest on Broadway's failure to meet its initial burden.

16a. Kern's response here is insufficient to keep the show on the road. Rule 56(e) specifically provides that a party may not avoid summary judgment by resting on contrary allegations in the complaint. All that Kern has done here is to say, "All right, you have evidence to prove Rogers was not acting in the scope of employment, but I say he was." This is mere persistence, not proof. The court knows that is Kern's position, but a summary judgment motion challenges him to show that he can prove it, not just allege it.

b. Once again, Kern is whistling Dixie. He has simply taken the scope of employment allegation in his complaint and restated it in his affidavit. If Kern cannot avoid summary judgment by resting on the allegation in his complaint, it hardly seems appropriate to allow him to achieve the same result by simply repeating the same allegation in an affidavit. This is not admissible evidence, but simply the opinion of an interested party as to how the factual issue should be resolved. If parties could avoid summary judgment by this tactic, it would hardly be an effective device.

c. This is an entirely different situation. Here Kern has offered admissible evidence, his own testimony, as to *facts* that tend to support the scope of employment allegation in his complaint. Summary judgment should be denied here because the evidence is contradictory, thus posing a triable issue of fact as to whether Rogers was on a delivery at the time he hit Kern. In this case, the show must go on.

---

6. Similar ambiguities in their own evidence led Ronan's lawyers to decide not to file their motion for summary judgment in *Schulansky v. Ronan*. See Chapter 28.

## Mixed Motions

17. In this case the defendant has moved to dismiss under Rule 12(b)(6) but submitted supporting evidence that indicates that the plaintiff cannot prove the favorable termination requirement of his malicious prosecution claim. Technically, this is improper since a Rule 12(b)(6) motion challenges the complaint alone, and the court does not consider any evidence in ruling on the motion. However, the fourth sentence of Rule 12(b) specifically provides that in such cases, in which the moving party has essentially filed a mislabeled motion for summary judgment, the court may treat it as such.

When the court decides to treat a 12(b)(6) motion as a motion for summary judgment, it must give the opposing party notice of that intent, so that she can produce evidence in opposition to the motion. Fed. R. Civ. P. 12(b), last sentence; compare Fed. R. Civ. P. 56(c) (summary judgment motion must be served at least ten days prior to hearing on the motion). Thus, Berlin will have the opportunity to submit evidence that the case was favorable terminated, and the court will then determine whether the parties have met their respective burdens on the summary judgment motion.

# 16

---

# *The Judge and the Jury, Part One: Directing the Verdict*

## Introduction

Every good citizen knows that the Constitution guarantees "the right to trial by jury." However, a good part of the civil procedure course is devoted to studying various hurdles that stand between the litigant who demands jury trial and actual jury decision of the merits of his case. As the last chapter demonstrates, the plaintiff's case may be cut short by a motion to dismiss under Rule 12(b)(6), which allows the judge to enter judgment for the defendant on the ground that the plaintiff's complaint does not state a legal claim for relief. If the plaintiff's case survives a Rule 12(b)(6) challenge, it may still meet an early demise on a motion for summary judgment if the judge concludes that there is "no genuine issue of material fact" for the jury to consider.

Although these two motions may preclude the parties from obtaining a jury trial, they are justifiable since both are based on the premise that there is really nothing for the jury to do. It comes as more of a surprise to students to learn that even after the beginning of trial and the presentation of evidence to the jury the judge may still snatch the case from the jury, or even more invasively, allow the jury to render a verdict and then enter judgment for the party who *lost* the jury verdict. This chapter and the one that follows are intended to help you understand three devices that the judge may use to control the jury's decision-making process: directed verdict, judgment not-withstanding the verdict, and new trial.

# The Plaintiff's Burden of Production

In order to understand these devices, it helps to have a preliminary under-standing of the plaintiff's burden to produce evidence at trial in support of his claim. Figure 16-1[1] represents varying degrees of evidence in support of the plaintiff's claim. At the extreme left is the case in which the plaintiff produces no evidence to prove his claim; as you move to the right along the line the strength of the plaintiff's evidence increases. The X line on the diagram indicates the point at which the plaintiff has produced evidence that is sufficiently persuasive that a jury, acting rationally, could find that he has proved each element of his case. If the plaintiff's evidence crosses this line, he is said to have satisfied his *burden of production*. Even though the judge may consider the plaintiff's evidence weak or less persuasive than the defendant's, if the evidence is sufficient to cross the X line the case falls in the realm of legitimate difference of opinion and must go to the jury for decision.

The Z line on the diagram represents the point at which the evidence is evenly balanced; that is, evidence of equal probative value supports the plain-tiff's position and the defendant's. In a civil case the plaintiff's burden of proof is to establish that his version of events is more probably true than the defendant's — that is, that a simple preponderance of the evidence favors the plaintiff's version of events. In terms of the diagram, his evidence must fall to the right of the Z line to carry his burden of proof. The Y line represents the point at which the plaintiff's proof becomes so strong that any reasonable jury would have to conclude that the plaintiff has proved his case.[2]

In the area to the left of the X line, a directed verdict for the defendant is proper. If the judge concludes that the plaintiff's case is so weak that no jury, acting rationally on the evidence before it, could find for him, allowing the case to go to the jury simply invites irrational decision making based on irrelevant or prejudicial factors. The directed verdict motion is intended to guard against such flawed verdicts by confining the jury's right to decide the facts to those cases in which there is legitimate doubt as to what those facts are. See *Rutherford v. Illinois Central R.R.*, 278 F.2d 310, 312 (5th Cir.), cert. denied, 364 U.S. 922 (1960) (directed verdict is "a method for protecting neutral principles of law from powerful forces outside the scope of law — compassion and prejudice."). The motion may be granted for plaintiffs as well as defendants (if the plaintiff's evidence is so strong as to pass the

---

1. A similar diagram in Landers and Martin, Civil Procedure (1981) was used, with permission, as the basis for this diagram.
2. In a criminal case, the state's burden of proof falls near if not on the Y line since the state must prove the defendant's guilt beyond a reasonable doubt.

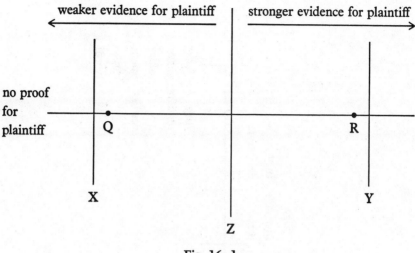

Fig. 16–1

hypothetical Y line), though for reasons discussed below this is much less common than directed verdicts for defendants.

The arena for legitimate differences of opinion as to the proper outcome — and hence the arena for jury decision — lies between the X and Y lines. Even though the judge concludes that the evidence falls at point Q, well to the left of the point where the balance of the evidence favors the plaintiff, he may not direct a verdict for the defendant. If the judge could direct a verdict in the area between X and Y, he could essentially usurp the role of the jury by substituting his own judgment for that of the jury any time they did not reach the same conclusion that he would. If reasonable minds can differ as to the result, the case is for the jury, not the judge.

Similarly, if the judge concludes that the balance of the evidence falls at point R on the spectrum, where the plaintiff's evidence substantially outweighs the opposing evidence (but is not so persuasive that the only reasonable verdict is for the plaintiff), the case must go to the jury. Even though the judge believes that the balance tips in the plaintiff's favor, at this point on the spectrum that conclusion is legitimately debatable (just as it is at point Q). If the jury could reasonably find for the defendant, it must be given the opportunity to do so even though the judge believes that the preponderance of the evidence favors the plaintiff.

In passing on the directed verdict motion, the judge may not determine the credibility of witnesses; the issue of which witnesses to believe is classically a jury decision. The test is not whether the judge believes the plaintiff's witnesses, but whether the jury, if it chooses to believe those witnesses, would have sufficient evidence to support a verdict for the plaintiff. Thus, in passing on the motion, the judge assumes that the jury will believe the witnesses for the nonmoving party and make all possible inferences in favor of that party.

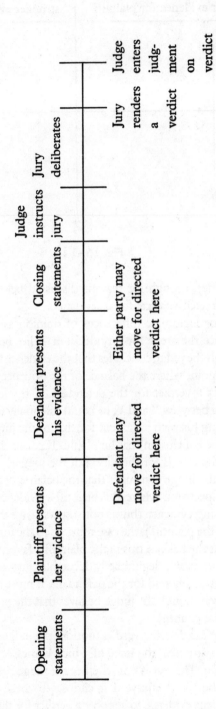

**Fig. 16–2**

# The Timing of the Directed Verdict Motion

As Figure 16-2[3] indicates, the plaintiff in a civil case presents his evidence first at trial. He has the burden during his case-in-chief to produce enough evidence on each element of his claim to pass the X line and reach the jury. At the close of the plaintiff's case-in-chief, the defendant may move for a directed verdict on the ground that the plaintiff's evidence does not cross the X line; that is, does not satisfy the plaintiff's burden to produce evidence in support of one or more elements of his claim. If the court agrees that the plaintiff has not produced enough evidence to support a rational verdict in his favor, it may direct a verdict for the defendant at this point.

If the judge denies the motion, the defendant will present his evidence to rebut the plaintiff's case or to establish any affirmative defense. After the defendant rests he may move again for a directed verdict. When the motion is made at this point it challenges the sufficiency of all the evidence, both plaintiff's and defendant's, to support a verdict for the plaintiff. As the diagram indicates, the plaintiff may also move for a directed verdict at this point, though not at the close of his own case.

## Two Fundamental Questions

1.   Why may the defendant, but not the plaintiff, move for a directed verdict at the close of the plaintiff's case?

2.   What will happen next if the judge directs a verdict for the defendant at the close of the plaintiff's case?

# The Standard for Directing a Verdict

Because the judge risks encroachment on the role of the jury in deciding the case on a directed verdict motion, it is important to have a clear picture of just where the X and Y lines fall. Unfortunately, while it is easy to draw diagrams conceptualizing the parties' burdens of production, it is a great deal harder to articulate a clear and workable *standard* for deciding when the evidence crosses those lines. Some courts have held that a directed verdict motion must be denied (and hence, the case left to the jury) if there is "a scintilla" of evidence to support the opposing party's case. See, e.g., *Hanson v. Couch*, 360 So. 2d 942 (Ala. 1978). Under this test, if the plaintiff has any evidence to support the elements of his claim he will get to the jury. This standard places point X almost on top of point W on the diagram. Obviously this stretches

---

3. The diagram and the accompanying discussion are a bit oversimplified. For example, after the close of the defendant's case, the court will often allow the plaintiff to reopen his case to offer rebuttal testimony.

the area between X and Y, giving the greatest latitude to the jury but at the expense of effective judicial control of irrational jury decision making.

Another standard found in the cases[4] requires the judge to consider *only* the evidence proffered by the nonmoving party (usually the plaintiff). Under this standard, the judge must assume the truth of all evidence offered by the nonmoving party, take all the inferences from the evidence in the light most favorable to that party, and direct a verdict only if that evidence would not support a verdict for the nonmoving party. *Wilkerson v. McCarthy,* 336 U.S. 53, 57 (1949). Suppose, for example, that Pavarotti sues Sills for negligence after he is hit by a red Chevrolet on Maple Street in Cleveland, Ohio. He presents evidence that Sills lives three blocks from the scene of the accident and owns a red Chevrolet bearing the license number 301-LJM. One of Pavarotti's witnesses testifies that she saw a red Chevrolet leave the intersection after the accident, driven by a blonde woman (assume that Sills is blonde) and read the first three numbers of the license number as 311. Although this evidence is hardly overwhelming, it may well be sufficient to allow a rational jury to find for Pavarotti. Under the "plaintiff's evidence" standard, the judge would probably deny a motion for directed verdict regardless of the evidence Sills presented in rebuttal.

A third statement of the standard for directing a verdict, and the formulation usually applied in the federal courts under Fed. R. Civ. P. 50(a),[5] requires the judge to consider the nonmoving party's evidence in its most favorable light (just as in the second test) but also to consider any evidence put forward by the moving party that is not impeached or contradicted by the opposing party's evidence. If, considering all of that evidence, there "can be but one conclusion" as to the verdict, the judge must direct a verdict for the moving party. 5A Moore's at ¶50.02[1]; see also *Carlson v. American Safety Equipment Corp.,* 528 F.2d 384, 385 (1st Cir. 1976) (when defendant moves for directed verdict, the court must examine the facts in the light most favorable to the plaintiff but without neglecting the uncontradicted evidence for the defendant).

Assume, for example, that Sills (after the plaintiff, Pavarotti, presents the evidence described above) offers the undisputed testimony of two eyewitnesses to the accident that she was not the driver of the car and documentary evidence that indicates that she was performing in an opera in Minneapolis at the time of the accident. On this state of the evidence, her directed verdict

---

4. Although Rule 50(a) authorizes use of directed verdicts in the federal courts, the rule itself tells almost nothing about what a directed verdict *is*. It is primarily devoted to eliminating certain antiquated aspects of directed verdict practice at common law. The standard for directing a verdict and other features of directed verdict practice must be ascertained from case law.

5. For easy reference, I will call this third standard the "federal" standard, although it is not unique to the federal courts and the phrasing of the standard given here is not universally accepted within the federal system.

motion at the close of all the evidence should be granted under the federal standard. The plaintiff produced enough evidence to support a legitimate (but not compelling) inference that Sills had hit him. But that inference is negated by the defendant's uncontradicted, unimpeached evidence to the contrary and leaves the jury without a reasonable basis to conclude that Sills is liable.

The questions that follow should help you to get a sense of the court's role in controlling jury action by the directed verdict motion. The questions are based on one of the old chestnut cases on directed verdicts, *Pennsylvania R.R. Co. v. Chamberlain*, 288 U.S. 333 (1933). The relevant evidence in *Chamberlain* is set forth immediately below, but you may want to read *Chamberlain* before considering the questions.

The decedent in *Chamberlain* was killed when he fell from a train he was riding while sorting groups of cars in a railroad yard.

> The lead track crossed a "hump," and the work of car distribution consisted of pushing a train of cars by means of a locomotive to the top of the "hump," and then allowing the cars, in separate strings, to descend by gravity, under the control of hand brakes, to their respective destinations in the various branch tracks. Deceased had charge of a string of two gondola cars, which he was piloting to track 14. Immediately ahead of him was a string of seven cars, and behind him a string of nine cars, both also destined for track 14. Soon after the cars ridden by the deceased had passed to track 14, his body was found on that track some distance beyond the switch. He had evidently fallen onto the track and been run over by a car or cars.

288 U.S. at 335-336. The plaintiff's theory was that the railroad's employees negligently caused the string of cars Chamberlain was riding to collide with the following string of nine cars, throwing him under the train.

# QUESTIONS

## The Plaintiff's Case

3.   In *Chamberlain* the plaintiff offered the following evidence as to the cause of the accident:

> The plaintiff's only witness to the event, one Bainbridge, then employed by the road, stood close to the yardmaster's office, near the "hump." He professed to have paid little attention to what went on, but he did see the deceased riding at the rear of his cars, whose speed when they passed him he took to be about eight or ten miles. Shortly thereafter a second string passed which was shunted into another track and this was followed by the nine, which according to the plaintiff's theory, collided with the deceased's. After the nine cars had passed at a somewhat greater speed than the deceased's, Bainbridge paid no more attention to either string for a while, but looked again when the deceased, who was still standing in his place, had passed the switch and onto the assorting track where he was

bound. At that time his speed had been checked to about three miles, but the speed of the following nine cars had increased. They were just passing the switch, about four or five cars behind the deceased. Bainbridge looked away again and soon heard what he described as "a loud crash," not however an unusual event in a switching yard. Apparently this did not cause him at once to turn, but he did so shortly thereafter, and saw the two strings together, still moving, and the deceased no longer in sight. . . . Until he left to go to the accident, he had stood fifty feet to the north of the track where the accident happened, and about nine hundred feet from where the body was found.

288 U.S. at 336-337.

Assume that the plaintiff in *Chamberlain* presented this evidence as to the cause of the accident and rested her case. The defendant moves for a directed verdict.

    a.  If the court applies the "plaintiff's evidence" standard, should the motion be granted?

    b.  Assume that the case is tried instead in a court that applies the federal standard, which also allows consideration of the moving party's uncontradicted, unimpeached evidence. Should the railroad's motion at the close of the plaintiff's case be granted?

4.  Suppose that Bainbridge was again the only witness and gave the same testimony but that he had made his observations while riding on a third string of cars following the nine-car string. If the railroad moved for a directed verdict at the close of the plaintiff's case, and the court applied the "plaintiff's evidence" standard, could it direct a verdict for the railroad?

## The Defendant's Case

5.  Should the railroad be allowed to move for a directed verdict at the close of all the evidence if it failed to do so at the close of the plaintiff's case?

6.  Suppose that the *plaintiff* moves for a directed verdict at the close of all the evidence. Paraphrase the plaintiff's position as to the state of the evidence when she makes such a motion.

7.  Suppose that the plaintiff in *Chamberlain* rests her case and the railroad rests its case without offering any evidence. The plaintiff moves for a directed verdict. Should it be granted?

8.  Assume that the court refuses to direct a verdict for the defendant in *Chamberlain* at the close of the plaintiff's evidence. Therefore, the railroad proceeds to present its case. (See Figure 16-2 supra). As the case report indicates, the railroad's case was as follows. "Three employees, riding the nine-car string, testified positively that no such collision occurred. They were corroborated by every other employee in a position to see, all testifying that there was no contact between the nine-car string and that of the deceased." 288 U.S. at 336.

a.  After presenting its case, the railroad moves for a directed verdict. Should the motion be granted under the plaintiff's evidence standard?

b.  Should the verdict be directed under the federal standard?

## A Few Variations

9.  Suppose that Bainbridge offered the same testimony as above, but there were only two trains, the two-car string and the nine-car string, in the yard at the time. How should the court rule if the railroad offers the same evidence as above and then moves for a directed verdict at the close of all the evidence? Assume that the federal standard applies.

10.  Suppose that Bainbridge's testimony was the same as that offered in the actual case, but that he testified that he actually saw the trains collide. Could the judge direct a verdict for the railroad? For the plaintiff?

11.  Suppose there had been only one witness for the defendant, the railroad yardmaster. Assume that he was standing near the spot where the decedent was found and testified unequivocally that no collision occurred. Could the verdict be directed for the railroad?

## Trial and Error

12.  Assume that the Chamberlain case was tried to the judge instead of a jury. The defendant's counsel rises at the close of the plaintiff's case and moves "for directed verdict on the ground that no reasonable jury could find for the plaintiff." What two grievous errors did defendant's counsel make? See Fed. R. Civ. P. 41(b).

## A Retrospective

13.  Let's back up a minute and assume that the railroad moved for summary judgment before trial and submitted affidavits in support of the motion from their employees. The affidavits all state that no collision took place between the two strings. The plaintiff submits an opposing affidavit of Bainbridge, stating his testimony as it is given in question 3. Should the railroad's motion be granted?

# ANALYSIS

## Two Fundamental Points

1.  Due process of law entitles every litigant to an opportunity to be heard before a court adjudicates his rights. If the court could direct a verdict for the plaintiff at the close of his case, the defendant would be deprived of his opportunity to present evidence, either to refute the plaintiff's case or to

establish an affirmative defense. Even if the judge concludes that the plaintiff's evidence has crossed the Y line, the defendant may well produce countervailing evidence that would leave legitimate doubt as to the facts, making the case an appropriate one for the jury. Thus, no matter how strong the plaintiff's evidence may be, the defendant will be given a chance to rebut it.

2.    The judge may only grant a directed verdict for the defendant if he concludes that the plaintiff has not produced enough evidence to support a rational verdict in his favor. If the judge concludes that the plaintiff's evidence has not made out "a prima facie case," there is no need to go on and hear the defendant's evidence. Judgment will be entered for the defendant on the basis of the directed verdict.

Under earlier practice if the judge decided to grant a directed verdict, the jury had to give its assent to the verdict (though the jury had no choice *but* to assent). This somewhat irksome relic of the common law is eliminated by the last sentence of Rule 50(a). The modern rule frankly recognizes that the directed verdict motion is not really a "verdict" at all but a withdrawal of the case from the jury.

## The Plaintiff's Case

3a.    Under the plaintiff's evidence standard, the motion should be denied if the jury, considering only the evidence supporting the plaintiff's case, could reasonably infer that the accident resulted from the railroad's negligence. Although the plaintiff's evidence that the two strings collided (thus indicating negligence by the railroad) is less than compelling, it is probably sufficient to support a rational inference that a collision caused the accident. If the jury credits Bainbridge's testimony, they would have evidence that a crash occurred, that the nine-car string was moving considerably faster than the two-car string before the crash, and that they subsequently were seen moving in tandem. In addition, the decedent was found dead on the tracks; this fact taken together with Bainbridge's testimony is probably sufficient to support an inference that a collision occurred. If such an inference could rationally be made, the jury should be allowed to make it (or reject it). The defendant's motion for a directed verdict at the close of Chamberlain's case should probably be denied.

b.    The result at this stage of the case should be the same under the federal test. At the close of the plaintiff's case the only evidence before the court is that offered by the plaintiff.[6] Thus, the defendant's motion at this point will usually be based on the position that the plaintiff's evidence is insufficient to cross the X line to satisfy his burden to produce evidence that would rationally support the conclusion that the accident resulted from the

---

6. Except, of course, for adverse testimony by the plaintiff's witnesses elicited by defendant's counsel on cross-examination.

railroad's negligence. As indicated above, the plaintiff's evidence in *Chamberlain* was probably sufficient to defeat this motion.

It is conceivable that the railroad's attorney would elicit evidence from the *plaintiff's* witnesses that would foreclose a verdict in the plaintiff's favor. For example, the railroad might get Bainbridge to admit on cross-examination that he is unable to see further than 25 feet without his glasses, which he was not wearing at the time. This evidence would be considered under the federal standard and if not impeached or contradicted by other evidence for the plaintiff, it could force the plaintiff's case back over the X line and lead to a directed verdict for the railroad even before it presents its own case. Assuming, however, that cross-examination does not produce such evidence for the defendant's case, the directed verdict motion will be denied.

4. Although the judge is required to view the case in the light most favorable to the plaintiff, there comes a point where the unlikely fades into the humanly impossible. As the case report indicates, Bainbridge apparently viewed the moving trains from a three-degree angle if he was standing *beside* the track. If he were actually on a train following the nine-car string (and there were no bend in the track) it would be impossible for him to observe a collision 900 feet in front of him on the same track. On this evidence, the reasonable judge could reasonably infer that only an unreasonable jury could find for the plaintiff.

It is true that the judge, by directing a verdict on these facts, exercises some judgment as to the strength of the plaintiff's case. A line must be drawn somewhere, between the inherently incredible and the unlikely-but-possible. If the court abdicates the responsibility of doing so, the jury becomes the unrestrained arbiter of the parties' rights regardless of the inadequacy of their proof.

## The Defendant's Case

5. Yes; there is no requirement that a defendant move for a directed verdict at the close of the plaintiff's case in order to preserve his right to do so at the close of all the evidence. Nor should there be; as stated in the introduction, the directed verdict motion raises distinct issues depending upon when it is made. When the defendant makes this motion at the close of the plaintiff's case the issue is whether the plaintiff has produced so little evidence that no reasonable jury could conclude that he had carried his burden of proof. When the defendant moves for directed verdict at the close of all the evidence, he may take the position that the plaintiff had initially presented a strong enough case to go to the jury, but the unimpeached and uncontradicted evidence that the defendant has presented forces the case back to the left of the X line on the diagram, where the judge must direct a verdict for the defendant. If that is true, then a directed verdict would be unwarranted at the close of the plaintiff's case, but appropriate at the end of all the evidence, if the federal standard applies.

6.   When the plaintiff moves for a directed verdict at the close of the case, his position is that the uncontradicted, unimpeached evidence in support of his case is so strong that the proof falls to the right of the Y line, where no reasonable jury could reach a verdict for the defendant. In passing on the plaintiff's motion, the court must assume that the jury would believe all of the defendant's evidence and reject all evidence for the plaintiff that had been contradicted or impeached. If, upon these assumptions, the only rational conclusion is that the plaintiff has proved each element of his case, the verdict may be directed.

As a practical matter, few verdicts are directed in favor of plaintiffs because they bear the burden of proof as to each element of their claim. Most cases turn at least in part on the credibility of witnesses. If the credibility of the plaintiff's witnesses has been challenged, the court will have to assume for purposes of the directed verdict motion that the jury will disbelieve them. If their testimony is necessary to establish any element of the plaintiff's claim, the motion will be denied.

7.   The directed verdict should be denied. As in the previous answer, the plaintiff's motion asserts that his evidence in support of the elements of his claim is so strong that no reasonable jury could fail to render a verdict in his favor. Even though the defendant has offered no evidence, it does not follow that the plaintiff has established his case beyond doubt. In *Chamberlain,* for example, if the jury only had the plaintiff's evidence before it, it would still have to infer from Bainbridge's circumstantial evidence that a crash occurred between the two-car string and the nine-car string. Reasonable jurors might make that inference, but they also might not. The evidence is strong enough to support a verdict for Chamberlain but not to compel it.

8a.   The answer to question 3 indicates that the plaintiff's evidence, taken alone, was sufficient to place the *Chamberlain* case in the middle area of the diagram, between the X and Y lines, where the jury must decide the contested issues of fact. If the plaintiff's evidence standard is applied here, the court must disregard all of the railroad's opposing testimony and the same result will follow in this case even though the defendant has introduced very strong contrary evidence.

b.   If the federal standard is applied, the court must consider not only Bainbridge's testimony for the plaintiff but also the uncontradicted and un-impeached testimony for the defendant. The crucial question is whether the defendant's witnesses, who testify directly that no crash occurred (and there-fore no negligence and no ground for recovery) are contradicted or im-peached by the plaintiff's evidence.

The Court holds, and I think rightly, that Bainbridge's and the defen-dant's versions of the incident are not contradictory. Bainbridge's testimony indicates that there was a crash and that the trains were moving along at the same speed after the crash. A jury could infer from this that the nine-car string collided with the two-car string. Alternatively, they could infer that a collision took place someplace else in the yard, and that these two strings were moving at the same speed because each had been braked to the same speed. The defendant's witnesses do not contradict Bainbridge; their testimony that the nine-car and the two-car strings did not collide simply eliminates one of the two possible inferences from his testimony. Unless the jury has some rational basis for rejecting their testimony, it is no longer possible to infer from Bainbridge's circumstantial version of events that these two strings actually collided.

It might be argued, however, that the jury could reject the testimony of the defendant's witnesses because they were all employed by the defendant and thus could be biased. The argument has some force, but the Court concluded in *Chamberlain* that the mere fact of employment by the defendant was insufficient to impeach their testimony. See also *Chesapeake & Ohio Railway Co. v. Martin,* 283 U.S. 209, 216-220 (1931). The case would likely be different if only one employee testified for the railroad and the evidence indicated that he was promoted the week after the accident.

Needless to say, the application of these standards for the direction of a verdict is hardly scientifically precise. In *Chamberlain,* the trial judge directed a verdict for the railroad. The court of appeals reversed, in a two-to-one decision, on the ground that the case should have been left to the jury. The eminent Judge Learned Hand wrote for the majority, and Judge Swan, another respected jurist, registered a strong dissent. 59 F.2d 986 (1932). The Supreme Court then unanimously reversed the court of appeals. Clearly, reasonable judges may differ about when reasonable jurors may differ. Yet the fact that there are close cases does not change the fact that the motion provides needed control of irrational jury behavior.

## A Few Variations

9.   This change in the facts introduces a direct contradiction between the plaintiff's and the defendant's evidence. If Bainbridge testifies that he heard a crash of the type made by trains colliding, and there only were two in the yard, the only possible inference (if you believe Bainbridge) is that those two strings of cars collided. Unlike the facts of the actual case, this testimony would directly contradict the testimony of the defendant's witnesses. Although there were six or seven witnesses for the defendant and only Bainbridge for the plaintiff, the court may not pass on issues of credibility in ruling on a motion for directed verdict; if there is a legitimate conflict in the evidence, the jury must resolve it. If the jury believes Bainbridge over the railroad's employees, it could reasonably find for the plaintiff and should be given the opportunity to do so.

10.   Here again Bainbridge's testimony directly contradicts that of the defendant's witnesses and should therefore raise a jury issue unless the court concludes that his testimony is inherently incredible. The Supreme Court

intimated that it may have been physically impossible for Bainbridge to actually see whether the two strings were in contact. *Chamberlain* at 342. Thus, it is not clear that direct testimony from Bainbridge of a collision would have changed the result. The court might disregard it as physically impossible and conclude that the plaintiff's case was built entirely on an inference that was negated by the defendant's direct evidence to the contrary. Many judges, however, would conclude (as the court of appeals did in *Chamberlain*) that Bainbridge's acute angle of vision is a fact for the jury to weigh in deciding whether to believe his testimony, rather than making that testimony inherently incredible.

A directed verdict for the plaintiff would obviously be inappropriate on this evidence. Although Bainbridge has offered direct testimony in support of the plaintiff's theory, the jury might well not believe it, either because of Bainbridge's angle of vision or for other reasons. In addition, the railroad has offered strong contrary evidence. If anything, the case on these facts hovers near the X line, not the Y line.

11. As suggested above, practice in this area is heavily fact-specific and unscientific. Consequently, distinctions that are conceptually clear do not always dictate results. In this case, the state of the evidence has not changed much when evaluated under the federal standard for directing a verdict. The plaintiff's case is still built upon inference, and it is still directly contradicted by evidence that the jury has little or no reason to discredit.

Yet many courts would not direct the verdict on these facts. There is not the same level of certainty about the defendant's case as there was in the real case, in which six witnesses unanimously denied a collision. A single witness might be unbiased but simply wrong. The argument for bias is stronger here as well since there is more incentive for a managerial employee of the railroad to testify falsely than for lower level yard workers to do so.

## Trial and Error

12. The railroad's attorney has made two mistakes here, one technical but the other substantial. *First,* he should not have called his motion a "directed verdict" motion because verdicts are rendered by juries and here the case was tried to the judge. Judges enter orders rather than rendering verdicts. The proper motion would have been for an order of involuntary dismissal under Fed. R. Civ. P. 41(b).

*Second,* and more important, the railroad's attorney has inappropriately asked the judge to apply the directed verdict standard for withdrawing a case from the jury to a case in which the judge is the factfinder. In a jury case the judge can only direct a verdict at the close of the plaintiff's evidence if the evidence so overwhelmingly favors the defendant that no reasonable jury could find for the plaintiff. In other words, the judge must decide whether the plaintiff has satisfied his burden to produce credible evidence in support of each element of his claim.

When the defendant in a nonjury trial moves for a directed finding at the close of the plaintiff's case, the judge's role is different. In a trial without a jury, the judge *is* the factfinder. When the defendant in a nonjury trial challenges the sufficiency of the plaintiff's case at the close of the plaintiff's evidence (by a motion for involuntary dismissal under Fed. R. Civ. P. 41(b)), the judge does not ask whether the evidence is strong enough that a reasonable jury could find for the plaintiff (i.e., whether it has passed the X line on the diagram) but rather whether the judge, as the factfinder, believes that the plaintiff has proved the elements of his cause of action by a preponderance of the evidence (i.e., whether the plaintiff's evidence has passed the Z line). If the plaintiff has not produced enough evidence to satisfy that standard, the judge may dismiss the case without hearing the defendant's evidence since the plaintiff has had a full opportunity to make his case and has not carried his burden of proof. See Fed. R. Civ. P. 41(b). See generally 5 Moore's at ¶41.13[4].

In making that determination, the judge may also consider the credibility of the witnesses; he is not deciding whether the jury *could* believe plaintiff's witnesses but rather whether he, the judge acting as the factfinder, *does* believe them. In other words, in a judge-tried case, the motion for a directed finding allows the judge to determine whether the plaintiff has carried his burden of *proof,* while in a jury case he must confine himself to considering whether the plaintiff has carried his burden of *production.*[7]

## A Retrospective

13. Summary judgment is only appropriate if there is "no genuine issue of material fact" to be resolved by the jury. It is sometimes said (and has been recently reiterated by the Supreme Court; see *Anderson v. Liberty Lobby Inc.,* 106 S. Ct. 2505, 2511 (1986)) that if the evidence is so one-sided that a judge would be required to grant a directed verdict, then no genuine factual issue exists and summary judgment is appropriate. Under this analysis, the difference between the directed verdict motion under Rule 50(a) and the summary judgment motion under Rule 56 is essentially procedural: The directed verdict motion is raised during the trial and decided on the basis of the testimony and documentary evidence offered at trial, while the summary

---

7. The analogy in a jury case would be if the judge sent the jury out after the plaintiff rested his case to determine whether the plaintiff's evidence had moved the case over the Z line (that is, satisfied his burden of proof) and dismissed the action if the jury concluded that the plaintiff had not. I suppose jury trials could be run that way: The jury would deliberate twice: first after the plaintiff's case to determine whether he had carried his initial burden of proof by a preponderance of the evidence, and a second time after the defendant's evidence to determine if he had pushed the case back over the Z line. However, such a system would break the flow of the evidence and confuse the jury as well. But the judge *can* do this in a nonjury trial since he is used to dealing with the concept of burdens of proof and can more easily break up the presentation of the evidence to consider the motion.

judgment motion is made before trial and determined on the basis of documentary evidence such as depositions, interrogatories, and affidavits. See *Anderson,* 106 S. Ct. at 2512.

While this is conceptually consistent, many courts are more reluctant to grant summary judgment than a directed verdict. Although in theory the judge must ask the same question in passing on both motions — whether the party opposing the motion has offered enough evidence that a reasonable factfinder could find in his favor — the context of the motions is strikingly different. In most cases summary judgment motions are decided on the basis of affidavits and other documentary evidence. The opposing party may submit his own evidentiary materials but will not have the benefit of cross-examination. In addition, the motion often comes fairly early in the litigation before the parties have exhaustively developed their cases. If the judge senses that the case will turn on questions of fact that are not fully elucidated by the record, he will likely conclude that the parties should have a full opportunity to present their evidence at trial before a decision is made to withdraw the case from the jury.

> In considering a motion for summary judgment, the district court must give the benefit of the doubt to the party who asserts he can prove a dubious proposition at trial. In considering a motion for a directed verdict, in contrast, the district court has had the benefit of seeing what the parties alleged they could prove prior to trial tested in the crucible of open court. Accordingly, the district court is entitled to grant a directed verdict even though some evidence supports the opposite position.

*Kim v. Coppin State College,* 662 F.2d 1055, 1059 (4th Cir. 1981). Consequently, it is not unusual for the court to deny summary judgment but subsequently grant a directed verdict for the same party. See 6 Moore's at ¶56.04[2] n.11.

In the *Chamberlain* case there is ample ground for a court to conclude that full trial of the issues might reveal a submissible case for the plaintiff. The evidence was largely testimonial; cross-examination might have revealed inconsistencies in the defendant's witnesses' testimony, or impeached their credibility. In such cases judges tend to give the party opposing summary judgment the benefit of the doubt by allowing the case to proceed to trial. See generally James and Hazard, Civil Procedure 273-277 (1985) (hereinafter cited as James and Hazard). Even if (as here) a verdict is ultimately directed, such forbearance gives the parties the fullest opportunity to satisfy their burden of production (and thus get to the jury) in close cases.

# 17

## The Judge and the Jury, Part Two: Whose Case Is This, Anyway?

## Introduction

A misguided minority of law students think that civil procedure is dull, but in truth it is full of surprises. You may well have been surprised to learn from the last chapter that a judge may snatch a case from the jury in the middle of trial by directing a verdict. It is perhaps even more surprising that the judge may actually allow the jury to deliberate and reach its verdict on the evidence but refuse to enter judgment on the verdict rendered. At first blush this seems the ultimate affront to the jury system, to allow the jury to go through the entire trial process and reach its decision, and then disregard or reverse it. Yet, as we shall see, there are good reasons to allow the judge to do so.

In the federal courts, two post-trial devices allow the judge to displace the jury's verdict. The first is the judgment notwithstanding the verdict, or j.n.o.v.[1] The j.n.o.v. motion is essentially a delayed (or, more accurately, renewed) motion for a directed verdict. The standard for granting the j.n.o.v. motion is the same as that for directing a verdict: In each case, the moving party will prevail on the motion only if the opponent's evidence is so weak

---

1. J.n.o.v., or judgment "*non obstante veredicto*," is Latin for judgment notwithstanding the verdict. The two terms are used interchangeably in practice and in this chapter.

that no reasonable jury could have reached a verdict for her. Of course, when the losing party moves for j.n.o.v. after the jury's verdict, a jury *has* found for the opposing party. Thus, the j.n.o.v motion asserts that the jury acted irrationally, in disregard of the evidence in reaching a verdict for the party opposing the motion.

You may well wonder what purpose is served by the j.n.o.v. motion. If the standards for granting the directed verdict motion and the j.n.o.v. motion are the same, why not simply grant the directed verdict before the jury deliberates? This will save the jury the trouble of unnecessary deliberations and avoid the affront of having their findings disregarded.

If the directed verdict decision was cut and dried so that the judge's decision to grant one would seldom be overruled on appeal, this argument would have considerable force. However, reasonable judges may differ — and often do — about whether a given case is strong enough to go to a jury. Because the decision that the evidence is too weak to go to the jury is often debatable, directed verdict decisions will frequently be appealed. If the trial judge grants a directed verdict and the appellate court disagrees,[2] it will reverse the decision and order a new trial. The case will then have to be tried again in its entirety thus leading to a wasteful repetition of the first trial.

If, on the other hand, the trial court withholds decision on the sufficiency of the evidence by denying the directed verdict motion at the close of the evidence, this scenario can frequently be avoided. If the evidence is really weak enough to lead the judge to consider directing the verdict, it is likely that the jury will agree and return a verdict for the moving party anyway. This is the best possible result: It avoids any apparent intrusion on the right to jury trial, leads to a verdict that the judge finds supportable on the evidence, and avoids the appeal that would frequently have followed if the judge had granted a directed verdict.

If the jury returns a verdict for the party (usually the plaintiff) against whom the judge considered directing the verdict, the judge can still enter judgment for the other party on a motion for j.n.o.v. In these cases the party whose verdict has been taken away will frequently appeal on the ground that the evidence was strong enough to support a rational verdict in her favor. If the appeals court agrees and reverses the entry of j.n.o.v., it can simply order judgment entered on the jury's verdict. Thus, the need to retry the case is avoided by waiting until after the verdict to decide whether the case is juryworthy.

There are several important limitations on the right to seek judgment notwithstanding the verdict. Under Fed. R. Civ. P. 50(b) (and many state

---

2. Because the decision to grant a directed verdict motion is based on the conclusion that the evidence is too weak as a matter of law to support a verdict for the other party, it is reviewed de novo by the appellate court under the same standard used by the trial judge. See 9 Wright and Miller at §2536 p.595.

rules modeled on it), the motion must be made within ten days of the entry of judgment on the jury's verdict.[3] In addition, a party may only move for j.n.o.v. if she has previously moved for a directed verdict. Fed. R. Civ. P. 50(b).

There are two reasons for this second requirement, one historical and rather silly, the other policy-based and entirely sensible. The historical reason has to do with the seventh amendment to the United States Constitution, which provides that "no fact tried by a jury, shall be otherwise reexamined in any Court of the United States, than according to the rules of the common law." Early cases held that it was unconstitutional for the judge to allow the jury to decide the facts and then "reexamine" them through the j.n.o.v. motion. *Slocum v. New York Life Ins. Co.,* 228 U.S. 364 (1913). However, the Supreme Court retreated from this position in *Baltimore & Carolina Line, Inc. v. Redman,* 295 U.S. 654 (1935). In *Redman,* the court held that it was permissible for the court to grant judgment notwithstanding the verdict if the moving party had sought a directed verdict before the jury deliberated and the court had reserved decision on the motion.[4] The first sentence of Rule 50(b) embodies the *Redman* fiction that the judge who denies a directed verdict has simply delayed decision upon it, rather than "reexamined" the jury's findings.

The second reason for requiring a directed verdict motion as a prerequisite for granting j.n.o.v. is more substantial. A party who moves for a directed verdict at the close of the case must state her grounds for concluding that the case should not be submitted to the jury. Fed. R. Civ. P. 50(a); see also Fed. R. Civ. P. 7(a). Thus, the motion will alert the court and the opposing party to the defects in that party's case before the jury has gone out, while there is still time to offer further evidence to cure the defect. Thus, the system by requiring the directed verdict motion in order to preserve the right to move for j.n.o.v. prevents a party from "sandbagging" her opponent by raising the defects in the opponent's evidence after the jury has been discharged, when it is too late to cure the defects. It may be frustrating to a careful lawyer to be forced to help a less perceptive opponent make her case by pointing out those defects. However, remember that the entire thrust of the Rules is to ensure

---

3. Entry of judgment occurs when the court clerk enters a notation of the judgment on the case docket. See Fed. R. Civ. P. 58, 79(a). It is also permissible to seek j.n.o.v. after the verdict but before entry of judgment; Rule 50(b) merely requires that the motion be made "not later than" ten days after entry of judgment.

4. This was regarded as permissible, despite the "reexamination" clause in the seventh amendment, because the court was deemed to have the power to direct the verdict for the defendant without ever sending the case to the jury. If the judge can do that, the *Redman* court reasoned, she should also be allowed to submit the case subject to a subsequent decision on the directed verdict motion. Instead of "reexamining" the jury's verdict, the judge is simply "examining" the sufficiency of the evidence for the first time, but a little late.

that suits are determined on the merits, not on the procedural skills of counsel.

## New Trial Distinguished

The judge may also deprive a party of a verdict by granting a new trial under Fed. R. Civ. P. 59. Unlike the j.n.o.v. motion, which leads to a judgment for the moving party, the grant of a new trial does not end the case but leads to a second trial on all or part of the case.

Rule 59 authorizes judges to grant new trials for any reasons for which they have been permitted under prior practice. A frequent ground for the grant of new trials under traditional practice was for errors in the trial process itself. Every litigant is entitled to "due process of law," including a fair trial procedure before her rights are determined. Any number of mistakes may be made in the course of trial, such as the improper admission or exclusion of evidence, improper instructions by the judge as to the legal principles the jury must apply, or juror contacts with witnesses outside the trial context. Errors of this sort may taint the jury's decision-making process, leading it to consider inappropriate information in reaching a verdict or to use the wrong rules of law in assessing liability or damages. See generally James and Hazard at §§7.17-7.19.

If the losing party moves for a new trial on the basis of such errors immediately after trial,[5] Rule 59 allows the judge to vacate the verdict and order the case retried in order to assure the parties a fair trial procedure. If she doesn't, the party prejudiced by the improper conduct at trial will doubtless appeal, the appellate court will reverse, and a new trial will be ordered anyway, after much additional litigation effort.[6] The judge can save the parties and the court much time by correcting her own error — always assuming, of course, that she is convinced that she made one.

In addition to new trials for procedural errors, the trial judge has traditionally had the power to grant a new trial if she believes the trial *process* was fair but the *result* is clearly wrong. In the federal system, cases indicate that the judge may grant a new trial if the jury's verdict is "against the 'clear weight,' 'overwhelming weight,' or 'great weight' of the evidence" (*Goldsmith v. Diamond Shamrock Corp.*, 767 F.2d 411, 416 (8th Cir. 1985)); when it is "quite clear that the jury has reached a seriously erroneous result" (*Lind v. Schenley Industries, Inc.*, 278 F.2d 79, 89 (3d Cir. 1960)); or when a new trial "is necessary to prevent injustice" (*Whalen v. Roanoke County Board of Supervisors*, 769 F.2d 221, 226 (4th Cir. 1985)). Under such formu-

---

5. The motion for new trial, like the Rule 50(b) motion for j.n.o.v., must be made within ten days of entry of judgment. Fed. R. Civ. P. 59(b).

6. In many cases, however, erroneous decisions in the course of trial will not affect the substantial rights of the parties. Such "harmless error[s]" will not support a grant of a new trial, j.n.o.v., or reversal on appeal. See Fed. R. Civ. P. 61.

las the judge cannot displace the verdict simply because she disagrees with the jury. But she may order a new trial in cases in which the evidence is strong enough to rationally support the jury's verdict, but she believes that verdict is seriously erroneous (represented, perhaps, by point Q on the diagram in the last chapter, p. 219; see also the comparative chart on p. 248 infra).

In passing on the new trial motion the judge may consider the credibility of the witnesses, unlike the directed verdict or j.n.o.v. motion, which requires her to assume the truth of the evidence for the nonmoving party. Thus, the judge in passing on the motion for a new trial acts to some extent as a "thirteenth juror," making an independent assessment of the evidence. The judgment to be made is not whether the verdict was totally irrational but whether the judge is convinced that it is so strongly suspect that it would serve the ends of justice to have another jury hear the case.

Arguably, the judge's power to grant a new trial on this ground is even more intrusive than directing a verdict since the standard for doing so is less stringent than the directed verdict/j.n.o.v. standard. However, it may be defended on the ground that a new *jury*, not the judge, will reconsider the case if the motion is granted. In fact, if a new trial is granted, the next step in the case will be to hold the second trial. Under federal procedure, the party who won the verdict may not immediately appeal the judge's new trial grant since it is an interlocutory decision. See 28 U.S.C. §1291; 6A Moore's at ¶59.15[1].

The judge may also grant partial new trials in appropriate cases. If, for example, the jury's verdict on liability is clearly supportable but the damages greatly exceed the losses reflected in the evidence, the judge may order a new trial as to damages only.[7] In other cases, the judge may find the verdict against one defendant clearly supported by the evidence but not against another and grant a new trial solely on the claims against the second defendant.

An important difference between new trials for trial error and for verdicts against the weight of the evidence is the standard of appellate review. Questions concerning the admission or exclusion of evidence or the proper instructions to the jury involve issues of law, which can be reviewed de novo by the courts of appeals. Appellate judges, after all, are specialists in such legal questions. However, whether the verdict goes against the great weight of the evidence is a delicate decision that requires a balancing of evidence, usually including live testimony, which only the trial judge has had a full opportunity to observe. Consequently, it is rare for appellate judges to second guess the trial judge's on the spot judgment that a new trial is warranted on this

---

7. In cases where the verdict is excessive, the judge may also offer the plaintiff a remittitur. Under remittitur practice, the court agrees to enter judgment for the plaintiff if she will accept a lesser sum than the jury's verdict. If the plaintiff refuses to accept the remittitur, the judge orders a new trial. See generally James and Hazard at §7.21, pp.395-400.

ground. Early federal cases suggested that the grant of a new trial on this ground was "unreviewable," that is, committed completely to the discretion of the trial court. See *Fairmont Glass Works v. Cub Fork Coal Co.*, 287 U.S. 474, 481-482 (1940). The current trend, however, is for the courts of appeals to review new trial grants under an abuse of discretion standard. See Friedenthal, Kane, and Miller at §12.4, pp.559-560.

The first questions that follow illustrate the relationship between directed verdict, j.n.o.v., and new trial. The second part of the chapter explores the procedural complexities of joint motions under Rule 50(c) and (d). Assume that all actions are brought in federal court.

# QUESTIONS

## Never Say Die

1.   Milne brings an action against Potter for interference with a copyright Milne holds on a book about a bear. The case is tried to a jury. Potter moves for a directed verdict at the close of Milne's evidence. The motion is denied. Potter renews the motion after presenting her own evidence. The motion is denied again. The jury is instructed, deliberates, and returns a verdict for Milne. May Potter now move for j.n.o.v.?

2.   Potter, the defendant, moves for a directed verdict at the close of the evidence. The motion is denied. The jury returns a verdict for Potter. Milne believes that the jury's verdict is completely unsupported by the evidence.

   a.   May Milne now move for j.n.o.v.?

   b.   May he move for a new trial?

3.   Assume, as in question 1, that Potter (the defendant) moved for a directed verdict at the close of Milne's evidence, but did not renew her motion at the close of all the evidence. The verdict went for Milne, and Potter now moves for j.n.o.v. Is the motion proper under the Rule?

4.   Potter moves for a directed verdict at the close of the evidence. The motion is denied, and the jury returns a verdict for Milne. Judgment is entered on the verdict. Potter believes that the verdict is completely unsupported by the evidence. Three days later, she moves for j.n.o.v. The judge denies the motion five weeks later. Potter now moves for a new trial, on the ground that the judge improperly excluded important evidence at trial and that the verdict is against the weight of the evidence. The judge, after research, agrees on the evidentiary point but not the "weight of the evidence" point. What should the judge do?

## Contingency Planning

5.   Assume the same basic facts as question 4, except that both parties have some complaints about the trial. The jury rendered a verdict for Milne, but Potter believes that the judge should have granted her directed verdict mo-

tion. She also objects to the judge's instruction on the standard for liability. Milne is satisfied with the verdict but is also convinced that his case would have been stronger if the judge had not excluded important evidence that he offered at trial.

    a.   How should Potter present her objections?

    b.   What should Milne do about his objection to the exclusion of the evidence?

6.   After trial the jury returns a verdict for Potter. Milne moves for a new trial on the ground that the judge improperly instructed the jury on the application of the copyright statute. Potter argues strenuously that the instructions were proper. The judge concludes that Milne is right and orders a new trial. What happens next? See 28 U.S.C. §1291.

7.   Once again, assume that Milne loses. In frustration, he reviews his trial notes and recalls that the judge allowed Potter to introduce hearsay evidence that probably should have been excluded. Although he had not objected at the time, he researches the evidentiary issue and concludes that the evidence was indeed improperly admitted. Within the ten-day period, he makes two motions, one for a new trial on the ground that the evidence should have been excluded and a second motion for j.n.o.v. on the ground that without the inadmissible evidence the case for Potter was too weak to go to the jury. Should the judge grant either or both motions?

8.   Assume that *Milne v. Potter* was tried before the judge, instead of a jury. After a full hearing, the judge finds for Milne and enters judgment accordingly. Potter believes that the judge improperly excluded important evidence she had offered on the liability issue.

    a.   How should Potter present her objection before the trial court?

    b.   What will the judge do if she agrees with Potter?

# Combined Motions and Appellate Review

As the questions above suggest, counsel for both parties may have multiple objections to the course of the trial, which they will seek to raise after trial by combined post-trial motions for j.n.o.v. and new trial or by motions for new trial asserting several grounds. Subsections (c) and (d) were added to Rule 50 in 1963 to guide the federal district courts and courts of appeals in disposing of such combined motions.

Under Rule 50(c)(1), the trial judge confronted with a combined motion for j.n.o.v. or new trial must not only rule on the j.n.o.v. motion but must also make a conditional ruling on the alternative motion for new trial. The purpose for requiring both rulings is to allow the court of appeals to address all the parties' objections to the trial in one consolidated appeal if the case is appealed. A similar purpose lies behind Rule 50(d), which allows a party who won the verdict below but has it taken away on appeal to assert objections to the original trial process.

The questions that follow should help you to see how the use of combined motions under these two intimidating provisions facilitates the disposition of cases on appeal. For some very helpful background you may want to read *Montgomery Ward & Co. v. Duncan*, 311 U.S. 243 (1940), in which the Supreme Court established the broad outlines of the procedure later embodied in Rules 50(c) and (d). However, you should be able to answer the questions from a careful reading of these parts of the rule.

# QUESTIONS

## No Stone Unturned

9.   Carroll sues Alcott for breach of contract. The jury returns a verdict for Carroll and judgment is entered on the verdict. Alcott moves for j.n.o.v. and in the alternative for a new trial on the ground that the verdict is against the weight of the evidence. The judge grants the j.n.o.v. motion and "conditionally" grants the new trial motion as well.

    a.   May Carroll appeal at this point?

    b.   Assume that when the case reaches the court of appeals that court holds that the evidence was sufficient to go to the jury, so that j.n.o.v. should not have been granted. What will the court do next?

10.   Alcott loses at trial and moves for j.n.o.v. and for a new trial on the ground that the verdict was against the weight of the evidence and that the judge's instructions to the jury were improper. The judge denies both motions. Alcott appeals. What will the court of appeals do if

    a.   it concludes that j.n.o.v. should have been granted?

    b.   it concludes that j.n.o.v. was properly denied and that the verdict was not against the weight of the evidence but that the instructions were improper?

11.   Assume that the jury returns a verdict for Carroll, the plaintiff, and Alcott makes a motion for j.n.o.v. as well as a motion for a new trial on the ground that the judge excluded admissible evidence crucial to her case. The judge denies j.n.o.v. but grants the motion for a new trial. May Carroll appeal? May Alcott?

## Delayed Reaction

12.   Assume that both Alcott and Carroll are unhappy with the trial. The jury returned a verdict for Carroll, but Alcott believes that the evidence was too weak to support the verdict. Carroll believes the verdict is proper but also believes that the judge improperly excluded evidence that would have strengthened his case. Alcott moves for j.n.o.v.; Carroll opposes the motion but makes none of his own. The motion is denied. Alcott appeals on the ground that j.n.o.v. should have been granted, and the court of appeals agrees. Where does the case go from here?

# ANALYSIS

## Never Say Die

1.   In this case Potter has already twice asked the judge to rule that Milne's evidence is too weak to go to the jury. Each time the judge has allowed the case to proceed. However, this does not bar Potter from renewing her challenge to the sufficiency of the evidence by seeking j.n.o.v. Every party who asks the court for j.n.o.v. will have moved for a directed verdict before the jury retires. As the introduction indicates, the rule requires this motion to preserve the right to move for j.n.o.v. The judge's denial of the directed verdict does not necessarily indicate that she believes the evidence poses a jury issue; she may simply wish to reserve judgment on the issue, so as to get the jury's verdict and save a complete retrial if the j.n.o.v. decision is reversed on appeal.

2a.   Rule 50(b) only authorizes a party who has moved for a directed verdict to seek j.n.o.v. for the reasons discussed in the introduction. Although Potter moved for a directed verdict at the close of the case, Milne did not. Thus, Milne's failure to seek a directed verdict will bar him from seeking judgment notwithstanding the verdict after the jury finds for Potter.

Potter may not argue that her motion is proper because Milne sought a directed verdict before the case went to the jury. As discussed in the introduction, the prior directed verdict motion is required in order to alert the opposing party to weaknesses in that party's case. Potter's motion was obviously directed to the weaknesses in Milne's case, not her own.

b.   Milne is barred from seeking entry of judgment in his favor under Rule 50(b), but Rule 59 contains no analogous requirement of a prior directed verdict motion in order to move for a new trial on the ground that the verdict is against the weight of the evidence. 6A Moore's at ¶59.04[5]. Since Milne believes the evidence was too weak to support a rational verdict for Potter, he presumably also believes that the verdict is against the great weight of the evidence. Thus, Milne can at least ask the judge to vacate the verdict and grant a new trial on this ground. That will not get him the judgment but will at least give him the opportunity to convince another jury of the strength of his case.

3.   It is established that a party must move for a directed verdict in order to preserve the right to seek j.n.o.v., but it is less clear when the directed verdict motion must be made. Even Rule 50(b) is unclear on this point. The first sentence ("Whenever a motion for a directed verdict at the close of all the evidence is denied . . .") suggests that the fiction about reserving judgment requires a motion for directed verdict at the close of all the evidence. But the second sentence simply refers to "a party who has moved for a directed verdict."

Rule 50(b) has usually been construed to require a directed verdict motion at the close of all the evidence. See 5A Moore's at ¶50.08. However, some recent cases have adopted a more flexible approach to this requirement and entertained motions for j.n.o.v. if the moving party has sought a directed verdict earlier in the trial. See, e.g., *Bohrer v. Hanes Corp.*, 715 F.2d 213, 216-217 (5th Cir. 1983). Although these cases may blink at the language of Rule 50(a), they are faithful to the policy underlying the prior directed verdict requirement. In this case, for example, Potter's motion at the close of the plaintiff's evidence should alert Milne to the unproved elements in his case since he will have already offered all the evidence he believes is necessary to make a prima facie case.

4.    The judge must deny the motion despite her conclusion that Potter has a valid claim that the trial was unfair. Under Rule 59, as under Rule 50(b), the motion must be made within ten days of the entry of judgment. Potter's original j.n.o.v. motion was timely, but her subsequent new trial motion was not, and the making of one post-trial motion does not suspend the time for making the other. Potter should have made both motions together within ten days of entry of judgment in order to assert all of her objections in a timely fashion. See Rule 50(b), third sentence, which authorizes combined motions for new trial and j.n.o.v.

Nor may the judge relieve Potter of her procedural mistake by granting the motion for a new trial on her own motion. Rule 59(d) authorizes the trial judge to grant a new trial sua sponte but requires her to do so within ten days of the entry of judgment. The implication is that she may not correct an error brought to her attention after this period has lapsed. This limitation seems unfortunate, at least where the judge becomes convinced of the error within the 30-day appeal period in Fed. R. App. P. 4(a)(1). If the judge is really convinced that she improperly excluded evidence that would have affected the result, it makes sense to allow her to grant the new trial. Otherwise, Potter will be forced to appeal and the court of appeals to hear and decide an appeal that could have been avoided by the grant of a new trial as soon as the error became apparent.[8]

The reason for the strict rule limiting the time for granting a new trial is the strong principle in favor of finality of judgments. Parties must know at some point that the decision rendered in an action will not be revised, so they can order their affairs accordingly. If the judge could reconsider at any time, the outcome would still remain uncertain despite the entry of a "final" judgment.

## Contingency Planning

5a.    It is not unusual for both parties to have some complaints about the conduct of a trial. Here, Potter believes that the outcome was unwarranted

---

8. The judge might be able to achieve the same result by granting relief from the judgment under Fed. R. Civ. P. 60(b), at least before the period for appeal of the judgment has run. See Chapter 18, question 15.

by the evidence and, in addition, that the process was tainted due to improper instructions. Milne is content with the outcome but believes that he could have made an even stronger case if all his evidence had been placed before the jury.

Potter, of course, should move for j.n.o.v. since she believes that the evidence was too weak to support a rational verdict for Milne. In addition, if she believes the evidence was so weak as to justify a directed verdict, she must also believe it was against the great weight of the evidence. Consequently, she should join with her j.n.o.v. motion a motion for a new trial on this ground. Last, she should assert the improper jury instruction as an alternative ground for a new trial. She may assert all three grounds in a combined motion, but must do so within ten days of entry of judgment.

b. Milne is in a slightly different position. Since he won the verdict, he has no cause to press his objection to the exclusion of evidence (unless, of course, the evidence went to the size of the verdict and he is unhappy with that). He prevailed without the evidence and presumably has no interest in trying the suit again just to have a perfect process. However, Milne is still somewhat at risk since Potter has asked the judge to displace the jury's verdict. If the judge grants j.n.o.v. for Potter on the ground that Milne had not produced sufficient evidence to pose a jury issue, Milne will surely wish to argue that he *could* have made a submissible case if the judge had not excluded important evidence.

Of course, the rulemakers have thought of everything and provided for this contingency. Rule 50(c)(2) allows Milne to move for a new trial on the ground that the evidence was improperly excluded within ten days after the judge deprives him of his victory by entering judgment notwithstanding the verdict. Thus, he need not raise the objection until it becomes apparent that the judge's evidentiary ruling may have prejudiced his case.

6.    Since Potter's position is that the instruction was proper, she would like to take an immediate appeal in hopes that the court of appeals will agree with her, reverse the new trial grant, and enter judgment on the jury's verdict. However, when a new trial motion is granted, the judge will enter an order for the case to be retried. As the introduction states (supra p. 237), Potter may not appeal the judge's decision to grant a new trial until after the new trial is held because in the federal system a new trial grant is not considered a final judgment in the trial court.

Thus, Potter will have to go through the second trial before appealing. If she wins at the second trial, she will presumably be satisfied with the result (though not the elongated process to reach it) and have no incentive to appeal the grant of the new trial. However, if she loses at the second trial and judgment is entered on the verdict for Milne, Potter will now be able to appeal the judge's earlier decision to grant the new trial since the court will render a final judgment on the second verdict (assuming no further motions for new trial are granted after the *second* trial). The court of appeals will then review the disputed instruction from the first trial. If it agrees with Potter that the original instruction was proper, it will enter judgment on the original verdict for her. If the appellate court upholds the trial judge's ruling that the initial instruction was wrong, it will uphold the grant of the new trial and (assuming no reversible error in the second trial) affirm the judgment for Milne.

Although there is logic to delaying review of the new trial grant in these cases, there is also much to be said for immediate appeal. If the case is reviewed before the new trial and the decision to grant the new trial is reversed, the parties and the court will not be put to the considerable effort of trying the case a second time, perhaps to no purpose. For these reasons some state systems allow interlocutory review of new trial grants. See Freidenthal, Kane, and Miller at pp.558-559.[9]

7.    The question here indicates that Milne did not object to the judge's error in admitting the evidence at the time that the error was made. In most cases the failure to object to the ruling during trial will foreclose relief on a motion for new trial afterwards. See 11 Wright and Miller at §2805, p.39 (in absence of a timely objection, new trial will not be granted "unless the error was so fundamental that gross injustice would result"). Although this rule seems draconian, especially given the pressures of trial, it makes good sense. If the error is brought to the judge's attention immediately, she may exclude the evidence and avoid a reversible error. If it is only raised after trial by the new trial motion, it is too late to save the trial.

Indeed, if Milne could raise such objections without having objected during trial, it would open the door to manipulation of the trial process. Milne might deliberately withhold objection to one or more arguably prejudicial decisions of the trial judge. Then if he lost the verdict, he could undermine the unfavorable verdict by pulling these objections out of his hat as grounds for a new trial.

The judge will also deny Milne's motion for j.n.o.v. Milne's argument here is that the evidence would have been too weak to go to the jury if the disputed evidence had not been admitted. Here again it is up to Milne to avoid the error by a timely objection rather than use it later to overturn the jury's verdict.

8a.   Parties have the same right to seek a new trial in cases tried to the judge as they do in jury cases. See Fed. R. Civ. P. 59(a)(2). Potter should make her motion for a new trial (often called a "rehearing" in nonjury cases) within ten days of entry of judgment, stating as her ground the exclusion of the disputed evidence.

---

9. In some cases, a grant of new trial may be subject to review by some extraordinary writ. The appellate court might, for example, hear a petition for interlocutory relief if the trial court had acted beyond its jurisdiction in granting the new trial. But such relief is not available simply to correct an error in the judge's ruling. See generally 6A Moore's at ¶59.15[2].

b. Although the procedure for presenting the motion is similar, the procedure on rehearing in a nonjury trial may differ significantly from a new trial in a jury case. In a jury case, the jury is discharged after a verdict is reached. They cannot be called back after the new trial is granted to hear the additional evidence that had been wrongly excluded. Thus, the only way to provide both parties with a full opportunity to be heard is to start over and present all the evidence to a new jury in a complete new trial.

In a nonjury case, however, the judge need not go back and start from square one. She has already heard all the evidence and decided the relevant legal rules to apply in reaching a decision. If Potter's only objection is that the judge failed to consider certain evidence (and if the judge concludes that she is right), the judge can reopen the hearing, hear that evidence, and reconsider the case taking the additional evidence into account. Thus the rehearing in such cases can be a relatively brief proceeding to simply augment the record with the additional evidence. See Fed. R. Civ. P. 59(a), second sentence.

If Potter's objection had been that the judge *admitted* evidence that should have been excluded, the "rehearing" might be even simpler. The judge could simply sustain the motion and reconsider the case without taking the inadmissible evidence into account. At least that's the theory. In practice it is obviously questionable whether the judge can really disregard persuasive evidence that she has already heard simply on the technical ground that it is inadmissible under the rules of evidence.[10]

## No Stone Unturned

9a. Carroll may appeal the judge's combined ruling, even though the new trial was "conditionally" (Fed. R. Civ. P. 50(c)(1)) granted. The judge has ordered judgment for Alcott as a result of the j.n.o.v. ruling, and the rule makes clear that that judgment is final. Fed. R. Civ. P. 50(c)(1), second sentence. Alcott is the winner and if no one appeals there will be no new trial. The purpose of requiring the judge to rule conditionally on Alcott's alternative motion for a new trial is to help the court of appeals to decide how to dispose of the case if it reverses the j.n.o.v. decision.

b. If Carroll appeals and the court reverses the j.n.o.v. decision, the judge's conditional ruling on the new trial motion assists the appellate court in deciding what should happen next in the case. Because the judge has ruled that a new trial should be granted, the court of appeals can review that conditional decision on appeal from the entry of j.n.o.v. If it concludes that

---

10. Indeed, if there is evidence in a case that is extremely persuasive but probably inadmissible under the rules of evidence, this may be a strong tactical reason for seeking a jury trial. In all cases the judge must see the evidence that is offered in order to pass on its admissibility. If she is also the factfinder, it will be difficult for her to disregard what she has seen. If the case is tried to a jury, however, the judge will see such evidence but the factfinder (the jury) will not.

the judge did not abuse her discretion in concluding that the verdict went against the clear weight of the evidence, the court can uphold the grant of the new trial and remand the case to the trial court for retrial. If, on the other hand, the court concludes that even the new trial motion should not have been granted (an unlikely decision, given the broad discretion accorded the trial court in making the new trial decision), it may reverse both decisions and order entry of judgment for Carroll. See Fed. R. Civ. P. 50(c)(1), third sentence.

The good sense of this procedure is highlighted by considering the alternative. If the trial judge decided only the j.n.o.v. motion, and that were reversed, the court of appeals would presumably have to remand for the judge to consider whether the alternative motion for new trial should be granted. If she granted it on remand, the new trial would proceed since the grant of a new trial is an interlocutory decision. Only after a second trial would Carroll be able to challenge the new trial grant, on a second appeal.

On the other hand, if the judge denied the motion for a new trial on remand after reversal of j.n.o.v., Alcott would appeal and a second trip to the court of appeals would be needed to fully dispose of the case. The Rule 50(c) procedure for conditional rulings on both motions allows consolidated treatment and decision on the motions and assists the appellate court in fully disposing of the case.

10a. If the court concludes that j.n.o.v. should have been granted because the evidence was too weak to go to the jury, it may enter j.n.o.v. itself. Unlike the discretionary decision as to whether the verdict was contrary to the clear weight of the evidence, which involves consideration of the credibility of witnesses, the j.n.o.v. decision is a question of law that the appellate court reviews de novo. The court must review all the evidence, consider it in the light most favorable to the nonmoving party (under the directed verdict/ j.n.o.v. standard), and make its own judgment as to whether Carroll's case was strong enough to submit to the jury.

b. If the court of appeals concludes that j.n.o.v. was properly denied and that the verdict is not against the weight of the evidence, it will also consider whether the new trial should have been granted due to legal error in the instructions. The issue of the proper rules for the jury to apply in deciding the case is obviously a question of law, which the court of appeals decides de novo. If the court concludes that the jury was not properly instructed, it can remand for a new trial. If the instructions were correct, it can affirm the denial of the new trial and (since it had already ruled that j.n.o.v. was properly denied) affirm the entry of judgment for Carroll. Either way the use of combined motions again allows the appellate court to dispose of all of the losing party's objections without remand for decision of further post-trial motions.

11. Neither party may appeal at the time of the judge's decision on the motions. Since j.n.o.v. was denied but a new trial granted, there is no final

judgment but rather a pending order for a new trial in the district court. Absent some ground for extraordinary review, the parties will have to go through the second trial. If Carroll loses at the second trial, he may appeal from the final judgment, asserting as error the judge's decision to grant a new trial (as well as any errors he claims took place in the second trial).

## Delayed Reaction

12. The situation here is similar to that in question 5b, in which the plaintiff won the verdict but had the victory snatched away when the judge granted j.n.o.v. for the defendant. Here, the same thing happened, except that it was the court of appeals rather than the trial judge that displaced the verdict. Until j.n.o.v. was granted on appeal, Carroll was content with the result of the original trial. Although he believed his case would have been stronger if the excluded evidence had been admitted, it was already strong enough to win. Thus Carroll had no reason to seek a new trial due to the exclusion of the evidence.

It is only after the court of appeals deprives him of his judgment by holding that j.n.o.v. should have been granted for Alcott that Carroll will wish to raise his objection to the evidentiary ruling. At that point, he will want to argue that the original trial was flawed and that he is entitled to a new trial at which the excluded evidence is placed before the jury. After all, it may be that his case was too weak to reach the jury precisely because that evidence was excluded.

Under Rule 50(d) Carroll may raise this argument at the appeal stage even if he did not seek a new trial in the district court or assert the evidentiary point on a cross-appeal. (Of course, he would have had to object at the time the evidence was excluded. See the answer to question 7.) In *Neely v. Eby Construction Co.*, 386 U.S. 317 (1967), the Supreme Court suggested that a party in Carroll's position could raise such objections either in the trial court (by a conditional motion for a new trial even though he was the verdict *winner*), in his brief as the appellee when Alcott appeals the denial of j.n.o.v. (even though he had no complaint with the final outcome of the trial), or even after the court of appeals reverses the entry of j.n.o.v., by a petition for rehearing in that court. See *Neely* at 328-329. If Carroll raises the issue after j.n.o.v. is granted by the court of appeals, that court may order a new trial or remand to allow the trial judge to address the motion. Fed. R. Civ. P. 50(d).

**Tab. 17–1:** The Judge's Power to Displace the Jury's Verdict: A Schematic

(This chart is a trifle oversimplified, but it should help you to see the general relation of the motions.)

| | ← weaker evidence for plaintiff | | Evidence Evenly Balanced | stronger evidence for plaintiff → | |
|---|---|---|---|---|---|
| Judge's assessment of the evidence | Evidence too weak to support a rational verdict for plaintiff | A verdict for plaintiff is supportable, but against clear weight of the evidence | Judge does not agree with jury, but cannot say verdict for plaintiff is against clear weight of the evidence | Judge and jury concur that preponderance of the evidence favors plaintiff | Judge concludes that evidence is so compelling that no reasonable jury could find for defendant (rare — see infra p. 228) |
| Judge's disposition of the case | Judge may enter directed verdict or j.n.o.v. for defendant | Judge may order new trial | Judge will order entry of judgment on the jury's verdict | Judge will order entry of judgment on the verdict for plaintiff | Judge enters directed verdict or j.n.o.v. for plaintiff |
| | X | | Z | | Y |

# PART FOUR

---

# *The Effect of the Judgment*

# 18

## Res Judicata: The Limits of Procedural Liberality

## Introduction

Perhaps you are thoroughly tired of hearing how *reasonable* the Federal Rules of Civil Procedure are. Certainly, one of the recurrent themes of the Rules is to create a flexible procedural system in order to prevent procedure from dominating substance, to assure that the merits of the parties' claims, not procedural missteps, determine the outcome of lawsuits.

For example, parties are given broad power to join claims and parties in a single suit. Fed. R. Civ. P. 13, 14, 18, 20, 24. They are given the latitude to plead all their possible claims against opposing parties, within the limits of good faith pleading. Fed. R. Civ. P. 8(a), 8(e)(2), 11. Pleadings are liberally construed, Fed. R. Civ. P. 8(f); *Conley v. Gibson,* 355 U.S. 41 (1957), and amendments freely allowed. Fed. R. Civ. P. 15(a). Even if amendments are not offered, the court can treat the pleadings *as though* they had been amended when justice so requires, Fed. R. Civ. P. 15(b), and may grant parties the relief to which they are entitled even though they never asked for it. Fed. R. Civ. P. 54(c). If the process still goes awry, despite all these opportunities to correct procedural errors, the court may grant relief from judgment, Fed. R. Civ. P. 60(b), or a new trial. Fed. R. Civ. P. 59.

Given all this procedural liberality, you might expect that the rules governing relitigation of claims would be correspondingly indulgent. However, the exact opposite is true. Once the parties have had a full and fair opportunity to be heard under the flexible rules reviewed above, all this paternalistic indulgence comes to an abrupt halt. Regardless of a party's reason for wishing to relitigate a dispute, the doctrine of res judicata stands like a brutish, unreflecting myrmidon, guarding the doors of the courthouse.[1] While the Rules are liberal, res judicata is strict and uncharitable. No matter how unfair the result in the first suit may seem or indeed, no matter how unfair it may actually have been, the myrmidon will not step aside.

For example, suppose that the plaintiff in the Schulansky case recovers $7,000 from Ronan for breach of contract. If Schulansky believes that the verdict was too low, she cannot bring a second action against Ronan for more. Or, if she discovers a statute that allows a more generous measure of damages, she cannot bring a new action based on that statute. If Schulansky loses but believes that her lawyer did not litigate the case energetically, she will be barred by res judicata from trying again with a new lawyer.

In the traditional terminology, Schulansky's claim was said to be "merged" into the judgment she had won. That is, the claim was extinguished and replaced by the judgment. Restatement (Second) of Judgments §§17, 18 (1982). Once the judgment was entered a suit could be brought to enforce that judgment if necessary (see Chapter 3, p. 38) but no further suit could be brought on the extinguished claim. Conversely, if Schulansky lost her claim was said to be "barred" by the adverse judgment so that no further suit could be brought on the claim.

The rationale for the doctrine is ancient and fundamental. From the point of view of the parties litigation is burdensome enough the first time without redoing it again whenever one of the parties is unhappy with the result. Parties must also get on with their affairs; without the certainty provided by res judicata, parties would not be able to rely on court decisions in planning their future conduct. Last, from the point of view of the system, there is no justification for multiplying the costs and delay of litigation by allowing parties to go at it again once they have had a full and fair opportunity to litigate a claim.

Of course, the efficiency of res judicata would not be justified if it were achieved at the expense of fairness to the parties in presenting meritorious claims. For example, it would be a hard system indeed that barred the plaintiff from amending his complaint to assert new theories for relief unearthed during discovery and also barred him from bringing a separate action based on those theories. But, if amendments are liberally allowed in the first suit, it is reasonable to bar a second. Thus, it is precisely because the Rules of Civil Procedure are so liberal in facilitating presentation of claims in the first action that the res judicata myrmidon can so stubbornly bar relitigation. Conversely,

---

1. A myrmidon is a servant who mindlessly but doggedly obeys his master's every command. The first myrmidons were ants, who were changed into men by Zeus to repopulate the island kingdom of Aegina. They were known for their loyalty and courage in following their leader, Achilles, in the Trojan War. See E. Hamilton, Mythology 296 (1969).

the specter of res judicata encourages parties to take full advantage of the Rules to present their claims initially since they know that they will not get a second chance to try the suit, that there will be no "second bite at the apple."

# The Basic Prerequisites

In most jurisdictions, there are four prerequisites for res judicata: (1) there must be a final judgment, (2) the judgment must be "on the merits," (3) the claims must be the same in the first and second suits, and (4) the parties in the second action must be the same as those in the first (or in privity with a party to the prior action). Most of the interpretive issues in applying the doctrine concern the requirements that the claims be the same in both suits and that the original judgment be on the merits.

The definition of a single "claim" for res judicata purposes varies from one jurisdiction to another. See generally Friedenthal, Kane, and Miller at §14.4. The federal courts and an increasing number of states have adopted the standard in the Restatement (Second) of Judgments §24 (1982), which essentially equates a party's claim for res judicata purposes with the "transaction or occurrence" test of the federal joinder rules. See 18 Wright and Miller at §4407, p.62. Under this view, a party who has asserted a right to relief arising out of a particular transaction or occurrence must join all claims he has arising from it, or the omitted claims will be barred by res judicata.

There is good sense to a theory that makes the scope of preclusion mirror the test for joinder under the Rules. If a party had the right to join two claims for relief arising from the same transaction in the first suit, it is reasonable to require him to do so instead of bringing two suits that will rehash the same facts. Conversely, if the scope of preclusion is to mirror the scope of permissible joinder, res judicata should *not* bar claims that could not have been joined in the first action. For example, before the development of the unified civil action under the Rules, parties could not always seek equitable and legal relief in the same proceeding: They might have been forced to split their claims between the law courts and the chancery courts. See generally James and Hazard at 14-17. In such cases, a party who had sought damages in an action at law was not precluded from seeking injunctive relief based on the same transaction or occurrence from a court of equity because he could not have obtained that relief in the prior action at law. Under the Federal Rules, however, parties may almost always assert all their claims in a single suit, and res judicata is correspondingly broad.[2]

Under the transaction or occurrence test, preclusion turns on the *right* to join the claim in the original action, not on whether the claim actually was

---

2. In some circumstances, however, the right to join claims under the Rules does not automatically lead to the conclusion that res judicata will bar a separate suit on those claims. See Chapter 19.

asserted. Consequently, claims need not have actually been litigated to be barred in a later action; they need only have been *available* to the plaintiff in the first suit. For example, it is clear that Schulansky after recovering $7,000 from Ronan in the contract action described in Part Five could not sue Ronan again for this claim on a breach of contract theory. However, res judicata will also bar Schulansky from suing Ronan for fraud even though she had never pleaded fraud in her first suit, never tried the case on a fraud theory, and in fact never thought of it. Indeed, the message of res judicata is that Schulansky (or, more particularly, Schulansky's lawyer) had *better* think of it, sooner rather than later.

Another res judicata prerequisite that has raised interpretive problems is the requirement of a decision "on the merits" in the first action. Clearly, a full trial followed by a verdict and judgment is the paradigm of a decision on the merits. At the other extreme, preliminary dismissals, such as dismissals for improper venue or lack of personal jurisdiction, do not bar a second action, on the rationale that the court never reached the merits in the first action, much less decided it after a full opportunity to be heard. The very basis of such dismissals is that the court does not have the power to reach the merits because the plaintiff has chosen an improper court under the "three-ring" analysis.

The toughest cases fall between these extremes. For example, jurisdictions differ as to whether a dismissal for failure to state a claim should bar a second action. The Restatement (Second) of Judgments concludes that such dismissals should bar relitigation on the theory that a plaintiff whose complaint is dismissed for failure to state a claim is allowed liberal opportunities to amend. Restatement (Second) of Judgments §19, comment d (1982). If he cannot amend to state a compensable claim on a second or third try, it is presumably because he has no right to relief under the law. If that is true, there is no reason to allow him to harass the defendant with a new action. This is the rule applied in the federal courts. However, some state courts allow a second action under these circumstances because comparatively little litigation effort goes into these preliminary dismissals and hence a basic value underlying res judicata, preservation of scarce judicial resources, is not compromised by allowing a new action.

A judgment must also be "final" before res judicata attaches. There is obviously little point in barring a second action on a claim that has not yet been fully resolved in the first. Suppose, for example, that Schulansky sues Ronan in federal court on breach of contract and fraud theories, and the court dismisses the fraud claim under Fed. R. Civ. P. 12(b)(6) but allows the contract claim to proceed. Generally, courts remain free to reexamine their rulings made in the course of suit, including a ruling dismissing one of the plaintiff's claims. See 18 Wright and Miller at §4478. Thus, the preliminary dismissal might be reconsidered and vacated by the judge in the first action and remains too uncertain to support a res judicata plea in a separate action between the parties.

However, many courts give res judicata effect to a judgment once it has become final in the trial court even if an appeal is pending. This is the Restatement view. Restatement (Second) of Judgments §13, comment f (1982). Under this approach, a judgment may bar relitigation even though the original case is still being litigated and is not yet enforceable by execution or otherwise. Other courts, however, prefer to suspend the operation of res judicata until the time for appeal has passed or the case has been finally resolved by the appellate court. James and Hazard at §11.4, p.592.

In working through the questions that follow assume that all suits are brought in federal court and that the Restatement principles discussed above apply. If you want further background, Professor Wright has a good short discussion of the doctrine. Wright at pp.678-682. For more detail, I recommend the Second Restatement itself, which is replete with helpful examples and comments. Restatement (Second) of Judgments §§13-26 (1982). But keep in mind (not for the questions below but for those long lawyering years ahead) that the doctrine varies from one jurisdiction to another; the Restatement may not be "the law" in your state. Even if the Restatement principles are generally followed, each jurisdiction is likely to have its own quirks and quiddities that can only be learned from studying local practice.

# QUESTIONS

## Fielder's Choice

1.    Rizzuto's eye is injured when his baseball glove breaks while he is fielding a vicious grounder. He sues Allston Leather Company for negligent manufacture of the glove. The case is tried and judgment is entered for Allston. Later, Rizzuto sues again. He argues that the judge in the first suit erroneously excluded important evidence from Rizzuto's expert on baseball glove manufacturing standards and that he should have a chance to have a trial with all the admissible evidence properly before the jury. Allston pleads res judicata. Will the defense bar Rizzuto's second action?

2.    After the judgment for Allston in Rizzuto's case, Boyer tells Rizzuto that he recovered judgment against Allston for an injury using the same type of glove, on a strict liability theory, thus avoiding the necessity to prove that Allston was negligent. Rizzuto files a new action against Allston based on the original accident but asserting a right to recover only on the basis of strict liability. Will the claim be barred?

3.    Assume that Rizzuto won his first suit against Allston and recovered $3,000 in compensatory damages. Boyer subsequently tells him that he had claimed gross negligence by Allston in a prior suit based on the same defective glove and recovered punitive damages. Rizzuto brings a second action against Allston for punitive damages based on gross negligence. Can Allston plead res judicata?

4.    Assume that Rizzuto recovered $15,000 dollars in an action against Allston, but Allston was in shaky financial condition and never paid. Rizzuto

later brings a new action against Allston after learning that its financial condition has improved. Does res judicata bar the second suit?

5. Assume that Rizzuto's proof of damages in his original action against Allston included evidence that he suffered impaired vision in his eye as a result of the accident and pain and suffering for several weeks. This is the only evidence he presented on damages. The jury finds for Rizzuto and awards him $10,000 damages. Three years later, after the judgment has been entered and paid, Rizzuto develops migraine headaches. The doctor tells him that these often result from an eye injury and are likely to continue indefinitely. Can Rizzuto sue Allston for damages for these headaches?

## An Absurd Hypothetical

6. Imagine that Rizzuto's vicious grounder breaks through his glove, whacks him in the eye, and bounces off Kubek, injuring him as well. Kubek sues Allston and recovers. Rizzuto testifies in Kubek's suit. Rizzuto now takes the cue and brings an action to recover for his injuries in the same accident. Allston pleads the inevitable res judicata. Is the suit barred?

7. At the time Rizzuto was injured using Allston's glove, he had an endorsement contract with them to promote the glove in television commercials. He had made the ads, but had not been paid by Allston.

Acting on the advice of his lawyers that asserting the contract claim in the negligence suit would confuse matters, Rizzuto did not assert his contract claim in the negligence suit against Allston. Instead, he sues separately on the contract claim after judgment in the negligence action. Allston pleads res judicata. Was the lawyer's advice sound?

8. Assume that Rizzuto's contract calls for royalties (or "residuals" in the language of the trade) to be paid to Rizzuto for each year that the commercials are used. Allston pays the residuals in the first year at 5 percent, while Rizzuto claims it should be 10 percent. Rizzuto sues and wins. At the end of the next year, Allston pays Rizzuto again at the 5 percent rate. Rizzuto sues again and Allston pleads res judicata. Is the second action barred?

9. Rizzuto sues Allston to collect under the endorsement contract. Allston defends the action and wins on the ground that Rizzuto had not performed his obligations under the contract because he abandoned filming after making several commercials. Allston subsequently brings a separate suit against Rizzuto for *his* breach of the contract. Is Allston's suit precluded by res judicata?

## Judgment on the Merits

10. Rizzuto sues Allston on the negligence claim in federal court. Allston moves to dismiss under Fed. R. Civ. P. 12(b)(1) for lack of subject matter jurisdiction on the ground that complete diversity does not exist because its principal place of business is in New York (Rizzuto's home state). The court

holds a full evidentiary hearing on the motion, including extensive testimony from officials of Allston as to the extent of Allston's business activities in New York and other states. After presentation of the evidence and briefs and argument by the parties, the court concludes that Allston's principal place of business is in New York and therefore dismisses the suit. Rizzuto now sues in a New York state court, and Allston pleads res judicata. Will the defense prevail?

11. Assume that the court in the case described in question 10 clearly has subject matter jurisdiction. Allston therefore answers Rizzuto's negligence complaint and subsequently moves for summary judgment on the ground that Rizzuto cannot prove any negligence of Allston. It submits supporting affidavits of its employees, stating under oath that they had examined the glove after the accident and it was not damaged or defective in any way. Rizzuto submits no opposing affidavit and summary judgment is entered for Allston. Subsequently, Rizzuto sues again. Is the second suit barred?

## Pendent or Independent?

12. Koufax sues Throneberry in federal court for violation of the federal trademark laws. He claims that Throneberry used a logo on his brand of baseball bats that copied the logo covered by Koufax's trademark. The court holds that the logo is sufficiently distinct that the trademark does not cover it and Koufax loses. Subsequently, he sues Throneberry in state court under a state unfair competition statute, based on the same acts. Will the second action be barred?

## "The Game Ain't Over 'till It's Over"

13. Berra sues Durocher for intentional infliction of emotional distress, arising out of an altercation behind home plate at Yankee Stadium. The court dismisses the suit under Fed. R. Civ. P. 12(b)(6) on the ground that under the New York case law[3] there is no right to recover for infliction of emotional distress unless the plaintiff also suffered physical injury. Judgment is entered for Durocher. Six months later, the New York Court of Appeals overrules its earlier cases and approves recovery for intentional infliction of emotional distress without proof of physical injury. Berra brings a new action to recover for the same incident. Is the suit barred?

14. Assume that Berra sued Durocher for intentional infliction of emotional distress in a New York state court. The court dismissed the suit on the ground that the applicable law did not allow recovery for infliction of emotional distress unless the plaintiff also suffered physical injury. Berra appealed.

---

3. New York law would apply in this federal diversity action under *Erie Railroad v. Tompkins,* 304 U.S. 64 (1938).

While the appeal was pending, the state supreme court held in a separate case that plaintiffs may recover for infliction of emotional distress without accompanying physical injury. Which rule should apply to Berra's case?

15. Assume that Berra learns of the change in the law six months after the judgment in his original suit became final. Rather than bring a new action on the claim, Berra takes a different tack: He brings a motion for relief from the *original* judgment, under Fed. R. Civ. P. 60(b), asking the court to reopen the case in light of the change in the applicable law. Should the court grant the motion?

# ANALYSIS

## Fielder's Choice

1. Res judicata will bar Rizzuto's second action. A judgment need not be right to preclude further litigation; it need only be final and on the merits. "Res judicata reflects the policy that sometimes it is more important that a judgment be stable than that it be correct." Friedenthal, Kane, and Miller at 616. Here, Rizzuto tried his case and lost, and final judgment was entered for Allston "on the merits," that is, based on a verdict by the jury that Allston was not negligent. That judgment bars a second suit by Rizzuto on the same claim even if evidence was wrongly excluded. If that exclusion was improper, Rizzuto should have appealed it in the first suit, not attempted to relitigate it in a second. See *Federated Department Stores, Inc. v. Moitie,* 452 U.S. 394, 398 (1981).

If Rizzuto could avoid the effect of the first judgment by claiming it was wrong, the res judicata doctrine would lose much of its value. A major purpose of the doctrine is to preserve judicial resources by barring rehearing of cases already litigated and decided. This purpose would be undermined if the evidence would have to be reheard in order to ascertain whether the first case was rightly decided. It would also place the judge in the second suit in the inappropriate position of reviewing the first trial to determine whether it was error-free in order to determine whether it should have res judicata effect.

2. Res judicata bars not only those claims that were asserted in the first suit but also any others arising out of that transaction or occurrence that could have been asserted but were not. Here, Rizzuto has simply switched theories of relief and sued again based on the same vicious grounder he complained of in the earlier suit. The suit will be barred.

The rigidity of this rule forces parties to litigate their claims fully in their first suit. Lawyers, knowing they will get only one bite at the apple, must consider all possible grounds for relief raised by the underlying facts and plead them in the first action. This is one reason why complaints often contain numerous counts based on different legal theories. It is better to be comprehensive in the original action[4] rather than try to battle the res judicata myrmidon in a subsequent action.

3.    Allston will also prevail on his res judicata defense here. In question 2, Rizzuto tried to "split his claim" by asserting one theory of relief in the first action and another in the second. Here he has tried a different type of claim-splitting, seeking different types of damages in different actions. Here too, the myrmidon says no. The claim for punitive damages could have been, and therefore should have been, asserted in the first action. No matter how clear Rizzuto's right to punitive damages, the court will not hear this claim.

In an earlier day many states allowed "claim-splitting" based on distinct types of damages. For example, plaintiffs in auto negligence cases were frequently allowed to seek recovery for their personal injuries and damage to their vehicles in separate actions, on the theory that these involved discrete rights protected by distinct causes of action. See, e.g., *Vasu v. Kohlers, Inc.*, 61 N.E.2d 707 (1945). This rule has given way in many jurisdictions to the view that all damages from a single accident must be sought in a single suit. See *Rush v. Maple Heights*, 147 N.E.2d 599, cert. denied, 358 U.S. 814 (1958) (effectively overruling *Vasu*).

4.    Rizzuto's problem here is not dissatisfaction with the relief he obtained in the first action but difficulty in collecting it from the defendant. The fact that the defendant has not satisfied the judgment does not give the plaintiff the right to bring a second action on the original claim. Under res judicata theory, his claim is "merged into the judgment"; his right to sue on the original claim is replaced by a right to enforce the judgment. In most jurisdictions a judgment remains enforceable for many years, as long as an execution is issued promptly after judgment. See, e.g., Wis. Stat. Ann. §815.04 (West 1977) (20 years); South Dakota Codifed Laws §15-18-1 (1984) (20 years). There is no need for Rizzuto to bring a new suit and relitigate matters already settled in his favor. When Rizzuto learns that Allston is in a position to pay, he should seek execution on the original judgment or bring an action on the judgment in another state where Allston has assets that can be taken on execution. See Chapter 3, p. 38.

5.    This is a hard case indeed. Here Rizzuto sought all his known damages in his original suit but did not seek recovery for a potential future consequence of the injury. Naturally when that consequence arises he feels entitled to compensation for it as well. And since res judicata only bars claims that could have been joined in the original action, he has a good argument for a new action.

Rizzuto's position is certainly sympathetic, but it has generally been rejected by the courts. Imagine the havoc that would result if plaintiffs could relitigate claims whenever their disabilities or medical expenses turned out to

---

4. Subject, of course, to the ethical constraints on pleading in Rule 11.

be more than expected at the time of trial. Judgments would never be final because they would be subject to revision in the light of future events. Defendants would be unable to rely on the finality of judgments in planning their future conduct and estimating their liabilities. In most cases the benefit of providing full relief based on subsequent evidence would be far outweighed by the burden of renewed litigation and the uncertainty that would result.

Consequently, the usual rule is that a plaintiff must recover for all his damages in the original action, including those suffered prior to trial and all future damages that are reasonably likely to ensue. Restatement (Second) of Judgments §25, comment c (1982)[5]; compare Fed. R. Civ. P. 60(b)(2), which allows a limited right to relief from the original judgment on the ground that newly discovered evidence should be considered. Here, for example, Rizzuto should have presented evidence in his original suit that victims of this type of eye injury are likely to develop headaches. The jury could then have assessed additional damages based on this foreseeable consequence of the injury. Admittedly, this is a very rough measure of Rizzuto's actual damages, but it is the best that the system can do without retrying Rizzuto's case repeatedly in future years.

## An Absurd Hypothetical

6.    The short answer to this question is that the four prerequisites for application of res judicata are not met since the parties are not the same in the second action. Rizzuto was not a party in the first suit; though Allston was, *both* parties must be the same (or in privity with the prior parties) for res judicata to apply. In addition, the "claim" is not the same in the second action. The rights of different plaintiffs to relief arising out of a single incident are not considered one "claim" simply because they arise out of one transaction or occurrence. Every potential plaintiff who suffers injury from a transaction or occurrence has a distinct claim for res judicata purposes. Here, for example, although Kubek's and Rizzuto's claims both arise out of the same incident, each has his own separate claim to damages. The fact that Kubek has sued for his injuries does not bar Rizzuto from suing separately for his.

If res judicata barred a second suit in a situation like this, all plaintiffs with claims arising out of a single incident would be forced to sue together. The usual rule in American courts is to the contrary: The "plaintiff is master of his claim" and *may* sue jointly with other plaintiffs (see Fed. R. Civ. P. 20(a))

---

5. Not all jurisdictions follow this rule however. See *Ross v. Johns-Mansville Corp,* 766 F.2d 823, 826 (3d Cir. 1985) (distinguishing New Jersey law, which recognizes separate causes of action for asbestosis and cancer caused by the same exposure to asbestos, from Pennsylvania law, which does not recognize a separate cause of action for asbestos-related cancer). For a case holding that the asbestos victim must recover all resulting damages in a single action, see *Gideon v. Johns-Mansville Corp.,* 761 F.2d 1129, 1136-1137 (5th Cir. 1985) (applying Texas law).

but need not. Even though Rizzuto knew of Kubek's suit, and appeared as a witness, he still has the right to sue separately.

7.   To the extent that the lawyer's advice is based on the conclusion that Rizzuto may sue separately on the contract claim without fear of the myrmidon, it is sound. Even though the contract claim had accrued at the time of the negligence suit (that is, the breach had occurred and Rizzuto had a right to sue on it), Rizzuto is not required to assert it in the negligence action. Under the Restatement definition of a single "claim," these are separate claims because they arise out of separate transactions. Restatement (Second) of Judgments §24 (1982). Rizzuto's first action was based on an accident on the playing field. His second is based on a separate transaction, the contract to promote Allston gloves on television.

This example highlights several important points. *First,* it is important to understand that Rizzuto's right to sue separately on these claims is not based on the fact that one action is for tort and the other for contract. In many cases a plaintiff may assert a right to recover under both tort and contract theories, based on a single incident. In the Schulansky case, for example, Schulansky asserts contract and tort claims against the defendants, which both arise out of the construction of the addition on her house. See the Schulansky complaint infra p. 38. If either of these were left out, res judicata would bar Schulansky from suing on it separately. By contrast, Rizzuto may sue separately here because his contract claim arises from a different set of historical facts.

*Second,* note that Rizzuto *could* have joined both of these unrelated claims in a single action under Fed. R. Civ. P. 18(a). It does not always follow that you must join claims in a single action simply because the Rules allow you to do so. (The relationship between res judicata and the joinder rules is explored in detail in Chapter 19.)

8.   On these facts Rizzuto's second action will not be barred. At the time of his first suit Rizzuto did not have a claim for the second year's royalties. He can hardly be expected to predict future defaults and sue for them before they occur. Even though the two suits arise out of a single contract, the separate breaches in successive years are different occurrences that may be sued on separately.

That would not be true, however, if Rizzuto had waited until the end of the second year to sue. At that point, the royalties for both years had accrued, and the usual rule is that Rizzuto must sue for them all as a single debt due on an account. Friedenthal, Kane, and Miller at 630-631. Similarly, a landlord who sues a tenant for back rent must seek recovery for all months' rent due but not future defaults. This reflects the basic premise that res judicata bars all claims arising out of a single transaction or occurrence that could have been raised in the original action. The claims for future nonpayment could not have been raised since the plaintiff has no right to sue for these claims until they accrue.

Although res judicata will not bar Rizzuto's second suit here, collateral estoppel will bar relitigation of issues that were litigated and decided in the first suit. For example, if the court held that the contract called for payment of all royalties at the 10 percent rate, Allston will be estopped from claiming that the rate should be 5 percent in the second action. See Chapter 20, p. 280.

9.    If you focused carefully on the prerequisites for res judicata discussed in the introduction, you should have concluded that the myrmidon will not bar Allston's suit against Rizzuto. As question 6 suggests, every separate party has a separate claim for res judicata purposes even though their claims arise out of the same incident. Thus Allston's claim against Rizzuto is not the "same claim" as Rizzuto's claim against Allston.

However, while traditional res judicata doctrine does not bar Allston's claim, many jurisdictions provide by court rule that counterclaims arising out of the same transaction or occurrence must be brought in the original action. See, e.g., Fed. R. Civ. P. 13(a) (counterclaim compulsory if it arises out of same transaction or occurrence as the opposing party's claim). If the defendant fails to join a compulsory counterclaim, he will then be barred from bringing it later in order to enforce the compulsory counterclaim rule, not because the common law res judicata doctrine applies. See James and Hazard at §11.14.

In a jurisdiction that does not have a compulsory counterclaim rule, Allston would remain free to assert its claim in a separate action. However, the crucial issues underlying its claim will likely have been decided in the original suit. In this case, for example, the earlier action determined that Rizzuto had breached his contract. In Allston's separate action, collateral estoppel will bar him from relitigating that issue.

## Judgment on the Merits

10.    Res judicata does not apply here because the claim has never been decided on the merits. Although an actual hearing was held and testimony and argument heard, the issue under consideration was the power of the court to hear the action, not the substance of Rizzuto's negligence claim. Because the court held that it lacked subject matter jurisdiction over the suit, it never reached the merits. Consequently, one of the prerequisites for res judicata is not met.

It would certainly be a hard rule if litigants in Rizzuto's position were barred from going to a second court after dismissal for lack of jurisdiction in the first. Under this approach, the second suit would be barred even though the first court never considered the merits of plaintiff's case and, in fact, never had the power to do so. To avoid this risk, the plaintiff would be forced to choose a court that certainly has jurisdiction even though he would prefer to sue in another that may well have it. The res judicata doctrine does not put the parties to such risks. The "on the merits" requirement assures that preliminary dismissals due to lack of jurisdiction or venue will not bar suit in another court that has the power to proceed.[6]

11. In this case, although Rizzuto's claim has been resolved without trial, it has been decided on the merits. Summary judgment in Allston's favor was based on the court's conclusion that Rizzuto has no evidence to support his contention that his accident resulted from Allston's negligence and therefore no jury could find for Rizzuto on the negligence issue. Since Rizzuto cannot prove an essential element of his claim, judgment for Allston is proper. This is "on the merits" because it represents an adjudication of Rizzuto's substantive claim for relief, not a preliminary issue. Similarly, a directed verdict is a decision on the merits that is given res judicata effect because it determines that the plaintiff's claim has so little "merit" that no reasonable jury could uphold it. Restatement (Second) of Judgments §19, comments g, h (1982).

## Pendent or Independent

12. Under the four prerequisites Koufax's second action would ordinarily be barred since he is suing the same defendant again on a claim arising out of the same events as the first suit. The procedural quirk here, however, is that it is not entirely clear that Koufax could have joined the unfair competition claim in the original action. It is a state law claim that would be within the court's pendent jurisdiction in the federal trademark suit, see Chapter 12, p. 159-160; however, under *United Mine Workers v. Gibbs,* 383 U.S. 715 (1966), the court has discretion to hear or dismiss pendent state law claims. It might not have heard Koufax's state law claim even if he had tried.

The general rule is that the plaintiff must join his pendent state claims in this situation or lose them by operation of res judicata. If the federal court entertains the pendent claims, it will contribute to judicial efficiency and consistency of decision making, two goals of the res judicata doctrine. If the court refuses to hear them, then they will not be barred since they could not be heard in the first action and the plaintiff has therefore not had an opportunity to litigate those claims. All that Koufax can do is ask; if he does and the court refuses, he is protected. If he doesn't ask, the potential benefits of joint litigation are lost through his own neglect and the myrmidon will be characteristically unsympathetic.

The same result would follow if the plaintiff sued in state court on a state claim but failed to join a federal claim that was within the concurrent jurisdiction of the state court. However, if he sued in state court and omitted a federal claim that was within exclusive federal jurisdiction, he should not be

---

6. The only argument for preclusion here is that the plaintiff has already caused the defendant and the courts to expend substantial time and energy in considering his case by choosing an inappropriate court. But this consideration is outweighed by the premium the system places on deciding cases on their merits, rather than allowing procedural defaults to dominate over substantive rights.

barred from asserting that claim in a separate action since the claim could not have been joined in the state court action. See Restatement (Second) of Judgments §26(c) (1982); 18 Wright and Miller at §4470, pp.686-688.

## "The Game Ain't Over 'till It's Over"

13. As indicated in the introduction, the federal courts give res judicata effect to dismissals under Fed. R. Civ. P. 12(b)(6) for failure to state a claim. See Fed. R. Civ. P. 41(b) (unless the court specifies otherwise, dismissals are with prejudice except for specified preliminary dismissals). Thus, Berra's second action will be barred unless the subsequent change in the substantive law provides a basis to avoid the usual effect of res judicata.

This subsequent change in the law will not allow Berra to start a new action. Parties are not entitled to have their cases decided under the law as it will be at some future time; each case must be decided under the law at the time it is considered. See 1B Moore's at ¶0.415. Imagine the confusion that would ensue if parties could bring new suits if the law changed after they lost a case. Finality of judgments would be meaningless since cases might be reopened (or nullified by the results in a later suit) at some indeterminate time in the future. How long would parties have to reopen the judgment? How much later could the law change and still be applied to a previously decided case?

Clearly, such a principle, even if circumscribed by some form of statute of limitations, would disserve the cause of judicial economy and certainty of judgments. Besides, rules may be fair at the time they are applied even though they change later when conditions have changed. Better to leave it at that than to undermine the finality of judgments by reconsidering them every time the underlying substantive law is reconsidered.

If Berra believed that the prior case law should be overruled, he should have appealed on that ground instead of waiting for a future plaintiff to carry the laboring oar. Perhaps the court would have changed the rule in his case instead of the next one six months down the line.

14. There is a crucial difference between this case and the last. Here, Berra's first action is still going on. Although he lost in the trial court, he has taken his appeal and asked the higher court to change the rule with regard to relief without physical injury. If the court had not adopted the new rule in the first case raising the issue, it presumably would have done so in his. He should not be disadvantaged by the fact that the appeal in the other case was heard first. Consequently, the general rule is that the court will apply the law as it stands when the pending appeal is decided, not the law as it stood at the time of trial.

15. If Berra could get the trial judge to reopen the original action, it would undermine the finality of the judgment just as clearly as allowing a new action would in question 13. Instead of starting a new suit, he could simply

revive the old and ask the court to retry the case under the new state of the law. The rule in the federal courts, therefore, is that the court may not grant relief from judgment due to a change in the substantive law once the period for appeal has passed. See, e.g., *Morris v. Adams-Millis Corp.*, 758 F.2d 1352, 1358-1359 (10th Cir. 1985); *Lubben v. Selective Service System Local Board No. 27*, 453 F.2d 645, 651 (1st Cir. 1972).

However, if the law changes while the period for appeal is still running (usually 30 days from entry of judgment in the trial court, see Fed. R. App. P. 4(a)(1)), Berra may seek relief from the judgment on this ground. This exception makes eminent good sense: If the trial judge could not acknowledge this change in the law and reopen the case during the appeal period, Rizzuto clearly would appeal. The appellate court would apply the new rule (see question 14), reverse the case for reconsideration under the new rule, and the case would be reopened anyway after a wasteful appeal. Allowing the trial judge to grant relief from judgment during the appeal period (but only during this period) will save the parties the expense of an unnecessary appeal with a foregone conclusion. Cf. 7 Moore's at ¶60.22[3], pp.60-185–60-186 (discussing related right of trial judge to correct error within time for appeal).

# 19

## Res Judicata and the Rules of Joinder: When Does May Mean Must?

## Introduction

In any reasonable civil procedure world, there ought to be a close relationship between the parties' right to join claims in their first lawsuit and the scope of res judicata in subsequent suits between them. If, for example, the rules of joinder did not allow plaintiffs to join counts for property damage and personal injury in a single lawsuit, it would be a rigid system indeed that barred the plaintiff who had sued for her property damage in one suit from bringing a separate action to recover for her personal injuries. Similarly, if the joinder rules limited a plaintiff to proceeding on a single theory, such as negligence, in her first suit, it would be unfair to bar her from starting a second action on a strict liability theory. One way or another, the system ought to offer parties a chance to have all of their claims heard, either through limited claims in multiple suits or multiple claims in a single suit.

The early English common law followed the first course, allowing multiple actions on different theories or seeking different relief. Under the common law system, the rigid limitations on joinder of claims frequently prevented plaintiffs from seeking full relief in a single action. For example, a plaintiff who sued at law for damages for trespass could not get an injunction against further trespasses in the same suit; she had to go to an equity court for that. Because the plaintiff was forced by these limitations to split her cause of action, the preclusion rules did not bar her from bringing the second action even though it arose out of the same occurrence as the first.

The federal courts and many state systems, as well, have chosen the second course, allowing many claims to be heard in a single action. Their approach is implemented by extremely broad rules governing pleading and joinder. See Rules 8(a)(3), 8(e)(2), 13, 14, 18, and 20. Under these liberal joinder rules, plaintiffs have broad power to join all their theories of recovery in their initial suit. Consequently, they will seldom be able to argue that they should be allowed to start a new action based on the same occurrence because they were unable to assert an omitted claim in the first suit.

For example, Fed. R. Civ. P. 18(a) allows joinder of virtually all possible theories of recovery in a single action. It is hardly unreasonable therefore under basic res judicata principles to bar any theory that is omitted from the first suit. In this situation the *may* of the rules clearly means *must* when the effects of res judicata are considered. If Elbers sues Doe Chemical Company for negligently manufacturing a drug, Rule 18(a) allows but does not require her to assert a separate strict liability claim against Doe based on the same events. See also Fed. R. Civ. P. 8(e)(2) (authorizing alternative or inconsistent pleading). However, if Elbers leaves out the strict liability claim, res judicata will bar her from asserting it in a later action. This is simply another theory of recovery for the same injuries already sued upon, and any claims arising from that occurrence that are not joined in Elbers's first action will be barred by res judicata doctrine. See Chapter 18, question 2.

There are a few instances when, despite Rule 18(a), initial joinder of a particular claim is not available. In such cases the res judicata myrmidon[1] grudgingly steps aside to allow the plaintiff to reenter the courthouse door. Suppose, for example, that Allen sues Moser under a state unfair competition statute, in state court. Suppose further that Allen might also recover against Moser for patent infringement, a federal claim over which the federal courts have exclusive jurisdiction. Here, Allen could not have included his federal theory in the first action because the federal courts have exclusive jurisdiction over patent claims. Consequently, he will not be barred from asserting the patent claim in a later suit. See generally Restatement (Second) of Judgments §26(1)(c) (1982).

It would make life a lot easier for civil procedure students, as well as practicing lawyers, if it were invariably true that every time a claim could have been joined in the initial action, the plaintiff were barred from bringing it separately. Alas, though this would be neat and symmetrical, it just isn't so. Although *theories* that could have been joined are generally barred, the scope of permissible joinder of *parties* is much broader than the dimensions of a single "claim" for res judicata purposes. Thus, in many cases claims against additional parties could be joined under the Rules but will not be barred by res judicata if they are not.

---

1. For a natural history of this creature, see Chapter 18, n.1.

For example, if Fellows is involved in a three-car collision with Rich and Rontowski, she could sue them as codefendants in a single lawsuit. Fed. R. Civ. P. 20(a). However, she doesn't have to: If she sues Rich alone, she is not precluded from suing Rontowski later in a separate action. A plaintiff's rights to recover from separate defendants are considered distinct "claims" under res judicata analysis, even though they arise out of the same occurrence. In addition, the "same parties" requirement of res judicata is not met in such cases since the defendants differ in the two actions.

This is puzzling at first, but if it were not true, the res judicata rules would convert permissive joinder under the Rules into compulsory joinder. Rule 20(a) says that Fellows *may* choose to sue Rich and Rontowski together. Clearly, the rulemakers have chosen to allow her to sue them jointly, but also given her the option not to. This reflects the traditional precept that the "plaintiff is master of her claim," free to choose when and where to sue each potential defendant. But, if res judicata barred Fellows from suing Rontowski because she had previously sued Rich without joining Rontowski, the *may* of Rule 20(a) would be converted to *must* under the preclusion rules: Fellows would be forced to sue them both in the first action. Although such a compulsory joinder of parties rule might make sense from an efficiency point of view, the rulemakers have favored freedom of choice over efficiency.[2] The res judicata rules should be crafted to protect that policy decision.

This principle that claims against different parties need not be joined even if the rules would allow it does not prevent the first action from having some preclusive effect, however. If Fellows loses her suit against Rich on the ground that she was contributorily negligent, Rontowski may be able to invoke collateral estoppel to establish Fellows's negligence if Fellows subsequently sues her. See *Blonder-Tongue Laboratories Inc. v. University of Illinois Foundation*, 402 U.S. 313 (1971); Chapter 21, pp. 296-298. Certainly, this inhibits Fellows's freedom of choice to some extent, since she cannot start her action against Rontowski with a completely clean slate.

The following questions will help you to sort out the relationship between the joinder and res judicata rules. Assume that all actions are brought in federal court and that subject matter jurisdiction is proper in each case. Consider in each case whether the omitted claim could have been joined under the rules and, if so, whether res judicata will bar the second action.

# QUESTIONS

## A Few Warm-Ups

1.   Roosevelt is hit by a car while walking across Park Avenue in New York City. The only occupants of the car were Kefauver and Warren, but each denies that he was driving. Roosevelt sues Kefauver, a Tennessee citizen, in

---

2. Some of the reasons for that choice are discussed in Chapter 10, question 1.

the federal court for the Middle District of Tennessee. She loses. Now Roosevelt sues Warren in the Southern District of New York.

    a.   Could Roosevelt have joined Kefauver and Warren in the first action?

    b.   Is Roosevelt's second suit barred?

2.   Roosevelt sues Kefauver in the Tennessee federal court for battery, based on the collision on Park Avenue. The jury finds that Kefauver did not hit Roosevelt intentionally, and judgment is entered for Kefauver. Subsequently, Roosevelt sues Kefauver in the Southern District of New York for negligently injuring her in the collision.

    a.   Could Roosevelt have joined the negligence claim in the first suit?

    b.   Is the second suit barred by res judicata?

3.   Roosevelt sues Kefauver for battery and for negligence based on the accident. She later sues Kefauver again in the same court for a breach of contract that took place before the accident.

    a.   Could Roosevelt have joined the contract claim in the first action?

    b.   Is the second suit precluded by res judicata?

4.   Stanton sues Anthony for her injuries in a two car collision, and recovers $17,000. Now Blatch, a passenger in Stanton's car, sues Anthony for her injuries in the collision.

    a.   Could Stanton and Blatch have joined as coplaintiffs in the first action?

    b.   Could Blatch have intervened in Stanton's suit against Anthony? See Fed. R. Civ. P. 24.

    c.   Is Blatch barred by res judicata from bringing her suit?

## A Hybrid Case

5.   Grasso sues Adams for breach of contract, arising out of a contract for the delivery of livestock to Grasso. Grasso loses. Subsequently, Adams sues Grasso for breach of the contract, seeking to collect the balance due under the contract.

    a.   Could Adams have joined his contract claim in the original action?

    b.   Is Adams's action against Grasso barred by res judicata?

6.   After Grasso sues Adams for breach of the livestock contract, could Adams start a separate action against Grasso on an unrelated fraud claim that accrued before the contract dispute?

7.   Grasso sues Adams and Johnson Drug Co. for personal injuries suffered as a result of using a drug made by Johnson and sold to her by Adams. She recovers judgment for $10,000 against each defendant. Adams pays the judgment and then sues Johnson for indemnification claiming that since the negligent manufacture of the drug caused Grasso's injuries, Adams should be indemnified by the manufacturer for the damages he paid to Grasso.

    a.  Could the claim have been asserted in the first action?

    b.  Is Adams barred from bringing the second suit?

## A Myrmidon in the Labyrinth

8.  Assume that Grasso sued Adams on the drug claim and recovered. Now Adams sues Johnson for indemnification.

    a.  Could Adams have asserted this claim in the original action?

    b.  Is his action against Johnson precluded?

9.  Smith, from South Dakota, sues Bryan, from Minnesota, for breach of a contract to construct a home for him. Smith claims that the foundation of the house was improperly poured. Bryan impleads Coolidge, a South Dakota subcontractor who poured the foundation, for indemnification. The court holds that the foundation meets the specifications and therefore judgment is entered for Bryan on the main claim and for Coolidge on the third-party claim. Subsequently, Bryan sues Coolidge to collect the wages of five laborers Bryan had lent to Coolidge to help him perform the foundation work.

    a.  Could Bryan have asserted the new claim in the first action?

    b.  Is the second suit barred by res judicata?

10.  Assume the same facts as question 9, but that the claim asserted by Bryan in the second action arose from an alleged breach of another contract between them.

    a.  Could Bryan have asserted the contract action in the first action?

    b.  Is he barred from bringing it in the second suit?

## When Does *May Not* Mean *Must*?

11.  Suppose that Smith sued Bryan for breach of the contract, as a result of defects in the foundation. Three years into the suit when the parties have completed discovery and trial is imminent, Smith moves to amend the complaint to assert a second claim against Bryan for negligence, on the ground that the foundation was inadequately poured. The court denies the motion to amend, on the ground that it is untimely, that it could have been brought earlier in the suit, and that allowance of the motion would delay the trial and prejudice Bryan's ability to prepare his defense. See generally *Foman v. Davis*, 371 U.S. 178, 181-182 (1962).

    The breach of contract claim is tried and Smith loses. He then brings a second action against Bryan, asserting only the negligence claim. (Assume that the applicable statute of limitations is six years, so that the action is not yet barred on this ground.) Bryan pleads res judicata.

    a.  If you represented Smith, how would you argue that the second action is not barred by res judicata?

    b.  How will the judge rule on the res judicata defense?

# ANALYSIS

## A Few Warm-Ups

1.   Joinder: Yes     Res judicata: No

a. This is a simple case of one plaintiff who has claims against two defendants. Rule 20(a) allows Roosevelt to sue them together because the claims arise from the same accident and will involve the common issue of who was driving the car. However, Rule 20(a) does not require Roosevelt to sue the defendants together; the rule says *may* and means it. In this case Roosevelt might have been well advised to sue them jointly. As is, the first jury may conclude that Warren was driving, and the second that Kefauver was, leaving Roosevelt a double loser. For one reason or another, Roosevelt has chosen to take that risk, as the joinder rules allow her to do.

b. Roosevelt's second action is not barred since her claim against Warren is distinct from her claim against Kefauver, and they are not the same parties. If res judicata did bar the second action, it would force Roosevelt to sue the two defendants together, thus undermining the choice given to Roosevelt by the rules. Consider the consequences that such a result would have for Roosevelt's case. It is unlikely that she could get personal jurisdiction in Tennessee over Warren for this New York accident. Consequently, if the res judicata rules forced her to sue the two together, Roosevelt would lose her choice of forum against Kefauver. She would be forced to sue in New York where she could obtain personal jurisdiction over both defendants because the claim arose there.

This is another example of the intricate interrelations of the various civil procedure doctrines. A change in this aspect of the res judicata rules would directly affect the joinder rules and the choice of forum rules. The rulemakers have chosen to preserve one value — the plaintiff's right to choose her forum against each defendant — and have had to mold the related joinder and preclusion rules accordingly.

As indicated in the introduction, however, it is still possible that the first suit will affect the second if the court in the second action allows Warren to invoke nonmutual collateral estoppel to bar relitigation of any issues decided in the first.

2.   Joinder: Yes     Res judicata: Yes

a. The issue here is joinder of "claims" (in the sense of theories of recovery) rather than joinder of parties. Rule 18(a), the epitome of liberality, allows a plaintiff to join any claims she has against a defending party. But again, the rule is permissive; under Rule 18(a) Roosevelt has the option but is not required to join the negligence claim in the first action.

b. The myrmidon[3] will stubbornly resist Roosevelt's efforts to bring this second action. Joinder of these "claims" may be permissive under the rules but is made mandatory by the res judicata principles applied in the federal courts. Under those principles, all theories for recovery arising out of a single transaction or occurrence constitute a single "claim" for preclusion purposes. See Chapter 18, pp. 253-254. A party who seeks relief based on a particular set of historical facts must join all her grounds for recovery on those facts in the first action or face the res judicata defense if she tries to sue later on one of these grounds. Thus, Roosevelt's second suit for negligence will be barred even though Rule 18(a) appears to give her the option to join or withhold it in the first action. Here, unlike the joinder of parties situation in question 1, the preclusion doctrine demands what the rule merely permits.

It makes no difference that Roosevelt's second action is brought in a different court. Under full faith and credit principles, each court within the system will honor the judgments of its sister courts by giving them full res judicata effect.

### 3.  Joinder: Yes     Res judicata: No

a. Rule 18(a) authorizes joinder of "claims," both in the sense of different theories arising out of the same events and also completely unrelated claims arising out of completely separate events. Thus, Roosevelt could have joined her contract claim with her other claims in the first action even though it arises from a separate transaction.

b. Roosevelt's second action is not barred. Unlike question 2, in which the omitted "claim" simply asserted a different theory of recovery for the same loss litigated in the first suit, the contract claim here arose out of a separate incident from the negligence and battery claims. Roosevelt's prior suit based on the accident will bar all future suits against Kefauver based on that accident but not other suits based on separate events.

Thus Roosevelt is free to bring a separate action on the contract claim even though she could have joined it in the first suit. Here, the *may* of the rule does not mean *must* under res judicata because the claim does not satisfy the res judicata definition of a single "claim." See Restatement (Second) of Judgments §24 (1982) (single claim under res judicata analysis includes all grounds for relief arising out of a single transaction).

### 4.  Joinder: Yes     Intervention: Maybe     Res judicata: No

a. Rule 20(a) authorizes, but does not require, Stanton and Blatch to sue jointly since they seek relief arising from the same occurrence and their

---

3. I will drop this metaphor eventually. There's no point in beating a dead myrmidon.

claims will involve a number of common questions of law or fact, including the central question of the cause of the accident.

b. Blatch could at least have tried to intervene under Rule 24(b) since her claim and Stanton's will involve a common question of fact — whether Anthony's negligence caused the accident. But intervention under Rule 24(b) is permissive; the court might have declined to allow Blatch into the suit for a variety of reasons.

It is less likely that Blatch could have intervened in Stanton's suit as a matter of right under Rule 24(a). She will not be prejudiced by the Stanton/Anthony litigation unless she will be barred from bringing her own action against Anthony. As explained immediately below, she will not be barred from doing so. In addition, even if Blatch meets the criteria for intervention as of right, she is still under no duty to intervene since Rule 24(a) authorizes intervention as of right but does not force parties to intervene even when they would have a right to do so.

c. Blatch's suit against Anthony is not precluded by Stanton's, because she is a different party from the original parties and because her claim against Anthony is not the same as Stanton's claim against Anthony. Thus, two of the prerequisites to res judicata are not met. While Blatch had several avenues for getting into the first action, they are both permissive, and *may* is not converted to *must* here because the separate requirements for preclusion are not met.

Blatch may obtain some benefit from Stanton's action, however; since Stanton has proved Anthony's negligence, Blatch may be able to invoke offensive nonmutual collateral estoppel to bar Anthony from relitigating the issue. See Chapter 21, pp. 298-300.

## A Hybrid Case

5.   Joinder: Yes    Res judicata: In a way

a. Adams's claim for the payments due under the contract was a compulsory counterclaim in the first action since it arose out of the same events as Grasso's original claim. Under Rule 13(a), Adams was required to assert this claim in the original action. The drafters of Rule 13(a) decided that the gain in litigation efficiency from hearing a defendant's related claims in the original action outweighed the defendant's usual right to choose her own forum. Consequently, they required such related claims to be asserted in the original action.

b. The rulemakers' goal will only be achieved if Adams is barred from suing separately on the omitted counterclaim. Under res judicata doctrine, however, Adams would not be precluded from suing separately on this claim because Adams's claim against Grasso is not the "same claim" as Grasso's claim against him. In this situation the courts have estopped parties in

Adams's position from suing separately on the omitted counterclaim, simply to enforce the policy underlying the compulsory counterclaim rule. This form of "rule-based res judicata" applies even though the same claim requirement of res judicata is not met. See Friedenthal, Kane, and Miller at §14.6, p.638.

In some state systems counterclaims are not compulsory whether or not they arise out of the same transaction as the main claim. In those systems Adams would not be barred from starting a second action on the counterclaim. However, such jurisdictions sometimes hold that a party waives her right to sue separately on an omitted counterclaim if the same issues were raised defensively in the prior action. Id. at 639-640.

6.    In this example, Adams's claim was available at the time of the original action and could have been joined as a permissive counterclaim under Rule 13(b). However, Adams need not join it in the first suit, and it will not be barred by res judicata if he omits it. A permissive counterclaim by definition arises out of a separate transaction from the main claim. See Fed. R. Civ. P. 13(b). Thus, it is not part of the "same claim" as the plaintiff's claim, nor is it barred by rule-based preclusion, as a compulsory counterclaim would be. Here, *may* really means *may*; Adams's fraud claim will not be barred.

If the claim were barred by res judicata if omitted from the first action, the preclusion rules would essentially make permissive counterclaims compulsory, undermining the rulemakers' choice and raising serious jurisdictional problems in many federal cases.

7.    Joinder: Yes       Res judicata: No

a. Adams could have joined his indemnification claim as a cross-claim in the original action, under Rule 13(g), which authorizes but does not require him to assert any related claim he has against the codefendant in the original action.

b. Res judicata will not bar Adams from seeking indemnification from Johnson in a second suit. Under the res judicata analysis, Adams's claim against Johnson is not the same as Grasso's claim against Adams, so that the assertion of the latter does not bar the subsequent assertion of the former. Again, this is the right result in terms of the policies established in the Rules. The rulemakers have chosen to make cross-claims permissive; if res judicata barred subsequent assertion of omitted cross-claims they would effectively be compulsory.

Compulsory cross-claims might actually not be a bad idea. As long as all the parties are already in the case, why not force them to litigate all claims among them arising out of the same transaction? The Rules make defendants do it under Rule 13(a) but draw the line at forcing the assertion of other related claims such as cross-claims and third-party claims.

## A Myrmidon in the Labyrinth

**8.    Joinder: Yes    Res judicata: No**

a. Adams could have impleaded Johnson for indemnification under Rule 14(a) since he seeks recovery from Johnson for the damages Grasso seeks from him.

b. If Adams is free to refrain from asserting his claim against Johnson in the last example, in which they are both already in the suit, he should similarly be free *not* to implead Johnson when sued by Grasso. Impleader is permissive, and Adams is free to sue Johnson separately for indemnification if he prefers. Tactically, it may be preferable to implead Johnson to prevent the risk of inconsistent judgments, but Adams may have his reasons for failing to do so, such as lack of personal jurisdiction over Johnson in the court where Grasso sued him. It would certainly be inappropriate to force Adams to join Johnson if he couldn't obtain personal jurisdiction over him. Such problems were undoubtedly in the minds of the rulemakers when they decided not to make Rule 14 impleader claims compulsory.

However, if Adams did implead Johnson, res judicata obviously would bar him from bringing a separate action against Johnson on the same claim. And Johnson may still be able to invoke collateral estoppel in the second action on some issues decided against Adams in the first.

**9.    Joinder: Unclear    Res judicata: Probably**

a. Bryan could have asserted this claim against Coolidge under Rule 18(a), which provides that a party seeking relief from an opposing party may assert as many claims as she has against that opposing party. Granted, Bryan could not have impleaded Coolidge on the basis of this claim alone because it does not satisfy the Rule 14(a) requirement that Coolidge may be liable to Bryan for all or part of the plaintiff's claim. See Chapter 11, pp. 148-149. But once Bryan has properly impleaded Coolidge on the indemnification claim, he may assert whatever claims he has against him, related or unrelated.

However, there is an additional problem here in determining whether this claim could have been asserted in the original action. While the court clearly had ancillary jurisdiction over the impleader claim for indemnification, it is less clear that ancillary jurisdiction will extend to an additional related claim such as the wage claim in this question. See *Owen Equipment & Erection Co. v. Kroger*, 437 U.S. 365, 376 (1978) (emphasizing the derivative nature of impleader claims as a basis for extending ancillary jurisdiction to them). Of course, the court would have had an independent basis for subject matter jurisdiction over the added claim if Bryan sought more than $10,000 in damages on the combined claims. Bryan and Coolidge are diverse and under the aggregation rules Bryan may aggregate the wage claim with the indemnification claim to satisfy the amount in controversy requirement.

b. Assuming that there was subject matter jurisdiction over the wage claim in the original suit, res judicata will bar Bryan from suing on the claim later. Res judicata applies not only to a plaintiff who has asserted claims against a defendant but to other parties in the suit who have become offensive parties by asserting claims. Here, Bryan has asserted a claim against Coolidge by impleading him on the foundation claim. Having done so, the res judicata rules require him to assert all claims he has against Coolidge arising out of that occurrence. Bryan omitted the wage claim, which also arose from the construction of the foundation, and he is therefore barred from asserting it in a new action.

Bryan had the option not to implead Coolidge at all, in which case he could have asserted the indemnification and wage claims in a separate suit (but *not* two separate suits). However, once he has joined issue with Coolidge on the foundation question, he must get it all out in that suit. Although Rule 18(a) says he *may* assert his related wage claim, the res judicata rules convert that to *must* in this situation.

Suppose, however, that there were no basis for subject matter jurisdiction over the wage claim in the initial suit. If that were so, the court in the second action will not know for sure whether the first court would have heard the wage claim or not; it would depend on the first court's interpretation of the *Kroger* decision. In these circumstances the court might conclude, "We can't be sure whether the court would have taken ancillary jurisdiction, but at least Bryan should have tried, since his claim arose from the same transaction as the impleader claim." (Compare the treatment of state law claims under the pendent jurisdiction doctrine; see Chapter 18, question 12.) Or I can imagine the court saying, "Since it was unclear whether the first court could have heard the claim, we should give Bryan the benefit of the doubt and allow him to bring it separately." To avoid any risk of being barred by res judicata, Bryan would be well advised to try to assert the wage claim in the first suit and see what happens. One thing that is clear in this situation is that if Bryan tried and the court refused, the claim will not be barred in a subsequent suit.

## 10. Joinder: Yes, with a caution    Res judicata: No

a. As in question 9, Rule 18(a) authorizes Bryan to assert this claim along with his third-party indemnification claim. Here, of course, the claim is completely unrelated to the impleader claim but Rule 18 doesn't seem to care. However, there would not be ancillary jurisdiction over this claim. Bryan would have to establish independent diversity jurisdiction as suggested in the answer to question 9.

b. Bryan is not barred from suing separately on this claim since the claim asserted in the second action does not arise out of the same transaction or occurrence as the impleader claim against Coolidge in the first suit. Therefore, it does not satisfy the "same claim" requirement of res judicata.

If Bryan were forced to join this unrelated claim, the symmetry of the res judicata and jurisdiction rules would be lost: The court would have ancillary jurisdiction over Bryan's indemnification claim, regardless of the amount in controversy or the citizenship of Bryan and Coolidge. See *Kroger,* 437 U.S. at 376-377. But ancillary jurisdiction would not extend to the unrelated claim. If the amount in controversy requirement were not met, Bryan would be forced by the preclusion rules to join this claim but prevented by the jurisdiction rules from doing so.

## When Does *May Not* Mean *Must?*

11a. Ordinarily, Smith's negligence claim would be barred because it arose out of the same transaction as the breach of contract claim. However, Smith may argue that he should be allowed to bring a second action on the negligence claim because he tried to join it in the first action but the court refused to hear it. The situation is roughly analogous to the case of pendent claims, which must be asserted in the original action, but will not be barred if the court refuses in its discretion to entertain them. See Chapter 18, question 12. Similarly, in this case Smith will argue that he sought but was denied the right to assert the claim in the original suit and should therefore be allowed to resurrect it here.

b. Smith's argument is clever, but the analogy is a bit too rough to carry the day. Here, the negligence claim was disallowed because it was asserted in an untimely manner. Once Smith brought suit against Bryan, Smith had to assert all his claims properly in that action. Although the amendment rules are liberal, Smith has no right to hold back some claims arising from the construction, and spring them on Bryan just before trial. At some point the defendant has a right to focus his trial preparation on those issues that have been properly placed in dispute and let the others go.

The irony here, of course, is that if Smith had waited for three years to bring the entire suit, he could have asserted all of his claims since the limitations period had not expired. But, once the suit has been commenced and the case approaches trial, fairness to the defendant and the need to expedite litigation may prevent the assertion of additional claims even though they would not be barred by the statute of limitations. In this case, the court's conclusion that Smith may not amend probably means that the omitted claims are lost.

# 20

## Collateral Estoppel: Fine-Tuning the Preclusion Doctrine

## Introduction

If law is a mysterious profession, it is partly because lawyers have such a knack for attaching intimidating names to relatively commonsense principles. Names such as res judicata and collateral estoppel, for example; handles like these are enough to intimidate any client and most lawyers. But once you rub elbows with these related doctrines for a while, they will lose their power to intimidate, and you will recognize them for what they are, essential and sensible tools of the trade.

Although they serve related functions, these two tools are different in character. Res judicata acts like a bludgeon, indiscriminately smashing all efforts of a party to relitigate events that have already been litigated and decided in a prior suit. Collateral estoppel, by contrast, operates like a scalpel, dissecting a lawsuit into its various issues and surgically removing from reconsideration any that have been properly decided in a prior action.

Speaking less metaphorically, res judicata bars Smith from suing Jones for any kind of relief arising from a particular transaction or occurrence if Smith had previously brought an action against Jones based on that transaction or occurrence and the prior action was decided on the merits. Restatement (Second) of Judgments §24 (1982).[1] Res judicata bars any relitigation of Smith's rights against Jones based on those events, including not only the claims that Smith did raise the first time around but also any other claims arising out of the same set of facts that Smith could have raised (but did not) in the first action.

Collateral estoppel is more narrowly focused. It only precludes Smith from relitigating issues that were actually litigated and decided in a prior action with Jones. If an issue could have been raised in the first case but was not explicitly raised and decided, collateral estoppel will not bar Smith from raising that issue in a subsequent action against Jones.

An example will help to distinguish the two. Smith sues Jones for trespass on her property. Jones defends on the ground that she holds an easement to enter on the land to cut firewood. The court concludes that the easement is valid and enters judgment for Jones. Res judicata would bar Smith from suing Jones again based on the same wood cutting incident. For example, Smith could not bring a new action on the theory that an implied condition of the easement was that Jones pay fair value for the timber cut. Nor could she seek damages for property damage done to her land during the cutting. When Smith sues Jones for that occurrence, res judicata forces her to bring forth all her theories of recovery in the original action, rather than plaguing Jones with successive suits based on the same incident but asserting new theories for relief.

Collateral estoppel, by contrast, would bar Smith from relitigating specific issues decided in the first action, such as the validity of Jones's easement. If Jones returns to cut wood again on Smith's land and Smith sues, her suit will not be barred by res judicata because she is not suing for the same incident as the original action. However, Smith will be collaterally estopped from trying again to prove that Jones's easement is invalid because that issue was litigated and decided in the original action. But Smith would be free to litigate other issues not resolved in the earlier action. For example, Smith could still claim in the second action based on the second incident that an implied condition of the easement required payment for the timber. This issue would not be barred by collateral estoppel because it was not raised and decided in the first action.

At this point you may be asking, "Well, who needs collateral estoppel?" If res judicata so broadly precludes relitigation, whether or not an issue was previously raised, what is the need for a separate doctrine with another

---

1. The discussion in this chapter is based on the principles of the Second Restatement of Judgments. These principles have been widely applied in the federal courts, see, e.g., *Montana v. United States,* 440 U.S. 147, 153, 162 (1979); *United States v. Stauffer Chemical Co.,* 464 U.S. 165, 171 (1984), and have been increasingly adopted by state courts as well.

mysterious name?[2] The answer is that collateral estoppel is needed because issues already litigated may come up again in later litigation based on separate events. For example, Smith's second action against Jones for the second wood cutting incident would not be barred by res judicata since this is a new "claim" that has not been litigated before. See Restatement (Second) of Judgments §24 (1982) (defining "claim" to include all rights arising out of a single transaction or occurrence). But the issue of whether Smith has an easement to cut timber will arise again in the new action. Collateral estoppel will preclude litigation of that issue even though res judicata is inapplicable.

This example shows that collateral estoppel is both broader and narrower than res judicata. It is narrower in that it does not preclude all possible issues that might have been raised in a prior action but only those actually decided in that action. But it is also broader in that it can foreclose litigation of a particular issue in an entirely new context. Once the validity of Jones's easement has been determined between the parties, estoppel may preclude either party from relitigating that issue in suits arising out of completely different underlying facts. Suppose, for example that Jones went to cut wood again on Smith's property and was injured when she fell in an abandoned well. Under common law negligence principles, the duty of care Smith owed to her might depend on whether she was a trespasser. In her negligence action Jones could estop Smith from defending on the ground that Jones was a trespasser. Although the context is different in the second action, Jones's right to be on the land is at issue in both suits and there is no reason to allow Smith to relitigate it.

## Prerequisites for Estoppel

Collateral estoppel is a flexible doctrine, which varies in its application from one jurisdiction to another. However, the basic prerequisites are fairly uniform. *First,* the issue in the second case must be the same as the issue in the first. In the example above, the issue in both suits is whether Jones has a legal right to enter upon Smith's property to cut wood. But if Smith sues Jones for breach of a contract made in June 1982, and Jones is held to have been incompetent to make the contract because she was a minor, it does not follow that Jones was incompetent to make another contract in October of 1983. Here, the issues are not the same, and the resolution of one should not preclude litigation on the other.

*Second,* the issue must have been actually litigated. Restatement (Second) of Judgments §27 (1982). This requirement will obviously not be satisfied when a party failed to raise an issue in the previous action, such as

---

2. With *two* mysterious names, actually. Collateral estoppel is also frequently referred to as "issue preclusion," and res judicata as "claim preclusion."

Smith failing to assert a right to be paid for the wood Jones cut in the first suit. But an issue may not have been "actually litigated" even though it was raised in a prior action. Suppose, for example, that Smith sues Jones for breach of contract and Jones admits in her answer that she made the contract but defends the action on another ground. Under the Restatement view, Jones may defend a second suit for a later breach of the same contract on the ground that she never made the contract since she never actually litigated that issue in the original suit.

> There are many reasons why a party may choose not to raise an is-sue, or to contest an assertion, in a particular action. The action may involve so small an amount that litigation of the issue may cost more than the value of the lawsuit. Or the forum may be an inconvenient one in which to produce the necessary evidence or in which to liti-gate at all. The interests of conserving judicial resources, of maintain-ing consistency, and of avoiding oppression or harassment of the adverse party are less compelling when the issue on which preclusion is sought has not actually been litigated before. And if preclusive effect were given to issues not litigated, the result might serve to discourage compromise, to decrease the likelihood that the issues in an action would be narrowed by stipulation, and thus to intensify litigation.

Restatement (Second) of Judgments §27, comment e (1982).

*Third,* even if an issue was litigated in a prior action, collateral estoppel will not bar relitigation unless the issue was actually decided in that action. Restatement (Second) of Judgments §27 (1982). Suppose, for example, that Smith sues Jones on patent infringement and breach of contract theories and the case goes to trial on both issues. If the court finds for Smith on the ground that Jones breached the contract, collateral estoppel will not bar relitigation of the patent infringement issue in another context even though both sides fully presented their evidence on the patent issue in the first case. The parties have fully litigated the issue, and it seems wasteful to have them relitigate it in another suit. However, it is a little hard to apply collateral estoppel without knowing which party to estop. Without a winner or loser on the patent issue, the court in the later action has no choice but to rehear it.

*Fourth,* it is usually said that collateral estoppel will not apply unless the decision on the issue in the prior action was necessary to the court's judg-ment. Restatement (Second) of Judgments §27 (1982). This requirement of the doctrine has raised some problems of interpretation. Suppose for exam-ple, that the court in Smith's patent and contract action finds that Jones breached her contract with Smith *and* that she infringed Smith's patent. Each issue has been actually litigated and actually decided, but the Restatement would deny collateral estoppel effect to either decision since it is impossible to tell which decision was necessary to the judgment:

> First, a determination in the alternative may not have been as care-fully or rigorously considered as it would have been if it had been

necessary to the result, and in that sense it has some of the character-istics of dicta. Second, and of critical importance, the losing party, although entitled to appeal from both determinations, might be dis-suaded from doing so because of the likelihood that at least one of them would be upheld and the other not even reached. If he were to appeal solely for the purpose of avoiding the application of the rule of issue preclusion, then the rule might be responsible for increasing the burdens of litigation on the parties and the courts rather than lightening those burdens.

Restatement (Second) of Judgments §27, comment i (1982). See *Halpern v. Schwartz*, 426 F.2d 102, 105-106 (2d Cir. 1970). However, this rationale has not been universally accepted; some courts have given collateral estoppel effect to *both* alternative determinations in these circumstances. See, e.g., *Winters v. Lavine*, 574 F.2d 46, 67 (2d Cir. 1978), in which the Second Circuit appeared to limit *Halpern* to bankruptcy cases. Other cases and com-mentators have suggested a flexible middle ground between these extremes, which would apply estoppel if the second court can determine from the record of the first that both holdings were given full consideration. See *Malloy v. Trombley*, 427 N.Y.S.2d 969 (1980); 18 Wright and Miller at §4221, p.208.

There are further wrinkles to the collateral estoppel doctrine. In particu-lar, the issues of "offensive" use of estoppel and nonmutual estoppel, consid-ered in *Parklane Hosiery Co. v. Shore*, 439 U.S. 322 (1979), add an additional level of complexity to the analysis, which is explored in the following chapter. For the moment, however, we will focus on the basics. In answering the following questions, assume that all actions are brought in federal court and that the "modern" Second Restatement principles of collateral estoppel apply.

# QUESTIONS

## First Principles

1. Vanderbilt enters into a contract with Fisk for the delivery of five tons of coal per week to Fisk's power plant, for the period from January 1980 to December 1985. In 1982 Vanderbilt sues Fisk for breach of contract. He claims that the coal delivered from March to August 1981 was "grade AB" rather than "first quality" coal, as required by the contract. Fisk denies the allegation that he delivered grade AB coal instead of first quality coal and prevails in a jury trial.

Subsequently, Vanderbilt again sues Fisk for breach of contract on the ground that the coal delivered between February and June 1983 was grade AB. Fisk denies the breach.

    a.   Why is Vanderbilt's second suit not barred by res judicata?

    b.   Does collateral estoppel bar relitigation of any issue decided in the first suit?

2. Assume that Vanderbilt claims in the first suit that Fisk delivered grade AB coal from March to August of 1981, which did not comply with the contract specification for "first quality" coal. Fisk admits that he delivered grade AB coal during that period but defends on the ground that AB coal satisfies the contract specification. The case is tried to a jury, which finds for Vanderbilt and awards him damages.

   a. Vanderbilt sues Fisk again for delivering grade AB coal from February to June 1983. Will collateral estoppel apply to any issue?

   b. If Vanderbilt sues for the second breach in 1983, could Fisk defend on the ground that the contract is void because the parties entered into it on the basis of a mutual mistake as to the type of coal to be delivered?

   c. Assume that in Vanderbilt's second action Fisk defends on the ground that AB coal satisfies the contract specifications. He offers expert testimony, not offered in the original action, that AB coal is universally accepted in the industry as "first quality" coal. Will the court bar him from relitigating the issue?

   d. Assume that Vanderbilt's second suit against Fisk is for delivering grade AB coal from September to December 1984. Fisk defends on the ground that Vanderbilt had agreed to an oral modification of the contract allowing delivery of grade AB coal due to a national shortage of "first quality" coal during those months. Will collateral estoppel bar Fisk from relying on this defense?

3. Vanderbilt sues Fisk for breach of the coal delivery contract, claiming that Fisk delivered AB coal from March to August 1981. Fisk defends on the ground that the contract was invalid due to mutual mistake and in the alternative that AB coal complies with the contract specifications. The jury renders a general verdict[3] for Fisk.

   a. In 1984, Vanderbilt sues Fisk for a subsequent breach of the contract by delivering AB coal from February to June 1983. Fisk again defends on the ground that AB coal satisfies the contract specifications. Does collateral estoppel bar relitigation of this issue?

   b. Assume that in the original suit described in this question Vanderbilt moved for a directed verdict on Fisk's mutual mistake defense, and the court granted the motion. The case went to the jury on the defense that AB coal was adequate under the contract, and the jury rendered a verdict for Fisk. Subsequently, Vanderbilt sues Fisk for the 1984 breach. Fisk raises the same defenses. May Fisk estop Vanderbilt from claiming that AB coal does not meet the contract specifications? May Vanderbilt bar Fisk from relitigating the mutual mistake defense?

---

3. A general verdict is a simple verdict for the plaintiff or defendant without specifying the ground upon which the decision is based.

     c.  Assume that the case went to the jury on both issues, and the jury rendered a verdict for Vanderbilt in the first suit. Now Vanderbilt sues for the second breach during 1983 and Fisk defends on the ground that the parties entered into the contract under a mutual mistake. May Vanderbilt estop Fisk from relitigating the issue of mutual mistake?

## Isn't This Question in the Wrong Chapter??

4.   Morgan sues Gould for violation of the federal antitrust laws, in the federal district court for the Southern District of New York. Gould moves to dismiss for lack of personal jurisdiction. The court allows discovery on the jurisdictional issue, takes evidence on the issue at a hearing, hears oral argument, and subsequently denies the motion. Gould defaults on the merits and Morgan gets judgment. He then brings an action to enforce the judgment in Florida. Gould opposes enforcement of the judgment.

     a.  Will collateral estoppel bar relitigation of the personal jurisdiction issue?

     b.  Will collateral estoppel bar relitigation of the merits of the antitrust claim?

5.   Carnegie sues Astor in California for manufacturing a type of railroad engine in that state. Carnegie bases his suit on two claims. First, he alleges that he has a patent on the engine under the federal patent laws and that Astor is infringing his patent by building the engine without his permission. Second, he claims that Astor is violating California's unfair competition laws by using Carnegie's engine design. The case is tried to a jury, which renders a general verdict for Carnegie and awards him damages.

    Subsequently, Astor resumes making the same engines in Nevada, which (we will assume) has no unfair competition statute. Carnegie sues him for patent infringement. Does collateral estoppel bar relitigation of the infringement issue?

## A Brainteaser with a Commonsense Answer

6.   Assume the same facts as question 5, except that Astor resumed making the engines in California. Carnegie sues him there again. He seeks to enjoin Astor from making the engines and argues that the decision in the prior suit bars relitigation of that issue. Will collateral estoppel bar Astor from relitigating the legality of his conduct?

7.   Assume that Carnegie's first suit against Astor was tried to the court rather than the jury and that the judge's written decision expressly finds that Astor is liable on both theories. Astor then begins production of the engines in Nevada, and Carnegie brings a second action against him there. Will collateral estoppel bar Astor from claiming that he has not infringed Carnegie's patent?

## Mega-Hypo: Exercise for the Enthusiast

8.    The examples above illustrate particular issues in the application of collateral estoppel. Often, though, cases are not so conceptually clean; it is necessary to cull through a long procedural history and voluminous record to prove that the requirements of collateral estoppel are met. Indeed, it may take as much litigation to prove that the issue is precluded as it would to relitigate it, thus undermining one of the policy reasons for allowing issue preclusion. For a taste of these complexities, try the following example.

Hill buys two identical blast furnaces from Villard. One of them explodes, and Hill sues Villard for his injuries. He asserts claims for negligent design, breach of warranty, and strict liability. He seeks compensatory damages on all three counts and punitive damages, which are only available on the negligence claim. Villard admits that he made the furnace, but denies that the design was negligent. He admits that a warranty of fitness for its intended use arose upon the sale but denies that he breached the warranty. He also denies that he is strictly liable for injuries resulting from the furnace. He also raises contributory negligence as a defense on the negligence claim and claims that Hill's negligence claim is barred by the statute of limitations. The judge dismisses the strict liability claim under Rule 12(b)(6), on the ground that the applicable law does not allow recovery on a strict liability theory. Villard seeks summary judgment on the statute of limitations defense, which is denied. At trial Hill moves for a directed verdict on the negligent design. The judge denies it. The jury returns a verdict for the plaintiff and awards compensatory and punitive damages.

Two weeks after the judgment in the original suit, the second furnace explodes and Hill sues Villard on the same theories. What issues will be precluded in the second action?

# ANALYSIS

## First Principles

1a.    It is important to distinguish at the outset the relitigation of claims from the relitigation of issues. Res judicata only bars relitigation of the same claim, that is, the same transaction or occurrence that was the subject of the first suit. See Chapter 18, pp. 253-254. Vanderbilt is not seeking to relitigate his original claim for a breach of contract that took place in 1981. Rather, he is litigating a new claim for a later breach of the same contract. This second breach is not the same transaction or occurrence as the first even though it involves the same contract. Indeed, since it had not occurred when Vanderbilt first sued Fisk, it obviously could not have been joined in the first action.

b.    Collateral estoppel, in contrast to res judicata, precludes relitigation of issues in a second suit that have previously been litigated in a prior action. Even though the second suit is for a separate claim, so that res judicata does not apply, a subsequent suit may involve issues already settled in an earlier suit between them. If so, it makes no sense to allow the same parties to relitigate those issues.

However, the first prerequisite for collateral estoppel is that the issues in the two suits must be the same. Therefore, analysis of collateral estoppel issues should always begin with a determination of what was decided in the first action. In this case the issue in the first suit was whether Fisk had delivered first quality coal from March to August 1981. The issue in the second suit was whether Fisk delivered first quality coal during a subsequent period. This is a different factual issue, which was not raised in the prior suit and must be litigated in the new one.

2a. The issue in the first suit was not whether Fisk actually delivered AB coal (he admits that he did), but whether AB coal was insufficient under the contract specifications. Since this was the basis for Vanderbilt's claim that Fisk breached the contract, and the jury found for Vanderbilt, they must have concluded that AB coal did not satisfy the specifications. Since that issue was litigated and decided in the first suit, the court in Vanderbilt's second action for a later breach will estop Fisk from defending the second suit on the ground that AB coal satisfies the specifications. Here, although the issue arises in the second suit on a claim resulting from a new transaction or occurrence (and thus would not be barred by res judicata), it will be barred by collateral estoppel since the issue was previously litigated and decided between the parties.

b. As indicated above, the issue that was raised and decided in the first suit was whether AB coal satisfied the contract specifications. Although the separate defense of mutual mistake at the time of entering into the contract was available to Fisk in the prior action, he failed to raise it. However, collateral estoppel does not bar him from doing so later in a second suit for a new breach of the contract. Collateral estoppel only bars issues that were litigated and decided in the prior action; it does not affect claims or defenses which *could have been* raised but were not.

Compare res judicata doctrine, which bars litigation of any issues that could have been raised in a prior suit on the same claim. Res judicata does not apply in this hypothetical because Vanderbilt's second suit is for a separate claim, the 1983 breach.

c. Essentially, Fisk's position here is that he should be able to relitigate the AB coal issue because, while he failed to prove his defense the first time, he can prove it now. This argument will most probably fall on deaf ears. This testimony could presumably have been offered in the original suit and should have been. There is no reason why preclusion should operate against parties who litigated carefully the first time around but not against those who did not. Nor is there a requirement that the original finding has to be "right" to preclude relitigation. If that were true, the second court would have to rehear the issue to decide whether it was correctly decided the first time, thus completely undermining the purpose of the doctrine itself.

In limited situations, a party who discovers new evidence on an issue may move for relief from judgment under Fed. R. Civ. P. 60(b)(2). Under this rule, Fisk could seek to reopen the *original* action and overturn the finding that AB coal was insufficient. If he succeeded, of course, that original finding would no longer be entitled to collateral estoppel effect in subsequent suits.[4]

d.  In this case the original finding that AB coal did not comply with the specifications could not be relitigated. However, Fisk's defense is not that AB coal is sufficient under the original contract but that a subsequent modification of the contract allows him to deliver AB coal. This is a new issue, which was not raised in the original action, has never been litigated or decided, and is available to Fisk as a defense to the new action.

3a.  Collateral estoppel does not apply unless the issue was decided in the prior suit. In this case Fisk raised two defenses to Vanderbilt's first claim. If the jury accepted either defense, they would have had to find for Fisk. Obviously, they did accept one of those defenses, but it is impossible to tell from the jury's general verdict for Fisk which one it was. When a case is submitted to a jury with a general verdict form, the jury is simply asked to find for the plaintiff or for the defendant (and if it finds for the plaintiff, to find the amount of the plaintiff's damages). In this case, the jury's general finding "for the defendant" does not indicate whether it found the contract void or, alternatively, that AB coal complied with the specifications. Because it is impossible to tell which issue was decided, Fisk will not be able to demonstrate that the issue of whether the coal was sufficient was actually decided or necessary to the judgment. Consequently, collateral estoppel will not bar relitigation of that issue.

b.  The result here is different because the procedural history of the suit clearly indicates what issues were decided. The directed verdict for Vanderbilt on the mutual mistake defense is a decision on that issue; it constitutes a finding that on the evidence produced by the parties no reasonable jury could find for Fisk on that issue. Thus, that issue was actually litigated and decided in Vanderbilt's favor. That left only one defense, that the AB coal complied with the contract specifications. The jury's verdict for Fisk must have been based on this defense.

In this case, therefore, unlike question 3a, it is clear that the AB coal issue was decided in Fisk's favor in the previous action and that it was the basis for the jury's verdict for Fisk. Consequently, Vanderbilt will be estopped from relitigating that issue; the court will grant judgment for Fisk if Vanderbilt sues him for damages on the ground that the coal was inadequate under the contract.

---

4.  Fisk will have an uphill fight in obtaining relief from judgment under Rule 60(b)(2). That rule only allows the court to reopen the suit due to newly discovered evidence within one year after judgment. In addition, the moving party on such a motion must show that the new evidence could not have been discovered in the exercise of due diligence in time for presentation at the original trial.

As this example indicates, collateral estoppel can work for either party. In question 2a, Vanderbilt used it to establish an issue crucial to obtaining relief. In this case Fisk uses it to establish a defense that had been previously litigated and decided in his favor.

Suppose, however, that Fisk raises the defense of mutual mistake. Could Vanderbilt estop him from relitigating the mutual mistake issue since it was litigated and decided adversely to Fisk in the first suit, by directed verdict? Unfortunately for Vanderbilt, the answer is "no" because the decision on the mutual mistake issue was not necessary to the original judgment. That judgment was for Fisk and was based on the jury's finding that Fisk had proved his defense that AB coal was adequate under the contract. It was not based on Vanderbilt's victory on the mistake issue. Even though that issue was litigated and decided, the court will deny collateral estoppel effect to the prior decision since it was not essential to the decision of the case.

Although this seems artificial, consider Fisk's point of view. Even if he believes that the court wrongly decided the mistake issue, he has no incentive to appeal since he won the verdict. If he did appeal for fear of the potential collateral estoppel effect of the decision on the mutual mistake issue, the appellate court would probably refuse to hear the appeal since Fisk won below and review of the mutual mistake issue would therefore serve no purpose. In a sense, then, there has been no final decision on the issue; Fisk should not be estopped by a potentially erroneous decision that he has no opportunity or incentive to correct.

c. Here, Vanderbilt may invoke collateral estoppel to bar Fisk from relitigating the mutual mistake issue. In this example Fisk raised two defenses in the first suit. If the jury accepted either one they would have found for Fisk. Since they found for Vanderbilt, they must have considered each of the defenses and concluded that Fisk had not proved either one. In addition, the decision on each defense was necessary to the judgment since they had to consider and reject each defense raised by Fisk in order to find for Vanderbilt.

## Isn't This Question in the Wrong Chapter??

4a. This situation should sound familiar: It echoes question 5 from Chapter 3. If you look at that question, you will see that the defendant was barred from relitigating whether the rendering court had personal jurisdiction over him because he had already raised and litigated that issue in the rendering court. Now it should be clear to you that this result is a straightforward application of collateral estoppel principles: The personal jurisdiction issue was raised, litigated, and decided in the original action and was necessary to the judgment as well since the court would not have entered judgment for Morgan if it had concluded that it lacked jurisdiction over Gould. Thus, all the requirements for collateral estoppel are met, and Gould will be barred from relitigating the issue.

Note that in this case the plaintiff invokes collateral estoppel on an issue that has nothing to do with the merits of the lawsuit, indeed, in a situation where the merits were never litigated at all. But a decision "on the merits" of the plaintiff's substantive claim is not necessary before collateral estoppel applies: So long as the particular issue, be it procedural or substantive, was litigated and decided and necessary to the judgment, issue preclusion will apply. This result makes good sense: Gould should not be allowed to reliti- gate the personal jurisdiction question if it has been fully and fairly decided in another court.

Distinguish res judicata, however. That doctrine only bars relitigation of *claims* once they have been decided on the merits. When a case is dismissed on procedural grounds, the merits have never been litigated and the plaintiff may sue again in a court that can properly reach the merits.

b. Collateral estoppel will not bar relitigation of the merits since the case was not litigated on the merits in the original suit. However, res judicata will bar Gould from litigating the merits. A default judgment is entitled to res judicata effect, and (unlike collateral estoppel) there is no requirement that claims have been "actually litigated" for res judicata to attach.

5. Carnegie will have to relitigate the patent infringement issue. Although he won the first suit, it is impossible to tell from the general verdict which claim prevailed before the jury. Thus, both the "actually decided" and "neces- sary to the judgment" requirements are not clearly met.

Because a general verdict obscures the basis of the jury's decision, one or both of the parties may want to request use of a special verdict form, under Fed. R. Civ. P. 49, if they foresee the possibility of future litigation involving the same issues. A special verdict asks the jury to make findings on particular issues, rather than finding generally for the plaintiff or defendant. See Friedenthal, Kane, and Miller at §12.1. In this case, for example, the jury could be asked specifically whether they find that Astor infringed Carnegie's patent and whether they find that he violated California's unfair competition laws. If they answered "yes" on the patent infringement issue but "no" on the unfair competition issue, then it would be possible to prove in subsequent actions that the patent question was actually decided and necessary to the decision of the original suit.

## A Brainteaser with a Commonsense Answer

6. At first glance, it seems that the answer here ought to be "no" in light of the answer to question 5. It is unclear whether the jury in the first suit found for Carnegie on the patent claim or the unfair competition claim. However, it is clear that they found that Astor's conduct infringed on Carnegie's rights on one ground or the other. This should be sufficient to preclude relitigation in some contexts, at least. Carnegie may invoke collateral estoppel to bar reliti- gation of Astor's right to make the engines, on the ground that the original

judgment necessarily decided that he had no right to do so. The court may not need to decide which of Carnegie's theories the jury accepted in the first action; it may be enough to support the injunction that they accepted one.

However, if Carnegie seeks damages from Astor in the second suit, it may not be possible for him to rely on the previous judgment. If the measure of damages under the two claims differs, it will be necessary to determine which theory of liability applies in order to assess the damages. Since Carnegie can only show that the first suit determined that Astor was barred from making the engines, but not which theory that determination was based on, the jury in a second damage action would have to decide anew whether Astor is liable and if so, on which ground.

7.   This question raises the "alternative holdings" problem discussed in the introduction. The judge's opinion leaves no doubt that both the patent and unfair competition issues were actually litigated and decided. However, there is a problem as to whether either is "necessary to the judgment" when either is sufficient to support the judgment. The Restatement (Second) of Judgments takes the position that neither holding is entitled to preclusive effect because it is impossible to tell whether each received full consideration and because the losing party has no incentive to appeal on one arguably incorrect ground if the other would support the judgment. As indicated in the introduction, however, other courts have not gone along with the Restatement.

Note that the issue here is whether *California* would give collateral estoppel effect to the alternative holdings, not whether Nevada would. Under the Full Faith and Credit Clause of the United States Constitution (Article IV, §1), the Nevada court must give the California judgment the same full faith and credit that it would be given by a California court in a second suit there. Thus, if California would bar relitigation of both issues, Nevada must do so as well.

## Mega-Hypo: Exercise for the Enthusiast

8.   This is not a particularly unusual scenario for a products liability action, yet it takes some doing to unravel the procedural history and ascertain whether any issues will be barred in the second suit.

A good place to start is to determine what issues were decided in the original action. Villard admitted that he made the furnace and that a warranty of fitness for use arose upon the sale. However, as the introduction points out, these admissions do not satisfy the "actually litigated" requirement for collateral estoppel purposes.

The denial of the motion for summary judgment on the limitations issue does not "actually decide" that issue; it simply indicates that both parties have some evidence on that issue and therefore ought to have the opportunity to go to trial on it. See Chapter 15, p. 204. Similarly, the denial of the directed verdict motion on negligent design does not satisfy the requirement that the issue be "actually decided." That denial simply indicates that there is enough evidence to support a rational verdict for Villard, the nonmoving party, on that issue.

By contrast, the judge's dismissal of the strict liability claim clearly indicates that he decided as a matter of law that there is no strict liability claim arising out of the sale. A dismissal under Rule 12(b)(6) is a decision "on the merits" that may bar future litigation on the same issue.

How about the verdict; can we discern what the jury actually decided in reaching their verdict for Hill? The case went to trial on breach of warranty and negligence (but not on strict liability since the judge dismissed that claim) and the jury's general verdict does not expressly indicate whether the jury found for Hill on one or both theories. However, the jury awarded punitive damages, which were only available under the negligent design claim. Thus the jury must have found for Hill on that claim. And in order to do so it must have rejected the defense that the negligence claim is barred by the statute of limitations and that Hill's contributory negligence bars relief.

The jury *may* have also found for Hill on the breach of warranty claim, but we can't tell, since compensatory damages are available on both theories. Even if the jury found for Hill on both theories, it would only award him his actual losses as compensatory damages. Thus the amount of the compensatory damages does not reveal whether the jury accepted both theories or only one.

We have identified four issues as actually litigated and decided: whether the statute of limitations barred the negligence claim, whether Hill's contributory negligence barred the negligence claim, whether the furnace was negligently designed, and whether Villard is strictly liable for the injuries resulting from the explosion. The first three were necessary to the judgment since the jury could not have found for Hill on the negligence claim without rejecting the statute of limitations and contributory negligence defenses and finding that the design was negligent. The dismissal of the strict liability claim is not necessary to the judgment, however, and Hill should be able to relitigate it in the second suit. After all, he *won* the first action on other grounds, so he had no incentive to appeal the dismissal of his strict liability claim.

Only three issues, then, satisfy the prerequisites. But two of those, the statute of limitations and contributory negligence[5] issues, are not likely to be the same in the two suits since the two explosions took place at different

---

5. In some circumstances, the contributory negligence issue might be the same, so that the rejection of the defense in the first action would bar Villard from asserting it in the second. Suppose, for example, that Hill installed the two furnaces in the same way at the same time, and Villard claimed in the first suit that inadequate installation contributed to the explosion. On those facts, the issue would be the same in the second suit and Villard would be barred by collateral estoppel from raising the defense again. But Villard would still have to prove that the furnaces *were* installed in the same way.

times and perhaps under different circumstances. Only the negligent design issue remains. That issue will presumably be the same since the two furnaces are identical.

Even though Hill will have to go through all of that to invoke collateral estoppel, he will still have a strong incentive to do so. If he can get the judge to travel this long road, at the end of it he will have established an issue crucial to his right to relief, without relitigating the merits of that issue or risking a different decision on it by the second jury. For Hill, the value of invoking collateral estoppel is not merely to save litigation time, but to assure the same favorable result he obtained in the first suit. Ironically, he may be willing to spend as much litigation time to obtain that result as it would take to try the issue again.

# 21

## The Obscure Kingdom: Nonmutual Collateral Estoppel

## Introduction

We began at the beginning (see page one), and we should end at the end . . . but nothing is quite that simple in civil procedure. A lawsuit "ends" when a final judgment is entered or an appeal of the trial court judgment is decided. But the suit may send out waves that break on very distant shores. Under collateral estoppel doctrine, issues decided in one lawsuit may have effects in another suit at a later time or in a different court. And, beyond this fairly well-mapped terrain lies the more obscure kingdom of nonmutual collateral estoppel.

Under traditional issue preclusion principles, a party may be estopped from relitigating an issue that she had litigated in a prior suit and lost. Restatement (Second) of Judgments §27 (1982); Chapter 20, pp. 281-283. Assume, for example, that Cartier sues La Salle, a tenant in his shopping center, for breach of a provision in the standard lease signed by all Cartier's tenants. If the court finds that the lease provision is invalid, La Salle may estop Cartier in a future suit involving the same lease from claiming that the disputed provision is enforceable. Conversely, if the provision had been held valid, La Salle would be estopped from defending a future action based on the same lease on the ground that the provision was invalid.

Nonmutual collateral estoppel goes a step beyond this basic doctrine by allowing a new party to invoke collateral estoppel against a party who litigated and lost on an issue in a prior action. Suppose, for example, that Cartier, after losing his suit against La Salle on the ground that the lease provision was unenforceable, sued Cortez, another tenant, who had signed the same standard lease. Under nonmutual preclusion principles, Cortez, the new defendant, could estop Cartier from claiming that the disputed provision was enforceable since Cartier had previously litigated that issue against La Salle and lost.

For many years, this frontier concept remained, if not undiscovered, at least unexplored by most courts. The general rule was that estoppels must be mutual, that is, the only parties who could invoke collateral estoppel were those who were involved in the suit in which the issue was initially decided. This "doctrine of mutuality" allowed La Salle to estop Cartier on the issue of the validity of the lease provision, but would not allow Cortez, a stranger to the first suit, to do so. The courts reasoned that La Salle had litigated in the first action; he took the risk that, if he lost on the issue, he would be bound by that finding in subsequent suits, under basic collateral estoppel doctrine, and therefore he — and only he — had earned the right to assert estoppel if he won. But Cortez was not a party to the first action; he took no risk of being bound by an adverse judgment if Cartier proved that the lease provision *was* valid. Consequently, since he would not be bound by an unfavorable finding, the mutuality doctrine barred Cortez from taking advantage of a favorable finding in the La Salle/Cartier suit.

## A Fundamental Question

1.   Why is it true, whether or not the mutuality rule applies, that Cortez could not be bound by a finding in the original suit that the lease provision was valid?

————————————

Courts that applied the mutuality rule were also influenced by an additional reason in confining estoppel to the original parties. If the litigants know that findings will only affect other suits with the same adversaries, they can fairly easily anticipate the future implications of an adverse decision in the original suit. However, if estoppel is available to new parties, the litigants may be forced to over-litigate issues in the original action for fear of unknown risks of estoppel in future actions involving new parties.

While the mutuality rule has had a respectable history and widespread acceptance, it has been abandoned in many jurisdictions since the landmark case of *Bernhard v. Bank of America National Trust & Savings Assn.*, 122 P.2d 892 (Cal. 1942). In *Bernhard*, Mrs. Bernhard claimed that certain funds held by Cook, the executor of an estate, belonged to the estate. Cook claimed they were a gift to him from the decedent, which he need not include in the assets of the estate. Bernhard challenged Cook's claim in a probate proceeding during the course of the settlement of the estate, and the court held that the funds were a gift to Cook. Bernhard then sued the bank that had been holding the funds and paid them to Cook, alleging again that the funds were assets of the estate that should have been paid to the estate rather than to Cook.

The bank pleaded collateral estoppel, arguing that Bernhard had already adjudicated the right to the funds in the probate proceeding, had lost, and should be precluded from relitigating the issue against the bank.

## Who's Who?

2.   Why was the bank's invocation of collateral estoppel in *Bernhard* "nonmutual?"

---

In *Bernhard*, Justice Traynor concluded that it was not categorically improper to allow a new party to take advantage of findings in an earlier suit to estop a party who had litigated the issue in the prior action. Instead of focusing on the "free ride" that the bank received by borrowing the favorable result achieved by Cook in the earlier case, Justice Traynor emphasized the fact that Bernhard, the party *against* whom the estoppel was asserted, had been a party to the first action and had had a full and fair opportunity to litigate the issue there. *Bernhard* at 895. In such circumstances, the court saw no reason to allow her to relitigate the decided issue by simply switching adversaries.

The United States Supreme Court first endorsed the use of nonmutual estoppel in the federal courts in *Blonder-Tongue Laboratories Inc., v. University of Illinois Foundation*, 402 U.S. 313 (1971). The situation in *Blonder-Tongue* was analogous to *Bernhard*. The University of Illinois Foundation sued one defendant for infringing a patent but lost on the ground that its patent was invalid. It then "switched adversaries," bringing suit against another defendant for infringement of the same patent. The Supreme Court reversed its long-standing rule allowing such relitigation and approved use of nonmutual collateral estoppel against the university on the issue of the validity of the patent. The Court noted the unfairness and waste of judicial resources that flows from allowing "repeated litigation of the same issue as long as the supply of unrelated defendants holds out." *Blonder-Tongue* at 329.

Like the *Bernhard* court, the Court in *Blonder-Tongue* emphasized that preclusion was only appropriate if the precluded party had had a full and fair opportunity to litigate the issue in the first action. *Blonder-Tongue* at 332-334. In addition, the Court emphasized the unique burdens that patent infringement actions impose on the courts. However, the lower federal courts have not construed the Court's holding as limited to patent cases.

Subsequent cases have applied nonmutual collateral estoppel in a wide variety of cases, at least when the posture of the parties in the successive actions is similar to that of the parties in *Blonder-Tongue* and *Bernhard*. See generally 18 Wright and Miller at §4464.

# Offensive and Defensive Estoppel

This matter of the posture of the parties introduces a further wrinkle to the nonmutual preclusion problem. In both *Blonder-Tongue* and *Bernhard*, the new party in the second action was a defendant who invoked estoppel to prevent the plaintiff from establishing a fact that he had been unable to establish in the first suit. Bernhard, for example, had essentially been a plaintiff in the first probate proceeding, trying to establish the estate's right to the bank account held by Cook. In the second action, she was again the plaintiff, attempting to prove the same issue in order to recover from the bank. The bank asserted estoppel "defensively," to prevent her from proving an essential element of her claim. Similarly, in *Blonder-Tongue*, the university foundation had brought the first suit and lost and was also the plaintiff in the second suit. The new defendant asserted defensive nonmutual estoppel to prevent the foundation from establishing the validity of a patent previously held invalid. See *Parklane Hosiery v. Shore*, 439 U.S. 322, 326 n.4 (1979) ("[d]efensive use occurs when a defendant seeks to prevent a plaintiff from asserting a claim the plaintiff has previously litigated and lost against another defendant"). Visually the sequence looks like this:

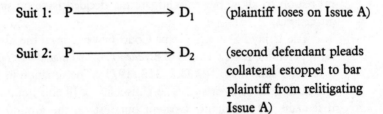

This defensive assertion of estoppel is more easily justified than the offensive use of estoppel discussed in *Parklane*. In defensive estoppel cases, the party being estopped was usually the plaintiff in the original suit and chose the forum and the defendant against whom to initially litigate the issue. When that is true, it hardly seems unfair to bind the plaintiff to the first resolution of the recurring issue.

By contrast, offensive use of collateral estoppel usually involves a new plaintiff who seeks to borrow a finding from a prior action to impose liability on a party who was a defendant in the prior action. See *Parklane* at 326 n.4 ("offensive use of collateral estoppel occurs when the plaintiff seeks to foreclose the defendant from litigating an issue the defendant has previously litigated unsuccessfully in an action with another party"). For example, sup-

pose that La Salle had brought suit against Cartier to enjoin him from
enforcing the disputed provision of the standard lease and the provision was
held invalid. If Cortez now sued Cartier for damages resulting from the
invalid provision and invoked collateral estoppel to prevent Cartier from
relitigating the validity of the provision, that would be offensive, nonmutual
estoppel. The new plaintiff, Cortez, would be taking advantage of the finding
against Cartier, a defendant in the prior action, to establish a claim against
Cartier in a new suit.

This is exactly what the plaintiff did in *Parklane*. In the first case to go to
judgment, the Securities and Exchange Commission had claimed — and the
court had held — that Parklane Hosiery had issued a false and misleading
proxy statement. Subsequently, the plaintiffs in a class action suit against
Parklane, based on the same proxy statement, invoked collateral estoppel
against Parklane on the question of whether the statement was false and
misleading. Since Parklane had litigated and lost that issue in the first suit, the
class plaintiffs argued that it had had its day in court on the issue and should
be barred from relitigating it. The plaintiffs sought to use estoppel offen-
sively, to establish the defendant's liability in a new action. The sequence of
suits looks like this:

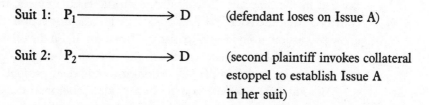

Suit 1:  $P_1 \longrightarrow D$        (defendant loses on Issue A)

Suit 2:  $P_2 \longrightarrow D$        (second plaintiff invokes collateral
                                          estoppel to establish Issue A
                                          in her suit)

In these offensive use situations, there are a number of reasons for the
courts to exercise particular caution in deciding whether to apply nonmutual
collateral estoppel. For one thing, the party against whom estoppel is asserted
in the second action (i.e., Parklane in the *Parklane* case and Cartier in the
preceding example) was a defendant in the first suit and did not choose the
forum in which the issue was initially decided. While it is possible to say that
the losing party in a defensive-use situation gave it her best shot in the
original action, this is not so clear in the offensive-use situation, in which
the estopped party did not choose the time and place of the first suit or the
adversary against whom to try the issue.

The Supreme Court in *Parklane* noted several other risks posed by offensive use of estoppel. *First,* the prospect of taking advantage of another plaintiff's victory to establish crucial issues without trial may lead plaintiffs to
"wait and see," that is, to hold back from joining in the first plaintiff's suit.
After all, if La Salle lost the first action against Cartier because the lease
provision was held valid, Cortez would not be barred from relitigating the
issue because he has never litigated it, and no party can be estopped until she
(or someone in privity with her) has had her day in court on the issue. But if

La Salle wins and the courts recognize nonmutual collateral estoppel, Cortez may be able to establish this crucial issue without trial and the resulting risk of losing on the issue altogether.

*Second,* the *Parklane* Court recognized that a party might not have litigated the issue aggressively in the first action if the stakes were small or the forum inconvenient. It may be inappropriate to apply estoppel in one context if the estopped party did not have the incentive to litigate the issue fully in another. *Third,* the Court noted that it may not have been possible for the losing party to litigate effectively in the first action if the procedural system of the court that decided the first case was more limited than that of the court hearing the second. Last, one or more prior inconsistent judgments on the issue may suggest that it would be unfair to give conclusive effect to any one of them.

In *Parklane* the Supreme Court did not categorically endorse or reject offensive nonmutual collateral estoppel. As modern courts are wont to do, the Court held that lower courts should exercise discretion in considering whether to allow such offensive assertions of estoppel. The court should consider, on the unique facts of each case, all the factors described above and any other factors that may indicate that the issue was not fully and fairly decided in the first suit. If, considering all the circumstances, the court is convinced that the issue was fully adjudicated in the first action, then it may allow preclusion, even in an offensive use situation. If, on the other hand, the court is doubtful, for whatever reason, that the party being estopped had a full "bite at the apple" in the first action, it should deny estoppel.

Although the *Parklane* case goes into more detail than *Blonder-Tongue* concerning the risks of nonmutual collateral estoppel, the two cases are entirely consistent. The Court in *Blonder-Tongue* emphasized that the court in the second action must be convinced that the estopped party had a full opportunity to litigate the issue in the first case. *Parklane* emphasizes the same fundamental prerequisite but spells out in more detail the factors to be considered in making that determination. In fact, most of the cautionary factors discussed in *Parklane* are equally applicable to defensive use situations, such as whether the estopped party had a strong incentive to litigate in the first suit, whether the procedural opportunities to do so were as broad in that action, and whether there are any prior inconsistent judgments. Other factors, however, such as whether the plaintiff should have joined in an earlier action are unique to offensive estoppel.

Let me end this introduction with a truism. Nonmutual collateral estoppel, whether of the offensive or defensive persuasion, *is* a form of collateral estoppel. As such, it must meet all of the basic prerequisites for application of estoppel discussed in the last chapter. In every case, mutual or nonmutual, the court must find that the issue is the same, that it was actually litigated and decided in the prior action, and that it was necessary to the judgment in the first action before it can apply estoppel in a second action. However, in nonmutual preclusion situations, the court must consider not only these basic requirements for estoppel but also the additional factors discussed above in order to determine whether it would be fair to preclude relitigation of findings from the prior action in a new suit involving a new party.

In answering the following questions, assume that contributory negligence constitutes a complete defense if it is proved. Also, assume that all actions are brought in state court unless otherwise specified.

# QUESTIONS

## Charting the Terrain

3.  Lewis sues Clark for trespassing on his property. Clark denies that Lewis owns the land. The court determines that Lewis owns the land and awards him damages for the trespass.

Subsequently, Lewis sues Fremont for trespass on the same piece of land.

   a.  Who would be likely to invoke collateral estoppel in the second action?
   b.  Would estoppel be allowed in a mutuality jurisdiction?
   c.  Would estoppel be allowed in a nonmutuality jurisdiction?

4.  Suppose that Lewis sued Clark for the trespass and the court found for Clark on the ground that Lewis does not own the land. Subsequently, Lewis sues Fremont for trespassing on the same property.

   a.  Who would be likely to invoke collateral estoppel?
   b.  Would this be mutual or nonmutual use of collateral estoppel?
   c.  Would it be defensive or offensive use of estoppel?
   d.  Could the court apply collateral estoppel in the second suit if the suits were brought in a jurisdiction that has abandoned the mutuality doctrine?

5.  Earhart brings a negligence action against Lindbergh for serious injuries suffered in an airplane accident. The jury finds for Earhart and awards her damages. Subsequently, Wright, a passenger in Earhart's plane, brings a separate action against Lindbergh for his injuries in the same accident. Wright invokes collateral estoppel to prevent Lindbergh from relitigating the issue of his negligence.

   a.  Is this offensive or defensive collateral estoppel?
   b.  Is it mutual or nonmutual?
   c.  Could the court apply collateral estoppel in the second action if both suits were brought in federal court?

## New Frontiers

6.  Mr. and Mrs. Byrd sue Da Gama for serious injuries suffered in a three-car collision. Da Gama pleads contributory negligence as a defense against

Mr. Byrd, who was driving the Byrd car, but not against Mrs. Byrd. The jury returns a verdict for Da Gama on Mr. Byrd's claim but for Mrs. Byrd on her claim for her own injuries.

Mr. Byrd now sues Smith, the third driver involved in the collision, to recover for his injuries. Smith pleads contributory negligence.

    a.   Who would seek to invoke collateral estoppel in the second action? On what issue?

    b.   Would this be offensive or defensive use?

    c.   Would it be permissible in a jurisdiction that requires mutuality?

    d.   Would it be permissible in a jurisdiction that has abandoned the mutuality doctrine?

7.   In 1981 Carol Burnett brought a libel suit in California against the *National Enquirer*, arising out of story in the *Enquirer* about her behavior in a Washington restaurant. Among other defenses, the *Enquirer* relied on a California statute, which allows a newspaper to avoid substantial liability by printing a timely retraction. See Cal. Civ. Proc. Code §48(a) (West 1982). A major issue in the case was whether the *Enquirer* was a newspaper that enjoyed the protection of the statute, or a magazine that would not. The court held that the *Enquirer* was a magazine and thus not entitled to the protection of the retraction statute. Burnett recovered a very substantial verdict.

The *Boston Globe* reported the verdict in a story on March 27, 1981, and went on to state:

> Burnett's case has been watched closely by other celebrities who have sued, or want to sue, the tabloid and other gossip publications over items they consider fiction and harmful to their careers.
>
>     Singer Helen Reddy and her manager-husband Jeff Wald were the most recent to sue the *National Enquirer*, asking $30 million this week for a March 3 article about them.

*Boston Globe*, March 27, 1981, p. 4.

Assume that the *Enquirer* printed a similar retraction of the Reddy/Wald article. After the decision in the Burnett case, Reddy and Wald bring suit against the *Enquirer*, and assert collateral estoppel on the issue of whether the *Enquirer* is a magazine or a newspaper.

    a.   Would this be offensive or defensive use of estoppel?

    b.   Would this be allowed if both actions were brought in California and California still applied the mutuality doctrine?

    c.   Would it be allowed if both suits were brought in California after California abandoned the strict mutuality approach?

## Outer Space

8.   Armstrong sues Ride and Gagarin in federal court for injuries arising out of an auto accident. Each defendant defends solely on the ground that he or

she was not negligent. After trial, the jury finds for Armstrong against Ride but finds Gagarin not liable.

Subsequently, Gagarin sues Ride for his injuries in the accident. Ride pleads contributory negligence.

    a.   Could Gagarin have joined his claim against Ride in the first suit?

    b.   Who would seek to invoke collateral estoppel in the second action?

    c.   Is this mutual or nonmutual estoppel?

    d.   Is it defensive or offensive?

    e.   Will the court allow use of estoppel on any issues?

# ANALYSIS

## A Fundamental Question

1.   We began this voyage by emphasizing that every litigant is entitled to due process of law before a court adjudicates her rights. See Chapter 1, p. 1. The very essence of due process is an opportunity for the parties to be heard, to litigate the issues before they are resolved for or against them. If Cartier won his suit against La Salle and then sued Cortez for violating the same lease provision, Cortez would be a new party who has never had an opportunity to litigate the validity of the provision. It would come as quite a surprise to Cortez to learn that he had effectively lost his action (because the crucial issue was already decided in Cartier's favor) before he had even reached the court-house, simply because La Salle had previously lost his suit. Cortez may well believe that he can litigate the lease question more effectively than La Salle, who may not have had the resources to litigate the issue aggressively or may have made a tactical decision to focus his defense on other grounds. Maybe Cortez won't do better but under the due process clause every party gets one chance to try, and Cortez has not yet had his "bite at the apple."

Although it would promote efficiency to estop Cortez from relitigating decided issues (just as it promotes efficiency to bar La Salle from doing so under traditional estoppel doctrine), efficiency is only one goal of the proce-dural system. In this case it is outweighed by the countervailing value of fairness to new parties.

## Who's Who?

2.   The Bernhard case is an example of nonmutual collateral estoppel be-cause the party seeking to invoke estoppel was not a party to the suit in which the issue was initially decided. That action was between the heirs (including Bernhard) and Cook. Under mutuality doctrine, only they could assert estop-pel in subsequent cases; the bank, a new party, was unable to assert estoppel because it was not a party to the original suit and hence took no risk of being estopped on the issue if it were decided in Bernhard's favor. Since the bank could not be burdened by the result in the original case (see question 1),

courts that adhered to the mutuality rule concluded that it should not be able to benefit from the prior decision if Bernhard lost.

## Charting the Terrain

3a.   The issue that is common to both actions is whether Lewis owned the land. Lewis won on this issue in the first suit and is therefore the party likely to assert estoppel in the second to establish his ownership of the property.

b.   Lewis will not be allowed to estop Fremont on the ownership issue because Fremont, like Cortez in the earlier example, has never had his day in court on the question of Lewis's title, and no court will estop him from litigating that issue until he has had a full and fair opportunity to do so. Besides, Fremont was not a party to the original action, and the mutuality doctrine confines estoppel to the parties to the original suit or those in privity with the original parties.

c.   Estoppel would also be denied in a nonmutuality jurisdiction. As indicated above, Fremont has never had an opportunity to litigate the issue of Lewis's title to the land; due process entitles him to an opportunity to do so. The abandonment of mutuality has *not* changed this basic tenet of the system. In every situation in which nonmutual estoppel has been applied, the estopped party (but not her opponent) had been a party in the first suit and therefore had had her chance to litigate the issue. Thus, the crucial question in such cases is the one emphasized in *Bernhard*: whether the party being estopped was a party in the prior action. Since Fremont was not a party in the first suit, estoppel would not bar him from relitigating the issue.

4a.   In this case, Fremont would seek to take advantage of the finding in the prior action that Lewis did not own the land. If he can estop Lewis from proving that he owned the land, he will defeat Lewis's claim, since a plaintiff must prove that he has an interest in the property to recover for trespass.

b.   Fremont would be invoking nonmutual collateral estoppel since he was not a party to the prior action. The only parties who could use mutual collateral estoppel are Lewis and Clark, the parties to the first suit. Here estoppel is invoked against a prior party by a stranger to the original action.

c.   This would be defensive collateral estoppel since Fremont, the defendant, would invoke estoppel to prevent Lewis, the plaintiff in the first suit, from relitigating the ownership issue that he had previously litigated and lost. Lewis is analogous to the foundation in *Blonder-Tongue*, which was barred from relitigating the validity of its patent against a second defendant after failing to prove it in a prior action. See the diagram on p. 298.

d.   In a jurisdiction that has abandoned mutuality, the court would have the authority to apply defensive nonmutual collateral estoppel to bar Lewis from relitigating the ownership issue. Under *Bernhard* and *Blonder-Tongue*, a court may allow the use of defensive estoppel by a new party, so long as the party being estopped was a party to the prior action and litigated the issue there. Those criteria are met here because Lewis was a party to the prior suit against Clark and litigated the ownership issue in that action.

However, the court would not automatically apply defensive estoppel to bar Lewis from relitigating. As the *Bernhard* court pointed out, and the Supreme Court reiterated in *Blonder-Tongue*, a party who has already litigated an issue should not be estopped from relitigating it unless she had a full and fair opportunity to contest the issue in the first action. Thus, the court will only apply estoppel if it is convinced, after review of the proceedings in the first suit, that Lewis had the incentive and opportunity to litigate the ownership issue tenaciously against Clark.

The burden to establish that the issue was fully litigated falls on Fremont, the party invoking estoppel. Friedenthal, Kane, and Miller at §14.11. Thus, the abandonment of mutuality opens the door to preclusion in situations like this, but the court must exercise caution in deciding who to let in.

5a. This is an example of offensive estoppel. Here, Wright invokes the negligence finding from the first action to *establish* an issue necessary for recovery against Lindbergh, the defendant in both the first and second suits. Wright seeks to use estoppel "as a sword," to establish a fact necessary to recovery, rather than as a "shield" against liability, as in question 4. See the diagram on p. 299 supra.

b. Because estoppel is invoked by Wright, a new party who did not litigate the negligence issue in the first action, this is nonmutual estoppel. Of course, Lindbergh *was* a party to the first suit; in every nonmutual estoppel case *one* of the parties in the second suit will have been a party (or in privity with a party) to the first, since estoppel may only be invoked against a party who litigated and lost on the issue before.

c. The Supreme Court held in *Parklane* that the federal courts may apply offensive nonmutual collateral estoppel in situations such as this in which a new plaintiff invokes estoppel to establish an issue the defendant lost on in a prior suit. Although Wright, the new party invoking estoppel, was not a party to the original action, the party against whom it was invoked (in this case Lindbergh) was there and litigated the issue in the first suit. Lindbergh has had an opportunity to be heard on the issue, the fundamental prerequisite to barring relitigation.

However, as in the defensive estoppel cases, the court will not automatically bar Lindbergh from relitigating. The court must examine the circumstances of the first case to determine whether Lindbergh had an adequate opportunity to litigate, and whether other cautionary factors (such as whether Wright sat out the first suit to see how Earhart would fare) counsel against application of estoppel.

In this case, several of these factors favor application of estoppel. *First,* since Earhart's injuries were serious, Lindbergh presumably had a strong incentive to defend her action vigorously to avoid paying substantial damages. *Second,* the question indicates that both suits were brought in federal court. Thus, there are not likely to be procedural advantages available to Lindbergh in suit two that were not available in suit one; both will be governed by the Federal Rules of Civil Procedure. Absent other factors suggesting unfairness to Lindbergh, this case looks like a good candidate for application of nonmutual offensive collateral estoppel.

## New Frontiers

6a.  The first step in analyzing this case, as in every collateral estoppel case, mutual or otherwise, is to determine what issues were decided in the first action that may recur in the second. In this case the verdict for Mrs. Byrd indicates that the jury found Da Gama negligent. But their verdict for Da Gama against Mr. Byrd indicates that they also found Mr. Byrd contributorily negligent.[1] It is this finding that is relevant to the second action: If Smith pleads contributory negligence as a defense to Mr. Byrd's suit and is able to invoke collateral estoppel to establish it, he will escape liability regardless of his own negligence.

b.  This is an example of nonmutual, defensive use of estoppel. The defendant in the second action invokes estoppel to preclude Byrd, a plaintiff in both the first and second suits, from relitigating an issue that he litigated and lost in the prior suit.

However, this case represents a slight twist from the typical defensive estoppel case. In cases such as *Blonder-Tongue,* the plaintiff lost on an issue that was an element of his prima facie case and was precluded in a later action from proving that element. In this case, however, the issue on which preclusion is sought was not essential to establish Byrd's claim in the prior suit but established a *defense* against the claim based on Byrd's contributory negligence. In the second action, Smith invokes estoppel to establish a similar defense to Byrd's claim against him. It is like the classic defensive use cases, however, in that it allows a defendant to prevent the plaintiff from recovering by borrowing the finding from an earlier suit in which the plaintiff lost on the same issue.

c.  Smith would not be able to assert collateral estoppel in a mutuality jurisdiction since he was not a party to the first suit and therefore was not allowed to take advantage of favorable findings in that action.

d.  In this case, as in question 4d, a court in a nonmutuality jurisdiction could allow Smith to invoke collateral estoppel even though he was not a party to the Byrd/DaGama suit in which Byrd's negligence was initially established. As in the Wright case, however, the court will only apply estoppel if it is convinced that Byrd had a full opportunity and incentive to litigate the issue of his negligence in the first action.

---

1. This assumes that the evidence of Mr. Byrd's injuries eliminates the possibility that the jury found that he had suffered no damages. Compare *Illinois Central Gulf R.R. v. Parks,* 390 N.E.2d 1078 (Ind. App. 1979).

7a. The *Enquirer* was the defendant in the first action, and lost on the issue of whether it is a newspaper within the meaning of the California statute. In the second action, two new plaintiffs try to use the finding from the first case to help establish their case against the *Enquirer*, a defendant in each suit. This is best classified as offensive collateral estoppel.

However, this is not quite the classic example of offensive nonmutual estoppel. As in question 6, the new plaintiff here asserts estoppel to preclude the defendant from proving a defense that failed in the first action. In the more typical offensive use situation, the plaintiff asserts collateral estoppel to establish an element of her prima facie case (such as the defendant's negligence) after another plaintiff proved that element against the same defendant in a prior action. In *Parklane*, for example, the plaintiffs in the second suit had to prove that the proxy statement was false and misleading in order to recover. They sought to do so by borrowing the court's finding to that effect in the earlier action.

b. Estoppel would be denied if California were still a mutuality jurisdiction since Reddy and Wald were not parties to the prior action or in privity with the plaintiff in that action.

c. The answer to this question is a cautious "maybe." The analysis must start with the truism at the end of the introduction. Nonmutual estoppel is a species of collateral estoppel; as such, it is only applicable if the basic prerequisites for estoppel are satisfied. Before collateral estoppel can ever be applied, the court must determine that the issue in the first and second actions is the same. Here, it is clear that the issue of the *Enquirer*'s status as a magazine or newspaper under the California statute was litigated and decided in the first action. But estoppel will only apply if the issue in the Reddy/Wald suit is the same, that is, if the California statute applies. If Reddy and Wald reside in Virginia and suffered most of their damages there, a court might not apply the California statute to their suit at all. It might apply Virginia law to the Reddy case; that law might authorize magazines as well as newspapers to escape liability by printing a retraction or not allow the retraction defense at all. Thus, the issue may be different in the second suit or irrelevant to it.

Assuming that the California statute would apply in the Reddy/Wald suit, the court would still have to consider the various factors that may make offensive nonmutual estoppel inappropriate. Although it certainly appears that the *Enquirer* had a strong incentive to litigate the issue in the Burnett case, the procedural opportunities might differ if the first suit were in federal court and the second in a state court or if important witnesses were unavailable to the *Enquirer* in the first case but can be produced in the second. Or if the court determined that Reddy and Wald had deliberately decided *not* to join in the Burnett case in order to get the advantage of nonmutual estoppel without taking the risk of losing on the issue in the first action, it might deny preclusion. Once again, the point is that the abandonment of mutuality opens the door to case-by-case consideration of whether estoppel should be available to the new party; it does not automatically lead to preclusion.[2]

## Outer Space

8a. Gagarin could have cross-claimed against Ride for his injuries in the first action, under Fed. R. Civ. P. 13(g), but was not required to do so. Since he did not have to do so, he may bring the claim separately. Res judicata does not bar the separate suit, because Gagarin's claim against Ride was never adjudicated in the first. See Chapter 19, question 7. In fact, he and Ride were never adversaries.

b. The verdicts in the first action indicate that the jury found Ride negligent, but not Gagarin. Gagarin would assert collateral estoppel in the second case to estop Ride from relitigating both her own negligence and Gagarin's.

c. If Ride and Gagarin each defended the first action by trying to prove that she or he was not negligent and that Armstrong was, they will not have litigated the issue of each other's negligence. If that is true, then use of estoppel in the second action would be nonmutual. Even though they were both parties to the prior suit, they were not adversaries and therefore did not risk preclusion (at least, under mutuality analysis) on issues that they did not litigate against each other. Consequently, they would not be able to assert preclusion against each other in a mutuality jurisdiction. The key to "mutuality" is not just having been a party to a prior suit but also actually having litigated issues against one another.

If, however, Ride and Gagarin had each defended against Armstrong by trying to show that the other was negligent, they *would* have litigated each other's negligence in the prior suit, even though they did not assert claims for relief against each other. On this assumption, they would each be bound by the decision on those issues, even in a mutuality jurisdiction.

d. Certainly, Gagarin's assertion of estoppel on the issue of Ride's negligence is an offensive use of estoppel: he invokes estoppel as a "sword" to establish Ride's negligence, a fact necessary to impose liability on Ride that was decided against her in the prior action. Assuming that Gagarin had not sought to establish Ride's negligence in the prior action, this would be nonmutual offensive collateral estoppel since he would be seeking to establish Ride's negligence on the basis of the fact that Armstrong had proved it in the first case.

Gagarin may also invoke estoppel to defeat Ride's contributory negligence defense. That is, he will claim that since he was found free of negli-

---

2. Although *Parklane* is not mandatory authority for state courts in establishing their own collateral estoppel rules, the factors enumerated in *Parklane* have been cited in state cases as well. See Restatement (Second) of Judgments §29 (1982) and accompanying Reporters' Note, pp.298-303.

gence in the first action, estoppel should bar relitigation of the issue. This would be nonmutual estoppel since Gagarin would be trying to estop Ride because Armstrong (the plaintiff in the prior action) had failed to prove that Gagarin was negligent.

e. Assuming that the two defendants did not attempt to prove each other's negligence in the prior action, the court will not allow Gagarin to estop Ride from relitigating Gagarin's negligence. Ride was under no duty to litigate Gagarin's negligence to defend the first suit, and she chose not to do so. Although they were both parties to the suit, they were not adversaries and were not required under the procedural rules to assert claims against each other. Although Armstrong was unable to prove Gagarin's negligence, Ride will be entitled to her opportunity to do so unless it is clear from the record of the first action that she tried to do so in that suit in the course of her defense.

The situation is different as to Ride's own negligence. Ride did fully litigate that question in the prior action and lost. Gagarin now seeks to use offensive estoppel to establish Ride's negligence in his own action for damages.[3] The court will have to review the proceedings in the first action to determine whether it would be appropriate, under the *Parklane* analysis, to apply collateral estoppel based on it. Ride will no doubt argue that Gagarin should have asserted his claim for damages as a cross-claim in the prior action. The court would have had ancillary jurisdiction over the cross-claim (see Chapter 12, question 3); perhaps Gagarin decided to "wait and see" what would happen in the first action, in hopes of using offensive collateral estoppel in the second. See *Parklane* at 330. He certainly had the right to withhold the claim in the first action, since cross-claims under Fed. R. Civ. P. 13(g) are permissive, but that does not mean the court has to grant him the further benefit of offensive collateral estoppel.

Few cases address whether a party will be barred from using offensive collateral estoppel because she failed to assert a claim in a prior action. This seems like a particularly strong case for denying estoppel, since Gagarin was already in the suit and the negligence issues were already being litigated against another party. However, refusing to apply estoppel in this case, in order to deprive Gagarin of the benefit of holding back his claim, also burdens the court system with additional litigation on an issue already resolved. If all the other prudential factors favor preclusion, it seems doubtful that the court will refuse to apply it simply because Gagarin exercised his right under the rules to bring his own action against Ride.

---

3. Of course, Gagarin will have to do more than prove that Ride was negligent in order to recover. He will also have to prove that Ride's negligence was the proximate cause of his injuries. The fact that Ride's negligence caused Armstrong's injuries does not automatically establish that it caused Gagarin's, though it very likely will if the claims arise from the same collision.

# PART FIVE

# *Thinking Procedurally: The Rules in Action*

# 22

# An Introduction to the Pretrial Litigation Process: Setting the Stage for the Schulansky Case

The materials in the first four parts of this book have dealt with the "substance" of civil procedure, that is, the various judicial rules and doctrines that govern the litigation process. The chapters that follow are intended to give you a sense of how the process actually works by chronicling the early stages of a typical (though hypothetical) civil case, *Schulansky v. Ronan*. Each chapter includes the court papers filed at a certain stage of the Schulansky suit, including typical pleadings, motions, and supporting documents. In addition, the materials provide a look at the legal and tactical questions that the attorneys considered in drafting those documents.

## Preparation for Filing Suit

In most cases the litigation process begins well before the parties get to court. Obviously, the first step is for the client to bring a dispute to a lawyer. The plaintiff's lawyer will obtain as much information as possible from the client. On the basis of this information and his assessment of the client, the lawyer must make a judgment as to whether to take the case. If he does agree to take it, he will propose a fee arrangement, and if the client accepts, a contract for services will be signed. In damage actions the agreement will frequently provide for a contingent fee, that is, an attorney's fee based on a percentage of any eventual recovery, frequently as high as 30 to 40 percent. The expenses of the action, such as deposition costs, expert witness fees, and other out-of-pocket expenditures, will also be paid out of the recovery.

Once the plaintiff's lawyer has agreed to handle the case, he will conduct a preliminary investigation of the events giving rise to the claim. He will obtain as much information as possible from his client and from other witnesses who are willing to discuss the case. He will gather and review documentary evidence, such as accident reports, business records, government reports, or other available materials. He will also do preliminary legal research if the case involves novel theories of recovery or other critical issues of law, in order to ascertain whether his client's injuries give rise to a right to relief.

On the basis of this preliminary development of the case, the plaintiff's attorney will usually send a claim letter to the defendant or discuss the claim with the defendant's counsel in order to explore the possibility of settling the claim without bringing suit. Many claims can be settled without the expense of litigation, particularly if there is little question as to liability and the only issue is the extent of the plaintiff's damages. However, in other cases the settlement value of a claim will depend on facts that have not yet been fully explored at this early stage. In the Schulansky case, for example, the defendant's judgment of the settlement value of the claim will turn in part on the parties' testimony as to their negotiations before the construction work began. The plaintiff's testimony as to those negotiations will only be available to the defendant through court-supervised "discovery" in the course of litigation. In such cases the parties will be less likely to reach an agreement until suit is brought and the facts are more fully developed.

The plaintiff's attorney must also consider a number of tactical issues in deciding whether to file suit. He must consider whether the case is strong enough and the value of a potential judgment high enough to justify the considerable expense of litigation. He must assess whether the client is patient enough and financially solvent enough to await a judgment several years down the road. He must consider possible alternative means of obtaining a remedy, such as invoking the assistance of a state agency or seeking an administrative remedy.

## Drafting the Complaint

Assuming that informal settlement efforts fail, and the plaintiff's attorney concludes that it makes sense to file suit on the claim, he will begin the lawsuit by filing a complaint, the first "pleading" required under the Federal Rules (and many similar state rules). Pleadings are the papers filed by the parties at the beginning of the action, in which they set forth their positions as to the facts in issue. Pleadings are not evidence; they are not even sworn testimony by the parties or their attorneys. They are simply statements of the parties' positions on the factual and legal issues in dispute.

In the simplest two-party suit the only pleadings required will be a complaint, in which the plaintiff sets forth his claim, and an answer, in which the defendant responds by stating his position as to each of the allegations in the complaint and asserting any other defenses he may have to the plaintiff's claim. See the plaintiff's complaint in the Schulansky case, infra p. 328, and Ronan's answer, infra p. 360. But further pleadings may be necessary if additional parties are brought into the suit or if counterclaims are asserted. See, e.g., Chapter 26, which includes a third-party complaint; see also Fed. R. Civ. P. 7(a), which describes the various pleadings that may be filed in appropriate circumstances.

Both the form and the content of the complaint are governed by the rules of procedure applicable in the court where the suit is filed. Since the Schulansky case was filed in the Massachusetts Superior Court, it must comply with the Massachusetts Rules of Civil Procedure. Chapter 23 illustrates in detail how the complaint was drafted to comply with those rules. In addition, most courts have local rules of procedure that supplement the general civil rules. For example, the Massachusetts Superior Court has its own supplementary rules that cover numerous details of practice before that court. The Superior Court Rules require plaintiffs in civil actions to file a cover sheet to facilitate administrative handling of the action. See Mass. Super. Ct. Rule 29; infra p. 335. Thus, all applicable local rules must be checked in order to comply with any additional requirements.

In drafting the complaint, counsel must also consider whether the procedural rules allow joinder of all the desired parties as plaintiffs or defendants. (The joinder rules are analyzed in Chapters 10-13.) The substantive law governing the plaintiff's claims must also be analyzed to ascertain whether there is good ground to file suit on the claims asserted in the complaint. A large part of the attorneys' memos in the following chapters is devoted to considering whether the law of contracts and negligence will support the claims for relief in *Schulansky,* and, if so, how those claims should be asserted in the pleadings.

# Tactical Considerations in Choosing the Forum

The plaintiff's counsel faces a number of "real world" tactical issues in deciding where to bring a lawsuit. To begin with, he must choose a court that has subject matter jurisdiction, personal jurisdiction over the defendant, and satisfies the applicable rules of venue. See Part One for a detailed analysis of those requirements. It may not always be clear from the facts whether jurisdiction and venue are proper in a particular court. (In *Schulansky*, for example, there is some doubt as to whether the Massachusetts court has personal jurisdiction over the defendants.) If so, the attorney will have to make a judgment as to whether the advantages of litigating in his chosen forum are outweighed by the risk that the suit will be dismissed on one of these grounds, causing additional expense to his client and possible statute of limitations problems.

The plaintiff's counsel must also decide whether to file suit in federal or state court, assuming, as will frequently be the case, that jurisdiction and venue are satisfied in both. Numerous factors may be important in making that choice. For example, the scope of pretrial discovery may be broader in federal court. Federal courts also have broader power to transfer cases than do state courts. On the other hand, the scope of interlocutory review may be broader in state court than federal court. (See, e.g., Chapter 3, question 9, concerning interlocutory appeal of decisions on motions to dismiss for lack of personal jurisdiction.) The right to join additional parties may differ, as may the court's power to exercise personal jurisdiction over them. (See Chapter 6, pp. 80-81.)

Other differences involving the trial process itself may be important in a case. For example, the rules of evidence in the state and federal courts may differ in crucial respects. The power of the court to subpoena witnesses will differ. The ethnic and economic characteristics of the jury will differ because a federal court jury will be drawn from a broader geographical area. The judges in one system may be more familiar with the type of case in suit. It may be possible to get to trial a good deal more quickly in one system than another (or in one state than another).

Convenience may also play an important role in the decision. The plaintiff's lawyer may be more familiar with practice in one system. One court may be more conveniently located for the plaintiff (or his attorney) or more inconvenient for the defendant (or his attorney). Attorney Ackerman's initial memo in the Schulansky case does not reveal all of the factors he considered in deciding to go to state court, but proximity to his client's home and his own office was undoubtedly an important one in such a relatively small case. Innumerable other such factors may also be significant in a particular case.[1]

## *Filing the Complaint*

In view of all these considerations, the attorney will draft the complaint, file it with the clerk of the appropriate court, and serve it on the defendant. (As to the proper methods of service, see Chapter 4.) If the defendant is already

---

1. For an excellent discussion of the tactical reasons for choosing state or federal court, see Steinglass, The Emerging State Court §1983 Action: a Procedural Review, 38 U. Miami L. Rev. 381, 412-424 (1984); see also 1A Moore's at ¶0.157[13].

represented by counsel, the plaintiff's lawyer may as a matter of courtesy call the defendant's lawyer to let him know that suit is being filed. In turn, the defendant's counsel may agree to accept service of the complaint and summons without compliance with the formal service rules. (As Chapter 14 indicates, the defendant may waive any objection to the manner of service by failing to object to it.)

It is only upon the filing of the complaint that the court gets involved in the case. At least initially, its involvement will be minimal. The clerk will assign a docket number to the case and establish a case file. All subsequent pleadings and other papers filed in the case will be "docketed," that is, entered on a docket sheet kept with the case file, and added to the file. In federal courts, the case will usually be assigned to a judge when the complaint is filed; that judge will then preside over the case for the duration.

In some state courts, however, the case is not permanently assigned; different proceedings will be heard by different judges depending on which judge is "sitting" at the time a motion comes up for hearing or when the case is reached on the trial list. For example, if the Schulansky case had remained in Massachusetts state court, the motion to dismiss might have been heard by Judge A, but the motion for summary judgment (had it been filed and marked up for hearing) by Judge B. Judge B would have no previous knowledge of the case but would have to review the pleadings and other papers before or during the hearing to familiarize himself with the suit. When the case reached trial, it might be tried before Judge C, who was assigned to the civil jury session at the time the case was reached on the trial list. By contrast, in federal court the same judge would preside over the suit from the outset and would develop a "feel" for the case through hearings on motions, discovery conferences, and other pretrial proceedings. As Chapter 28 indicates (see infra pp. 405, 421), knowing which judge will preside over the case can have an important effect on the attorneys' tactical decisions.

## Responding to the Complaint

Once the defendant or his counsel receives the complaint, he must respond. In most cases, the defendant will answer the complaint. If the defendant has certain preliminary objections to the suit, however, he may move to dismiss instead. See the motion to dismiss for lack of personal jurisdiction filed by Jones, the third-party defendant in *Schulansky*, infra p. 389. (Chapter 14 reviews in detail the circumstances in which a motion to dismiss may be filed instead of an answer.)

It is important to understand the difference between a pleading and a motion. A motion is not a pleading. See Fed. R. Civ. P. 7(a) and (b), which provide separately for pleadings and motions. The pleadings set forth the positions of the parties on the claim. A motion, by contrast, is a direct application to the court for an order. Whenever a party seeks action from the court, a motion is the appropriate way to do so. For example, a defendant's motion to dismiss for lack of personal jurisdiction is a direct request to the court to dismiss the case.

Although many types of motions are specifically provided for in the rules (see, e.g., Fed. R. Civ. P. 12(b), (e); 56), the motion is a flexible device for seeking any type of action from the court. Other common examples are motions for further discovery, motions to place a case on the trial list, to convene a discovery conference, to implead a third party, to amend the complaint or answer, to extend the time to answer, or for any other assistance in the litigation process. (One well-known pro se litigant in Massachusetts is rumored to have filed a "Motion for a Landmark Decision"!)

If the defendant answers the complaint instead of moving to dismiss, his answer must set forth his position on the allegations in the complaint. As Chapter 23 demonstrates, the Federal Rules of Civil Procedure require the plaintiff in federal suits to set forth his allegations in numbered paragraphs. The defendant's answer must respond to each allegation, paragraph by paragraph. The defendant may also assert affirmative defenses or counterclaims in the answer, as Ronan has done. The answer must be filed with the court and served on the plaintiff. The rules require the answer or motion to dismiss to be filed within 20 days, but extensions of time to answer are frequently granted, often with the consent of the opposing party.

## Discovery

Once the pleadings are complete, the case will move into the *discovery phase*. Discovery is the process by which the parties obtain information from each other and outside witnesses through several commonsense devices authorized by the rules of procedure. In the federal courts, three primary discovery devices are used to develop factual evidence in preparation for trial. *Interrogatories*, authorized by Fed. R. Civ. P. 33, are written questions sent by one party to another, which must be answered under oath. *Requests for production of documents*, under Fed. R. Civ. P. 34, are requests from a party for an opposing party to produce documents that may be relevant to the issues in suit, for inspection or copying by the requesting party. The third basic discovery tool[2] is the *oral deposition*, authorized by Fed. R. Civ. P. 30. A deposition is a procedure for taking oral testimony from a witness.

Usually counsel will take the depositions of crucial witnesses for the other party, in order to prepare for trial and to get the witness's testimony

---

2. Two other basic discovery devices are the *request for admission*, under Fed. R. Civ. P. 36, used to narrow the scope of trial by obtaining admission of undisputed facts, and the *physical or mental examination*, authorized by Fed. R. Civ. P. 35 in cases in which a party's mental or physical condition is at issue in the lawsuit.

"on the record." The deposition is taken before a licensed court reporter, usually at the office of one of the parties' attorneys. The witness testifies under oath and may be represented by counsel. Counsel for opposing parties are entitled to cross-examine, but usually do not do so extensively. Chapter 28 contains an excerpt from the plaintiff's deposition in the Schulansky case.

Despite the emphasis in this book on procedural rules and doctrines, the most crucial phase of a lawsuit is the development of the evidence through the discovery process and investigation by the attorneys. Most cases are won, lost, or settled on the basis of the strength of the facts, and it is through discovery that the facts and the credibility of the crucial witnesses can be evaluated. Typically, the discovery phase will take at least a year in a reasonably substantial case, but it may take considerably longer.

# Attorney Cooperation in the Discovery Process

Throughout this period, it is the attorneys who conduct the litigation by using the discovery tools provided in the rules, providing discovery to the other side, and developing the evidence to support their cases at trial. In many cases judicial involvement may be minimal right down to the time of trial. The attorneys carry the laboring oar by filing their pleadings, sending and responding to requests for discovery, scheduling and conducting depositions, and where possible, agreeing to stipulations of the undisputed facts to shorten the trial.

Because discovery is conducted primarily by the attorneys, it is important for opposing counsel to cooperate in the discovery process. The formality of the civil procedure rules and the adversary nature of litigation practice frequently lead beginning attorneys to conclude that they are not serving their clients unless they resist every request of opposing counsel. In the long run, however, unrestrained belligerence is counterproductive. It is entirely feasible for counsel to work together to facilitate moving a case to trial without in any way compromising their clients' substantive rights.

For example, many questions will arise during the pleading and discovery phases of the suit that can be resolved by agreements of counsel. Extensions of time to file pleadings can be agreed to, saving the need to argue a contested motion for an extension. Stipulations of agreed facts can be drawn up to obviate the need to prove those facts at trial. Disagreements as to the scope or timing of discovery, claims of attorney-client privilege, or limits imposed by a preliminary injunction may often be worked out by counsel instead of taking court time. In addition, scheduling of depositions and hearings on pretrial motions can be arranged with opposing counsel. In these and other ways, the process will run much more smoothly (and inexpensively) for all concerned if the attorneys cooperate.

# The Changing Judicial Role in Litigation

Under the traditional model (still followed to a degree in many state courts) the court itself plays a largely passive role in litigation. The parties file the pleadings, conduct discovery, initiate settlement discussions, and seek a trial when ready. Under this system, there is no active periodic review of pending cases by a judge. For example, a judge will not review complaints as they are filed to determine whether the court has personal jurisdiction over the defendant or the complaint states a claim upon which relief can be granted. It is up to the attorneys to seek court decision of such questions by filing an appropriate motion. The court is simply there as a referee to respond to motions by the parties if the pleading or discovery process goes awry and to supply a judge to preside over the trial when and if a trial is necessary. If the attorneys choose to litigate at a leisurely pace, the court under this model does little to force them to trial.

However, the litigation process is moving away from this "hands off" model as the volume of litigation increasingly strains court resources. Particularly in the federal courts, judges are taking an activist role in managing cases by monitoring the discovery process, limiting the issues in pretrial conferences, and setting deadlines for discovery and trial. For example, the court in federal cases is now required to enter a scheduling order in many cases, setting deadlines for the joinder of additional parties, amendment of pleadings, and completion of discovery. See Fed. R. Civ. P. 16(b). The court may also schedule discovery conferences with the attorneys to monitor the progress of discovery, to narrow the issues, and to encourage settlement discussions. See Fed. R. Civ. P. 26(f).

# Moving towards Trial

As discussed in Chapter 15, lawsuits may be cut short by pretrial dismissal or summary judgment. However, most cases survive these hurdles and, if not settled during the discovery phase, continue on track toward the culmination of the litigation process: a trial on the merits. As the discovery process nears completion, the court will usually hold a pretrial conference to resolve pending motions, address evidentiary issues, encourage stipulations as to undisputed facts, explore the possibility of settlement, and set a final schedule for trial. See Fed. R. Civ. P. 16. In some systems, trials may be fairly prompt, but in others the court's caseload forces long delays before the case is reached on the trial list. If the parties persevere, they will eventually get a trial, but it is almost impossible in many systems to predict or control exactly when that will be.

Most cases, even if they are actively litigated through the discovery phase and are set down for trial, are never tried. Upwards of 90 percent of all civil actions are ultimately settled, many on the eve of trial. However, the considerable effort that goes into discovery and pretrial preparation in such cases is not wasted. It is the intensive development of the facts and the parties' increasingly sophisticated understanding of the strengths and weaknesses of their positions that makes an equitable settlement possible. In addition, the incentive to settle increases markedly as trial becomes an impending reality rather than a distant possibility. (For a good discussion of the tactical considerations involved in settlement discussions, see J. Kelner and F. McGovern, Successful Litigation Techniques 6-1 – 6-12 (1981).)

# The Attorney's Experience of Litigation

All of this is very well, but it still gives little impression of what the experience of litigation is like for the lawyers who conduct it. In practice, litigation is episodic. A lawyer may have anywhere from 20 to 50 or more active cases at a time, at various stages from pre-filing investigation to post-trial motions. At any given time, there will not be much happening in many of those cases: The lawyer might be awaiting responses to discovery requests in one, awaiting judicial action on a motion to dismiss in another, discussing responses to interrogatories with his client in another, drafting an answer in another, awaiting a trial date in another, and so on.

Much of the average litigator's time is spent in detailed factual investigation: reviewing depositions and documents produced under discovery requests, interviewing witnesses, meeting with clients or witnesses, tracking down other sources of proof, and preparing and organizing testimony for trial. The work requires a painstaking attention to detail; a good memory and a methodical approach to trial preparation helps. In addition, a good deal of time is spent drafting pleadings and motions, supporting affidavits, and other materials. There is frequently legal research to be done (especially by junior attorneys in the office), and memoranda to be written in support of or opposition to pending motions.

A litigator's cases have a way of "acting up" unexpectedly. The morning mail may bring a motion for summary judgment in a case that has been sitting on the back burner, a motion for sanctions in a case based on allegedly inadequate response to a request for production of documents, notice of a deposition of an important witness, or an order from the court to appear for a pretrial conference. Often these litigation events require a prompt response — a memorandum in opposition to a motion, an appearance in court to argue a motion, a conference with a client to draw up answers to interrogatories, or preparation for and attendance at a deposition.

Thus, a litigator is constantly juggling a number of cases, trying to keep all the balls in the air at once. The unexpected happens frequently and a constant procession of deadlines beckons. Periodically, the process is punctuated by trials, which usually involve intensive periods of long hours and single-minded attention to one case (with consequent reshuffling of commitments in other cases). However, for most litigators, trials are infrequent; litigation practice resembles continuously preparing for exams, most of which are then called off at the last minute. Some lawyers find it exhilarating; others, simply nerve-wracking. Few find it dull.

# 23

## First Moves: Schulansky Goes to Court

## The Drafting Request

### MEMORANDUM

**TO:**    David E. Howard,
           Associate

**FROM:**  Phyllis Slater

**RE:**    Schulansky construction dispute
          Our file No. 85-1248

**DATE:**  November 20, 1985

------------------------------------------------

Deborah Schulansky, a client of ours, has consulted me concerning a dispute that has arisen between her and a contractor who recently built an addition to her vacation home. It appears that this problem cannot be resolved without filing suit. I would like you to help me with the case.

Although Schulansky lives here in Plymouth, Massachusetts, she also owns an antique colonial home in Alton, New Hampshire, which she uses as a vacation home. The house dates from 1782, and is listed in the National Register of Historic Places. Last spring, Ms. Schulansky met Richard Ronan, a New Hampshire contractor, while he was restoring a house in Plymouth. After some negotiations at her home in Plymouth, the parties agreed that Ronan would build an addition on the back of the Alton house. Ronan mailed a "Proposal and Estimate" to Schulansky in Plymouth, and she signed and returned it. I have attached a copy of the Proposal and Estimate for the job, signed by both the parties. [See p. 332.—ED.]

The work involved taking out part of the back wall of the house and building a 14′ × 20′ addition behind the living room, with a full cellar under the addition. The contractor was to excavate the earth from the original foundation, excavate the adjacent area to be occupied by the addition, lay a cellar floor and walls in the excavated area to support the addition, and build the addition above the new cellar area. In order to provide access to the new cellar, the contractor was to break a doorway through the original foundation of the main house adjacent to the addition.

There were problems from the beginning of the construction work. Ronan hired a bulldozer operator, named Jones, to do the excavation work, as he had told Schulansky he would. When Jones excavated the earth from the original foundation with his bulldozer, he discovered that the lower part of the foundation was simply loose rubble. Evidently, in colonial days it was fairly common to simply pile large rocks around the perimeter of the house site and build brick and mortar foundations on top of the rocks. These rubble foundations apparently last remarkably well as long as they are undisturbed, but are less stable if exposed, as was necessary here to construct the cellar for the new addition.

Apparently, there was some discussion during the negotiations about possible problems with the old foundation. Schulansky asked Ronan if he anticipated any problems due to disturbance of the foundation. He responded that he doubted that it would be a problem, but if anything was loose he would do whatever was needed to provide adequate support for the addition. When Schulansky visited the site and observed the excavation, she became concerned about the stability of the original foundation. For one thing, she could see that the foundation was just loose rubble, with no mortar or other support except the surrounding earth. For another, the bulldozer had repeatedly ploughed into the old foundation in the course of excavating the new cellar, and loose rocks from the foundation were lying in the ditch next to the foundation. Schulansky asked Ronan several times if the old foundation was adequate and asked him to reinforce or rebuild it. Ronan refused to do any major reconstruction, on the ground that he had not agreed to do so and that it was unnecessary. Instead, he simply told the foundation subcontractor to pour some cement in between the rocks and left it at that.

In May, when the job was virtually complete, Schulansky began to notice cracks in the plaster walls of the living room, in the bedroom above it, and in the addition itself. She also observed some sagging in the floor at the joint between the main house and the addition. She had a friend who is a structural engineer come and look at the house. He concluded that the cracks resulted from settling of the old foundation, evidently due to shifting of the rubble after exposure during the excavation. He is unsure whether the settling resulted from negligent excavation (that is, the rubble being disturbed by the bulldozer), or from the removal of the supporting earth on the outside of the old foundation.

In either case, his opinion is that the settling will continue, causing major structural damage, unless the foundation is rebuilt. Because the addition is now completed, that reconstruction will be substantially more expensive than it would have been if it had been done during construction of the addition. He estimates that it will cost a minimum of $12,000 for reconstruction of the foundation and another $5,000 to repair the damage to the house due to settlement of the foundation.

Schulansky has tried to work this out with Ronan, but he denies any responsibility. Consequently, she refused to make the final payment under the contract. I have talked to Ronan myself, and written him a demand letter, but it is clear that he will refuse to provide any satisfaction to our client. Instead, he has threatened to file suit himself if Schulansky does not pay him the last progress payment under the contract.

I intend to initiate suit against Ronan personally and against Ronan Construction Company for breach of contract and negligence. Although we could probably bring suit in federal court on the basis of diversity (Ronan lives in Nashua, Ronan Construction is incorporated in New Hampshire, and its principal place of business is probably in New Hampshire), I would prefer to litigate here in Plymouth Superior Court.

I realize that we may have a claim against Jones as well. At the moment, however, I am not even sure of Jones's full name, much less where he lives, whether he is solvent, and whether he is subject to personal jurisdiction here. We will have to learn more about Jones through discovery and amend to add him if necessary. But I have some hope that this can be settled quickly without the expense of lengthy, multi-party litigation.

Please draft a complaint and summons to initiate this suit in the Superior Court for Plymouth County. If you need further information, talk to me or call Ms. Schulansky directly. As you know, Rules 8-11 of the Massachusetts Rules of Civil Procedure are almost identical to Rules 8-11 of the Federal Rules of Civil Procedure. The one important distinction for our purposes is that it is unnecessary under the Massachusetts version of Rule 8 to allege the basis for subject matter jurisdiction. Compare Fed. R. Civ. P. 8(a)(1).

We will also want to assert our right to a jury trial. See Mass. R. Civ. P. 38(b) (identical to Fed. R. Civ. P. 38(b)).

# The Associate's Response

## MEMORANDUM

**TO:**     Phyllis Slater

**FROM:**   David E. Howard

**RE:**     Complaint in *Schulansky v. Ronan*
            Our file No. 85-1248

**DATE:**   December 1, 1985

------------------------------------------------------------

I have attached a draft complaint and summons in the Schulansky matter. Please note that I have made both Richard Ronan and Ronan Construction Company defendants in the suit. (I refer to them collectively as "Ronan" in this memo.) The contract is signed by Richard Ronan, but on the stationery of Ronan Construction Company. At this stage, it is not clear whether Ronan signed on behalf of the corporation or individually, or both. Since either or both may be liable, I have named both as defendants.

As my draft complaint indicates, Schulansky may be entitled to relief on two separate theories, breach of contract and negligence. Ronan may have breached the contract in several ways. First, Ronan may have agreed to reconstruct the foundation if necessary, but failed to do so. The Proposal and Estimate is hardly clear on this; the only relevant provision is paragraph two, which requires construction of ". . . foundation walls to support 14′ × 20′ addition." However, an argument can be made that the old foundation wall at the juncture of the house and the addition is part of the foundation of the addition, and therefore the contractor had a duty to make sure that that part of the foundation was solid as well. Paragraphs twenty-three and twenty-four of the draft complaint assert this basis for recovery for breach of contract.

Our argument that paragraph two required Ronan to reconstruct the foundation is bolstered by the negotiations between Ronan and Schulansky concerning possible reconstruction of the foundation if it turned out to be inadequate. The potential problem here is that these discussions took place before the Proposal and Estimate was signed. The defendants will no doubt argue that the written contract embodies the entire agreement between the parties, that on its face it does not include any obligation to reconstruct the old foundation, and that the parol evidence rule bars evidence of prior negotiations to vary the terms of the contract. See generally, Farnsworth, Contracts §7.12 (1982). We will have to argue that paragraph two is ambiguous, so that evidence of the prior negotiations is proper to demonstrate the intent of the parties.

Alternatively, it may turn out that the settling resulted from damage done to the foundation by Jones in the course of excavating the cellar. If this is true, Ronan would still be liable on a breach of contract theory. Certainly, an implied term of the contract between Ronan and Schulansky is that the work will be carried out in a workmanlike manner, including the work which Ronan chooses to delegate to his employees or agents. See Restatement (Second) of Contracts §318(3) (1981) (delegation of duties under contract does not discharge delegating party from its duty to perform those duties). Even if it was Jones who damaged the foundation with the bulldozer, this would constitute a breach of Ronan's duty to perform the contract work carefully. Thus, even if we cannot prove that Ronan had agreed to rebuild the foundation, this would constitute a separate breach of the contract, which gives rise to a claim for whatever subsidence resulted from the damage. I have included this allegation in paragraph twenty-five of the draft.

The second claim for relief in my draft complaint is based on the theory that the negligent excavation by Jones led to the subsidence. If Jones acted as Ronan's employee in performing the excavation work, Ronan will be liable for Jones's negligent acts on the basis of respondeat superior. Restatement (Second) of Agency §219 (1958). It is not clear at this stage whether Jones operated as an employee or independent subcontractor in performing the excavation work. The legal distinction between an employee and independent contractor turns on the employer's right to control the details of the work. *Cowan v. Eastern Racing Assn.,* 330 Mass. 135, 141-142 (1953); Restatement (Second) of Agency §220 (1958). If Ronan exercised control over Jones in the manner of digging the new cellar, Jones acted as Ronan's employee, and Ronan would be liable for Jones's negligence. However, if Ronan simply hired Jones to complete the excavation work in his own manner for an agreed price, Jones may have acted as an independent subcontractor.

There is some reason to believe that Jones acted as Ronan's employee, since (according to Schulansky) Ronan appeared to direct him in the course of the excavation work. Thus, I have drafted the second claim for relief on this theory. An important goal of discovery on our second claim for relief will be to ascertain the exact course of dealing between Ronan and Jones, to determine whether Jones acted as Ronan's employee or as an independent contractor.

Once you have reviewed the draft and made any changes, I will arrange for filing of the complaint and service on the defendants in New Hampshire.

# The Resulting Documents

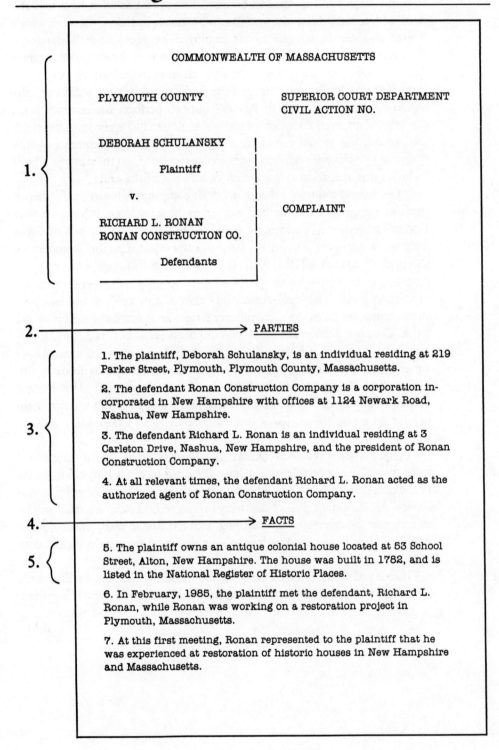

1.

COMMONWEALTH OF MASSACHUSETTS

PLYMOUTH COUNTY                SUPERIOR COURT DEPARTMENT
                              CIVIL ACTION NO.

DEBORAH SCHULANSKY

    Plaintiff

    v.                        COMPLAINT

RICHARD L. RONAN
RONAN CONSTRUCTION CO.

    Defendants

2. → PARTIES

3.

1. The plaintiff, Deborah Schulansky, is an individual residing at 219 Parker Street, Plymouth, Plymouth County, Massachusetts.

2. The defendant Ronan Construction Company is a corporation incorporated in New Hampshire with offices at 1124 Newark Road, Nashua, New Hampshire.

3. The defendant Richard L. Ronan is an individual residing at 3 Carleton Drive, Nashua, New Hampshire, and the president of Ronan Construction Company.

4. At all relevant times, the defendant Richard L. Ronan acted as the authorized agent of Ronan Construction Company.

4. → FACTS

5.

5. The plaintiff owns an antique colonial house located at 53 School Street, Alton, New Hampshire. The house was built in 1782, and is listed in the National Register of Historic Places.

6. In February, 1985, the plaintiff met the defendant, Richard L. Ronan, while Ronan was working on a restoration project in Plymouth, Massachusetts.

7. At this first meeting, Ronan represented to the plaintiff that he was experienced at restoration of historic houses in New Hampshire and Massachusetts.

8. In early March, 1985, the plaintiff met with Ronan at her home in Plymouth, Massachusetts, to discuss the possibility of hiring him to build an addition on her house in Alton, New Hampshire.

9. During that meeting, the parties discussed the need for extensive rebuilding of the foundation of the main house adjacent to the planned addition.

10. During that meeting, the defendant Richard L. Ronan agreed that any necessary reconstruction of the old foundation would be included as part of the construction of an adequate foundation for the addition.

11. After the March meeting, Richard L. Ronan sent a Proposal and Estimate to the plaintiff in Plymouth, Massachusetts, describing the work to be done and offering to perform the work for $19,200. A copy of the Proposal and Estimate is attached to this complaint as Exhibit A.

12. The plaintiff accepted the defendants' offer by signing and mailing the Proposal and Estimate to the defendants, at their office in Nashua, New Hampshire, on April 3, 1985.

13. The defendants commenced work on the addition on April 15, 1985, and continued until June 3, 1985.

14. In the course of the work, the defendants or their agents excavated the earth from the outside of the foundation of the main house to a depth of approximately seven feet.

15. This excavation revealed that the base of the foundation consisted of loose rocks piled on top of each other and held in place by the surrounding earth.

16. In the process of excavation, the defendants or their agents damaged the foundation of the main house by digging up and displacing large boulders, which formed part of that foundation.

17. As a result of the removal of the supporting earth outside the foundation, or the damage done to it during the excavation, or both, it became necessary to reconstruct this part of the foundation to adequately support the main house and the addition.

18. Despite their agreement to do so, the defendants failed to reconstruct the original foundation to provide adequate support for the house and the addition.

19. Even after the plaintiff brought the problem to the defendants' attention during construction, and demanded that they reconstruct the foundation in accordance with their agreement, the defendants refused to do so.

20. As a result of the inadequate foundation work, the main house and the addition have sustained major structural damage, including cracks in the walls and sagging of the first floor immediately above the affected area.

**7.** ──────────────────────→ FIRST CLAIM FOR RELIEF:

BREACH OF CONTRACT

**8.** ──────→ 21. The plaintiff repeats and realleges the allegations in paragraphs 1-20 of the complaint.

22. The Proposal and Estimate signed by the defendant Richard L. Ronan and the plaintiff constitutes a written contract for a valuable consideration between the defendants and the plaintiff.

23. Under paragraph two of the contract, the defendants agreed to construct an adequate foundation to support the addition and adjacent portion of the main house.

24. The defendants breached the contract by failing to perform their obligation to construct an adequate foundation for the addition.

25. The defendants also breached the contract by failing to perform the excavation work required by the contract in a workmanlike manner, which resulted in damage to the existing foundation of the house.

26. The plaintiff made all progress payments under the contract in a timely manner, until she became aware of the defendants' breach.

27. As a result of the defendants' breach, both the main house and the addition have sustained severe structural damage, which will require extensive repair and reconstruction.

SECOND CLAIM FOR RELIEF:

NEGLIGENCE

28. The plaintiff repeats and realleges the allegations in paragraphs 1-20 of the complaint.

29. In the course of the construction of the addition, the defendants or their employees negligently excavated the area adjacent to the foundation of the main house.

30. As a result of this negligent excavation, the foundation of the main house was displaced and damaged, causing subsidence of the foundation and structural damage to the main house and the addition.

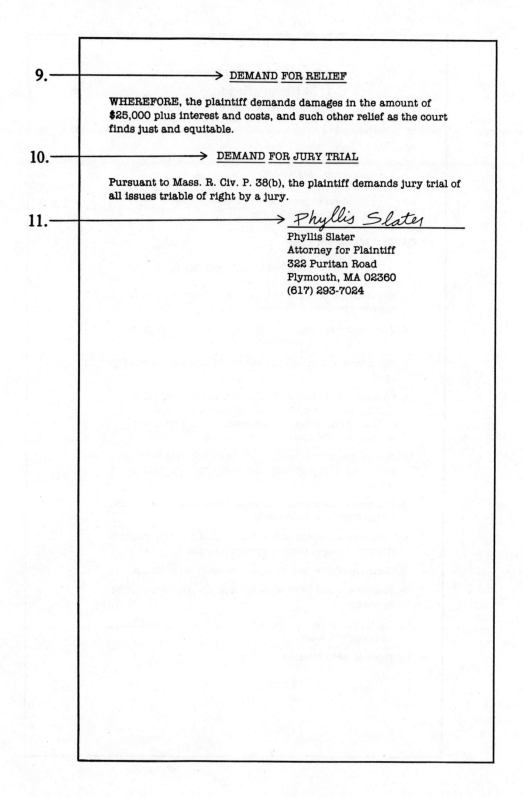

**9.** → <u>DEMAND</u> <u>FOR</u> <u>RELIEF</u>

**WHEREFORE**, the plaintiff demands damages in the amount of $25,000 plus interest and costs, and such other relief as the court finds just and equitable.

**10.** → <u>DEMAND</u> <u>FOR</u> <u>JURY</u> <u>TRIAL</u>

Pursuant to Mass. R. Civ. P. 38(b), the plaintiff demands jury trial of all issues triable of right by a jury.

**11.** → *Phyllis Slater*

Phyllis Slater
Attorney for Plaintiff
322 Puritan Road
Plymouth, MA 02360
(617) 293-7024

## RONAN CONSTRUCTION CO.
1124 Newark Road
Nashua, New Hampshire 03061


TO:    Deborah Schulansky
219 Parker Street
Plymouth, MA 02360

RE:    Addition to premises at 53 School Street,
Alton, New Hampshire

DATE:    March 15, 1985

### PROPOSAL AND ESTIMATE

1. Excavate 14' x 20' x 7' deep area at right rear of house; remove fill.

2. Construct footings, cellar floor, and foundation walls to support 14' x 20' addition.

3. Cut doorway through present foundation into new cellar area.

4. Construct one-story addition with peaked roof and unfinished attic crawl space — standard frame construction, including cedar clapboard siding and asphalt shingle roof.

5. One standard double-hung window each side (west and east), and 6' bay window (double glazed) on main south wall.

6. Interior walls standard drywall construction; clear maple finish floor and baseboards.

7. Remove wall where addition abuts house; support upper floors with steel beam spanning opening.

8. Clean-up of site; broom clean, no seeding or planting.

9. Electrical work to be done by separate contractor hired by owner.

10. Contractor reserves the right to sub-contract excavating and concrete work.

11. Work to be completed by June 20, 1985.

Estimated Cost:      $19,200

Payment schedule:    $2,000 on completion of excavation
$3,000 on completion of foundation
$3,000 on completion of framing
$4,000 on completion of exterior finish work
balance upon completion of job.

*Richard L. Ronan*
Richard L. Ronan

Bid accepted:       *Deborah Schulansky*
Deborah Schulansky

COMMONWEALTH OF MASSACHUSETTS

PLYMOUTH, ss.

SUPERIOR COURT DEPARTMENT OF THE
TRIAL COURT OF THE COMMONWEALTH

CIVIL ACTION

NO. 27,982

Deborah Schulansky ...................................., Plaintiff(s)

**vs.**

Richard L. Ronan,
......Ronan Construction Co...................................., Defendant(s)

## SUMMONS

To the above-named defendant   :

    You are hereby summoned and required to serve upon Phyllis Slater, Robbins,
plaintiff    attorney, whose address is 322 Puritan Rd. Plymouth, MA, 02360 an answer to the
complaint which is herewith served upon you, within 20 days after service of this summons upon you,
exclusive of the day of service.  If you fail to do so, judgment by default will be taken against you for
the relief demanded in the complaint.  You are also required to file your answer to the complaint in the
office of the Clerk of this court at Plymouth either before service upon plaintiff    attorney or within a
reasonable time thereafter.

    Unless otherwise provided by Rule 13(a), your answer must state as a counterclaim any claim which
you may have against the plaintiff    which arises out of the transaction or occurrence that is the subject
matter of the plaintiff    claim or you will thereafter be barred from making such claim in any other action.

    Witness, THOMAS R. MORSE, JR., Esquire, at Plymouth, the .............Sixth..... day of
.......December............., in the year of our Lord one thousand nine hundred and eighty- five ....

*Francis R. Powers*

CLERK.

## NOTES

1. This summons is issued pursuant to Rule 4 of the Massachusetts Rules of Civil Procedure.
2. When more than one defendant is involved, the names of all defendants should appear in the caption.  If a separate summons is used for each defendant, each should be addressed to the particular defendant.
3. To plaintiff's attorney: please circle type of action involved — Tort — Motor Vehicle Tort — Contract — Equitable Relief — Other.

## PROOF OF SERVICE OF PROCESS

    I hereby certify and return that on ..................................................., 19    , I served a copy
of the within summons, together with a copy of the complaint in this action, upon the within-named
defendant    , in the following manner (See Mass. R. Civ. P. 4 (d) (1-5): ...... ...    ...... ..

.......................................................................................................................................

.......................................................................................................................................

Dated:                     , 19        .........................................................................

N. B.   TO PROCESS SERVER:—
        PLEASE PLACE DATE YOU MAKE SERVICE ON DEFENDANT IN THIS BOX ON
        THE ORIGINAL AND ON COPY SERVED ON DEFENDANT.

|  |
| --- |
| , 19   . |

FORM 1 RP SM

*NOTICE TO DEFENDANT — You need not appear personally in court to answer the complaint, but if you claim to have a defense, either you or your attorney must serve a copy of your written answer within 20 days as specified herein and also file the original in the Clerk's Office.*

TYPE OR USE BALL POINT PEN — BEAR DOWN FIRMLY

**MASSACHUSETTS TRIAL COURT**     SUPERIOR COURT DEPARTMENT

_____PLYMOUTH_____ . SS.

CIVIL ACTION COVER SHEET
(To be filed with each Complaint)

NO. _____

| PLAINTIFF(S) | DEFENDANT(S) |
|---|---|
| DEBORAH SCHULANSKY | Richard L. Ronan<br>Ronan Construction Company |
| ATTORNEY(S) (Firm Name, Address, Tel.)<br>Robbins, Slater and Goldman<br>322 Puritan Road<br>BBO # Plymouth, MA 02360 Tel. 617-293-7024 | ATTORNEY(S) (If known) |

**Place an ☒ in one box only**

ORIGIN

☒ 1. F01  Complaint
☐ 2. F02  Removal to Sup. Ct. c.231, s.104
☐ 3. F03  Retransfer to Sup. Ct. c.231, s.102C

☐ 4. F04  Dist. Ct. Appeal c.231, s.97
☐ 5. F05  Reactivated after Rescript; Relief from judgment/order (Mass. R. Civ. P. 60)

**Place an ☒ in one box only**

NATURE OF ACTION

**CONTRACT**
☒ A01  Services, labor and materials
☐ A02  Goods sold and delivered
☐ A03  Commercial paper
☐ A08  Sale or lease of real estate
☐ A99  Other (specify) _____

**TORT**
☐ B03  Motor vehicle negligence-personal injury/property damage
☒ B04  Other negligence-personal injury property damage
☐ B05  Products liability
☐ B06  Malpractice-medical
☐ B07  Malpractice-other (specify) _____
☐ B08  Wrongful death, G.L. c.229, s.2A
☐ B15  Defamation (libel-slander)
☐ B99  Other (specify) _____

**REAL PROPERTY**
☐ C01  Land taking (eminent domain)
☐ C02  Zoning appeal, G.L. c.40A
☐ C03  Dispute concerning title
☐ C04  Foreclosure of mortgage
☐ C99  Other (specify) _____

**EQUITABLE REMEDIES**
☐ D01  Specific performance of contract
☐ D02  Reach and apply, G.L. c.214, s.3(6)-(9)
☐ D06  Contribution or indemnification
☐ D07  Imposition of trust
☐ D08  Minority stockholder's suit
☐ D10  Accounting
☐ D12  Dissolution of partnership
☐ D13  Declaratory judgment, G.L. c.231A
☐ D99  Other (specify) _____

**MISCELLANEOUS**
☐ E02  Appeal from administrative agency, G.L. c.30A
☐ E03  Action against Commonwealth or Municipality, G.L. c.258
☐ E04  Taxpayer suit, G.L. c.40 s.53
☐ E05  Confirmation of arbitration awards, G.L. c.251
☐ E06  Massachusetts Antitrust Act, G.L. c.93
☐ E08  Appointment of receiver
☐ E09  General contractor's surety bond, G.L. c.149, ss.29, 29a
☐ E10  Summary process appeal
☐ E11  Workman's Compensation
☐ E12  Small Claims Appeal
☐ E13  Labor Dispute
☐ E14  Chapter 123A Petition — SDP
☐ E15  Abuse Petition, G.L. c.209A
☐ E16  Auto Surcharge Appeal
☐ E17  Civil Rights Act, G.L. c.12, ss.11H-1
☐ E99  Other (specify) _____

IS THIS A JURY CASE?     ☒ YES     ☐ NO

**SUPERIOR COURT RULE 29.**   Requirement of statement as to money damages to prevent the transfer of civil actions to District or Municipal Court Departments.

1.   Superior Court Rule 29, as amended requires the statement of money damages on the reverse side be completed.

2.   Failure to complete the statement, where appropriate, will result in transfer of this action (Superior Court Rule 29(2).

SIGNATURE OF ATTORNEY OF RECORD                                               DATE:

**(OFFICE USE ONLY—DO NOT WRITE BELOW THIS LINE)**

**DISPOSITION**

**A. Judgment Entered**
☐ 1.  Before jury trial or non-jury hearing
☐ 2.  During jury trial or non-jury hearing
☐ 3.  After jury verdict
☐ 4.  After court finding
☐ 5.  After post trial motion

**B. No Judgment Entered**
☐ 6.  Transferred to District Court under G.L. c.231, s102C

Disposition date _____

RECEIVED
BY:
DATE:

DISP ENTERED
BY:
DATE:

**CLERK'S OFFICE COPY**

mtc003-07/84

# Comments on the Schulansky Complaint

Although Schulansky's complaint has been drafted to comply with the pleading requirements of the Massachusetts Rules of Civil Procedure, (Mass. R. Civ. P. 8-11), those rules are identical in most respects to Rules 8-11 of the Federal Rules of Civil Procedure. The following comments therefore refer to the rules generically unless the federal and state versions differ on the particular point under discussion.

1.   While some of the contents of pleadings are a matter of custom in a particular court or personal preference of the drafting attorney, the Rules specifically govern many aspects of pleading. For example, Rule 10(a) requires every pleading to have a caption such as that in Schulansky's complaint. Under Rule 10(a), the caption must include the name of the court (*Commonwealth of Massachusetts, Plymouth County, Superior Court Department*), the docket number of the action (*Civil Action No.*), the names of the parties, and a designation of the pleading (*Complaint*).

  The docket number is a number assigned to each case by the court clerk, for administrative purposes. On Schulansky's complaint, the docket number is left blank because the case will not be assigned a docket number until the complaint is filed with the clerk.

2.   Note that Howard has included a number of subheadings in the complaint. While these are not required by the Rules, such subheadings are frequently included for the sake of clarity. Particularly in a lengthy complaint that asserts a number of claims, or where the factual allegations are complex, separate sections for *Parties, Facts,* and *Claims for Relief* make it easy for the court and the parties to quickly find and review parts of the complaint during motion arguments and other proceedings.

  In federal actions, a *Jurisdiction* subheading is frequently added because Fed. R. Civ. P. 8(a)(1) specifically requires the plaintiff to allege the basis for subject matter jurisdiction over the action. (Such an allegation is not required under Massachusetts Rule 8 because, unlike the federal district courts, the Superior Court is a court of general jurisdiction.)

  For many simple cases, such as an action on a note or a straightforward motor vehicle tort case, the complaint may be so brief that subheadings are unnecessary. See the Appendix of Forms accompanying the Federal Rules of Civil Procedure, Forms 3-18 for examples of such complaints. These forms are sufficient under the Rules. Fed. R. Civ. P. 84.

3.   The rules do not explicitly require separate paragraphs identifying the parties to the action. However, it is customary to begin the complaint with descriptions of the plaintiff(s) and the defendant(s). This information is important to various issues, including personal jurisdiction, venue, capacity to

sue and be sued, and, (particularly in federal court diversity actions) subject matter jurisdiction. In Schulansky's complaint, for example, the allegation that Schulansky resides in Plymouth County indicates the plaintiff's basis under state law for laying venue there. See Mass. Gen. Laws. ch. 223, §1 (venue proper in county where plaintiff lives).

4. Many complaints will include a subheading entitled *Facts,* or *Factual Allegations,* setting forth chronologically the events that gave rise to the plaintiff's claim for relief. This type of breakdown is useful, particularly in complex cases, to distinguish the underlying facts giving rise to the claim from the plaintiff's asserted claims for relief arising out of those facts.

In Schulansky's case, for example, there is enough factual background that a separate facts section facilitates a clear understanding of her claims. It is true that Rule 8(a)(2) only requires a "short and plain statement of the claim," and that very brief, general allegations will suffice to avoid dismissal. *Conley v. Gibson,* 355 U.S. 41, 47-48 (1957). But a little more detail than the absolute minimum needed under the pleading rules will give the court a clearer picture of the case, from the plaintiff's point of view. And, since Rule 8(b) requires the defendant to respond paragraph by paragraph to the allegations in the complaint, a more detailed complaint will elicit more specific denials or admissions in the defendant's answer.

5. The Rules require all allegations in the body of the complaint to be set forth in numbered paragraphs. Rule 10(b). This facilitates quick reference to the allegations in the complaint. It also allows defendants to respond to each of the plaintiff's allegations by number, and allows the plaintiff to incorporate allegations by number in later parts of the complaint, as Howard has done in paragraphs twenty-one and twenty-eight of the Schulansky complaint.

Rule 10(b) also provides that the allegations in each paragraph of the complaint "shall be limited as far as practicable to a statement of a single set of circumstances. . . ." However, reducing specificity to the atomic level (for example, by breaking Schulansky's paragraph five into three paragraphs), would make the complaint unduly tedious. The allegations in paragraph five all relate closely to the issue of the age and value of the house and form a logical grouping for a single paragraph. The Rule does not limit each paragraph to a single fact, but to a single "set of circumstances," and calls for the breakdown of allegations "to the extent practicable."

6. The Rules authorize parties to attach exhibits to their pleadings, as Schulansky has done here. Rule 10(c). Such exhibits become a part of the complaint for all purposes. Parties should exercise care in incorporating documents in the complaint, however, since doing so may constitute an admission at least of the authenticity of the documents if not their accuracy. Here,

for example, Schulansky's inclusion of the Proposal and Estimate, together with her allegation that it constitutes the contract between her and Ronan, may weaken her argument that Ronan had an additional duty, arising from their prior discussions, to repair the old foundation. See the Third Defense in Ronan's answer, infra.

7.    In paragraphs 21-27 and 28-30, Howard has recast the factual allegations in terms of claims for relief for breach of contract and negligence. These sections of the complaint are intended to show the court that the facts alleged satisfy the elements of legally recognized claims that, if proved, entitle Schulansky to relief.[1] The subheading *Claim for Relief* tracks the language of Rule 8(a)(2), which requires the complaint to include a "short and plain statement of the claim showing that the pleader is entitled to relief." Here, Schulansky has asserted a right to relief under two distinct theories. If the court concludes that she has proved a right to recovery on either her contract theory or her tort theory, it will grant her whatever relief is proper under that claim. This "pleading in the alternative" is expressly authorized by Rule 8(e)(2).

The rules do not require the pleader to state the legal theory on which she claims a right to relief. A brief description of the "claim," that is, the events giving rise to the action, is sufficient. See 2A Moore's at ¶8.14 (1986). However, it is certainly appropriate and helpful to allege the elements of each claim clearly, especially in cases involving multiple theories of relief based on the same underlying facts. See *O'Donnell v. Elgin, J. & E. Ry. Co.*, 338 U.S. 384, 392 (1949) ("We no longer insist upon technical rules of pleading, but it will ever be difficult in a jury trial to segregate issues which counsel do not separate in their pleading, preparation or thinking.").

Separate pleading theories are often labelled as different "counts" instead of Claims for Relief. In simple complaints, such subdivisions are unnecessary. See, e.g., Appendix of Forms accompanying Federal Rules of Civil Procedure, Form 17, which asserts two theories of relief quite clearly without separate counts or subheadings.

8.    Rule 10(c) authorizes a pleader to incorporate prior allegations by reference in later parts of her pleading. Here Howard has done so in order to make clear that the breach of contract claim is based on the facts alleged in the cited paragraphs.

9.    At the end of the complaint, Howard includes a demand for the relief Schulansky seeks on both claims, as required by Rule 8(a)(3). In this case, the

---

1. Schulansky might have other claims for relief in addition to the two asserted in the complaint. For example, other claims might be based on the failure of Ronan to properly supervise Jones or negligent selection of Jones as the subcontractor. For illustration purposes, however, I have tried to keep the complaint to a manageable length.

relief sought is damages, but in other actions different types of relief are also commonly sought, such as specific performance, an injunction, or a declaration of the rights of the parties.

In Schulansky's complaint, the demand for relief is set forth in a separate subsection. A single demand at the end of the complaint is appropriate here, since Schulansky seeks the same measure of damages on each of her claims. However, if the elements of damages on the various claims differ, it is appropriate to insert a demand for relief after each claim. For example, if Schulansky were seeking specific performance of the contract with Ronan, inserting separate demands for relief after each claim for relief would help to make it clear that specific performance is sought under the contract claim rather than the negligence claim (which would not support a demand for specific performance). Since she seeks only damages on each claim, however, and the measure of damages on each theory is apparently the same, either a single demand at the end of the complaint or demands after each claim would be appropriate. Compare the separate demands for relief in Ronan's third-party complaint, infra p. 376.

10. Rule 38(b) provides that a demand for jury trial "may be endorsed upon a pleading." The jury demand is often included in the complaint. Since the right to trial by jury is waived if not demanded within ten days of the close of the pleadings (see Rule 38(b)), it is wise to at least consider inserting the demand for jury trial in the complaint. Otherwise, plaintiff's counsel may forget about it, and the period for seeking jury trial may slip by unnoticed.

11. Rule 11 governs signature of the complaint and other pleadings.[2] It requires the attorney to sign the complaint, and state her address. The rule also imposes important ethical duties on attorneys who sign complaints and other court papers. Under Federal Rule 11, an attorney's signature on a complaint certifies to the court that the attorney has read it and believes, after reasonable inquiry, that it is well-grounded in fact and warranted by existing law or an argument for change in the existing law, and that the complaint is not filed for any improper purpose.

The "reasonable inquiry" requirement was added to Federal Rule 11 in 1983 to strengthen the attorney's obligation to the court to avoid frivolous or unethical pleadings. See Advisory Committee Note to 1983 Amendment to Rule 11, U.S.C.S. Rules of Civil Procedure R. 11, p.343 (1984). This language does not require Slater and Howard to complete their research or investigation before filing suit against Ronan, but it does require them to have some factual basis beyond mere opinion or speculation to support the

---

2. The complaint is shown here with the attorney's signature affixed. Subsequent pleadings and motions have not been signed because they are suggested pleadings for the partner's review and have not yet been filed in court.

pleaded facts, as well as a colorable argument for the legal positions asserted in the complaint.

The factual standard in Rule 11 would be met by the information Schulansky gave her attorneys about the construction problem before they drafted the complaint. They knew that the damage appeared shortly after the construction work began, in the area where the work was being done. They also knew that an engineer had viewed the damage and concluded that it resulted from the inadequate construction work. That is a reasonable basis to support the factual allegations in the Schulansky complaint. The rule does not require certainty or admissible evidence, but only a reasonable pre-filing inquiry.

The legal standard in Rule 11 is also satisfied in the Schulansky case. Howard and Slater had a copy of the contract, which required Ronan to construct walls to support the addition. If the damage to the house resulted from inadequate support, that would arguably constitute a breach of the contract. In addition, the discussions between Ronan and Schulansky during the negotiations may well support a claim that Ronan had agreed to reinforce or rebuild the foundation. Similarly, if the engineer's alternative conclusion that the bulldozer damaged the foundation is accurate, that would certainly constitute actionable negligence.

# Comments on the Summons and Cover Sheet

Rule 4(d) requires both a summons and complaint to be served on the defendant. The complaint is written by the plaintiff or her attorney, setting out the allegations against the defendant. The summons, by contrast, is an official order from the court requiring the defendant to respond to the complaint. Hence, Rule 4(b) requires that the summons bear the seal of the court and be signed by the clerk.

In many courts printed summonses like the one used here, already signed and sealed, may be obtained in blank from the clerk's office. In some courts, the seal is actually printed on the summons; in others, the court clerk embosses the seal on the summons by hand. (The Plymouth County clerk's office uses an embossed seal, so it does not show up on the form illustrated here.)

The plaintiff's attorney fills in the blanks and arranges for service of the summons with the complaint. Compare the printed summons with the detailed requirements of Rule 4(b). (Mass. R. Civ. P. 4(b) closely parallels Federal Rule 4(b).) The summons includes the seal of the court, the name of the court, space for the names of the parties, and the name and address of the plaintiff's attorney. It also warns the defendant, as required by Rule 4(b), that she must answer within 20 days or default judgment will be entered against her. See Rule 55, which authorizes entry of a default judgment if the defendant fails to respond to the complaint.

The first paragraph of the summons quite properly distinguishes between service and filing of the defendant's answer. Rule 12(a) requires the defendant to *serve* her answer on the plaintiff within 20 days of service of the complaint. See Chapter 4 for a discussion of methods of service of process, particularly question 15, which discusses proper methods for service of the Schulansky complaint. Rule 5(d) also requires the defendant to file the answer (and all other papers in the case) with the clerk of court, so that a complete official record of the documents in the case is available to the court and the parties. As the summons states, the answer must be filed before it is served or within a reasonable time thereafter.

Nothing in Rule 4(b) requires inclusion of the second paragraph of the summons, warning defendants that they must assert compulsory counterclaims under Rule 13(a). Other courts, operating under the same version of the rule, do not include it. The purpose of the warning is obviously to remind defendants, who must respond within a short time, that they must assert any compulsory counterclaims in their answer or risk loss of those claims.

The printed summons usually includes space (here, at the bottom of the page) for the sheriff, constable, or other official process server to provide proof of service. See Rule 4(g). The server fills out the form, indicating the date and manner in which service was made, and files it with the court.

If service is made directly by the plaintiff's attorney (for example, in a case such as this one, where service on the out-of-state defendants will likely be made by mail), a separate, sworn affidavit must be filed setting forth the time and manner in which service was made.

As Chapter 22, the introduction to these pleading materials, indicates, most courts have their own local rules governing various details of local practice. Such local rules must always be checked before filing suit or taking other actions that may implicate the local rules. The Massachusetts Superior Court rules, for example, require plaintiffs to include a Civil Action Cover Sheet with complaints filed in the court. Mass. Super. Ct. Rule 29. As you can see from the cover sheet for *Schulansky v. Ronan,* the cover sheet provides administrative information for the court.

# 24

## A Change of Forum: Ronan Petitions for Removal

## The Drafting Request

**MEMORANDUM**

**TO:**    Marcia Losordo
             Associate

**FROM:**  Arthur Ackerman

**RE:**    *Schulansky v. Ronan*
             Plymouth Superior Court No. 27,982

**DATE:**  December 19, 1985

----------------------------------------------------

As you know, this office frequently handles litigation for Federal Security Insurance Company, a large insurer specializing in construction accounts. Federal Security has just asked us to represent one of their insureds, a New Hampshire contractor named Richard Ronan. On December 10 Ronan was served with process in a suit commenced against him and Ronan Construction Company in the Plymouth Superior Court. A copy of the complaint is attached.

Ronan was in this morning for an initial interview on the case. (I would have asked you to sit in, but you were in court.) Although I didn't have much time, I did get the relevant background information on the case. The suit arises out of some work Ronan did for the plaintiff, Deborah Schulansky, on her second home in Alton, New Hampshire. Schulansky claims that Ronan agreed to build an addition to the house but failed to reinforce the foundation adequately, causing the main part of the house to settle. Ronan denies that the house has settled, or if it has, that it resulted from his work.

My initial reaction was that it seems doubtful that Ronan is subject to personal jurisdiction in Massachusetts for this claim, since the work was done out of state and Ronan is from New Hampshire. However, he did negotiate the contract with the plaintiff in Massachusetts, so he does at least have some relevant contacts here.

If Ronan is subject to jurisdiction in Massachusetts, I would prefer to litigate in federal district court here in Boston rather than down in Plymouth. Ronan lives in Nashua, New Hampshire, and Ronan Construction Company is incorporated in New Hampshire with its principal place of business in Nashua, so the case is removable on diversity grounds.

I need some quick information on removal of this case. Could you please write me a short memo answering the following questions:

1. Should the petition be filed in the state or federal court?
2. What documents must be filed with the removal petition?
3. Can we file our motion to dismiss for lack of personal jurisdiction in the state court and wait for a decision on that motion before removing the suit?
4. Do we have to answer or move to dismiss before removing? If not, when is our response due in federal court?
5. The plaintiff has demanded trial by jury in her state court complaint. If we also want a jury, do we have to request it again in the federal court after removal?

If we have to remove right away, rather than waiting for the state court to resolve the personal jurisdiction issue, please draft a petition for removal as well. Even though the holidays are imminent, please get to this during the next week; I believe there is a 30-day limit on removal, and we've already lost nine of them.

# The Associate's Response

## MEMORANDUM

**TO:**     Arthur Ackerman

**FROM:**  Marcia Losordo

**RE:**     Removal of *Schulansky v. Ronan*
           Plymouth County Superior Court No. 27,982

**DATE:**  December 23, 1985

-----------------------------------------------

I have researched your questions on removal of the Schulansky case. In addition, since I conclude that we must file the removal petition within 30 days even if the state court lacks personal jurisdiction, I have also drafted a removal petition and other required documents, which I attach for your review.

The answers to your questions are as follows:

1. Should the petition be filed in the state or federal court?

The petition for removal must be filed in the federal district court "for the district and division within which such action is pending." 28 U.S.C. §1446(a). A copy of the petition must then be filed in the state court. 28 U.S.C. §1446(e).

2. What must be filed with the removal petition?

Under 28 U.S.C. §1446(a), copies of "all process, pleadings and orders" served upon the defendants must be filed with the removal petition. In this case that includes only the summons and complaint served on each defendant.

The petition must be verified, that is, the facts in the petition must be affirmed under oath. 28 U.S.C. §1446(a); see 1A Moore's Federal Practice ¶0.168 [3.-4] (1986). However, the party making the verification need not have direct personal knowledge of the facts alleged in the petition; it is sufficient to affirm the facts on the basis of "information and belief" obtained from others with knowledge of the facts. Thus, it is proper for the defendant's attorney to sign the verification, and I have prepared a verification form on the assumption that you will do so.

The petition must also be accompanied by a bond, to assure payment of costs the plaintiff may incur as a result of improper removal. 28 U.S.C. §1446(d). The removal statute does not specify the amount of the bond, but the local rules of the District of Massachusetts provide that a $250 bond is sufficient. United States District Court, District of Massachusetts, Local Rule 25.

A party who petitions for removal must give written notice of the filing to all other parties to the action "promptly after filing the petition and bond."

28 U.S.C. §1446(e). I have prepared a notice, as well as copies of the petition and bond, for service on the plaintiff and a copy of the petition to be filed in the state court.

3.  Can I file my motion to dismiss for lack of personal jurisdiction in the state court and wait for a decision on that motion before removing the suit?

It is certainly permissible to file the motion to dismiss before removing. Until removal is sought, the case is governed by the state court rules, which require a response to the complaint within 20 days. Mass. R. Civ. P. 12(a).

However, §1446(b) provides that the petition for removal must be filed within 30 days after the defendant is served with the complaint. Nothing in the statute suggests that the 30-day period is suspended by any pending motions, and it is very unlikely that the motion to dismiss would be acted on before the 30 days elapse. Therefore, we cannot await decision on the motion before petitioning to remove. We should remove the case; the federal court will then decide the pending motion.

4.  Do I have to answer or move to dismiss before removing? If not, when is my response due in federal court?

As indicated in the previous answer, the Massachusetts rules require a response within 20 days after service of the complaint and summons. If you do not remove within the first 20 days, a response to the complaint will be due and you will have to file one or be in default. You should either remove before the response is due, or file an answer or motion to dismiss in the state court. If you do answer before removing, the answer will stand as the answer in federal court, unless that court orders otherwise. Fed. R. Civ. P. 81(c).

If you remove before responding to the complaint, Fed. R. Civ. P. 81(c) provides that you must answer within 20 days of service of the complaint or 5 days after the petition is filed, whichever is longer. Thus, we had better begin preparing an answer immediately, or move for an extension of time in which to answer, under Fed. R. Civ. P. 6(b).

5.  The plaintiff has demanded trial by jury in her state court complaint. If we also want a jury, do we have to request it again in the federal court after removal?

Rule 81 (c) provides that a party who has properly requested jury trial prior to removal need not renew the request in the federal court. Once the case is removed, the federal rules will govern the action (Fed. R. Civ. P. 81(c)), including Fed. R. Civ. P. 38(d), which provides that a jury trial demand cannot be withdrawn without the consent of the parties. Therefore, this action will be tried to a jury unless both sides later consent to trial before the court.

However, I am not sure whether the plaintiff's general demand for jury trial would apply to any counterclaim we may assert in our answer. If the case reaches the point of filing an answer, and you decide to assert any counterclaims, a separate demand for jury trial should be made as to them.

# The Resulting Documents

1.

2.

3.

4.

5.

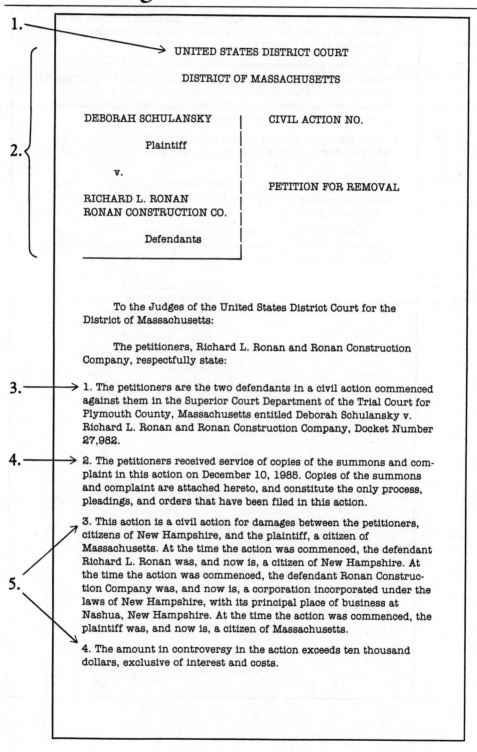

UNITED STATES DISTRICT COURT

DISTRICT OF MASSACHUSETTS

DEBORAH SCHULANSKY

Plaintiff

v.

RICHARD L. RONAN
RONAN CONSTRUCTION CO.

Defendants

CIVIL ACTION NO.

PETITION FOR REMOVAL

To the Judges of the United States District Court for the District of Massachusetts:

The petitioners, Richard L. Ronan and Ronan Construction Company, respectfully state:

1. The petitioners are the two defendants in a civil action commenced against them in the Superior Court Department of the Trial Court for Plymouth County, Massachusetts entitled Deborah Schulansky v. Richard L. Ronan and Ronan Construction Company, Docket Number 27,982.

2. The petitioners received service of copies of the summons and complaint in this action on December 10, 1985. Copies of the summons and complaint are attached hereto, and constitute the only process, pleadings, and orders that have been filed in this action.

3. This action is a civil action for damages between the petitioners, citizens of New Hampshire, and the plaintiff, a citizen of Massachusetts. At the time the action was commenced, the defendant Richard L. Ronan was, and now is, a citizen of New Hampshire. At the time the action was commenced, the defendant Ronan Construction Company was, and now is, a corporation incorporated under the laws of New Hampshire, with its principal place of business at Nashua, New Hampshire. At the time the action was commenced, the plaintiff was, and now is, a citizen of Massachusetts.

4. The amount in controversy in the action exceeds ten thousand dollars, exclusive of interest and costs.

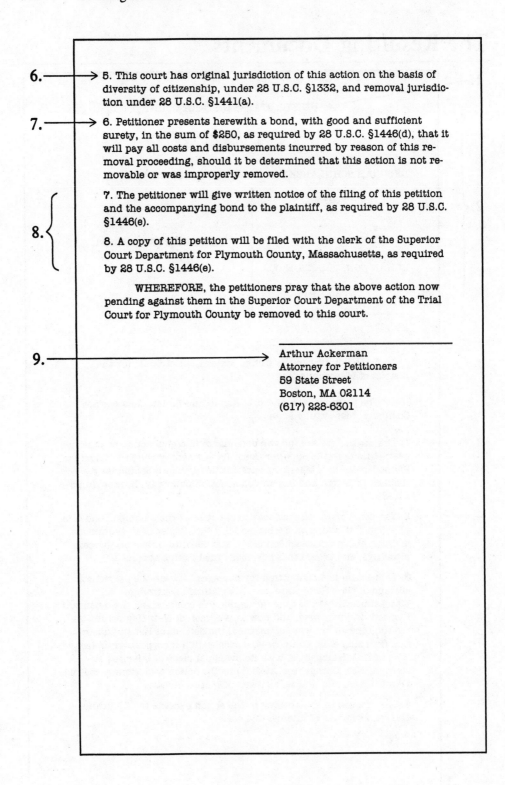

**6.** → 5. This court has original jurisdiction of this action on the basis of diversity of citizenship, under 28 U.S.C. §1332, and removal jurisdiction under 28 U.S.C. §1441(a).

**7.** → 6. Petitioner presents herewith a bond, with good and sufficient surety, in the sum of $250, as required by 28 U.S.C. §1446(d), that it will pay all costs and disbursements incurred by reason of this removal proceeding, should it be determined that this action is not removable or was improperly removed.

7. The petitioner will give written notice of the filing of this petition and the accompanying bond to the plaintiff, as required by 28 U.S.C. §1446(e).

**8.** 8. A copy of this petition will be filed with the clerk of the Superior Court Department for Plymouth County, Massachusetts, as required by 28 U.S.C. §1446(e).

WHEREFORE, the petitioners pray that the above action now pending against them in the Superior Court Department of the Trial Court for Plymouth County be removed to this court.

**9.** → Arthur Ackerman
Attorney for Petitioners
59 State Street
Boston, MA 02114
(617) 228-6301

UNITED STATES DISTRICT COURT

DISTRICT OF MASSACHUSETTS

| | |
|---|---|
| DEBORAH SCHULANSKY | CIVIL ACTION NO. |
| Plaintiff | |
| v. | |
| | VERIFICATION ←————————— 10. |
| RICHARD L. RONAN | |
| RONAN CONSTRUCTION CO. | |
| Defendants | |

Commonwealth of Massachusetts

County of Suffolk } ss:

    Arthur Ackerman, being duly sworn, deposes and says that he is the attorney for Richard L. Ronan and Ronan Construction Company, the petitioners for removal of this action, that he has read the foregoing petition and that the contents thereof are true to the best of his knowledge, information, and belief.

_____

Arthur Ackerman

Subscribed and sworn to before me this twenty-sixth day of December, 1985.

_____

Notary Public

My commission expires:

_____

UNITED STATES DISTRICT COURT

DISTRICT OF MASSACHUSETTS

| | |
|---|---|
| DEBORAH SCHULANSKY | Civil Action No. |
| Plaintiff | |
| v. | NOTICE OF REMOVAL ← ———— 11. |
| RICHARD L. RONAN | |
| RONAN CONSTRUCTION CO. | |
| Defendants | |

TO:   Phyllis Slater
      Attorney for Plaintiff
      322 Puritan Road
      Plymouth, MA 02360

Please take notice that the defendants in the above-entitled
action have this date filed their petition and bond for removal of this
action in the Office of the Clerk of the United States District Court for
the District of Massachusetts. Copies of the petition and bond are
attached hereto.

You are further advised that the defendants, upon filing of the
petition and bond for removal, also filed a copy of this petition with
the Clerk of the Superior Court Department for Plymouth County,
thus effecting removal under 28 U.S.C. §1446(e).

Date: December 27, 1985

Arthur Ackerman
Attorney for the Petitioners
59 State Street
Boston, MA 02114
(617) 228-6301

# Comments on the Removal Petition and Accompanying Documents

1.  The heading of the removal petition reflects the fact that the petition is filed in the federal district court, not in the state court in which Schulansky filed suit.

2.  Although Fed. R. Civ. P. 10(a) only governs the caption for pleadings, and a petition for removal is not a pleading (see Fed. R. Civ. P. 7(a)), it is customary to use the same type of caption in all papers filed in the suit. (Indeed, this may be required by local rule of the federal district, as it is in Massachusetts. See United States District Court, District of Massachusetts, Local Rule 11.) Of course, the title of the paper (*Petition for Removal*) will change, but the court, names of the parties, and docket number will appear on all filed papers. Note again that the docket number has not been filled in since the case will receive a new federal court docket number when the petition for removal is filed.

3.  Although the removal statutes are not entirely clear on the point, the courts have held that all defendants must join in the removal petition. See Chapter 7, question 7. Paragraph one indicates to the court that this requirement is met.

4.  The allegation as to the date of service of the complaint indicates to the court that the removal petition is timely, since the 30-day removal period begins to run on the date of service of the summons and complaint on the defendants. 28 U.S.C. §1446(b). This paragraph of the petition also indicates that the defendants have complied with the requirement of 28 U.S.C. §1446(a) that "a copy of all process, pleadings and orders served upon him or them" be filed with the petition.

5.  It will not always be clear from the plaintiff's complaint that a case meets the requirements for original or removal jurisdiction of the federal court. For example, Schulansky's state court complaint did not allege where Ronan Construction Company's principal place of business was, since it was not necessary to do so to invoke the state court's jurisdiction over the action.

Section 1446(a) authorizes the removing defendant to state facts in the petition that are necessary to demonstrate that the federal court has jurisdiction. The information in paragraphs three and four of the removal petition is intended to show the court that this is a proper diversity case, which could have been brought originally in federal court. These paragraphs also demonstrate that none of the defendants is a citizen of the forum state, a separate requirement in 28 U.S.C. §1441(b) for removal of diversity cases.

6.  The fundamental requirement for removal is that the case could have been brought initially in federal court. In paragraph five, the defendants state that original jurisdiction existed, and that removal is therefore proper under 28 U.S.C. §1441(a).

7.  Paragraph six is also intended to demonstrate that the defendants have complied with the removal requirements. See 28 U.S.C. §1446(d), which requires that a bond be filed to assure payment of costs incurred by the plaintiff in securing remand of an improperly removed action.

8.  Paragraphs seven and eight indicate that the removing defendants will comply with the requirements of 28 U.S.C. §1446(e), that the plaintiff be notified of the removal and that a copy of the petition be filed in the state court.

9.  The ethical requirements in Rule 11 apply not only to pleadings, but also to "other paper[s]" filed with the court throughout the litigation. Thus, as with Slater's signature on the complaint, Ackerman's signature certifies to the court that he has made a preliminary inquiry both as to the supporting facts and legal right to file the petition, and concluded that he has adequate grounds to support the positions asserted in it.

10.  Verification is a formal requirement that the petitioner, his attorney, or some other person with knowledge of the facts swear to the facts in the removal petition. It is intended to give some assurance of the truth of the facts in the petition. Note, however, that it is permissible for the party signing the verification to swear to the facts on "knowledge, information, and belief." 1A Moore's at ¶0.168[3.-4]. Under this standard, the person verifying the petition need not have direct knowledge of all the facts alleged, but may rely on information supplied by other witnesses. This is certainly a lesser standard than personal knowledge of the underlying facts, but it lends some additional solemnity to the petition beyond the basic requirements of Rule 11.

11.  The notice of removal is a fairly commonsensical document drawn up to comply with the requirement of 28 U.S.C. §1446(e) that the defendant give notice to the adverse parties of the filing of the petition and bond. As with the petition itself, it is intended to demonstrate to the court and the plaintiff that the defendants have complied with the removal requirements.

---

The third question Ackerman asks in his memo is interesting. It seems like an unnecessary hassle to go through the formalities of removal if the action is likely to be dismissed for lack of personal jurisdiction anyway. However, as the answer indicates, the removal statute does not allow the defendants to litigate preliminary objections in the state court before exercising their right to remove; removal must take place within 30 days, regardless of objections the plaintiff may have to jurisdiction, venue, or other matters relating to the court's competence to entertain the action. Ironically, even if the defendant claims the state court lacks *subject matter* jurisdiction (in which case removal is improper), he must remove within the 30 days if he prefers federal court and then argue that the case was not properly before the state court to begin with.

This may lead to another awkward result for the defendants. The federal courts have taken a very broad view of the scope of personal jurisdiction under the Massachusetts long-arm statute and minimum contacts analysis. See, e.g., *Hahn v. Vermont Law School,* 698 F.2d 48 (1st Cir. 1983). If personal jurisdiction were the only issue in the case, Ackerman might prefer to stay in a Massachusetts court, which, ironically, might construe its own jurisdictional reach more narrowly than the federal court would. However, Ackerman does not have the choice to litigate some issues in the one court and some in the other; removal brings the entire action into the federal court. Ackerman may not have considered this possible adverse effect of removing the case; when the case came into the office nine days of the removal period had already elapsed, leaving little time to research all potential ramifications of removal. On the other hand, he may be willing to accept the greater risk of losing on the jurisdictional defense in order to obtain other tactical benefits from litigating in federal court.

# 25

## The Defendants' Perspective: Ronan's Answer and Counterclaim

## The Drafting Request

### MEMORANDUM

**TO:**    Marcia Losordo
          Associate

**FROM:**  Arthur Ackerman

**RE:**    Answer and Counterclaim in *Schulansky v. Ronan*
          U.S. District Court No. 86-67

**DATE:**  January 8, 1986

----------------------------------------------------

Thank you for your informative memo and removal documents in this case. I have filed the removal petition today and notified the plaintiff and the state court, so we are officially in federal court.

I have decided to file an answer to the complaint (instead of a Rule 12(b) motion), and would appreciate your assistance in drafting it. I realize that you have not yet had any Christmas vacation, but as your memo indicates, we are under the gun because Fed. R. Civ. P. 81(c) requires us to respond to the complaint within five days of removing the case.

Not surprisingly, Dick Ronan's version of the facts in this case differs significantly from the allegations in Schulansky's complaint. First of all, although there was some discussion about the old foundation during their negotiations, Ronan's position is that he never assumed responsibility for any extensive reconstruction work. He never said anything about rebuilding the foundation, except that he doubted it would be necessary. He did say he would pour cement into any gaps in the exposed boulders, but definitely did not agree to anything more than that. He points out that reconstructing the foundation on a house that old is a very substantial job; he could never have quoted her the price he did if such reconstruction were included in the work.

Second, according to Ronan, he and Schulansky discussed the problem again after the old foundation had been exposed. She asked him whether it ought to be rebuilt, and Ronan said that he did not think it was necessary and that it was beyond the scope of the contract. He specifically recalls telling her at that time that he thought the foundation would be sufficient if he filled in the gaps with concrete, but "you can never be 100 percent sure — old houses are unpredictable." She agreed to his suggestion, and that is what he did.

Ronan also denies any negligence in excavating the foundation. There were some loose boulders in the excavated area near the foundation, which Schulansky assumed had been knocked out by the bulldozer. Ronan admits that the bulldozer hit the foundation a number of times, but he thinks those rocks were probably excavated from the new cellar area instead. He also states that digging the earth away from the foundation did not weaken it. According to him, it is the direct downward pressure of the structure on top of the rocks in the foundation, not the surrounding earth, that keeps the foundation — and the house itself — in place.

Last, Ronan denies that Schulansky's house has settled as a result of his construction work or any defect in the old foundation. He claims that most of the cracks she refers to were already there when he inspected the house before he bid on the job; after all, the house is over 200 years old, and there is evidence of settling in every room of the house. While he does not doubt the good faith of the plaintiff, he thinks she simply had not noticed these problems until the construction work caused her to take a close look at the structure of the house.

Please draft an answer to the Schulansky complaint, based on Ronan's understanding of the facts outlined above. Feel free to contact Ronan directly for any further information you need.

Our answer should not only respond to the individual allegations in Schulansky's complaint, but also raise several additional defenses. First, I think we should take the position that the Proposal and Estimate constitutes the entire agreement between the parties and that Ronan is under no duty to rebuild the foundation if the Proposal and Estimate does not require it. Even if there was some prior discussion in which Ronan arguably agreed to rebuild the foundation, it is the contract itself, not the discussions leading up to it, that defines the parties' obligations. As you know, where a contract is clear and complete on its face, the parol evidence rule bars either party from varying or contradicting the terms of the contract by evidence of prior inconsistent negotiations. Here, the contract is clear: Paragraph two requires Ronan to build a foundation for the addition, not to rebuild the preexisting foundation.

Second, Ronan states (and the plaintiff's complaint admits), that Schulansky was present when the foundation was exposed. Ronan told her what he planned to do, and she evidently accepted his proposal to reinforce it rather than rebuild it. Thus, I think we can make a strong argument that Schulansky has waived any right to reconstruction of the old foundation.

Our answer should also raise the objection that the court lacks personal jurisdiction over both defendants. I realize that we could postpone answering by filing a motion to dismiss on this ground, but I have decided to answer instead. I am somewhat doubtful that the court will dismiss on this ground. If the court postpones decision on the motion (as it may under Fed. R. Civ. P. 12(d)), I would rather have our answer to the complaint, setting forth our position on the merits, before the court from the beginning of the litigation.

Please also include a counterclaim for the final payment under the contract, which Schulansky has never made. In addition, it is our position that Richard Ronan signed the contract as an agent of Ronan Construction Company, not on his own behalf. Consequently, he was not a party to the contract and is not personally liable for any breach of that contract. Please be careful in drafting the answer to observe this distinction in responding to the allegations in the complaint and in drafting the counterclaim.

We may also wish to file a third-party complaint against the excavation subcontractor, Arlen Jones. Please let me know whether this must be filed with the answer. I certainly would prefer to have more time to decide whether to file a third-party claim and, if so, whether there will be any jurisdictional problems involved. (Jones is apparently from New Hampshire, but I am not sure whether he may be subject to personal jurisdiction here on some ground.)

# The Associate's Response

## MEMORANDUM

**TO:**  Arthur Ackerman

**FROM:**  Marcia Losordo

**RE:**  Answer and Counterclaim in *Schulansky v. Ronan*
U.S. District Court No. 86-67

**DATE:**  January 10, 1986

I have attached a proposed answer and counterclaim in the Schulansky case. I have also attached a certificate of service to go with it.

I have based my responses to the plaintiff's allegations on the facts as you set them out in your memo and on direct conversations with Dick Ronan. In responding to the plaintiff's first claim for relief, for breach of contract, I have consistently taken the position that Ronan's only obligation was to construct foundation walls for the addition, not for any part of the main house.

The plaintiff's second claim for relief on a negligence theory is evidently premised on the assumption that Jones was an employee of either Ronan personally or Ronan Construction Company, so that one or the other would be liable for his negligence under respondeat superior principles. However, it is not at all clear that Jones was an employee, as opposed to an independent contractor with Ronan. The decision turns on whether Ronan had the right of control over Jones in the detailed performance of the work. Restatement (Second) of Agency §220 (1958). If he did, Jones was an employee; if not, he acted as an independent contractor.

From what Ronan tells me, it is unclear whether the court would characterize Jones as an employee of Ronan or an independent contractor. On the one hand, Jones was paid a flat fee for the job and used his own bulldozer, factors that suggest that he was independent. Restatement (Second) of Agency §227 (1958). On the other, Jones worked for Ronan on a regular basis, did not have any written agreement for the work, and generally did whatever Ronan told him to do. These facts would support a finding that Jones was an employee. Ibid. Where the facts could reasonably support the conclusion that Jones was independent, I conclude that it is proper under Fed. R. Civ. P. 11 to deny that he was Ronan's employee, and I have done so. See paragraph twenty-nine of the First Defense and the Sixth Defense.

If you decide to file a third-party complaint against Jones, it need not be filed with the answer. You may serve a third-party complaint without leave of court within ten days of serving the answer in the original action. Fed. R. Civ. P. 14(a). After that you will need leave of court, after notice to the plaintiff, to file any third-party claims. Id. However, even if we file within the ten-day period for filing as of right, the court does not have to entertain the third-party claim. The decision to allow or dismiss a third-party claim is a discretionary one in each case. Wright at 509. If the court concludes that entertaining the additional claim would not advance the efficient and fair resolution of the entire dispute, it may dismiss it at any time.

Please note that the answer is due by January 13. Fed. R. Civ. P. 81(c) is not entirely clear as to whether the answer must be *filed* or *served* within five days after removal. Under Fed. R. Civ. P. 12(a), the answer must be *served* within the 20-day period. It is reasonable to assume, by analogy to Rule 12(a), that an answer is timely under Rule 81(c) if it is served within the five-day period. I did some quick research to confirm this interpretation but was unable to find any authority on point.

Since Fed. R. Civ. P. 5(d) provides that service by mail is complete upon mailing, we will have to get this in the mail on Monday, January 13. Even though the 11th and 12th are weekend days, please remember to save time to review the documents before that date.

One last point you may wish to consider. Is it possible that, by seeking affirmative relief from Schulansky in our counterclaim, we will waive our objection to the court's jurisdiction? I have not researched this point but will do so if you think this is a possible problem.

# The Resulting Documents

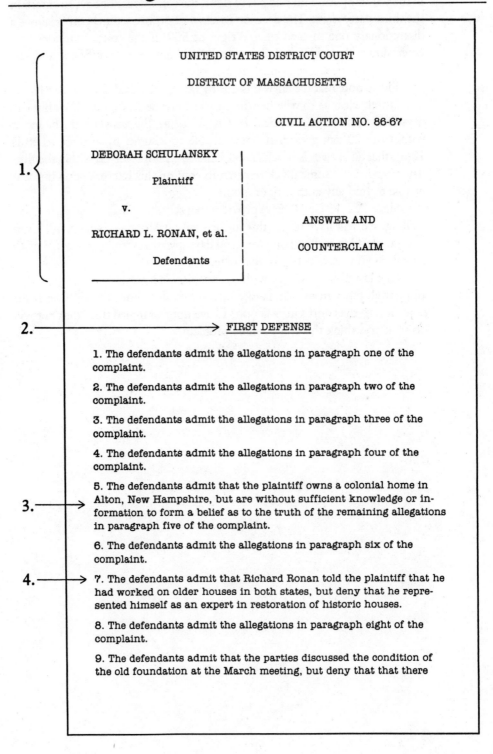

UNITED STATES DISTRICT COURT

DISTRICT OF MASSACHUSETTS

CIVIL ACTION NO. 86-67

**1.**

DEBORAH SCHULANSKY

Plaintiff

v.

RICHARD L. RONAN, et al.

Defendants

ANSWER AND

COUNTERCLAIM

**2.** FIRST DEFENSE

1. The defendants admit the allegations in paragraph one of the complaint.

2. The defendants admit the allegations in paragraph two of the complaint.

3. The defendants admit the allegations in paragraph three of the complaint.

4. The defendants admit the allegations in paragraph four of the complaint.

**3.** 5. The defendants admit that the plaintiff owns a colonial home in Alton, New Hampshire, but are without sufficient knowledge or information to form a belief as to the truth of the remaining allegations in paragraph five of the complaint.

6. The defendants admit the allegations in paragraph six of the complaint.

**4.** 7. The defendants admit that Richard Ronan told the plaintiff that he had worked on older houses in both states, but deny that he represented himself as an expert in restoration of historic houses.

8. The defendants admit the allegations in paragraph eight of the complaint.

9. The defendants admit that the parties discussed the condition of the old foundation at the March meeting, but deny that that there

was any discussion of a possible need for extensive reconstruction of the foundation.

10. The defendants deny that they, or either one of them, agreed to reconstruct the foundation, or that such reconstruction was part of the construction of the foundation for the addition agreed to in the contract between the plaintiff and Ronan Construction Company.

11. The defendants admit that the defendant Richard Ronan sent a Proposal and Estimate to the plaintiff. The defendants further state that the Proposal and Estimate constituted an offer by the Ronan Construction Company, not by the defendant Richard Ronan individually.

12. The defendants admit that the plaintiff signed and returned the Proposal and Estimate on or around April 3, 1985, but further state that the Proposal and Estimate constituted an offer solely by Ronan Construction Company.

13. The defendants admit the allegations in paragraph thirteen of the complaint.

14. The defendants admit the allegations in paragraph fourteen of the complaint.

15. The defendants admit that the foundation consisted of loose boulders without mortar, but deny that they were held together by the surrounding earth.

16. The defendants deny the allegations in paragraph sixteen of the complaint.

17. The defendants deny the allegations in paragraph seventeen of the complaint.

18. The defendants admit that they did not completely reconstruct the preexisting foundation, but deny that such reconstruction was necessary to provide adequate support for the house or the addition. The defendants did heavily reinforce the preexisting foundation with concrete in the course of constructing the addition.

19. The defendants deny that the plaintiff demanded that they reconstruct the foundation or that the contract required them to do so.

20. The defendants deny the allegations of paragraph twenty of the complaint.

5.————▶ 21. The defendants repeat and reallege their responses to the allegations in paragraphs one to twenty of the complaint.

22. The defendants admit the allegations in paragraph twenty-two of the complaint.

23. The defendants admit that, under the contract, the defendant Ronan Construction Company agreed to construct an adequate foundation for the addition. They deny that the the contract imposed any obligation upon Ronan Construction Company to reconstruct the foundation of the main house.

24. The defendants deny the allegations in paragraph twenty-four of the complaint.

25. The defendants deny the allegations in paragraph twenty-five of the complaint.

26. The defendants admit that the plaintiff made the first four progress payments under the contract, but deny that they breached the contract. The defendants further state that the plaintiff has refused to make the final payment due under the contract, although the defendant Ronan Construction Company has performed all of its obligations under the contract in a timely and satisfactory manner and has demanded payment of the balance due under the contract.

27. The defendants deny the allegations in paragraph twenty-seven of the complaint.

28. The defendants repeat and reallege their responses to paragraphs one to twenty of the complaint.

29. The defendants deny that the area adjacent to the foundation of the main house was negligently excavated. They further deny that the excavation was performed by employees of either defendant.

30. The defendants deny the allegations of paragraph thirty of the complaint.

**6.** ⟶ <u>SECOND</u> <u>DEFENSE</u>

This action must be dismissed because the court lacks personal jurisdiction over the defendants under the Fourteenth Amendment and the Massachusetts Long-Arm Statute, Mass. G.L. c. 223A, §3.

<u>THIRD</u> <u>DEFENSE</u>

The plaintiff's claim fails to state a claim upon which relief can be granted, because the Proposal and Estimate does not require any reconstruction of the original foundation, and any evidence of negotiations that preceded the written contract is barred by the parol evidence rule.

**7.** ⟶ <u>FOURTH</u> <u>DEFENSE</u>

If the defendants had any obligation under the contract to reconstruct the preexisting foundation, the plaintiff waived performance of that obligation on or about April 15, 1985, when she agreed that the defendants could fulfill their obligations under the contract by reinforcing the preexisting foundation with cement.

### FIFTH DEFENSE

The plaintiff's first claim for relief fails to state a claim upon which relief can be granted against the defendant Richard L. Ronan, because he was not a party to the contract.

### SIXTH DEFENSE

If there was any negligence in the excavation of the foundation, that negligence was solely the act of Arlen Jones, an independent contractor for whose negligence the defendants cannot be held liable.

**8.** ⟶ WHEREFORE, the defendants request that the court dismiss the plaintiff's complaint and award the defendants their costs, together with such other relief as the court finds just and equitable.

**9.** ⟶ COUNTERCLAIM OF RONAN CONSTRUCTION COMPANY —

### BREACH OF CONTRACT

The defendant Ronan Construction Company counterclaims against the plaintiff as follows:

**10.** ⟶ 1. This court has subject matter jurisdiction of this action under Article III, §2 of the United States Constitution and 28 U.S.C. §1332. This counterclaim is a compulsory counterclaim under Fed. R. Civ. P. 13(a), which is subject to the court's ancillary jurisdiction.

**11.** { 2. The signed Proposal and Estimate attached to the plaintiff's complaint constitutes a valid contract between the plaintiff and the defendant Ronan Construction Company.

3. Under that contract, the plaintiff agreed to pay Ronan Construction Company $19,200 for the construction of an addition to her home at 53 School Street, Alton, New Hampshire.

4. The defendant Ronan Construction Company has fully performed all of its obligations under the contract.

5. Although the defendant Ronan Construction Company has demanded payment of the final balance due under the contract, the plaintiff has failed to pay Ronan Construction Company the final progress payment of $7,200.

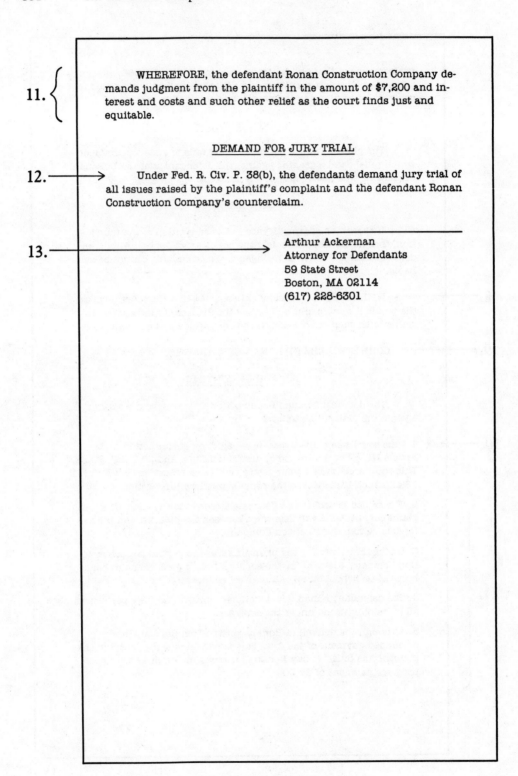

11. WHEREFORE, the defendant Ronan Construction Company demands judgment from the plaintiff in the amount of $7,200 and interest and costs and such other relief as the court finds just and equitable.

## DEMAND FOR JURY TRIAL

12. Under Fed. R. Civ. P. 38(b), the defendants demand jury trial of all issues raised by the plaintiff's complaint and the defendant Ronan Construction Company's counterclaim.

13.

Arthur Ackerman
Attorney for Defendants
59 State Street
Boston, MA 02114
(617) 228-6301

UNITED STATES DISTRICT COURT

DISTRICT OF MASSACHUSETTS

CIVIL ACTION NO. 86-67

DEBORAH SCHULANSKY

Plaintiff

v.

RICHARD L. RONAN, et al.

Defendants

CERTIFICATE OF

SERVICE

I, Arthur Ackerman, attorney for the defendants, hereby certify that on this date I served copies of the attached Answer and Counterclaim on the plaintiff's attorney in this action by mailing a copy thereof, first class mail, postage prepaid, to Phyllis Slater, Robbins, Slater and Goldman, 322 Puritan Road, Plymouth, Ma. 02360.

_____
Date

_____
Arthur Ackerman
Attorney for Defendants
59 State Street
Boston, MA 02114
(617) 228-6301

# Comments on the Answer and Counterclaim

1.    Rule 10(a) governs the caption of the answer as well as the complaint and all other pleadings. Note that the federal docket number is now known and will be used in all subsequent pleadings and other papers.

2.    Rule 8(b) specifically requires the defendant to respond to each allegation in the complaint, by admitting or denying the allegations, stating the parts that are true and denying the remainder, or stating that the defendant does not have enough information to assess the truth of the allegation. In his *First Defense,* Ronan complies with this requirement by responding, paragraph by paragraph, to the allegations in the plaintiff's complaint. Rule 10(b) requires these responses to be set forth in numbered paragraphs, and the drafting attorney here has numbered her admissions and denials to correspond to the appropriate paragraphs in the complaint. This will make it easy for the parties and the court to compare the pleadings during the course of the suit, in order to quickly ascertain the positions of the parties on the various issues.

   In some cases, the defendant may group her responses to parts of the complaint in a single sentence. For example, the answer might state that "the defendant admits the allegations in paragraphs one to eleven and sixteen to twenty-one of the complaint." See, e.g., Official Form 20, accompanying the Federal Rules of Civil Procedure. This saves space and time, but in cases with a large number of paragraphs and varied responses it is less helpful for quick reference in comparing the complaint and the answer.

3.    It is permissible for a party to respond by stating that she lacks sufficient information to admit or deny an allegation. Fed. R. Civ. P. 8(b). The defendants here probably have no particular knowledge of the National Register of Historic Places and are under no duty to scurry around and find a copy to verify this allegation in order to answer the complaint.

4.    Rule 8(b) requires the defendant to respond clearly and forthrightly to the allegations of the complaint. ("Denials shall fairly meet the substance of the averments denied.") It would not be proper for the defendants here to simply deny the entire allegation in paragraph seven, because Ronan had told the plaintiff that he had worked on old houses. However, the defendants do not accept the plaintiff's characterization of his statements and have therefore crafted their response to paragraph seven to negate any inference that Ronan represented himself as an expert in this area. A number of the defendants' other responses also admit some parts of the allegations but deny other parts or recharacterize allegations in the complaint. See, e.g., paragraphs eleven, fifteen, eighteen, and twenty-six.

5.   Rule 10(c) authorizes adoption by reference of parts of a pleading in another part of the pleading. The language of the rule is general, so it is clear that a defendant — or any other pleader — may do so as well as a plaintiff. Since Schulansky incorporated all of her factual allegations by reference into her First Claim for Relief, Ronan has similarly incorporated his answers to the earlier paragraphs in his answer to her First Claim for Relief.

6.   As you are probably aware, defending parties will frequently have further defenses to the plaintiff's claims, in addition to denials of the allegations in the complaint. After responding in the First Defense to each of the allegations of the complaint, the answer goes on to set forth several further defenses. This breakdown is proper under Rule 10(b), which provides in part that "each defense other than denials shall be stated in a separate count or defense whenever a separation facilitates the clear presentation of the matters set forth."

The defendant's Second Defense here is an objection to the court's power to adjudicate, on the ground that it lacks personal jurisdiction over the defendants. This objection could be raised by pre-answer motion under Rule 12(b), but it does not have to be. It is always proper to include this objection in the answer instead of raising it by pre-answer motion, so long as no pre-answer motion is made on other grounds. See Chapter 14, p. 187. As Ackerman's comments indicate, the decision to answer rather than move to dismiss is a tactical one.

7.   The defendant's Fourth Defense raises an affirmative defense. The defendant takes the position that, even if the contract required reconstruction of the foundation, and the defendant failed to do so, the plaintiff waived performance of this obligation by her assent to Ronan's alternative suggestion. An affirmative defense asserts new facts that avoid liability even if the plaintiff proves her basic allegations. It is akin to the old common law "confession and avoidance" device, except that the defendant need not confess before he can avoid. Under Rule 8(e)(2), the defendant may plead inconsistently, and that is what the *Schulansky* defendants have done in their answer. In their First Defense, they deny that they agreed to reconstruct the foundation. In their Fourth Defense, they assert that, even if they did agree to do so, the plaintiff waived performance of that obligation.

The order of the various defenses is not prescribed by the rules. On occasion, you will see an answer that begins with objections and affirmative defenses, and leaves the admissions and denials until later. Of paramount importance, of course, is that all defenses be raised in the answer, to avoid waiving any by omission.

8.   Defendants frequently include a paragraph like this at the end of the answer, asking the court, on the basis of the defenses and denials in the

answer, to dismiss the complaint. In the federal courts (and state systems as well), a prevailing defendant is entitled to recover certain costs of defending the action, such as witness fees and the costs of service of process. See 28 U.S.C. §1920. It is customary to ask for these in the answer as well. And, in a lawyerly excess of caution, to append a request for any other relief the court finds "just and equitable" as well.

9.   It is entirely proper to include a counterclaim within the answer. It should be set apart from the rest of the answer, however, and clearly labeled as a counterclaim. If a counterclaim is not clearly labeled as such, it may look a good deal like an affirmative defense. (Compare, for example, paragraph twenty-six of the answer, which could be construed to seek relief from Schulansky for the unpaid balance under the contract.) Unless it is clearly labeled and set apart from the various defenses, it may be unclear whether Ronan is defending on the basis of Schulansky's failure to fulfill her obligations under the contract, or seeking independent, affirmative relief by way of counterclaim.

Note that Losordo has consistently taken the position in drafting the answer that the contract is between Ronan Construction Company and Schulansky. See paragraphs ten, eleven, twelve, twenty-three, and twenty-six of the First Defense. Thus, the company is the proper party to assert the counterclaim for breach of the contract. Indeed, Losordo might have chosen to emphasize the difference in the positions of Ronan and Ronan Construction Company by filing completely separate answers for them. The rules do not require the defendants to file a joint answer, and in cases where their interests are clearly divergent, they will not do so.

10.   Federal Rule 8(a) requires "a pleading which sets forth a claim for relief" to include a statement of the grounds for the court's jurisdiction. A counterclaim is such a pleading, and Losordo has according asserted here that the court has jurisdiction based on ancillary jurisdiction. Ancillary jurisdiction is proper for this claim because it is a compulsory counterclaim. See Chapter 12, question 4.

Strictly speaking, this is probably overpleading. Rule 8(a)(1) does not require a jurisdictional allegation if the court already has jurisdiction (i.e., if an earlier pleading has already provided a basis for jurisdiction over the action), and the new pleading does not require "new grounds" for jurisdiction. In this case, the court has jurisdiction over the main claim based on diversity. Ancillary jurisdiction is arguably not a "new ground" for jurisdiction over the compulsory counterclaim since it follows from the jurisdiction on the main claim. See 2A Moore's at ¶8.07[4], [5]; Official Forms 20, 21. However, since Schulansky's complaint was originally filed in state court, it contained no explicit allegation as to the basis of jurisdiction, and it is certainly appropriate, even if not required, to assert the ground of jurisdiction in the counterclaim.

The Rule 8(a)(1) requirement to state the ground of the court's jurisdiction refers to subject matter jurisdiction, not personal jurisdiction. *Sterling Homex Corp. v. Homasote Co.*, 437 F.2d 87, 88 (2d Cir. 1971). It is not necessary to assert in a pleading that the court has personal jurisdiction over the defendant, but of course, the court must have it in order to proceed.

11. The general rules of pleading govern the allegations in a counterclaim, including the use of numbered paragraphs and inclusion of a demand for relief. Like an original complaint, a counterclaim may include a number of claims for relief based on different theories. It is even permissible to assert completely unrelated counterclaims (see Fed. R. Civ. P. 13(b)), although these will not be within the court's ancillary jurisdiction.

Unlike the common law, where the parties might plead back and forth a number of times before a single issue was reached, the answer usually ends the pleadings under the Federal Rules. However, Fed. R. Civ. P. 7(a) does require the plaintiff to reply to a counterclaim "denominated as such." This limitation relieves plaintiffs from the obligation to guess whether vague allegations in an answer are affirmative defenses, denials, or counterclaims. Schulansky would be required to file a reply to this counterclaim, since Ronan's counsel has clearly labeled it as such, putting Schulansky on notice that Ronan is claiming affirmative relief from her.

The plaintiff's reply is governed by the same pleading requirements as Ronan's answer, and should include responses to each of the paragraphs in the counterclaim as well as affirmative defenses. Of course, the reply will only address the allegations in the counterclaim itself, since the parties' positions on the main claim are already established by the complaint and the answer. The reply must be served within 20 days after service of the answer. Fed. R. Civ. P. 12(a).

12. Losordo has followed her own suggestion in her memo on removal (see infra p. 346) and included a demand for jury trial on the counterclaim. It may be that the jury demand is unnecessary, but at most it is redundant. Rather than invest substantial research time (and the client's money) in finding a definitive answer to this question, Losordo has simply erred on the side of caution by including it in the answer. Just to cover all the bases, she has also demanded jury trial on the main claim as well.

13. The answer, like the complaint and all other pleadings and motions, must be signed by the attorney, and is subject to the ethical constraints and sanctions set forth in Fed. R. Civ. P. 11.

———————

Losordo raises an interesting question at the end of her memo, concerning the possibility that asserting the counterclaim might waive the defendant's objection to personal jurisdiction. In fact, if Ronan's attorneys look into this issue, they will find that the courts are split on this question. Some cases have held that a defendant waives her objection to personal jurisdiction by asking the court to adjudicate a counterclaim. Others, however, have recognized that this puts the defendant in an awkward position, because Fed. R. Civ. P. 13(a) *requires* her to assert any counterclaim that arises out of the same events as the plaintiff's claim. (Of course, the defendant could present the personal jurisdiction issue by pre-answer motion, thus obtaining resolution of that issue before answering.) See generally 5 Wright and Miller at §1397, which reviews the issue and suggests that assertion of a compulsory counterclaim should not waive the personal jurisdiction defense.

One of the things that makes a litigation practice unnerving is the number of uncertainties that arise in the course of a case, in circumstances that make it impossible to give those issues the full attention they deserve. Here, the attorneys are under the gun to get their responsive pleading in and are doubtless handling many other matters as well. Many lawyers would never even have thought of this rather subtle ramification of the counterclaim. Even if their client could afford to have exhaustive research done on this point, it would have been hard for Ronan's lawyers to find the time to do it. And they probably would not have found a definitive answer if they had.

# Comments on the Certificate of Service

Be careful to distinguish service of the original complaint from service of subsequent pleadings and other papers in the suit. The elaborate service provisions of Fed. R. Civ. P. 4 only govern service of the complaint. Subsequent papers may be served under the simpler provisions of Fed. R. Civ. P. 5(b), which authorizes service by personal delivery or regular mail to the attorney for the opposing party. The certificate of service constitutes a representation by the serving attorney that he has complied with the requirements of Rule 5(b).

Most attorneys have blank Certificates of Service in their offices and simply fill them out and attach them to all papers served in the course of the suit. Thus, the certificate will frequently have a fill-in-the-blanks format and not include the caption of the case: The local rules for the District of Massachusetts now provide that the certificate of service must appear in the margin of the pleading or motion itself, rather than on a separate sheet. Local Rule 11, effective July 1, 1986. This certificate would be improper in that court if filed after that date.

# 26

## Chain Reaction: Ronan Brings In Jones

## The Drafting Request

### MEMORANDUM

**TO:** Marcia Losordo
Associate

**FROM:** Arthur Ackerman

**RE:** Third-party, complaint in *Schulansky v. Ronan*
U.S. District Court No. 86-67

**DATE:** January 14, 1986

---

I have reviewed and filed your answer and counterclaim in the Schulansky case. I have also discussed with Dick Ronan the possibility of filing a third-party complaint against Arlen Jones, the bulldozer operator who did the excavation work on the job. On the basis of that discussion, I have decided to proceed with the third-party complaint.

As you are no doubt aware, Fed. R. Civ. P. 14(a) allows us to implead Jones if he "is or may be liable to [our clients] for all or part of the plaintiff's claim" against them. In other words, we can implead Jones if we have a right to reimbursement from him for any damages Schulansky recovers from us. In my judgment, we may be able to obtain indemnification from Jones if Schulansky recovers on either her breach of contract claim or her negligence claim.

Please let me know if you agree with the following line of reasoning, which leads me to that conclusion.

As you suggested in your earlier memo, it is not clear whether Jones acted as a subcontractor to Ronan or as Ronan's employee in doing the excavation work. The accepted test is the extent of control Ronan could exercise over Jones in the course of the work, and the facts on this are ambiguous. On the one hand, Ronan did not have a written contract with Jones for the excavation work; he simply called Jones up and asked him to do the work for $1,400. The facts that Jones worked for a flat price and used his own equipment support the argument that he acted as an independent contractor. On the other hand, according to Ronan, he consistently directed Jones in the course of the work and considered Jones (who worked quite regularly for Ronan) an employee, even though he usually paid him by the job. In addition, the informality of their arrangement suggests an employment relationship more than a contract. Given the ambiguity in the evidence, it will likely be up to the jury to determine whether Jones acted as an employee or independent contractor. Restatement (Second) of Agency §20, comment c (1958).

If the jury were to find that Jones was Ronan's employee, Ronan would be liable for his negligence, under respondeat superior principles (Restatement (Second) of Agency §219 (1958)) but would have a right to indemnification from Jones. Thus, if Schulansky proves that Jones negligently disturbed the existing foundation during the excavation, and we can prove that Ronan had sufficient control over Jones to make him an employee in doing the work, Schulansky will recover judgment from us, but Jones will be liable to indemnify us for the entire judgment.

Alternatively, if the jury finds that Jones was not directly under Ronan's control, and therefore acted as a subcontractor to Ronan, Ronan should still have a right of indemnification from him under contract principles. If his negligent excavation caused a breach of the main contract between Ronan and Schulansky, Ronan would be liable directly to Schulansky for the breach by his subcontractor. However, Jones would have breached his (unwritten) subcontract with Ronan by failing to perform the work properly, and we would have a cause of action against him for breach of the subcontract. Our damages for this breach would include the judgment we incurred to Schulansky, as well as the attorneys' fees we incurred in defending her claim. Thus, if Schulansky recovers on her breach of contract claim, we should be entitled to recover these damages from Jones under the subcontract.

If you agree with my reasoning, please draft a third-party complaint against Jones for indemnification on both of the plaintiff's claims. I realize that our theories for indemnification are based on inconsistent allegations, since we will allege on the negligence claim that Jones was an employee, but on the contract claim that he was a subcontractor. However, Rule 8(e)(2) expressly allows us to plead inconsistent versions of our claim. Nor do I view this as inappropriate under the ethical pleading requirements in Rule 11, since there is factual support for characterizing Jones either as an employee or an independent contractor. Where the jury could properly reach either conclusion, it is appropriate to assert whatever rights we may have against Jones based on either theory.

As you pointed out in our discussions, it is also a little awkward to deny that the foundation was damaged at all during the excavation (as we did in our answer), but to turn around and implead Jones for causing that damage. Ronan tells me that, in his judgment, Jones did an adequate job; he does not believe that the digging destabilized the foundation, or that anything did. But there is some evidence to support a finding that Jones was negligent. Apparently Jones did hit the foundation a number of times with his bulldozer, and the excavation turned up some loose rocks along the edge of the foundation. Schulansky was present at the time, and this is probably what is behind her negligence claim.

I do not think the Rules require us to disregard our possible rights against Jones just because we denied in our answer that any negligence took place. As indicated above, the Rules specifically authorize inconsistent pleading. Of course, we must have reasonable grounds to support the allegations under Rule 11, but I believe Ronan's observations about Jones's encounters with the foundation during the excavation meet this test. This evidence is probably sufficient to support a finding that Jones damaged the foundation in the course of the excavation. If that is true, we shouldn't have to abandon our right to indemnification against Jones just because we plan to defend the main action on the ground that he was not negligent.

We may have a serious problem obtaining personal jurisdiction over Jones in Massachusetts. Jones lives in New Hampshire, agreed to do the work in a telephone conversation with Ronan, and performed all the work in New Hampshire. According to Ronan, Jones does work occasionally in Massachusetts, but I doubt that this occasional work in the state is sufficient to support personal jurisdiction over Jones for a claim unrelated to his work here in the state. On the other hand, Ronan tells me that Jones is currently working on a condominium development in Methuen, Massachusetts. If he is not subject to personal jurisdiction on some other basis, perhaps we can serve process on him there and obtain jurisdiction on that basis. Please give me your thoughts.

I realize you have not yet had a chance to open your Christmas presents, but please get on this right away. I would like to file this within the ten-day limit for filing the third-party complaint without leave of court.

# The Associate's Response

## MEMORANDUM

**TO:**      Arthur Ackerman

**FROM:**  Marcia Losordo

**RE:**      Third-party complaint in *Schulansky v. Ronan*
             U.S. District Court No. 86-67

**DATE:**   January 17, 1986

-----------------------------------------------------------

I have attached a draft third-party complaint against Jones in the Schulansky case. I agree with your analysis of Jones's potential liability to us, but have several additional observations. First, it is conceivable that Schulansky would recover from us for breach of contract on both grounds alleged in her complaint. It may turn out that the structural damage resulted in part from Ronan's failure to rebuild the foundation, and in part from damage caused by Jones's bulldozer. If the jury finds that both causes contributed to the settling, we would have a right to partial indemnification from Jones, since presumably the court would apportion the damages between the two causes, and Jones only contributed to one of them.

It is proper to implead a third party for partial as well as full indemnification; Rule 14(a) authorizes impleader of a party who "is or may be liable to him for all *or part* of the plaintiff's claim . . ." (emphasis supplied). Thus, I have asserted two claims for relief based on the theory that Jones breached his subcontract with Ronan, one for full indemnification and a separate claim for partial indemnification.

Second, note that our claim against Jones for the attorneys' fees we incur in defense of Schulansky's claim does not satisfy the Rule 14 requirement, since we are not seeking reimbursement from Jones for fees we must pay Schulansky. These fees represent separate consequential damages our clients have suffered as a result of Jones's breach of the subcontract, and the resulting need to defend Schulansky's law suit. However, it is proper to assert this additional claim in the third-party complaint. Once a defendant has asserted a proper impleader claim under Rule 14(a), he may also assert independent claims against the third-party defendant under Fed. R. Civ. P. 18(a).

As you suggest, the fact that Jones does occasional business in Massachusetts is not sufficient under the *International Shoe* minimum contacts test to support personal jurisdiction over him for a claim unrelated to the in-state business. See *Helicopteros Nacionales de Columbia, S.A. v. Hall,* 466 U.S. 408, 414-415 (1984) (where claim does not arise out of contacts with forum state, the defendant must have continuous and systematic contacts there to support jurisdiction). Since Jones only works in Massachusetts occasionally, it is doubtful that he would be subject to general in personam jurisdiction here. However, it appears likely that personal jurisdiction can be obtained over Jones by serving process on him here in Massachusetts, under the hoary doctrine of *Pennoyer v. Neff.* Although the Supreme Court cast some doubt on the sufficiency of such "transient personal service" in *Shaffer v. Heitner,* 433 U.S. 186 (1977), a quick look at the post-*Shaffer* case law indicates that the lower courts have continued to uphold jurisdiction on this basis. See, e.g., *Amusement Equipment, Inc. v. Mordelt,* 779 F.2d 264, 267-271 (5th Cir. 1985); *Driver v. Helms,* 577 F.2d 147, 156 n.25 (1st Cir. 1978) (dicta).

Alternatively, it may be possible to serve Jones under Fed. R. Civ. P. 4(f), the "100-mile bulge" provision for service on certain additional parties to actions in federal court. Under Rule 4 (f), a defendant may be served with process outside the forum state but within 100 miles of the courthouse. This provision authorizes service on Jones in New Hampshire, as long as he is served within 100 miles of the courthouse in Boston. However, I am not sure whether the 100-mile bulge provision authorizes a federal standard of amenability to jurisdiction, or whether it simply authorizes a manner of service. If the latter is true, we might still have to satisfy fourteenth amendment standards of personal jurisdiction, even if we serve Jones in New Hampshire. See, e.g., *Quinones v. Pennsylvania General Ins. Co.,* 804 F.2d 1167 (10th Cir. 1986).

There are some very sophisticated personal jurisdiction issues involved here, which may require extensive research and briefing. However, Jones may not raise an objection to personal jurisdiction. I suggest that we serve him on the job site in Methuen and see if he moves to dismiss. (Please note that the complaint and summons must be served under the provisions of Fed. R. Civ. P. 4, not under Rule 5.) If he submits to jurisdiction, we may save our clients a good deal of expense in a relatively small-stakes case.

# The Resulting Documents

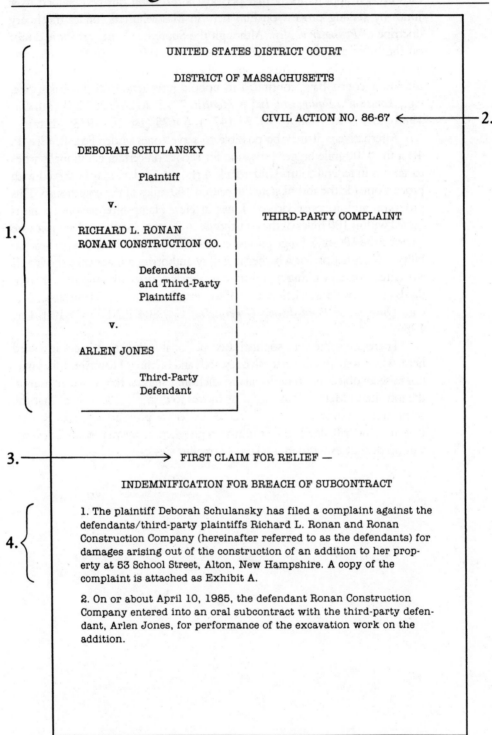

UNITED STATES DISTRICT COURT

DISTRICT OF MASSACHUSETTS

CIVIL ACTION NO. 86-67 ← ———————— 2.

DEBORAH SCHULANSKY

Plaintiff

v.

RICHARD L. RONAN
RONAN CONSTRUCTION CO.

THIRD-PARTY COMPLAINT

Defendants
and Third-Party
Plaintiffs

v.

ARLEN JONES

Third-Party
Defendant

1.

3. ————————→ FIRST CLAIM FOR RELIEF —

INDEMNIFICATION FOR BREACH OF SUBCONTRACT

4.
1. The plaintiff Deborah Schulansky has filed a complaint against the defendants/third-party plaintiffs Richard L. Ronan and Ronan Construction Company (hereinafter referred to as the defendants) for damages arising out of the construction of an addition to her property at 53 School Street, Alton, New Hampshire. A copy of the complaint is attached as Exhibit A.

2. On or about April 10, 1985, the defendant Ronan Construction Company entered into an oral subcontract with the third-party defendant, Arlen Jones, for performance of the excavation work on the addition.

3. Under that contract, the third-party defendant agreed to perform all the excavation work required by the main contract, using his own labor and equipment, and the defendants agreed to pay the third-party defendant the sum of $1,400 upon completion of the work.

4. The excavation work was performed entirely by the third-party defendant, on or about April 15-18, 1985.

5. The First Claim for Relief in the plaintiff's complaint alleges a right to relief for breach of contract, on the ground that the defendants breached their contract with her by failing to perform the excavation work in a workmanlike manner, resulting in damage to the existing foundation of the house.

6. If defendants breached their contract with the plaintiff by failing to perform the excavation work in a workmanlike manner, that breach and any resulting damage was caused solely by the acts of the third-party defendant.

7. If the third-party defendant failed to perform the excavation work in a workmanlike manner, that failure constituted a breach of the contract between the defendants and the third-party defendant.

**5.** →  8. If the plaintiff recovers against the defendants on the ground that the damage to the foundation in the course of excavation constituted a breach of their contract, the third-party defendant is liable to the defendants for any damages adjudged against them in the main action described in paragraph one.

**6.** →      WHEREFORE, the defendants demand judgment against the third-party defendant as follows:

   a. For any and all sums that may be adjudged against them in the plaintiff's main action against them.

**7.** →   b. For all costs, including attorneys' fees, incurred in defense of this action.

   c. For such other relief as the court deems just and proper.

SECOND CLAIM FOR RELIEF —

PARTIAL INDEMNIFICATION FOR BREACH OF SUBCONTRACT

9. The defendants repeat and reallege the allegations in paragraphs one to seven of the third-party complaint.

10. If the plaintiff recovers from the defendants both on the ground that they breached their contract with the plaintiff by negligently excavating the foundation and on the ground that they failed to rebuild

it, the third-party defendant is liable to the defendants under the subcontract for that part of the damages resulting from the negligent excavation.

WHEREFORE, the defendants demand judgment from the third-party defendant as follows:

a. For any and all sums that may be adjudged against them for breach of contract resulting from the third-party defendant's negligent excavation.

b. For that part of the defendants' attorneys' fees and costs in defending this action that are attributable to the plaintiff's claim for negligent excavation.

c. For such other relief as the court deems just and proper.

### THIRD CLAIM FOR RELIEF —

### INDEMNIFICATION FOR NEGLIGENCE

11. The defendants repeat and reallege the allegations in paragraph one of the third-party complaint.

12. The Second Claim for Relief in the plaintiff's complaint alleges a right to recover from the defendants on the ground that the defendants were negligent in excavating the area in which the addition was to be constructed.

13. On or about April 10, 1985, the defendants employed the third-party defendant Jones to perform the excavation work for the addition.

14. The excavation work was done entirely by the third-party defendant in the course of his employment for the defendants.

15. If the excavation work was negligently performed, any negligence in the work was due solely to acts of the third-party defendant.

16. If the plaintiff recovers from the defendant on her Second Claim for Relief, the defendants are entitled to indemnification from the third-party defendant for any and all damages that they are ordered to pay to the plaintiff on that claim.

WHEREFORE, the defendants demand judgment from the third-party defendant as follows:

a. For all damages that the defendants are ordered to pay to the plaintiff on her second claim for relief.

8.

b. For all costs incurred in this action.

c. For such other relief as the court deems just and proper.

9.  ————————————————————→   Arthur Ackerman
                                          Attorney for the Defendants
                                          59 State Street
                                          Boston, MA 02114
                                          (617) 228-6301

# Comments on the Third-Party Complaint

1.  The contents of the caption of the third-party complaint are again governed by Rule 10(a), which applies to "every pleading." Note that the title of the action has grown to include the third party as well as the original parties.

2.  The docket number on the third-party complaint is the same as that assigned to the original action. This reflects the very important fact that the third-party action is *not* a separate action, but an additional claim asserted by the defendant against a new party in the original action. This new claim will be litigated along with the main claim unless the court orders separate trials. Thus, all three parties will be entitled to seek discovery from each other (see, e.g., Fed. R. Civ. P. 33, 34, 36), all motions and other papers will be served on all other parties, all parties will participate in any hearings or pretrial proceedings, and all claims will be tried at the same time.

3.  A third-party complaint is a pleading that asserts a right to relief against a new defendant. Thus, its contents are governed by Rule 8(a), which applies to any "pleading which sets forth a claim for relief, whether an original claim, counterclaim, cross-claim or third-party claim. . . . " Like an original complaint, the third-party complaint must contain an allegation as to the court's basis for subject matter jurisdiction (unless the ground for jurisdiction appears in a previous pleading),[1] a short and plain statement of the plaintiff's claim, and a demand for relief.

Because it is subject to the regular pleading rules, the defendants' third-party complaint is organized much like an original complaint, with separate claims for relief asserting the defendants' various theories for holding Jones liable to them, and demands for relief following each claim. The defendants have not included a separate *Facts* section as in Schulansky's complaint, because most of the relevant facts are already in the original complaint and the additional facts can be set forth clearly within the *Claim for Relief* sections.

4.  The underlying premise of the defendants' impleader claims is a right to recover from Jones for damages they are ordered to pay Schulansky in this lawsuit. They therefore begin their third-party complaint by alleging the existence of the primary suit, which gives rise to their claims for indemnification.

---

1. The defendants have not included an allegation of jurisdiction, since there is ancillary jurisdiction over third-party claims. Thus the claims do not need "new grounds" (Fed. R. Civ. P. 8(c)) to support them. See my comment 10 on the answer and counterclaim, supra p. 368. However, there is some doubt (not yet noticed by Ronan's attorneys) as to whether ancillary jurisdiction will extend to the fees claim as well as the indemnity claims, since the fees claim is not derivative of the main suit.

A third-party claim requires an answer conforming to the same rules as the original answer. See Fed. R. Civ. P. 7(a), which specifies that proper pleadings include an answer to a third-party complaint. In order to properly respond to Ronan's claim against him, Jones will need to have Schulansky's original complaint before him as well as the third-party complaint. For example, Rule 14 allows Jones to raise defenses that *Ronan* may have to Schulansky's primary complaint, on the theory that, if Ronan is not held liable to her, then Jones cannot be held liable to Ronan. Jones can only do this if he has the original complaint to work with in formulating an answer. The defendant should therefore append a copy of the original complaint to the third-party complaint.

5.   The defendants may bring in Jones if he is or may be liable to them for all or part of Schulansky's claim against them. The third-party complaint properly seeks recovery from Jones for damages that the defendants are held liable to pay Schulansky.

6.   Since the third-party complaint is governed by the pleading requirements of Rule 8(a), it must include a demand for relief. Again, since Ronan seeks recovery over against Jones, his main demand for relief (subsection a) is for the damages he must pay Schulansky. In their third-party complaint, the defendants have included separate demands for damages after each claim for relief. Since the potential damages differ under at least the first two claims, including separate demands after each claim makes it easier to understand each claim. Compare the original complaint, supra p. 328, and comment 9 following it, supra p. 338.

7.   The associate's point about the right to attorneys' fees is a perceptive one. While Ronan's claim to recover from Jones any damages he pays to Schulansky is derivative under Rule 14, his claim for fees is for a separate loss he suffered as a result of Jones's acts. Essentially, Ronan's fees claim is based on the theory that he would not have had to defend Schulansky's suit if Jones had done his job right. Thus, the fees expended in the defense are a consequential loss resulting from Jones's breach, although they are paid to Ronan's lawyer, not to Schulansky. They constitute a distinct claim that does not satisfy Rule 14 but may be asserted along with it under Fed. R. Civ. P. 18(a). Compare Chapter 13, question 9. It is not entirely clear that ancillary jurisdiction will extend to the fees claim because although it is related to the main claim, it is not derivative. See *Owen Equipment & Erection Co. v. Kroger,* 437 U.S. 365, 376 (1978) (emphasizing the "logical dependence" of impleader claims on the main claim); see also *Schwab v. Erie Lackawanna R.R. Co.,* 438 F.2d 62, 68-72 (3d Cir. 1971) (a pre-*Kroger* case approving ancillary jurisdiction in similar circumstances).

8.  In paragraphs thirteen and fourteen of the third claim for relief, Ronan alleges that Jones acted in the scope of his employment for Ronan. Compare paragraphs two and three of his first claim for relief against Jones, which allege a contractual relationship. As Ackerman's memo indicates, the two theories of relief are premised on differing underlying factual conclusions that the jury might reach. Consequently, the factual allegations in the two claims for relief reflect these inconsistent positions.

9.  The attorney's signature on the third-party complaint, as on any other pleading or motion, is subject to the ethical requirements of Rule 11. As Ackerman's memo indicates, he gave considerable thought to those requirements before including inconsistent allegations concerning Jones's status in the third-party complaint.

———————————

Any practicing lawyer will attest that innumerable complex issues arise in the practice of law. Sometimes, it is evident from the outset that a case will turn on such an issue. In other cases, the issue may be potentially important, depending on the course of the suit, the evidence turned up in discovery, and whether the case goes to trial. Attorneys constantly make very pragmatic judgments about which issues to spend their time and their clients' money researching. Frequently, those complex issues just go away, for one reason or another.

In this case, for example, the issue of Jones's amenability to jurisdiction, either under Fed. R. Civ. P. 4(f) or on the basis of transient service in the state, is a complex one. But it may never need to be decided, if Jones does not object, or if he does but the case settles before the issue is litigated. Here, Losordo has noted the potential problem with bringing in Jones, but has quite sensibly delayed extensive research on the issue until it becomes clear that it will have to be resolved.

# 27

---

## *Preliminary Objections: Jones Seeks a Way Out*

## The Drafting Request

### MEMORANDUM

**TO:**    Phillip Torres
           Associate

**FROM:**  Don Philbrook

**RE:**    Arlen Jones Construction Case

**DATE:**  January 28, 1986

------------------------------------------------

    I represent Arlen Jones, a neighbor of mine who is in the excavation business. He has just been served with process in a federal court suit down in Boston, arising out of some work he did on a house over in Alton. I have attached the original complaint in the action and the third-party complaint against Jones. He is surprised and puzzled by the suit, since he thought the job went fine and the owner was happy. He is also concerned about defending an action down in Boston. Arlen is a local guy with a small business; he is hardly in a position to pay big city legal fees. (I'm not even sure he'll be able to manage mine . . . . I'll probably have to put in a pool so he can pay me off by doing the excavation!)

    Naturally, Jones would rather litigate up here than down in Boston, or, better still, get out of this suit entirely. It seems to me that we may have several grounds for dismissal of this action by motion. First, it seems dubious to me that Jones should be subject to personal jurisdiction in Massachusetts on this claim. He negotiated with the general contractor, Ronan Construction Company, here in New Hampshire. He did the work in New Hampshire. The job was a small one at that, only a few days' work for something like $1,400. Whatever damages the owner suffered were suffered here. Thus, this claim does not arise out of any "minimum contacts" Jones has with Massachusetts. Nor is he subject to general in personam jurisdiction there — he lives next door to me here in Littleton, and though he works in Massachusetts once in a while, he does not do business there regularly.

However, Jones *was* served with process in the suit in Massachusetts. Traditionally, that was always good enough, and I know it is still done all the time, but I'm not sure it is a valid basis for forcing Jones to defend there. I'm just an old country lawyer, and you young fellas may know more about these things than I do, but hasn't the Supreme Court recently pulled in the reins on this kind of transient service of process?

Please check the current state of the law on this. If we have grounds for filing a Rule 12(b) motion to dismiss (remember, we are litigating under the Federal Rules here, not the crusty old New Hampshire common law rules), I would like to do so. Please draft an appropriate motion for my signature.

We may also be able to move to dismiss for lack of subject matter jurisdiction, since we are from the same state as Ronan, the third-party plaintiff, and this is a state law claim. I'm unclear as to whether this affects the court's jurisdiction or not. Please research and advise me on this as well.

If we can't get the claim against Jones dismissed under Fed. R. Civ. P. 12(b)(1) or (2), perhaps we can convince the court to transfer this action to the District of New Hampshire under 28 U.S.C. §1404(a). It seems to me that it makes much more sense to litigate this case here than in Boston. The work was done here, both of the defendants and the third-party defendant live and do business here, and any damages resulting from the job were suffered here. I assume that most of the witnesses other than Schulansky will be from New Hampshire, since Jones tells me that all of Ronan's employees are also local.

Please take a look at the case law on the grounds for transfer of venue. If the cases support our argument for transfer, please draft a separate motion to transfer this action to the District of New Hampshire and advise me as to whether you think we should file it along with our motion to dismiss or hold off until decision of that motion. Be sure to check the local rules of the District of Massachusetts for any special requirements pertaining to motions filed in that court. Feel free to call Jones directly if you need further information from him.

Our response is due within 10 days (the 20-day period under the rule minus the 10 days it took Jones to come to me), so please take care of this right away.

# The Associate's Response

## MEMORANDUM

**TO:**    Donald Philbrook

**FROM:**  Philip Torres

**RE:**    Preliminary Motions in *Ronan v. Jones*
Mass. Federal Dist. Ct. Civil Action No. 86-67

**DATE:**  February 6, 1986

-------------------------------------------------

1. It appears that we do not have a valid objection to subject matter jurisdiction over Ronan's claim against Jones. The rule is clearly established that the citizenship of an impleaded third party is not relevant to establishing diversity jurisdiction. Several prominent authorities indicate that, if the original action is a proper diversity action, the addition of a third party does not affect the court's jurisdiction. See 3 Moore's Federal Practice ¶14.26 (1985); Glannon, Civil Procedure: Examples and Explanations 152 (1987). Jurisdiction over the claim against Jones is based on ancillary jurisdiction, which extends to proper third-party claims in diversity cases. See *Owen Equipment & Erection Co. v. Kroger,* 437 U.S. 365, 375-376 (1978). Consequently, I have not included this defense in the motion to dismiss.

2. I spent about six hours researching the issue of whether personal jurisdiction was properly established over Jones in this case based on service of process within Massachusetts. On the basis of that research, I conclude that we have good ground to support a motion to dismiss for lack of personal jurisdiction, but that the court will probably not accept our argument.

Under Fed. R. Civ. P. 4(e), the federal court may exercise jurisdiction in this case if the Massachusetts courts could do so. State court jurisdiction has traditionally been held proper on the basis of service of process within the forum state. See *Pennoyer v. Neff,* 95 U.S. 714 (1877). However, there is some debate as to whether the Supreme Court undermined this basis for jurisdiction in *Shaffer v. Heitner,* 433 U.S. 186 (1977). In *Shaffer,* the Court held that exercising jurisdiction over absent defendants based solely on the presence of unrelated property in the state was inconsistent with the minimum contacts analysis of *International Shoe v. Washington,* 326 U.S. 310 (1945). The Court in *Shaffer* broadly concluded that "all assertions of state-court jurisdiction must be evaluated according to the standards set forth in *International Shoe* and its progeny." 433 U.S. at 212.

Since the decision in *Shaffer,* a number of commentators have argued that in-state service is no longer sufficient to support personal jurisdiction over nonresident defendants who are not subject to jurisdiction under minimum contacts analysis. See Friedenthal, Kane, and Miller, Civil Procedure

§3.17 (1985); Scoles and Hay, Conflict of Laws §8.7 (1982). However, the majority of the post-*Shaffer* cases have continued to approve jurisdiction based solely on service of process within the forum state. See, e.g., *Amusement Equipment, Inc. v. Mordelt*, 779 F.2d 264, 267-271 (5th Cir. 1985); *Opert v. Schmid*, 535 F. Supp. 591, 593-594 (S.D.N.Y. 1982); *Humphrey v. Langford*, 273 S.E.2d 22, 22-24 (Ga. 1980); but see *Harold M. Pitman Co. v. Typecraft Software Ltd.*, 626 F. Supp. 305, 310-314 (N.D. Ill. 1986) (rejecting transient service in a well-reasoned opinion).

The First Circuit has approved the majority view, upholding the sufficiency of jurisdiction based on transient service. See *Driver v. Helms*, 577 F.2d 147, 156 n.25 (1st Cir. 1978), cert. denied, 439 U.S. 1114 (1979), in which the First Circuit stated in dictum that in-state service remains an adequate basis for personal jurisdiction after *Shaffer*. The court had taken a similar position just before *Shaffer* was decided. *Donald Manter Co. v. Davis*, 543 F.2d 419, 420 (1st Cir. 1976). The Supreme Court has denied certiorari in several such cases, including *Helms* and *O'Brien v. Eubanks*, 701 P.2d 614 (Colo. Ct. App. 1984); a cert. petition has recently been filed in another case reaching the issue. See *Kirchner v. Kirchner*, 54 U.S.L.W. 3285 (October 11, 1985).*

In view of this case law, our position is clearly a minority view. It is doubtful that the district court could grant the motion, since the *Manter* case would be mandatory authority in the District of Massachusetts (as in all courts in the First Circuit), and the same conclusion was endorsed again in *Helms*. However, our position does draw substantial support from the commentators and the strong language of the Supreme Court in *Shaffer*. We will certainly be within the ethical constraints of Rule 11 in moving to dismiss on this ground, since our position is "warranted by . . . a good faith argument for the extension, modification or reversal of existing law" (Fed. R. Civ. P. 11) established by the Court in *Shaffer*. In addition, filing the motion will preserve our objection; in the event that the Supreme Court strikes down transient service while our case is pending, we will be able to renew our motion, whereas we will waive it if we don't raise it now.

3. Our strongest argument is for transfer of the case under 28 U.S.C. §1404(a). Under §1404(a), the court may transfer cases "for the convenience of the parties and witnesses, in the interest of justice." The primary factors to be considered are those established in *Gulf Oil Corp. v. Gilbert*, 330 U.S. 501 (1947) (decided under the related doctrine of forum non conveniens), including the plaintiff's choice of a forum, relative ease of access to sources of proof, availability of compulsory process, convenience of willing witnesses, possibility of a view, and advantages of enforceability of a judgment. See generally 1 Moore's at ¶0.145[5].

---

* The Supreme Court denied certiorari in *Kirchner* on January 28, 1986. 54 U.S.L.W. 3498 — ED.

Many of these factors point to transfer of this action. As you indicate, the events that gave rise to the suit took place in New Hampshire, and all witnesses and parties except for Schulansky live here. In fact, it will not be possible to compel all of Ronan's employees to testify in Massachusetts, because Jones tells me that several of them no longer work for Ronan and they are not subject to the subpoena power of the Massachusetts court. It may also be necessary for the court and the jury to view the house, which would obviously make trial here more appropriate.

In addition, while I have not yet had the time to research the issue, it seems likely that the Massachusetts federal court, applying Massachusetts conflicts of law doctrine (see *Klaxon Co. v. Stentor Co.*, 313 U.S. 487 (1941)) would apply the contract and tort law of New Hampshire to this case, since most of the events giving rise to the action took place here, the property is located here, and the damage was suffered here. A number of cases have concluded that the need to apply the law of another state is a factor in favor of transfer. See, e.g., *Hotel Constructors, Inc. v. Seagrave Corp.*, 543 F. Supp. 1048, 1052 (N.D. Ill. 1982); but cf. *Houk v. Kimberley-Clark Corp.*, 613 F. Supp. 923, 932 (W.D. Mo. 1985) (applicable law not given great weight unless it is complex or unsettled).

An important limitation on transfer is the requirement that the suit "might have been brought" in the transferee district. 28 U.S.C. §1404(a). The Supreme Court held, in *Hoffman v. Blaski*, 363 U.S. 335, 342-343 (1960), that this phrase limits transfer to districts in which venue was proper and service could have been made on the defendant. This requirement is obviously met here, since venue would be proper under 28 U.S.C. §1391(a) and all defendants and third-party defendants would be subject to personal jurisdiction here.

Because a major reason for transfer under §1404(a) is for the convenience of the parties, it would certainly bolster our position if the defendants were willing to join in the motion to transfer. You may wish to call Ronan's counsel to see if he is willing to do so. Ironically, while it might well be more convenient for Ronan personally to litigate up here, it would be less so for his lawyers, because Smith, Hollings, and Korn only have offices in Boston. You might get a more enthusiastic reception if you could suggest this directly to Ronan. However, I realize this would be improper under the Code of Professional Responsibility.

I have attached draft motions to dismiss and to transfer, along with supporting affidavits from Jones. Tactically, we could file the motion to dismiss under Fed. R. Civ. P. 12(b)(2), and hold our motion to transfer, as there is no requirement that the transfer motion be filed before answering the complaint. However, since it looks doubtful that the court will dismiss for lack of personal jurisdiction, we may want to file both motions together. This will give the judge the option to transfer the case at the outset. Perhaps he will latch on to that option as a means of avoiding the more complicated personal jurisdiction question. Since we will have to participate in discovery while the motions are pending, it may be best to present both motions in hopes of getting out of the Massachusetts court as soon as possible.

Thank you for reminding me to check the local district court rules. Rule 12 of the Local Rules of the District of Massachusetts specifically deals with motions and provides that affidavits and other supporting materials, including supporting memoranda, must be filed with the motion. Otherwise, they may only be filed with leave of court. In view of this rule, I suggest that we file a motion for an extension of time to file a responsive pleading under Fed. R. Civ. P. 6(b) or ask Ronan's counsel to assent to an extension, to give us adequate time to prepare a supporting memorandum of law to file with these motions. Alternatively, I have included a request in each motion for leave to file supporting memos at a time specified by the court.

# The Resulting Documents

UNITED STATES DISTRICT COURT

DISTRICT OF MASSACHUSETTS

CIVIL ACTION NO. 86-67

DEBORAH SCHULANSKY

Plaintiff

v.

RICHARD L. RONAN
RONAN CONSTRUCTION CO.

Defendants

v.

ARLEN JONES

Third-Party
Defendant

THIRD-PARTY DEFENDANT'S

MOTION TO DISMISS THE

THIRD-PARTY COMPLAINT FOR

LACK OF PERSONAL

JURISDICTION

The third-party defendant, Arlen Jones, moves to dismiss the third-party complaint against him under Fed. R. Civ. P. 12(b)(2) on the ground that the court lacks personal jurisdiction over him on this claim. In support of the motion the third-party defendant states as follows:

1. The third-party defendant is not domiciled in Massachusetts or doing business in Massachusetts on a regular basis, as more fully appears from the Affidavit of Arlen Jones, paragraphs one and three, attached as Exhibit A to this motion.

2. This claim arises out of construction work performed by the third-party defendant in Alton, New Hampshire, as more fully appears from paragraphs one to four of the Third-Party Complaint, and paragraphs four and five of the attached Affidavit of Arlen Jones.

3. The third-party defendant has no contacts with Massachusetts that are related to this claim, as further appears from the Affidavit of Arlen Jones.

4. The exercise of personal jurisdiction over the third-party defendant in these circumstances is improper under Fed. R. Civ. P. 4(e) and the Due Process Clause of the Fourteenth Amendment to the United States Constitution.

The third party defendant requests twenty minutes for oral argument on this motion, pursuant to Local Rule 12(c)(1), and leave to file a supporting memorandum at a time specified by the court.

Donald R. Philbrook
Attorney for Third-Party
  Defendant
11A Grove Street
Littleton, New Hampshire 03561
(603) 471-8200

UNITED STATES DISTRICT COURT

DISTRICT OF MASSACHUSETTS

CIVIL ACTION NO. 86-67

DEBORAH SCHULANSKY

Plaintiff

v.

RICHARD L. RONAN
RONAN CONSTRUCTION CO.

Defendants

v.

ARLEN JONES

Third-Party
Defendant

AFFIDAVIT OF ARLEN JONES

IN SUPPORT OF MOTION TO

DISMISS THIRD-PARTY

COMPLAINT

State of New Hampshire

County of Littleton

ss.:

Arlen Jones, being first duly sworn, states as follows:

1. On January 18, I was personally served with a summons and Third-Party Complaint in the above-captioned action. Service was made at Methuen, Massachusetts while I was engaged in a small excavating project for a condominium complex there.

2. At the time of service and at all other times relevant to this action I resided at 88 Warner Avenue, Littleton, New Hampshire, and conducted a small excavating business from that address as a sole proprietor.

3. Although I occasionally (approximately once per year) do small excavation jobs in Massachusetts, I am not licensed to do business in

Massachusetts, do not conduct business there on a regular basis, and receive less than 5% of my income from Massachusetts business.

4. This action arises out of renovation work performed by Richard Ronan on the plaintiff's house in Alton, New Hampshire. The third-party complaint alleges a right to relief for faulty excavation work performed as part of the renovation work at the Alton site.

5. All negotiations, agreements, preparation, and performance of the work giving rise to this claim took place in New Hampshire. I did not solicit this job in Massachusetts nor perform any act related to the events in suit in Massachusetts, nor was I aware until I received process in this action that the plaintiff resided there.

6. I have never consented to suit in Massachusetts on this claim.

_____

Arlen Jones

    Subscribed and sworn to before me this 5th day of February, 1986.

_____

Notary Public

My commission expires:

_____

UNITED STATES DISTRICT COURT

DISTRICT OF MASSACHUSETTS

CIVIL ACTION NO. 86-67

DEBORAH SCHULANSKY

    Plaintiff

    v.

RICHARD L. RONAN         THIRD-PARTY DEFENDANT'S

RONAN CONSTRUCTION CO.

                          MOTION TO TRANSFER UNDER

    Defendants          28 U.S.C. §1404(a)

    v.

ARLEN JONES

        Third-Party
        Defendant

The third-party defendant, Arlen Jones, moves to transfer this action to the federal district court for the District of New Hampshire, under 28 U.S.C. §1404(a), for the convenience of the parties and in the interest of justice. In support of the motion, the third-party defendant states as follows:

1. This action arises out of construction work performed on the plaintiff's home in Alton, New Hampshire, as more fully appears from paragraphs 5 and 14-20 of the plaintiff's complaint and paragraphs 7-9 of the Affidavit of Arlen Jones, attached hereto as Exhibit A.

2. The defendants on the main claim are a New Hampshire resident and a New Hampshire corporation, as more fully appears from paragraphs 2-3 of the plaintiff's complaint.

3. All negotiations between the defendant and the third-party defendant concerning the excavation work took place in New Hampshire, as more fully appears from the Affidavit of Arlen Jones, paragraph 8.

4. All of the construction work giving rise to both the plaintiff's claims against the defendants and the defendants' claims against the third-party defendant took place in Alton, New Hampshire, as more fully appears from the Affidavit of Arlen Jones, paragraph 9.

5. Any damages suffered by the plaintiff or the defendant were suffered in New Hampshire, where the premises involved in this action are located and the defendants are located.

6. All potential witnesses who worked on the construction of the addition reside in New Hampshire, as more fully appears from the Affidavit of Arlen Jones, paragraph 10.

7. At least some of the potential witnesses in this action are beyond the subpoena power of this court, as more fully appears from the Affidavit of Arlen Jones, paragraph 10.

8. This claim could have been brought in the District of New Hampshire because the claim arose there and all defendants are subject to service of process in that district.

The third-party defendant requests one half hour for oral argument of this motion, and leave to file a supporting memorandum at a time specified by the court.

Donald R. Philbrook
Attorney for Third-Party
  Defendant
11A Grove Street
Littleton, New Hampshire 03561
(603) 471-8200

UNITED STATES DISTRICT COURT

DISTRICT OF MASSACHUSETTS

CIVIL ACTION NO. 86-67

DEBORAH SCHULANSKY

Plaintiff

v.

RICHARD L. RONAN
RONAN CONSTRUCTION CO.

Defendants

v.

ARLEN JONES

Third-Party
Defendant

AFFIDAVIT OF ARLEN JONES

IN SUPPORT OF MOTION TO

TRANSFER UNDER

28 U.S.C. §1404(a)

State of New Hampshire

County of Littleton

ss.:

Arlen Jones, being first duly sworn, states as follows:

1. I reside at 88 Warner Avenue, Littleton, New Hampshire, approximately 125 miles from Boston, and have resided there at all times relevant to the events involved in this action.

2. I operate a small excavation business, as a sole proprietor. The business is operated out of my home and grosses about $60,000 per year.

3. Over 90% of my business is done in New Hampshire, most of it in the Littleton area of northern New Hampshire. While I occasionally

do small jobs in Massachusetts, I do not work there more than approximately once a year. I do not currently have any orders for future jobs in Massachusetts.

4. I am currently booked solid for the new construction season with jobs all over New Hampshire. Since I am a small proprietor, and must attend to my business every day, it would seriously inconvenience me to litigate this action, which arises out of one of the smallest jobs I did last year, in Massachusetts.

5. At no time did I have any direct negotiations with the plaintiff in this action, nor was I apprised of the fact that she lives in Massachusetts or of any other facts which would have led me to expect to have to defend this claim in a Massachusetts court.

6. On information and belief, the defendants Richard Ronan and Ronan Construction Company are primarily engaged in residential construction in New Hampshire.

7. Sometime during the first week of April 1985, Richard Ronan called me in Littleton concerning an excavation job on the Schulansky house in Alton, New Hampshire.

8. After several phone calls between Ronan and me, all of which took place in New Hampshire, I agreed to do the excavation work on the Alton job, for $1,400.

9. I commenced work on the Schulansky job on April 15, 1985, and completed the work on April 17. All preparation and performance of the work took place in either Littleton, New Hampshire or Alton, New Hampshire.

10. I have done at least twenty excavation jobs for Ronan and/or Ronan Construction Company during the past three years. I am acquainted with all of Ronan's employees who worked on the Schulansky job. All of those employees live in New Hampshire, and at least four of them in the Littleton area, more than 100 miles from Boston.

11. Since the Schulansky job in April 1985, several of the carpenters who worked on the job have left Ronan's employ.

_____
Arlen Jones

Subscribed and sworn to before me this 5th day of February, 1986.

_____
Notary Public

My commission expires:

_____

# Comments on the Third-Party Motions

1. The same formal rules that govern captions for pleadings also apply to motions and to affidavits as well. See Fed. R. Civ. P. 7(b)(2). In addition, the ethical constraints on pleadings in Rule 11 also apply to motions. Fed. R. Civ. P. 7(b)(3). Under Rule 11, as amended in 1983, attorneys must investigate both the factual and legal bases for filing motions before doing so. Under earlier practice, defense counsel would frequently respond to a complaint with a motion to dismiss including a long laundry list of dubious objections. Such habits, while they die slowly, are now clearly inconsistent with the Rule 11 requirements for reasonable inquiry and supporting grounds.

2. Rule 7(b) provides that a motion shall "state with particularity the grounds therefor." In both the motion to dismiss and the motion to transfer, Jones's counsel has set forth briefly the reasons that support the particular order sought in the motion. This satisfies the requirement of "particularity" and assists the court in understanding the basis of the motions.

However, the motion is not the right place to *argue* the merits of the motion, or to set forth in detail the facts that support the motion. The supporting arguments and discussion of authority should be set forth in an accompanying memorandum of law. Any facts necessary to support the motion should be provided in supporting affidavits, deposition transcripts, interrogatories, business records or other evidentiary documents.

3. An affidavit is a sworn statement by a witness. It is usually notarized and is signed subject to the pains and penalities of perjury. The "ss." in the heading is a legal formalism frequently found in affidavits. It stands for "silicet," which roughly means "to wit" or "let it be known," and simply indicates that the affiant publicly asserts the facts in the affidavit.

It is entirely proper to submit affidavits in support of a motion, to establish the facts necessary for the court to rule on the motion. See Fed. R. Civ. P. 43(e). In the case of Jones's motion to dismiss for lack of personal jurisdiction, for example, the earlier pleadings do not indicate whether Jones has contacts with Massachusetts sufficient to support jurisdiction over him for this claim. Jones's affidavit provides the court with admissible evidence (since it is sworn personal testimony of the affiant), which supports the position taken in his motion.

If the other parties have countervailing evidence, they may submit their own affidavits or other materials in opposition to the motion. The court may decide the motion on the basis of the facts presented, or, if issues of credibility are involved or further evidence needed, may take testimony from the witnesses in a full evidentiary hearing on the motion.

**4.** You may have been puzzled as to why Jones's lawyers have included a paragraph in the affidavit stating that several potential witnesses no longer work for Ronan and do not live within 100 miles of Boston. This fact may be relevant to the motion to transfer because if these witnesses still worked for Ronan they would presumably be subject to his control and therefore would appear to testify at a trial in Massachusetts. If they no longer work for Ronan, however, and are outside the subpoena power of the Massachusetts federal court, they will probably not be available to testify at a trial in Boston. See Fed. R. Civ. P. 45(e)(1) (authorizing service of subpoenas within the judicial district where suit is pending or within 100 miles of the place of trial). A New Hampshire court, however, could subpoena witnesses from any place within New Hampshire, thus supporting the argument for transfer.

**5.** It is entirely proper to file combined motions for more than one form of action by the court. Jones's lawyers could, for example, decide to file a combined "Motion to Dismiss for Lack of Personal Jurisdiction, or in the Alternative to Transfer Venue under 28 U.S.C. §1404(a)." Torres drafted the two separately because the tactical decision whether to file them together or separately had not yet been made.

**6.** Torres's suggestion that Philbrook contact Ronan's counsel is interesting. It would certainly lend credence to the motion if the original defendants also sought transfer. Although Jones and Ronan are adversaries on the merits, their interests may coincide on this issue or others in the suit. As the introduction to these pleading materials points out, it is appropriate to contact Ronan's counsel to discuss a possible joint motion or any other such issues that arise in the course of the litigation.

Further, the point that Torres makes about the potential difference in interests between Ronan and his attorneys is a delicate and interesting one. If the case is transferred, the insurance company may retain local counsel in New Hampshire to handle it, and the Boston firm will lose the case. However, Ronan's counsel is there to represent his clients' interests, not his own, and should join in the removal petition if Ronan prefers to litigate in New Hampshire, or if other tactical considerations point to New Hampshire as the preferable forum.

**7.** This book writing business is frustrating. I started out to create a fairly straightforward case for illustration purposes, but like all lawsuits, *Schulansky v. Ronan* refuses to be simple. The motion to transfer presents a good example. If the defendants will not join in Ronan's motion to transfer, there is some doubt as to whether the court can grant the motion. Wright and Miller suggest that a third-party defendant should not be able to object to venue or, apparently, move to transfer. 6 Wright and Miller at 242. They suggest that the court should consider inconvenience to the third-party defendant in deciding whether to allow impleader (which is always at the court's discretion under Rule 14(a)) but should not transfer the entire suit on motion of the third-party defendant. See also *Pelinski v. Goodyear Tire & Rubber Co.*, 499 F. Supp. 1092, 1095 (N.D. Ill. 1980) ("some question" whether a third-party defendant can seek transfer under §1404(a)).

To be truthful, your humble author never knew that arcane bit of procedural lore until his research assistant stumbled on the point in researching the standards for transfer. It is hardly surprising that Jones's attorneys have not yet discovered it. They well may when they reach the stage of briefing the transfer issue. Or they may not. If they don't, the issue will probably be raised by one of the other parties or the judge. If at that point the court decides that Jones lacks standing to seek a transfer (or that transfer is not warranted, since the plaintiff and defendants are happy with the forum), he may still take the course suggested by Wright and Miller, and dismiss the third-party claim in his discretion under Rule 14(a).

**8.** It is fortunate that Philbrook, a New Hampshire practitioner,[2] remembered to have Torres check the local rules for the District of Massachusetts. Most federal districts have their own rules, in addition to the Federal Rules of Civil Procedure, and they frequently cover important aspects of local practice. In this case, Rule 12(a) of the Local Rules for the District of Massachusetts specifically provides that supporting affidavits and memoranda must be filed with the motion, or else only with leave of court.

**9.** Local Rule 12(c) also requires that a request for a hearing be included in the motion if the moving party wants one and that the party seeking a hearing indicate in the motion the amount of time needed for oral argument.

The Local Rules for the District of Massachusetts also impose a requirement that may trap the unwary litigant. Under Local Rule 12(a)(2), a party who *opposes* a motion must file an opposition to the motion within ten days. There is nothing in the Federal Rules of Civil Procedure that requires that an opposition be filed. It is thus imperative to be familiar with the local rules as well as the Federal Rules themselves, which apply generally to *all* federal district courts.[3]

---

2. Philbrook will not automatically have the right to appear on behalf of Jones in the Massachusetts Federal District Court, unless he is a member of the Massachusetts bar. However, Rule 6 of the Massachusetts District Court Local Rules authorizes the district court to allow an attorney admitted to practice in another state to appear in particular cases.

3. To make matters worse, the rules may change. Substantial amendments to the Local Rules for the District of Massachusetts became effective on July 1, 1986, after the papers in these chapters were filed, but while the case was still going on.

Massachusetts state practice presents an even more subtle trap for the unwary. The Massachusetts Superior Court has issued so-called standing orders governing various aspects of practice in that court. These standing orders are not even published in the rule books; you have to go to the clerk's office and ask for them. All of which is old news to an experienced practitioner, but can present real problems for new members of the bar or out-of-state attorneys who occasionally appear in the Superior Court.

# 28

## A Tactical Dilemma: Ronan's Motion for Summary Judgment

## The Drafting Request

### MEMORANDUM

**TO:** Marcia Losordo

**FROM:** Arthur Ackerman

**RE:** Summary judgment in *Schulansky v. Ronan,*
U.S. District Court No. 86-67

**DATE:** September 8, 1986

-----------------------------------------------------

Now that the judge has denied Jones's motion to transfer this action (somewhat to my surprise, actually), I think we should review the file to determine whether we might be able to get at least some of the claims in this case dismissed on a motion for summary judgment.

In particular, it seems to me that we may be able to get summary judgment on Schulansky's claim (see Complaint, paragraphs twenty-three and twenty-four) that Ronan agreed to rebuild the old foundation wall. Schulansky virtually admits in her complaint (paragraphs 11-12, 22-23) that the Proposal and Estimate is the entire contract between the parties. If that is true, Schulansky will have to prove that the terms of the Proposal and Estimate itself required Ronan to rebuild the old foundation. The only provision of the contract that arguably addresses this issue is paragraph two. We may be able to convince the court that the proper interpretation of that paragraph required Ronan to build supporting foundation walls for the three walls of the addition itself, but not to rebuild the original foundation as well.

Schulansky will probably argue that the Proposal and Estimate did not embody the entire agreement between the parties, and that she and Ronan had a separate understanding about the scope of the work to be done on the old foundation wall. However, as I recall, Schulansky's deposition testimony strongly supports our position that there were no other agreements or implied terms of the agreement apart from the written terms of the contract.

If the court agrees that the contract is complete on its face, won't the parol evidence rule bar Schulansky from introducing evidence of any prior representations by Ronan concerning rebuilding the foundation? And if such evidence is inadmissible, shouldn't we be entitled to summary judgment based on the language of paragraph two, which only requires Ronan to build walls to support the new addition itself?

In order to determine whether this motion has a reasonable chance of success, I think we should go over the evidence relevant to this issue in detail. Please review the Schulansky deposition and pull out her testimony concerning the negotiations on the foundation problem. Also, talk to Ronan and draw up an affidavit that we could submit in support of our motion, setting out his testimony as to the course of their discussions. Last, please draw up a draft motion for summary judgment, and briefly give me your assessment of the likelihood of prevailing on the motion, based on the evidence set forth in the affidavit and deposition. Please do not draft a memorandum in support of the motion at this time, in case we decide not to file the motion.

# The Associate's Response

## MEMORANDUM

**TO:**    Arthur Ackerman

**FROM:**  Marcia Losordo

**RE:**    Partial Summary Judgment in *Schulansky v. Ronan*
U.S. District Court No. 86-67

**DATE:**  September 16, 1986

------------------------------------------------

As you requested, I have reviewed Deborah Schulansky's deposition and pulled out her testimony concerning the negotiations on the reconstruction of the old foundation and the signing of the Ronan contract. I have attached the relevant pages of the deposition to this memo. I have also discussed this aspect of the case in detail with Richard Ronan and drawn up an affidavit for his signature that sets forth his version of the facts. I also attach a draft motion for partial summary judgment on the issue of Ronan's contractual duty to rebuild the foundation.

After reviewing the documents and spending about four hours researching Massachusetts law on the parol evidence rule and contract interpretation, my preliminary conclusion is that the court will probably deny our motion for summary judgment in this case. Summary judgment will only be granted if our evidence demonstrates that there is no disputed issue of fact for the jury to resolve, and that, on the undisputed facts, we are entitled to judgment as a matter of law. Fed. R. Civ. P. 56(c). I doubt that we will be able to make that showing in this case. Given the expense to the client, it may not be worth litigating the motion in a case of this size.

You are correct in stating that Schulansky would be barred from proving any separate agreement with Ronan if the Proposal and Estimate is "fully integrated," that is, constitutes the complete and final agreement of the parties. *Shain Investment Co. v. Cohen,* 15 Mass. App. 4, 13 (1982); Restatement (Second) of Contracts §215 (1981). A fully integrated contract is one that includes "all of the matters agreed upon." Restatement (Second) of Contracts §210, comment a (1981). If a contract is fully integrated, prior negotiations (like the March discussion in this case) are irrelevant, since they have been superseded by the contract, which includes all the rights and obligations of the parties. *Thomas v. Christenson,* 12 Mass. App. 169, 176 (1981); Restatement (Second) of Contracts §215 (1981). If the contract is not fully integrated, evidence of other agreements would be admissible.

However, in order to determine whether a contract is "fully integrated," the court may consider all the evidence of prior negotiations. Restatement (Second) of Contracts §214 (1981). Thus, (somewhat ironically) the court will hear the evidence as to the negotiations between Ronan and Schulansky about the old foundation, if only to determine whether a separate agreement existed that covered additional matters not addressed in the written contract. See *Wang Laboratories Inc. v. Docktor Pet Centers,* 12 Mass. App. 213, 219-220 (1981); Restatement (Second) of Contracts §210, comment b (1981) (court has "wide latitude" to inquire into the intent of the parties in determining whether a contract is fully integrated).

In deciding whether the Proposal and Estimate constitutes the complete agreement of the parties, the court will probably not give too much weight to Schulansky's answers to your questions in the deposition (pp. 9-10) about the existence of additional agreements. Although she does appear to concede that there were no other agreements, her answers indicate some confusion as to exactly what you were asking. She probably was not aware of the legal significance of your questions; she may have thought you were asking whether there were any other formal contracts, rather than oral agreements.

Slater's objections suggest that she is aware that the issue of a possible separate agreement regarding the foundation is crucial. If we file our motion, supported by the deposition testimony, Slater will doubtless file a counter-affidavit of Schulansky stating that she did not fully understand your questions, that she did not mean that there were no separate understandings about rebuilding the old foundation, and that such a separate oral agreement did in fact exist.

Our strongest argument for summary judgment is that the plaintiff's complaint itself relies exclusively on the Proposal and Estimate as the source of the contractual duty to rebuild the old foundation. See paragraphs twenty-two and twenty-three. Frankly, I don't understand why her counsel wrote the complaint so narrowly. If the court does not allow an amendment, Schulansky may effectively be barred from proving that she and Ronan had a separate agreement about the old foundation, since she has based her right to relief exclusively on the terms of the Proposal and Estimate. We can argue that any proof of collateral agreements is outside the scope of the complaint. Therefore, if no obligation is created by the terms of the written contract, Ronan is entitled to judgment on the contract claim.

However, this argument may still not carry the day. First, Slater is likely to move to amend the complaint, to add an allegation that the parties had an additional oral agreement concerning the old foundation. At this stage of the case, the court is likely to allow the motion. (Indeed, Schulansky's deposition itself indicates that we are already litigating the issue of possible additional agreements; thus it will be hard to argue that the amendment should be denied due to surprise or prejudice to us.)

Second, even if the court accepts our argument that it is solely the Proposal and Estimate that governs the work, there is still a question as to the interpretation of its terms. If the meaning of a contract term depends on the credibility of witnesses or conflicting inferences as to the intent of the parties, interpretation of the term poses a question of fact for the jury. Restatement (Second) of Contracts §212(2) (1981).

In this case, the court will probably conclude that paragraph two of the contract is susceptible of several interpretations. The obligation to build foundation walls "to support the addition" might have meant only the three new walls. Alternatively, it could be construed to include the fourth wall, the old foundation wall adjoining the addition. If the evidence before the court would support either interpretation, the issue must be resolved by the jury, and summary judgment will be denied.

After review of the deposition, I think that Judge Meliotis would likely find that there is a genuine issue of material fact as to the meaning of paragraph two. Although Schulansky never states that Ronan explicitly agreed to rebuild the foundation, if the jury believed her testimony they could find that Ronan agreed to do whatever was necessary to make the foundation solid. Schulansky understood him to say that he would do whatever had to be done to stabilize the old foundation. See Schulansky deposition at 12 (Ronan "would take care of it"); pp. 12-13 (she got the impression that "he would rebuild it if it had to be done").

I agree with you that Ronan's testimony is more precise and is supported by the fact that he did exactly what he says he agreed to do, stabilize the foundation with concrete. See Affidavit of Ronan, paragraphs seven, twelve. In addition, Schulansky's own testimony tends to support Ronan's position. Deposition, p. 12 (Ronan said he would "use concrete to fix" the foundation). However, as long as a reasonable jury *could* infer from Schulansky's testimony that Ronan had agreed to do more, a factual issue is posed and summary judgment must be denied. See Fed. R. Civ. P. 56(c) (summary judgment appropriate where there is "no genuine issue of material fact").

Please let me know whether you intend to file the motion; I assume you will want me to write a memorandum in support of the motion if you do.

## MEMORANDUM

**TO:**     Marcia Losordo

**FROM:**  Arthur Ackerman

**RE:**     Summary judgment in *Schulansky v. Ronan*
U.S. District Court No. 86-67

**DATE:**  September 19, 1986

-----------------------------------------------------

Thank you for your memo on the complexities of contract interpretation in this case. Given the expense of briefing and arguing the motion and the obstacles to prevailing on it, I have decided not to seek summary judgment at this time. Although I think we have a very strong case for our interpretation of the contract, I reluctantly agree that getting a judge to say, as a matter of law, that paragraph two *must* carry our meaning is less than a 50/50 proposition.

Several other points in your memo also suggest that we might be better advised not to file the motion, at least at this stage of the case. Your memo reminded me that Judge Meliotis has this case. Judge Meliotis is affectionately referred to as "Try It" Meliotis among experienced members of the local bar, for his well-known propensity to give plaintiffs their "day in court" by denying pretrial motions to dismiss.

In addition, I agree that the plaintiff's allegations in the complaint may ultimately limit her right to prove a collateral agreement at trial, since those allegations would not support relief based on a separate oral agreement to rebuild the foundation. If we move for summary judgment this early in the case, you quite rightly point out that the court is likely to allow an amendment. However, if the plaintiff does not amend before trial, the court might refuse to allow her to do so at trial. At that point, we will be able to argue that the motion is unduly delayed and that our trial preparation has been shaped by the original pleadings. Under the circumstances, we should probably not educate the plaintiff now about possible defects in those pleadings.

Since the Parnell case has just settled unexpectedly, and we will not be filing the summary judgment motion in the Schulansky case, maybe you should try to catch a few days off. Don't we owe you some time from last Christmas?

# The Resulting Documents

UNITED STATES DISTRICT COURT

DISTRICT OF MASSACHUSETTS

CIVIL ACTION NO. 86-67

DEBORAH SCHULANSKY

Plaintiff

v.

RICHARD L. RONAN et al.

Defendants

v.

ARLEN JONES

Third-Party
Defendant

DEFENDANTS' MOTION FOR

PARTIAL SUMMARY JUDGMENT

The defendants move for summary judgment under Fed. R. Civ. P. 56 on the plaintiff's Claim for Relief for breach of contract set forth in paragraphs twenty-one through twenty-four of the complaint. In support of this motion, the defendants state that, based on the complaint (including the Proposal and Estimate, attached as Exhibit A to the complaint), the answer, the attached excerpt from the deposition of Deborah Schulansky, and the attached affidavit of Richard L. Ronan, there is no genuine issue of material fact as to this claim and the defendants are entitled to judgment as a matter of law.

In support of this motion, the defendants state:

1. The plaintiff's complaint alleges a right to relief for breach of a contract between her and the defendants, dated March 15, 1985, and entitled "Proposal and Estimate."

2. The plaintiff admits that she signed the Proposal and Estimate (see complaint, paragraphs eleven, twelve) and that it constitutes the final and complete contract between the parties for the work to be done on

the Alton house. Complaint, paragraph twenty-two; Deposition of Deborah Schulansky, pp. 9-10.

3. Paragraph two is the only provision of the Proposal and Estimate that covers foundation work to be done under the contract.

4. Paragraph two does not create any obligation on the part of the defendants to rebuild the foundation of the main house.

Pursuant to Rule 12(c)(2) of the Local Rules of the District Court of Massachusetts, the defendant requests one half hour for oral argument on this motion.

Arthur Ackerman
Attorney for the Defendants
59 State Street
Boston, MA 02114
(617) 228-6301

UNITED STATES DISTRICT COURT

DISTRICT OF MASSACHUSETTS

CIVIL ACTION NO. 86-67

DEBORAH SCHULANSKY

Plaintiff

v.

RICHARD L. RONAN et al.

Defendants

v.

ARLEN JONES

Third-Party
Defendant

DEPOSITION OF DEBORAH SCHULANSKY, taken on behalf

of the defendants Richard Ronan and Ronan Construction Company,

pursuant to notice under the Federal Rules of Civil Procedure, before

Alexander Barlow, a Registered Professional Reporter and Notary

Public in and for the Commonwealth of Massachusetts, at the office

of Smith, Hollings and Korn, 59 State Street, Boston, Massachusetts,

on Wednesday, May 14, 1986, commencing at 10:00 a.m.

Q. Now, Mrs. Schulansky, I show you this document, headed "Proposal and Estimate," which is attached to your complaint and marked Exhibit A. Are you familiar with that document?

A. Yes, that's the paper Richard Ronan sent me to sign about the job.

Q. Is this the contract between you and Ronan Construction Company for the construction of the addition?

A. Yes, that's it.

Q. Did you make any additions or changes to this agreement before you signed it and returned it to Ronan?

A. No, I didn't change anything on it.

Q. Did you make any written changes or modifications in the agreement <u>after</u> it was signed, either before the work commenced or while it was being done?

A. No.

Q. Is this the only contract you had with Ronan or Ronan Construction Company relating to the construction of the addition?

A. Yes.

Q. You didn't enter into any other agreements with Ronan concerning the work?

A. I'm not sure just what you mean...

Q. Did you sign any other documents describing the work to be done or other terms of the agreement?

A. No, that was the only thing I signed.

Q. Did you have any other oral agreements about the job, apart from the Proposal and Estimate?

Ms. Slater: Objection. You are asking for a legal characterization of the negotiations between the parties.

Q. Well, I think the plaintiff is qualified to testify to her own understanding of what happened. Let me rephrase the question.

Was it your understanding that there were other agreements between you and Ronan Construction Company, or between you and Richard Ronan, governing the work to be done on the addition?

A. No, I didn't have any other agreements with him. Just that contract you have there that I signed in March. But I'm still not sure I know what you mean.

Q. So this Exhibit A, the Proposal and Estimate, was the only agreement you had for the construction?

A. Yes, it was the only thing I signed.

Q. And it represents the complete agreement between you as to how much you would pay, the work to be done, the timing, all the terms of the contract?

Objection: The question calls for a legal conclusion.

A. That's the only agreement I signed, if that's what you're getting at.

Q. Now, Mrs. Schulansky, could you tell us what was the first time that you discussed the foundation of the house with Richard

Ronan?

A. It was the second time we talked. He came to my house —

the one in Plymouth, that is — to go over the details of the project.

After we met the first time, he went over and took a look at

the house in Alton so we could talk more specifically about what had

to be done. Then we sat down in Plymouth to go over the details.

Q. Who brought up the subject of the foundation at that time?

A. Well, I don't really remember. I remember that it was a

concern of mine, and I planned to ask him about it, but I can't say

whether I brought it up or he did. I think probably I did, but I'm not

sure.

Q. Could you tell me as accurately as you can recall just what

the sequence of the conversation was about the foundation?

A. Well, I think I asked him whether he thought there would

be any problem with the foundation, and he said he didn't think so.

Q. Did you specify problems with the old foundation, as

opposed to the foundation to support the addition?

A. Well, I don't think I was as specific as that, but I'm sure he

knew what I was talking about. In fact, I remember saying that one

reason I had some concerns about it was that we were going to cut a

door through it into the new cellar.

Q. Exactly what did you ask him about the foundation?

A. As I said, I asked him whether it would be O.K., whether it

would be disturbed by the construction and whether it would have to be rebuilt when he dug a new cellar.

Q. Did you use the word "rebuilt"?

A. I really couldn't say what words I used, but that was the gist of what I was asking.

Q. And what did Ronan answer?

A. Well, he said that he didn't think it would be a problem, that it had been there for 200 years and would probably be there for 200 more, something like that. But if there was a problem he would take care of it.

Q. Were those his exact words?

A. I really don't remember exactly what he said, but it was something about if anything was loose he would take care of it, or fix it, or something like that.

Q. Did he say he would rebuild the foundation?

A. I don't remember whether he used those exact words, but I do remember him saying he would use concrete to fix it. He definitely said he would use concrete, he would fix it with concrete, which I assume means the same thing as rebuilding it.

Q. But he didn't use the word "rebuild"?

Ms. Slater, Objection as to the form of the question.

A. I can't swear that he used that exact word, but that was the impression I got, that he would rebuild it if it had to be done.

Q. Did he say he would "reinforce" the foundation?

A. Again, I just can't say, it was over a year ago and I didn't expect to get in a lawsuit over this thing. I can't say he said "re-build" or "reinforce" but it was clear to me that he was going to take care of any problems with the foundation, because that was part of the job.

Q. Was there any discussion about the type of foundation that was there, what it was made up of or how it was put together?

A. I think he said he couldn't tell for sure until it was exposed during the excavation, but that it was probably stones and cement, or I guess they called it mortar back then.

Q. Did Ronan say that he would fix it no matter what he found when he got in there?

A. I already told you, he said he didn't think it would be a problem, but he would take care of it.

Q. Did he discuss any different methods he would use to fix it, depending on what he found when it was exposed?

A. Well, he said he would reinforce it, fix it with concrete.

Q. But he didn't make any distinction between what he would do if it was a mortar foundation or a rock foundation, anything like that?

Ms. Slater: Objection as to the form.

A. No, he just assured me it would be all right.

Q. Was that all of the discussion you had concerning the old foundation?

A. At that time, yes.

Q. Did you discuss it again later?

A. Yes, when they were doing the excavating and that guy with the bulldozer started tearing it to pieces...

Q. But you didn't discuss it again at any time before the job started, before you signed the Proposal and Estimate?

A. No, just the one time. I thought we had a clear understanding on it; I didn't bring it up again.

Q. Was there anything in the Proposal and Estimate about rebuilding the foundation?

Ms. Slater: Objection, the question calls for a legal interpretation.

Q. I will withdraw the question. When you got the Proposal and Estimate from Ronan did you have any question about whether the proposal covered rebuilding the foundation?

A. No, it seemed to me to cover the ground... he was going to build the addition as we discussed and I was going to pay him $19,000, or whatever it was.

Q. Did you contact Ronan with any questions about the Proposal and Estimate?

A. No, I just looked it over and signed it. It looked all right to me, but I'm a stockbroker, not a lawyer. I wasn't planning on getting into a lawsuit over this thing. He seemed like he knew what he was talking about, and he did a good job for my neighbor, so I assumed he would do the job right.

Q. Now, Mrs. Schulansky, moving on, when was the next time, after your March meeting, that you discussed possible problems with the old foundation with Ronan, or any other employee of Ronan Construction Company?

A. Well, I guess it was when I drove up to Alton, when they started the work, in mid-April.

Q. You didn't discuss it with Ronan between signing the Proposal and Estimate and the time the work started?

A. No, I didn't see him again until then.

Q. No phone discussions prior to the beginning of the work?

A. No.

Q. Could you tell me how the subject arose when you went to the job site?

A. Well, I went there when they started the job, to check out any last minute problems and see how the excavation went. When I arrived the bulldozer man was already in there digging out the new cellar, and I started to get nervous about the foundation problem. So I stayed to see what the foundation was like. It wasn't until after lunch that he really started to excavate around the foundation, but as soon as he did I could see there were going to be problems.

Q. Did you talk to Ronan at that point about the foundation?

A. Yes. I was upset because the bulldozer kept smashing into the rock foundation, and I could see he was loosening up the rocks that hold up the house. So I spoke to Ronan about it.

UNITED STATES DISTRICT COURT

DISTRICT OF MASSACHUSETTS

CIVIL ACTION NO. 86-67

DEBORAH SCHULANSKY

Plaintiff

v.

RICHARD L. RONAN et al.

Defendants

v.

ARLEN JONES

Third-Party
Defendant

AFFIDAVIT OF

RICHARD L. RONAN

IN SUPPORT

OF MOTION FOR

SUMMARY JUDGMENT

Commonwealth of Massachusetts

Suffolk County

} ss:

I, Richard L. Ronan, being first duly sworn, depose and say:

1. I am the president of Ronan Construction Company, a New Hampshire corporation with offices at 1124 Newark Road, Nashua, New Hampshire.

2. Ronan Construction Company is engaged in residential construction work in New Hampshire and Massachusetts.

3. In March of 1985, I entered into negotiations, on behalf of Ronan Construction Company, with Deborah Schulansky, the plaintiff in this case, concerning an addition that she wished to build onto the back of her home in Alton, New Hampshire.

4. During one of the meetings I had with the plaintiff concerning the work to be done as part of the construction of the addition, the plaintiff asked me about possible reconstruction of the old house foundation, where the addition adjoined the living room of the main house.

5. At that time, I stated that such reconstruction would probably not be necessary, because the foundation appeared to be stable, had been there for many years and was unlikely to shift.

6. However, I further stated that you can never be sure about a foundation that old, and that it was impossible to tell for sure what the foundation was like until we uncovered it in the process of excavating the new cellar.

7. I further stated that it was likely that it was a rock and mortar foundation, or a plain rock foundation, and that if there were holes in it I would fill them in with cement.

8. At no time during this conversation did I indicate that I would completely rebuild the foundation, or that I could guarantee that the foundation would last for any period of time or never be subject to subsidence.

9. This was the only discussion that I or anyone else on behalf of Ronan Construction Company had with the plaintiff concerning the old foundation until the actual excavation began.

10. Complete reconstruction of even a small part of the original foundation, without disturbing the structure above it, is a delicate and expensive job, that could easily cost as much as the entire bid I made on the Schulansky job.

11. Such reconstruction would normally be done separately, by a masonry contractor, not as part of a construction job such as the one in issue in this case.

12. After exposure of the foundation, it became clear that the foundation was stable, although no mortar had been used in the original construction. In accordance with my earlier statements to the plaintiff, I had the mason pour cement into the holes among the rocks.

13. At no time did I state that I would rebuild the old foundation, or do anything more than add small amounts of concrete to the existing foundation.

_____
Richard L. Ronan

Subscribed and sworn to before me this 14th day of
September, 1986

_____
Notary Public

My commission expires:

_____

# Comments on the Motion for
# Summary Judgment

1. A motion for summary judgment, like any other motion, is governed by Rule 7(b) of the Federal Rules of Civil Procedure. It must be in writing, and must state "with particularity" the grounds of the motion. The four numbered paragraphs of Ronan's motion briefly state the supporting reasons for the motion.

2. As the motion indicates, the defendants only seek partial summary judgment, on part of Schulansky's first claim for relief. Even if they prevail on their argument that Ronan had no duty to rebuild the old foundation, Schulansky has also sought relief for breach of contract on the ground that Jones, acting on behalf of the defendants in performing the contract work, damaged the foundation with the bulldozer. See Complaint, paragraph twenty-five, supra p. 330. That issue (and, of course, the negligence claim in the second claim for relief) would still have to be litigated, even if summary judgment were granted on the duty-to-rebuild issue.

3. As Chapter 15 indicates, a motion for summary judgment is based on the assertion that there is no "genuine issue" as to the material facts. To support that position, the moving party must submit admissible evidence that supports its version of the facts.[1] In this case, Losordo has reviewed the deposition, pulled out those pages that contain relevant testimony, and attached them to the motion. The defendants' position, if they file the motion, is that Schulansky's testimony (at pp. 9-10) when read together with the Ronan affidavit, demonstrates that the Proposal and Estimate constitutes the complete agreement of the parties and that nothing in that contract required Ronan to rebuild the foundation.

4. As the introduction to these materials indicates, depositions are arranged by the parties. The evidence is taken under oath, by a licensed court reporter. After the deposition, the reporter prepares a transcript and sends it to the party who scheduled the deposition and a copy to opposing counsel if requested. The parties usually agree that the deposition will not be filed with the court.

Depositions are an extremely effective means of discovery, since they provide the opportunity to examine the witness in person and to follow up

---

1. In cases in which summary judgment is sought against the party who bears the burden of proof, the moving party may rely on the absence from the record of any admissible evidence to support the opposing party's case. See *Celotex Corp. v. Catrett*, 106 S. Ct. 2548, 2551-2555 (1986). But in most cases the moving party will submit evidence to establish its own version of the facts.

immediately on issues that arise from the deponent's answers. However, they are also expensive. A typical deposition might run anywhere from 50 to 200 pages or more. As of July 1986, court reporters in Boston were charging $2.35-2.55 per page for taking a deposition and providing the transcript to the attorney who took the deposition. Preparation for taking the deposition takes time, and of course the lawyer charges for his time during the deposition. In view of the expense involved, counsel must exercise judgment in deciding whether the size of the case and the likelihood that the deposition will be productive justify taking a particular deposition.

**5.** Tactically, the defendants should probably submit only that part of the Schulansky deposition (pp. 9-10) that deals with the existence of other agreements. They would probably not submit the following pages (11-14) of the deposition, since the testimony about the March negotiations may raise a question of fact as to whether the parties had a separate agreement about the old foundation, or, if not, about the meaning of paragraph two of the Proposal and Estimate.

Of course, if the defendants did not submit this part of the testimony, Schulansky's lawyers probably would. When a motion for summary judgment is made and supported by evidence that supports the movant's version of the facts, the party opposing summary judgment must come forward with evidence that shows that there is a factual dispute for the jury. As Losordo's memo suggests, Schulansky's testimony about the March discussions probably is sufficient to raise a factual question as to whether a separate agreement existed, and if so, what it required Ronan to do.

**6.** Losordo's memo points out a real problem with the plaintiff's complaint. Paragraphs 22-24 of the complaint allege that Ronan had a duty under the Proposal and Estimate to rebuild the foundation. No mention is made of a possible separate understanding regarding this part of the work. Ackerman's questions in the Schulansky deposition have undoubtedly alerted Schulansky's counsel to the fact that the defendants will argue that any obligation to rebuild must be based on the Proposal and Estimate. Slater might well seek to amend the complaint to assert, in the alternative, that the parties had a separate oral agreement regarding reconstruction of the foundation.

Such an amendment would likely be granted at this stage of the case. The spirit of the federal "notice pleading" system is to have the parties set forth their positions at the outset, but to allow them to clarify those positions as the discovery process provides more detailed information about their claims and defenses. That is precisely what has happened here. As the parties proceed with discovery and focus in on the pivotal issue of the exact terms of the agreement between the parties, Schulansky's counsel will refine their understanding of both the facts and the (somewhat amorphous) law of contract formation.

Absent undue delay or other demonstrable prejudice to the defendants, they should be allowed to amend their pleadings to reflect that clearer understanding of the case. However, as Ackerman's second memo suggests, the likelihood that such an amendment will be allowed decreases as trial approaches. If Schulansky's attorneys do not seek an amendment promptly, they risk the possibility that the court will deny a motion to amend later on. If that happens, they could be precluded from proving that a separate agreement existed, because they failed to give the defendants timely notice that the issue would be raised.

7. Ackerman's comment about Judge Meliotis raises an interesting tactical point. As the introduction indicates cases in federal court in Massachusetts are assigned to one judge, who presides over the case from start to finish. Thus, Ronan's attorneys know who will hear their motion for summary judgment and will naturally take into account whatever they know about that judge's predilections.

While ours is supposedly "a government of laws, not of men," any practicing lawyer will tell you that it makes a difference which judge hears your case. If Judge Meliotis is conservative in interpreting the rules of procedure, he may be less likely to grant summary judgment, given the requirement that there be "no genuine issue" of material fact. Or, if he is particularly sensitive to reversal on appeal, he may see denial of the motion as the safest course, since denial of the motion is much less likely to be reversed than a grant of summary judgment. These and many other considerations may influence a judge's decision, and hence must be taken into account (to the extent they are known) by the parties litigating before that judge.

8. Obviously, an essential component of the defendants' motion for summary judgment will be an accompanying memorandum of law, explaining why there are no material facts in dispute and why, as a matter of law, the court should enter judgment in their favor. See Local Rule 12(a)(1) of the District of Massachusetts, which authorizes filing a memorandum along with a motion.

Although *Schulansky* is a relatively low-stakes case, the legal issues involved are not correspondingly simple. For example, Losordo's memo demonstrates that the summary judgment motion raises complex issues of contract interpretation. In addition, an even more complex issue may be lurking in the case: Which state's contract law should apply to this case ?

Under *Erie Railroad Co. v. Tompkins,* 304 U.S. 64 (1938), the federal court must apply state law to this diversity case — but which state's law, Massachusetts's or New Hampshire's? In *Klaxon Co. v. Stentor Electric Mfg. Co.,* 313 U.S. 487 (1941), the Supreme Court held that the court must apply the law that the state court would apply if the case were in state court. Under *Klaxon,* the federal judge must determine whether the Massachusetts court would apply Massachusetts or New Hampshire law, under "choice of law" principles. The defendants' lawyers might spend a good deal of their clients' money to research that issue and still only come up with an educated guess. The plaintiff's counsel will also have to research these issues and write a memorandum in opposition to the motion for summary judgment.

One of the difficult calls lawyers must make all the time is how much time to put into particular issues, given the client's ability to pay, the likelihood that the issue will arise, the likelihood that research will yield helpful results, and the amount at stake in the case. Losordo could easily spend 20 hours researching the contract issues raised above and drafting an effective memorandum in support of the motion. At $75 per hour, that amounts to $1,500 just to file the motion. Additional time will have to be spent preparing to argue the motion and writing a reply to the plaintiff's memorandum in opposition to the motion.

Obviously, this is only one stage in the case; trial will doubtless involve substantially more hours (often billed at a higher rate), and other time has already gone into the pleadings and discovery. Although litigation provides a means for resolving disputes, it is neither simple nor fast in most cases.